ALSO BY DEBORAH JOWITT

Jerome Robbins: His Life, His Theater, His Dance

Meredith Monk (editor)

Time and the Dancing Image

The Dance in Mind

Dance Beat

ERRAND INTO THE MAZE

ERRAND

∼ INTO THE ∼

MAZE

·

THE LIFE
AND WORKS OF
MARTHA GRAHAM

·

DEBORAH JOWITT

FARRAR, STRAUS AND GIROUX   NEW YORK

Farrar, Straus and Giroux
120 Broadway, New York 10271

Library of Congress Cataloging-in-Publication Data
Title: Errand into the maze : the life and works of Martha Graham /
    Deborah Jowitt.
Description: First Edition. | New York : Farrar, Straus and Giroux, [2023] |
    Includes bibliographical references and index.
Identifiers: LCCN 2022055025 | ISBN 9780374280628 (Hardcover)
Subjects: LCSH: Graham, Martha. | Dancers—United States—Biography. |
    Choreographers—United States—Biography. | Modern dance.
Classification: LCC GV1785.G7 J69 2023 | DDC 792.8/2092 [B]—dc23/
    eng/20230109
LC record available at https://lccn.loc.gov/2022055025

Designed by Abby Kagan

Our books may be purchased in bulk for promotional, educational, or business use.
Please contact your local bookseller or the Macmillan Corporate and
Premium Sales Department at 1-800-221-7945, extension 5442, or by email at
MacmillanSpecialMarkets@macmillan.com.

www.fsgbooks.com
Follow us on social media at @fsgbooks

1 3 5 7 9 10 8 6 4 2

CONTENTS

PREFACE

I N 2011, I QUIT MY JOB at *The Village Voice*, a weekly paper, where I had written articles forty-eight weeks a year since 1974. Blogging for *ArtsJournal*, although it paid no money, helped me through the transition and continues to make me happy. I was no longer a full-time teacher in the Dance Division at New York University's Tisch School of the Arts. I had published a biography about Jerome Robbins and his work. What came next?

I had read Don McDonagh's 1973 biography of Martha Graham, the one that Agnes de Mille published in 1991 (the year Graham died), and a number of relevant others. Looking back on myself of ten years ago, I realize that I had some nerve in attempting this book, assuming that as a dancer, choreographer, and writer, I had one foot up the ladder. I had taken morning classes at the Martha Graham Studio, seen many of her dances, and written about them. Dressed in one of her Yves Saint Laurent pantsuits, she had nodded briefly to me as I waited on a bench to meet and interview Margot Fonteyn, who, along with Rudolf Nureyev, was preparing to premiere Graham's *Lucifer.*

What I hadn't counted on was the remarkable generosity and support that has sustained my efforts. Janet Eilber, artistic director of the Martha Graham Center of Contemporary Dance, not only spoke with me, but allowed me to read Graham's letters to her younger sister Georgia, walked me through the company's wardrobe of costumes at Westbeth after Hurricane Sandy, honored me at an event in 2011, and answered my innumerable questions about productions. At her behest, Oliver Tobin, director of Martha Graham Resources, kindly copied and sent me DVDs of major Graham works.

The Graham teacher and former company dancer extraordinaire Peggy Lyman invited me to her Connecticut house, where she laid out her beautifully organized scrapbooks for my perusal, fed lunch to me and my husband, and answered my questions. Stuart Hodes sent me a heavy box of galleys so I might read his *Onstage with Martha Graham* before its 2021 publication. The Graham dancer Terese Capucilli shared material and memories with me. So did a number of dancers now deceased: Bonnie Bird, Dorothy Bird, Jane Dudley, Jean Erdman, Nina Fonaroff, Martha Hill, Mary Hinkson, Helen Priest Rogers, Bessie Schönberg, Ethel Winter, and Yuriko (Kikuchi).

When I traveled to Washington, D.C., to peruse the Library of Congress's Martha Graham Collection and related others, Elizabeth Aldrich, then curator of dance, took me home with her, where her husband, Brian Russell Olson, cooked and served our dinner, and their three-legged dog escorted me to bed.

When I needed to do some research in Santa Barbara, where Graham spent her adolescence, Ninotchka Bennahum put me up at her house, cooked dinner while I entertained her then-little daughter Marianna, arranged for me to deliver a lecture-demonstration at the University of California, Santa Barbara, where she was at the time a professor, and walked with me through avenues I needed to see and a house on Garden Street in which Graham's family had once lived.

Sitting next to Douglas Nielsen at a New York performance resulted in an invitation to spend five days in Tucson at the University of Arizona, where he was dean and director of dance. There, I lectured to Jim Clouser's Dance History students and performed my talking-dancing solo *Body (in) Print*. More important, Doug took me to the Desert Lodge, where Graham had visited her retired younger sister "Geordie," took me up Sabino Canyon, and invited me to visit classes and performances and join a faculty dinner. He also made sure that I saw relevant holdings relating to Graham in the university library and made it possible for me to interview Dan Leach, who had known Graham years before.

When I visited Bennington College, faculty member Dana Reitz—dancer, choreographer, teacher—led me and my husband into the small upstairs theater in which a number of Graham's works were first seen, showed me the studios where she had taught and the rooms in which she had been housed, and talked with me at the coffee shop in town. The great expanse of grass looked much as it had when the luminous New York faculty members strode across it, and they still live in the photos and films taken by their students.

Sometimes people I wrote to or talked with (pestered?) gave me a sudden flashing memory, a word, a fact, a story, an image. I am thankful for valuable contributions from Clinton Atkinson, Karen Bell-Kanner, Kathleen Brewster, Selma Jeanne Cohen, Agnes de Mille, Lucia Dlugoszewski, Deborah Friedes, Ann Hutchinson Guest, Erick Hawkins, Martha Hill, Stuart Hodes, Elizabeth Kendall, Francis Mason, Don McDonagh, Barbara Morgan, John Mueller, Ron Protas, Bertram Ross, Jane Sherman, Janet Mansfield Soares, and Elizabeth Zimmer.

Prominent among those I must thank are the curators who have helped me over the years, such as Tanisha Jones, Linda Murray, Madeleine Nichols, and Jan Schmidt at the Jerome Robbins Division of the New York Public Library for the Performing Arts, plus the library assistants both in New York City and at the Library of Congress who lugged heavy boxes to me and found things I hadn't expected to see.

I am deeply grateful to my agent and friend, Robert Cornfield, whose astute commentaries on my manuscript helped give the book its final shape, to my longtime friend and colleague Marcia B. Siegel for her advice and help, and to my West Coast friend and colleague Martha Ullman West. I honor and thank my late husband, Murray Ralph, who loved and encouraged me almost every step of the way; my supportive son, the drummer Tobias Ralph; and everyone who said a few words that ignited my brain.

ERRAND INTO THE MAZE

$$\sim 1 \sim$$

FROM COAL-FED ALLEGHENY TO SANTA BARBARA'S OCEAN

I
N 1971, MARTHA GRAHAM SPOKE deprecatingly and with win-
ning frankness to an interviewer. Among the three daughters of
Dr. George Graham, she had not, she said, been the pretty one:
"Mary was blond and gorgeous. Geordie had curly auburn hair and
big beautiful eyes. And then there was little old slit-eyed me."

But it was, of course, Martha, the eldest of the three, whose cheekbones photographers came to adore and who—as a dance artist adven-
turing into new, somber, and challenging territory—was often
caricatured in her skeletal glory by newspaper cartoonists.

In any case, it was never conventional beauty that made people
look twice at Graham. Even when she was a rather plain little girl by
the standards of the day, she had a sense of herself and could summon
an imperious manner when she thought a situation called for it. Dis-
liking the experience of being on a train, four- or five-year-old Martha informed the conductor, "I'm Dr. Graham's daughter, and I want
out of here!"

She was proud of the fact that her dainty little mother, Jane Beers
(usually "Jenny" or "Jeanie"), could trace her lineage back to Myles
Standish, the well-born military officer who arrived on the *Mayflower*
in 1620, hired to help organize that first British colony on American
soil. Miss Beers, the eldest of three sisters, would have been about

twenty-two years old in 1893 when she eloped with George Graham, fourteen years older than she and a covert ladies' man. The family was strictly Presbyterian. The daughters—Martha (b. 1894), Mary (b. 1896), and Georgia (b. 1900)—attended Sunday school (Martha even taught there at one point). On the Sabbath, the only toys they were allowed to play with were brown-and-white blocks with biblical scenes on them (which the often-rebellious eldest daughter detested and declined to touch).

In the many interviews Graham gave over the decades, she polished the memories that remained the most pungent to her and that could be said to have influenced her work. She divided her childhood from her birth until she came of age into two distinct parts, the first spent in her father's hometown of Allegheny, Pennsylvania (swallowed up by Pittsburgh in 1907), and the second in Santa Barbara, California, where the Graham family moved when she was fourteen. It was not just her metamorphosis from little girl to adolescent that she stressed, but the differences between life in the two cities and the birthmarks that both left on her art. Many of the dances that later made her famous drew on the dualities of restraint and freedom, decorum and wildness that molded her bisected early years.

The city of Allegheny was cradled by the Monongahela and Allegheny rivers as they join to flow into the Ohio. From Pittsburgh's steel mills across the river, effluvia more noxious than river water also bathed the town. Even when deprecating the pollution, writers marveled at the vision of power harnessed and transformed. In his 1907 book, *The Romance of Steel: The Story of a Thousand Millionaires*, Herbert W. Casson could not resist painting a heroic image of Pittsburgh's mills.

> The city has always its pillar of cloud by day and pillar of fire by night. A yellow haze hangs over the region, as though reflecting the gold-making that is going on below. Floating rivers of dense black smoke flow from hundreds of chimneys and flood the streets between the skyscrapers. At night the scene is one of lurid grandeur—a continuous fire festival.

When Martha and her sisters left their Fremont Street home, silk veils covered their hats and faces, and they wore gloves winter and summer. They were allowed to play in the open air when they visited their mother's sister Anna and her family in the more rural town of Mars. The Grahams sometimes went to Atlantic City at Easter, too, and photos show them in Hot Springs, Arkansas, where one of Dr. Graham's five brothers lived and where Martha's father, "in his sweet way," said she years later, would take the waters "to get boiled out of him his naughtiness" (probably not a thought that occurred to her at the time). The brothers, she said approvingly, were all "hellers."

In later life, Graham couldn't remember having any friends her age when she was a small child, unless you counted her "slew of cousins" (Jenny's two sisters, Mary and Anna, had ten offspring between them—all girls). Nor did she ever mention where she received her primary education ("We didn't go to school too early," she said to an interviewer). Their young mother invented playtimes that Martha remembered as "enchanting" and may have been educational as well.

Elements of theatricality infused the sisters' recreation. They loved dressing up in their mother's silk petticoats, which took its toll on the petticoats, so Mrs. Graham stitched little skirts with trains for her girls (they insisted on trains), and they swept grandly about, impersonating grown-up ladies. Their parents returned from a trip to California with three pairs of what Graham called "little Fu-Manchu shoes" to add to their disguises.

At some point, a cardboard theater, telling the tale of Little Red Riding Hood, made its way into the house, and Martha—fascinated early on by the interplay between darkness and light—left the room where her siblings, mother, cousins, and aunts were playing and returned to the toy theater. Something, she realized, wasn't quite right: How could Little Red Riding Hood find her way to grandmother's house unless there was a light in the window to guide her? Martha struck a match and put it in place, with predictable results. By the time the adults had smelled smoke and come running, the prudent child had already thrown a rug over the burning toy.

Late in life, she christened the little paper theater as her first stage set—her "first attempt to make another world."

Accounts of her early temper fits also suggest a sense of drama that could be interpreted as presaging a career on the stage. Once, hating the dress she was supposed to wear to school, she tore it off herself. (Her mother told her they'd mend it and she would wear it to school.)

Lizzie Prendergast, the family's young Irish cook and nursemaid, also stimulated the girls' imaginations. An engaging storyteller and singer with a good voice, she could entertain them even as she prepared the family dinner. George Graham—before marrying, starting a family, and moving his practice into their large hillside home—had served as a medical doctor in nearby Dixmont, at the Western Pennsylvania Hospital, an institution specializing in mental disorders. He had treated the orphaned Lizzie at some point—apparently for severe dog bites. She credited him with saving her life and, according to family legend, showed up on the Graham doorstep soon after Martha was born, offering her services.

The household seems to have had surprising fissures in the rules of discipline, morality, and ladylike behavior that reflected nineteenth-century Christian values. During Dr. Graham's childhood, when he and his brothers had lived for a time in Hannibal, Missouri, the only church nearby was Roman Catholic, and the family opted to forgo theological differences and attend services; mistrusted Christianity was apparently better than none. When he and his wife were out of town, they had no objection to Lizzie's taking the girls with her to the Catholic church in Allegheny, where Martha became fascinated with the vestments, the statues and paintings, the incense, the colors, the music—in short, the theatricalized ritual of the services.

Mrs. Graham disapproved of professional theater (as, no doubt, did her own mother and formidable grandmother, with her black silk gowns and white widow's caps). Yet George Graham took four-year-old Martha to a Punch-and-Judy show and paid little attention to what she was reading in his considerable library. One afternoon he escorted her to a play, scandalizing his wife. It isn't recorded what

Jenny thought on the occasions when he took his eldest girl to the races and helped her place one-dollar bets. These gambling forays were possibly the source for a remark of Dr. Graham's that Martha cherished and often quoted: "You're like a horse that runs best on a muddy track."

In 1908, a tragedy and a change of residence resulted in a profound alteration in the family's way of life. Jane Graham bore a son, William, who died before his second birthday, leaving her not only bereft but in delicate health. In light of this and Mary's worsening asthma, the Graham family (including Lizzie) left Allegheny for Santa Barbara and cleaner air. According to Graham, this wasn't the first long train trip they made to the West Coast. "Mother said, 'I can't live here. I can't live in this god-forsaken city' [meaning the Pennsylvania coal town]. So we picked up everything and went to California again and stayed there." Dr. Graham maintained his practice in Allegheny for several years and took Santa Barbara vacations as often as he could, finally retiring in 1912. His wife's sister Mary ("Auntie Re") was widowed in 1910, and over the next few years Mrs. Graham persuaded her husband to bring both her sisters' families to Santa Barbara.

Graham, like the pioneering American dancers who preceded her, was given to recounting epiphanies. Loïe Fuller, performing in a play when the lighting system accidentally dimmed, filled time by rushing around the stage brandishing an overlong skirt that she happened to be wearing: "It's a butterfly!" cried the enchanted crowd (and so began Fuller's transformative solos with fabric and light). Isadora Duncan experienced her revelation in the Parthenon ("I had found my dance, and it was a prayer"). Ruth St. Denis wrote of being steered into the spiritual reaches of Orientalism by a cigarette poster in a Buffalo drugstore window that showed the goddess Isis on her throne. The facts do not fully support these inspirational claps on the head as jump starters for careers, but—polished by memory and repeated many times—the stories provided iconic assists for the women's attempts to dignify dancing and separate it from popular entertainment.

One of Graham's early epiphanies was Santa Barbara—the burgeoning city and everything about it. Picnicking on the high, flat tongue of a peninsula known as the Mesa and referred to by Martha as "the old Diblee estate," she and her siblings cavorted like young horses. "I remember running in absolute ecstasy into the sun with my arms open to the wind . . . And I'd get so tired I'd fall down and then I'd get up and run some more. But it was the sense of light, the sense of freedom, and the sense of the beginning of NOW, that terrific beginning of one's impulse." She was seventy-seven years old when she recollected this feeling—not for the first time. And, although the Grahams attended the Presbyterian church in Santa Barbara, she felt in retrospect that "no child can develop as a real puritan in a semitropical climate. California swung me in the direction of paganism, though years were to pass before I was fully emancipated."

However selective memories of childhood can be, anyone who has gone from an industrial city in northeastern America to the western shores of the continent can understand how a fourteen-year-old girl in 1908 may have experienced California as a place in tune with her own developing body and sensuality. The sunny days and balmy temperatures in a small city nestled between the tempestuous Pacific to the west and the Santa Ynez Mountains to the east were as heady as the scents of eucalyptus and manzanita on the bluffs and orange blossoms, magnolia, and jasmine in the gardens. Two blocks from the house on Garden Street, where the Grahams eventually settled, huge trees unfamiliar to an easterner graced Alameda Park. Everywhere flowers bloomed and fruits ripened. Crimson bougainvillea vines draped over porches, jacaranda trees sprouted lavender blossoms, and agave plants reared their leafy swords. A girl could step outside and pick guavas and figs for breakfast or lemons to spice the dinner. Uphill stood the eighteenth-century Franciscan mission. A trolley running down State Street led to the harbor and the beach.

The population of Santa Barbara was not quite as variegated as its flora. However, it included the Spaniards and Mexicans who were part of its founding years, Chinese, Japanese, and a dwindling tribe of Chumash Indians. The Chinese workers who did the Grahams' cooking, housework, and laundry adored pretty, blond Mary. Little Geordie was the favorite of a fat old friar at the mission.

Martha—and soon, Mary—could easily walk from the first Graham residence on De la Vina Street to the Santa Barbara High School, a substantial, somewhat grim stone edifice, out of keeping with any adobe-walled, tile-roofed buildings that acknowledged California's Spanish history. When the family moved to the Garden Street house, the trips to school would have taken longer, and the walk home was a steep, uphill one, perhaps entailing a trolley ride. Graham's strength and physical adroitness initially found an outlet in basketball; according to schoolmates, she was a nimble, slippery devil on the court. Anyone considering her high school career would think her the typical bright student. She joined the Quorum, the school's debating society; organized a school dance; and contributed to the yearbook, *Olive and Gold*, and edited it during her senior year. She adored her English teacher, Jane Carroll Byrd, and learned to sew expertly.

Santa Barbara wasn't quite the cultural backwater Graham once claimed it was. ("Nothing ever erupted there but a nice day.") In 1908, the year the Grahams settled there, the city boasted four theaters that presented plays, including the Potter (part of the gigantic seaside Potter Hotel). The others showed a mix of vaudeville and silent movies. Influxes of wealthy people seeking space, sunshine, and clean air swelled the population, which, in the 1910 census, reached eleven thousand. And in 1912 the Ace American Picture Company (known, because of its trademark symbol, as "The Flying A") set up a branch in Santa Barbara, the following year building a studio that covered two downtown blocks.

The initial group of twenty (actors, crew, and a cadre of cowboys) arrived on July 6, and by noon the next day, the Flying A had completed its first locally made one-reeler, *The Greaser and the Weakling* (Mexicans weren't always treated respectfully in these mini sagas). During Graham's last year of high school, one- and two-reelers were being filmed not just on outlying ranches and on the studio lot but on city streets. Citizens could hardly avoid bumping into a shoot.

Everyday life mingled with celluloid visions of the Old West, with its Indian maidens, Spanish missions, and cowboys both gallant and villainous.

However, the experience that apparently kindled in Graham the desire for a life in the theater was a single live performance. On May 3, 1911, Ruth St. Denis was scheduled to present in Santa Barbara the program of solo dances she had been touring with since December 1910, and Graham saw a poster advertising it downtown. Oddly, it was one of St. Denis's six shows presented in late April at the Mason Opera House in Los Angeles, to which Martha had persuaded her father to take her. They did not travel the ninety-odd miles on the train that linked San Francisco with Los Angeles, but made their way south on the schooner that regularly plied the coast. The outing—as well as the corsage of violets Dr. Graham had bought for his daughter—must have seemed exciting from the start to a girl approaching her seventeenth birthday.

St. Denis had embarked on her career as a soloist only four years prior to this, her second American tour. Her performances often baffled spectators to whom dancing was what they saw on the vaudeville circuit. The images she presented onstage were both alluring and high-minded, sometimes simultaneously. Although, as a girl, St. Denis had paraded her high kicks and splits at Worth's dime museum in New York and learned stagecraft from performing in plays produced by David Belasco, her ideas about movement were influenced by the Delsarte System of Expression, devised by François Delsarte (1811–1871) and further developed by such American exponents as Genevieve Stebbins. In an era when dancing was viewed as licentious, Delsarte's system analyzed gestures and positions of the body in terms of the balance among the spiritual, the mental, and the physical.

As young Martha Graham would have noticed, Ruth St. Denis's art involved transformation on two levels. She embedded herself in cultures where dance was associated with religion as well as with entertainment. And although she didn't stint on exotic sets, fake jewels, wigs, and gauzy fabrics, a number of her solos involved an inner transformation; the character she impersonated rose to a higher state of self-knowledge or received a spiritual revelation.

St. Denis hadn't studied the dance styles of the Asian countries she represented onstage; her light steps, whirlings, and stampings had little to do with, for example, Indian tradition. Instead, at a time when Orientalism was all the rage in theater, literature, art, and design, it was the philosophy and the iconography of various cultures that she plundered for her dances, along with exotica she had observed in Coney Island's 1904 "Durbar of Delhi exhibit with performers" and in the 1892 extravaganza *Egypt Through Centuries* at the Eldorado Amusement Park in Weehawken, New Jersey, on the palisades just across the Hudson River from New York City. What Graham and her father saw that day in Los Angeles (and perhaps again in Santa Barbara?) struck the high school girl as startlingly beautiful—and something more. The program consisted of three solos that had figured in St. Denis's first New York recital in 1906, *Radha*, *The Incense*, and *The Cobras*; two, *The Yogi* and *The Nautch*, that she had composed during her successful European appearances between 1908 and 1910; and three excerpts from *Egypta*, an elaborate dance-drama with a cast of fifty that she had premiered in New York in December 1910. The piano scores for all these were by Western composers. (Radha went through her transformations to pseudo-oriental extracts from the opera *Lakmé* by Léo Delibes.)

At thirty-two, St. Denis was a charismatic performer (and remained so into old age), and the theatrical savvy she had acquired while performing in Belasco's productions made her aware of how to balance a program. In *The Cobras*, for instance, she played a snake charmer, coiling and rippling her remarkably flexible arms while a jeweled ring on each hand formed the serpents' eyes. In *The Incense*, those sinuous arms took on the image of the smoke rising from the incense that she, as a devout woman, had scattered from a bowl into each of two braziers—her sari-draped body swaying and settling into soft curves, as if she had become elevated by the fumes into communion with the deity she had come to worship.

She opened her California programs with the "Palace Dance" from *Egypta*. Red-wigged, bejeweled, and flourishing a tambourine, she re-created herself as an exotic court entertainer. Several hours later, the evening ended with the more complex *Radha*, an ingenious amalgam of the desires of the flesh and the triumph of the spirit.

Seated on her throne, wearing more jewels than fabric, St. Denis as Radha, the beloved of Krishna, rose to demonstrate to her assembled priests ("Hindu" extras that sometimes included St. Denis's brother) the dangerous delights absorbed through the five senses. To convey Sight, she caressed a string of pearls; she sipped from a cup of wine for Taste and shook little ankle bells for Hearing. The scent of a garland of roses, draped over her arching body, led to the "Delirium of the Senses," in which—now wearing a full skirt—she spun herself into ecstatic collapse. Having illustrated the senses so seductively, she then rejected them all and returned to her niche, purified. *Radha* undoubtedly sent members of that Los Angeles audience home congratulating themselves that they had seen something morally uplifting.

The program certainly inspired Martha Graham. Perhaps for the first time, she beheld a performer presenting herself as a mysterious and glamorous presence, as a magician with fabric and lighting, as a goddess. Interviewed in 1986, when the Martha Graham Dance Company revived *The Incense*, Graham recalled St. Denis's uncanny, seemingly boneless arm ripple as "one of the treasures of the world. It went from the spine through the entire body and was in touch with all the vibrations of the universe."

After seeing St. Denis perform, Graham veered onto a new course—appearing as one of thirty-seven "geishas" in a downtown performance based on Gilbert and Sullivan's *The Mikado* and acting in plays at Santa Barbara High. She undertook the female lead in a classroom effort, *Dido and Aeneas*, and, in her last year, had no time for basketball. After she appeared as one of the heroine's three aunts in the senior play, *Prunella, or Love in a Dutch Garden*, a 1904 romantic fantasy by Laurence Housman and Granville Barker, she received what may have been her first review, which she, as editor of *Olive and Gold*, was doubtless pleased to publish in its pages:

> The interpreter of "Privacy," the aunt who remains in the forlorn garden waiting for Prunella's return, was a fine bit of acting. Miss Graham's voice exactly suited the part and she was careful not to overact when she discovers that the man who bought her house is he who lured Prunella away. Sincere and artistic appreciation of proportion marked every moment of Miss Graham's admirable work.

After graduation, Graham didn't apply to Vassar as her father hoped she might, instead enrolling in the Cumnock School of Expression in Los Angeles, which turned out to be quite near where Ruth St. Denis and her new husband, Ted Shawn, opened a school in 1915.

Why Cumnock? It's likely that Graham first heard the name when Hope Westen, a Santa Barbara High School alumna who was studying at Cumnock, returned to her alma mater to stage some dances for *Prunella* (the play involved a Pierrot and a troupe of traveling players). This all-female college, built to resemble Shakespeare's half-timbered domicile in Stratford-upon-Avon, was not designed as a jumping-off place for girls bent on a career in the burgeoning motion picture industry. Cumnock, like many of the "schools of expression" that peppered the United States during the first third of the twentieth century, was founded by a former student of Robert McLean Cumnock, who headed the School of Oratory at Northwestern University and based its teaching on his methods and lofty principles.

Dr. and Mrs. Graham would have been reassured about the school's mission, as stated in words similar to these:

> The purpose of a true School of Expression should be to develop character and prepare one to live. Our aims are therefore:
> First—Upbuilding the inner man;
> Second—Preparing the body to express the inner man;

Third—Developing the individual. It is absolutely essential that one should learn to express himself from the heart out. The result is a genuineness of character, a naturalness and simplicity, together with personal power.

Cumnock students studied literature (Shakespeare and Browning were high on the list) and the history of art. They developed their voices and delivery for public speaking, while "Physical Training" primed their bodies for expressive gestures. They studied pedagogy and practiced teaching. They acted in plays and learned about play production. Staying for four years, as Graham evidently did, meant being certified to teach oral and dramatic expression in high schools.

Martha had a role in the school's production of Arthur Wing Pinero's 1898 play, *Trelawny of the "Wells."* The heroine, a successful actress in popular melodramas, abandons her career to marry a respectable suitor. It's not long before she yearns to return to the stage and leaves her husband, only to realize that she has outgrown her former theatrical style and taste. Fortunately, she meets a young playwright who is ambitious to write material more serious, restrained, and realistic than that found in melodramas, and she becomes the star of his play. (Meanwhile, her former husband has, unbeknownst to her, become an actor too, so the ending is satisfactory on all counts.)

Except for the husband, one might be tempted to see in this a parallel with Graham's own early career as she moved from performing numbers in vaudeville and on Broadway toward deeper and more innovative forms of expression.

She must have enjoyed her years at Cumnock (1913–1917). A photo taken in 1916 shows a plumpish, jolly teacher seated outside with six students surrounding her. Some are grinning shyly, two are sober, but only Martha leans slightly sideways at an angle, the better to beam a big, delighted smile at the photographer. If you glance at the picture, she immediately catches your eye. She's the one offering herself wholeheartedly to the camera and the occasion.

The years that Graham spent at Cumnock and at home in Santa Barbara were ones of upheaval in the world. The 1913 Armory Show in New York blasted art circles with new visions from abroad, pointing the road to full-fledged modernism. Paintings by such outstanding Americans as Edward Hopper and Maurice Prendergast vied for attention with more than one hundred works by European Futurists, Cubists, Impressionists, and Post-Impressionists. The *Titanic* had sunk in 1912 from a collision with an iceberg, but when the British liner *Lusitania* went down in May 1915, the cause was a torpedo launched by a German U-boat. The act and its ramifications helped galvanize the United States' entry into World War I two years later.

A more personal upheaval occurred in Graham's private life. In 1914, after her first year at Cumnock, her father died. In later years, she spoke of embezzlement by a partner of her father's concerning the purchase of some land and of privations in the ensuing years, but he appears to have left his family moderately well-off. His half share of a ranch in Goleta, planted mostly in walnuts, yielded some income. Each Graham daughter stood to inherit $6,000 (the equivalent of approximately $167,000 in 2022 in terms of buying power). Martha used some of her portion to return to Cumnock, and in the summer of 1916 she felt confident enough to enroll in a school on a Los Angeles hill—the school that called itself Denishawn—and learn from the dancer she had idolized for almost six years.

$$\sim 2 \sim$$

DENISHAWN DAYS: LEARNING FROM MISS RUTH AND TED

GRAHAM WAS TWENTY-TWO when she appeared at Denishawn for the organization's second summer course. Her age, her solid little body, and her lack of dance experience did not instantly impress either St. Denis or her husband of two years, Ted Shawn. Shawn, a dozen years younger than his wife, had risen quickly to a position of power in her career. Like Graham, he had seen St. Denis perform in 1911, when he was a nineteen-year-old Denver divinity student wondering how he might combine his two interests: dancing and religion. In 1914 he did so with an ardor St. Denis couldn't resist. Vernon and Irene Castle had made exhibition ballroom dancing popular, and Shawn, with Hilda Beyer as his partner, became a feature of St. Denis's touring program, then became *her* dancing partner and her spouse.

Shawn hadn't yet turned twenty-five the summer that Graham became a committed dance student, but he had already begun to cast himself, onstage and off, as St. Denis's entranced suitor as well as her master. In his *Arabic Suite* (1914), St. Denis appeared as a dancing girl, an almeh, practicing seductively while alone in her tent, then sinking to a couch to await his coming. In Shawn's words, "I entered, burnoose flying and white turban twisted high. Brandishing a curved sword, I executed a dashing vigorous dance full of leaps and turns accented by pounding feet." Presenting a manly image—like that recently introduced to a doubtful and puritanical American public by Mikhail Mordkin in his performances with Anna Pavlova—became one of Shawn's missions. He had to work to achieve stereotypical masculinity; his body was strong and well-proportioned but lacked obvious muscular definition; his facial features were small and his cheeks fleshy. It must have stung when Redfern Mason wrote of him in the *San Francisco Examiner*, "It is well enough for a woman to be orchidaceous, but one dislikes it in a man."

During the first months of 1916, Serge Diaghilev's Ballets Russes appeared in American cities with a repertory of ballets that included Mikhail Fokine's savage Orientalist *Schéhérazade* and his Russian folktale *The Firebird*. Perhaps influenced by these colorful one-act works, Shawn busied himself expanding the ideas that fueled some of St. Denis's solos into duets or ensemble settings. In 1907 St. Denis had presented herself as an Indian nautch dancer entertaining in the streets of Delhi and as a yogi seeking enlightenment; nine years later, during Graham's first summer at Denishawn, Shawn cast himself as a disguised holy man and St. Denis as a nautch dancer reformed by her devotion to him. He added ballroom duets and Spanish-dance scenarios whose fiery edge provided contrast to St. Denis's more spiritual vignettes.

No concert or vaudeville tours were possible in the slack summer months for the small company that starred St. Denis—"assisted by Ted Shawn." In 1915, to earn additional money, Shawn masterminded the creation of the Denishawn School. In all his arrangements—whether academic or artistic—St. Denis was complicit, but not especially happy. After all, before marrying Shawn, she had performed at a benefit for the National Woman Suffrage Association, and she had asked that the word "obey" be omitted from their wedding ceremony in New York City; she refused to wear a wedding ring. Nor did she like to teach; she was, as she later admitted, not very good at it, but she could, in her words, "inspire like hell."

In 1915 Los Angeles was a city of 550,000, the hub of major agricultural activity; there was also a great deal of open space within the city proper. Shawn and St. Denis had no difficulty acquiring a Spanish-style mansion on a hill, surrounded by acres of land. Students boarding there for the summer could cool off in the swimming pool and, wearing their uniform black bathing suits, take dance classes on an outdoor wooden platform built for that purpose or study yoga with "Miss Ruth" in a small indoor studio. When on tour, the couple promoted the school with a film of them having tea on a veranda, St. Denis leading students in an outdoor yoga class, and pretty young women handing their wraps to a dark-skinned servant in a turban before they headed to the outdoor studio (or the pool). Parents might have assumed that they would be sending their daughter to an artistically inclined, spiritually elevated finishing school.

Memorializing St. Denis after her death, in 1968, Graham wrote in *The New York Times* of "those morning hours of counsel as we sat on a small balcony and she read certain texts from the Bible, which I had known all my life, and from East Indian literature, which I had not known."

St. Denis and Shawn had discovered at their first meeting that they had much in common. They both knew and revered Emerson's writings. She was raised in Christian Science; he, too, had found Mary Baker Eddy's writings stimulating. François Delsarte's principles of expression had shaped her dancing; he had recently studied them. As Suzanne Shelton noted in her biography of St. Denis, the couple modeled their school on the utopian arts colonies that had figured in their own lives prior to their meeting—she inheriting the precepts of the Eagleswood community in Perth Amboy, where her parents had met, he through his whirlwind studies at the Triunian School of Personal Harmonizing in New Haven, where poet Bliss Carman was in residence.

Denishawn might have taken its tone from Carman's 1908 book, *The Making of Personality*, in which he accorded Terpsichore, the muse of dance, a high position in the business of enlightenment:

> To follow her commandments, keeping proper time, proper force and
> form, in every motion we create, is to bring ourselves, body and spirit
> and understanding, hourly into happier accord with the orderly

rhythms of infinitude. By doing so we lose timidity and strangeness and distrust of ourselves; we learn number, proportion, accuracy, skill; and we become assured, gracious, composed and glad. For art not only holds the keys to the realm of beauty, but to the realms of knowledge and benevolence as well. This is the truth which every artist divines, and which all must one day come to perceive.

Even as Denishawn presented itself as enlightened and enlightening, with lectures on philosophy and the history of dance, Shawn also endeavored to turn it into a successful business. He taught ballroom dance and ballet. The previously mentioned Denishawn film shows him guiding a little girl who is attempting to balance on pointe. "Greek," "Egyptian," and "oriental" dancing were also part of the curriculum. At Denishawn, a student could learn a solo and purchase the right to perform it, along with sheet music and instructions on making the appropriate costume. Denishawn franchises were negotiated for a fee. An aspiring dancer who, like Graham, arrived for the 1916 summer session, paid $500 for room and board and twelve weeks of classes and lectures. Those taking single classes put a dollar into the box provided for that purpose. A private lesson cost $5.00.

During Graham's first summer at Denishawn, instruction in dyeing fabric, crafting costumes, and fashioning props was put to immediate practical use, since Shawn and St. Denis were preparing a massive spectacle, *A Dance Pageant of Egypt, Greece, and India*, which premiered in Berkeley at the University of California's Greek Theatre on July 29, 1916. The program advertised a company of one hundred. Denishawn's musical director, Louis Horst, conducted forty members of the Steindorf Orchestra. Martha Graham, Ada Forman, Katharine Laidlaw, and Ernestine Myers are listed as "Dancers with Musical Instruments," although for the performance in San Diego on August 5, Margaret Severn replaced Graham. A photograph of Graham in Egyptian garb, properly two-dimensional and holding two sistra, may have been taken at a later date; Shawn and St. Denis ransacked their previous work for some of the dances and lifted material from the pageant for their tours for years to come.

The most valuable principles taught at Denishawn may have been Delsartian. From lectures by Henrietta Russell Hovey, who had studied with the master, and in classes with Shawn, the students learned how movement revealed character, and they practiced exercises that helped them portray feelings through posture and gesture. Decades later, in her New York school, Graham on at least one occasion evoked Delsarte (without mentioning him). While teaching a class in her own technique, she demonstrated the various shifts that could alter a simple turn of the head to the side to signify abandon (by tilting it back at the same time) or speculation (by tilting it forward).

Delsarte's ideas explicated and promoted the emotion-driven tensions within the body that infused modern dance after Graham and fellow Denishawn dancers Doris Humphrey and Charles Weidman had severed their connections with the school and company and begun to develop their own styles. And it may have been in part the Delsarte exercises that attracted silent film actors to visit Denishawn and take classes. D. W. Griffith sent such stars as Lillian and Dorothy Gish to the school (Lillian rented the original school premises when Shawn and St. Denis set off on a vaudeville tour with their company in 1916–17). St. Denis, in her autobiography, *An Unfinished Life*, remembered the screen actresses Mabel Normand, Ina Claire, Ruth Chatterton, and Colleen Moore coming to absorb principles of expressive movement. Shawn choreographed dances for Lillian Gish and Rozsika Dolly (of the Dolly sisters) in Griffith's 1915 *The Lily and the Rose*.

Stars were also "discovered" at Denishawn. The hordes of dancers on the steps of Babylon before its fall in Griffith's 1916 *Intolerance* came from the school and were led by the future film actress Carol Dempster. Margaret Loomis went from being one of St. Denis's favorites to having a considerable career in 1920s movies. (No doubt her training in Denishawn exotica prepared her well for the role of O. Noto San in the fifty-minute 1917 comedy *Hashimura Togo*, starring Hollywood's notable Japanese star Sessue Hayakawa.) Five years later, Louise Brooks graduated from Denishawn into movie stardom. Shawn himself, garlanded in flowers, romanced Gloria Swanson in the "Vision of Love" sequence in Cecil B. DeMille's 1919 *Don't Change Your Husband*. That same year, Graham evidently performed as a court dancer in the Babylon dream sequence in DeMille's *Male and Female* (although most of her number was cut).

By 1919 Graham had made her mark in Denishawn. Prior to about 1918, she had impressed Shawn and St. Denis primarily by her intelligence and her diligence. In 1939, St. Denis recalled the young student as being initially "exceedingly shy and quiet, with the same fascinating, homely face that she has today. Most of the time in my class she sat very still and listened. When she spoke it was only to ask an intelligent question." (She was being tactful; Shawn recounts that St. Denis's first opinion of Graham—after the individual session required for all new students—was, "She's hopeless.") Eventually St. Denis made Graham a helper, seamstress, and sometime confidante, but reserved her greatest admiration for Doris Humphrey, a red-haired, lyrical beauty who arrived at Denishawn in 1917, already an experienced dancer and teacher with an interest in choreography. It was only later that St. Denis could write with confidence, "If one saw Martha do a certain dance, it was rendered innocuous and pale when any other girl attempted it."

Graham's shyness and reserve, then, didn't entirely mask the ferocious intensity she possessed. Horst—later Graham's musical director, mentor, and lover—said, "The first time I ever saw Martha she was running across the tennis courts at Denishawn. I watched her from my window, her black hair flying. She had a special quality—like a wild animal." Shawn had his epiphany about her somewhat later. In the course of a lesson, he often taught the students an entire dance to see what they'd make of it. One day, the dance was *Serenata Morisca*, a solo he had devised to music already in print, which he described years later as "a dance with a circular skirt, which was a blend of Spanish and North African that you could say was a mish-mash. All right, so it was. It was good theater. The music was very dashing, strongly rhythmic." As the students went through the dance during that session, he said, "Suddenly for the first time since Martha had come to us my eye was caught. There at the back of the class she had come to life, she was glowing. Ah-hah! So after class I kept her. I told her, 'Martha, we've hit on something!'" According to Shawn, Graham made what may have been her professional debut performing *Serenata Morisca* in the prologue accompanying a feature film in a Los Angeles theater run by Samuel Rothafel, whose nickname, "Roxy," became attached to the immense movie palace he opened in New York in 1932 (at which time Martha Graham and Dance Group appeared on the opening program). The *Serenata Morisca* that was resurrected in 1986 for the Martha Graham Dance Company may not be exactly the solo that Graham herself performed. The former Denishawn dancer and author Jane Sherman based her reconstruction on what she believed to be the same number—renamed *Ballerina Real* in 1925, when it was performed by Doris Humphrey during Denishawn's Far East tour. If Sherman is correct, Shawn must have revised the dance somewhat. Graham danced to Ruperto Chapi's guitar piece of the same name (arranged for piano), while Humphrey performed to Mario Tarenghi's *Serenata*, op. 13.

It's clear from photos, however, that the dancer wore a tight bodice; a long, full skirt; jewelry; and maybe a flower behind her ear. That she portrayed an entertainer—whether at a sheik's court or not—is beyond dispute. Graham must have been adept at displaying the smolder that accompanies a certain kind of flirtatiousness. The skirt served the dancer as a prop as well as a costume—something to gather around her, hold up, swish from side to side as she took her little traveling steps, and make spiral in the air when she circled her leg high. When she spun, the audience that she eyed much of the time could receive a rewarding glimpse of flesh.

Martha, adoring St. Denis, became Shawn's protégée. St. Denis made only brief use of her as an uncredited Japanese servant boy assisting her in a solo, "Arranging the Flowers" (drawn from St. Denis's 1913 *O-Mika*). Shawn had seen something sexier and more volcanic about her. With her dark hair and eyes and the hint of a fiery temper, she fit into his growing interest in Spanish and Hispanic culture. In 1917, Denishawn moved and expanded, taking over the campus of the Westlake School for Girls at the corner of Alvarado and Sixth streets, across from Westlake (now MacArthur) Park, and created a four-hundred-seat outdoor theater. The L.A. *Graphic* of August 20 described and pictured a tiny, tented stage with an immense apron, on three sides of which the spectators sat. There the advanced students— Graham among them—honed their performing skills in Monday-night performances.

It's remarkable how quickly Graham progressed in her dancing, considering that she spent the 1916–17 academic year at Cumnock, returning to Denishawn for the 1917 summer session. St. Denis, Shawn, and the company had recently come home from their strenuous tour on the Orpheum Circuit (October 22, 1916, through June 11, 1917), part of the income from which went into purchasing Liberty Bonds in support of America's entrance into World War I. At some point, Graham's sisters joined her there. Pretty Mary, who'd been a lure for all the boys at Santa Barbara High, didn't stay long. As Graham recalled, "[She] said she wasn't interested: 'Why should I have to work so hard?'" Mary married a doctor, but big-eyed Georgia set out to rival her eldest sister and inherited a number of Martha's roles after the latter left Denishawn.

After America joined the fight in April 1917, St. Denis and Shawn's professional and marital difficulties were temporarily soothed by absence. St. Denis set off on a vaudeville tour with only Margaret Loomis sharing the program, and in December, when being drafted began to seem inevitable, Shawn enlisted in the Ambulance Corps. Since he was stationed at Camp Kearney near San Diego, he was able to teach at Denishawn on weekends. The brochure for the summer of 1918 advertised an array of classes: Delsarte; Ballet; Egyptian, Greek, and Oriental Dance; Plastique; Creative; and Geisha (a qualified Japanese woman had turned up to provide it). When not dancing, students rolled bandages in the curriculum item labeled Red Cross, and they, along with St. Denis, made trips to San Diego to perform for the troops.

Shawn was demobbed in December 1918, following the Armistice, while St. Denis was on tour with Doris Humphrey and three young female dancers, one of whom, Betty Horst (Louis's wife), performed *Serenata Morisca*, the solo Graham came to own. Louis Horst played piano for the performances. Denishawn was temporarily dissolved, most of the buildings sold, and Graham, with less than two years of training under her belt, taught classes to children and beginners in the renamed Ted Shawn Studio and lived on the top floor. Lizzie Prendergast came down from Santa Barbara to cook for her and for Shawn, who had a few pounds to shed after his less active days in the army.

The relationship between Shawn and Graham was a changeable one, judging from their later words about each other. Certainly both he and St. Denis were wounded when Graham contributed an essay to Oliver Sayler's 1930 *Revolt in the Arts*, in which she advocated a fresh American vision of dance as opposed to ballet or dances that purveyed "the weakling exoticism of a transplanted culture." Humphrey later accorded Shawn the lesser role in Denishawn, artistically speaking, and one detrimental to St. Denis's career as a soloist. In a 1970s interview, Graham said that she was never "deeply fond" of Shawn and that she wouldn't call him Papa Denishawn as the other students did (not surprising, however, since the age difference between them amounted to only three years). He was Mr. Shawn or Ted to her. She would never forgive him for "things he did about Miss Ruth." She did, however, appear to have forgiven him when she appeared in the 1950s at Jacob's Pillow, the school he founded in the Berkshires, to give a Sunday-night talk, resplendent in a tight, floor-length taffeta gown in wide bands of black and gold. When she was honored with a Capezio Award in 1960, she acknowledged Shawn and Horst, who were sitting together, as the two men who had "profoundly and constructively influenced her life and career" and said that she was happy that Shawn was there to see her get the award.

In 1923, after her last Denishawn performance before going into the Broadway revue *The Greenwich Village Follies*, she wrote him a letter that belies her later critical words: "The artist in me was born in Denishawn—and because that is fundamentally the me—I was born there. It's always B. D. (Before Denishawn) and A. D. (after Denishawn). Oh I wish I could tell you how much I thank you for it all . . . On little external things I may not always agree—or sympathize—

but in my heart—you are a god." Unless she was being hypocritical (Shawn had given her permission to perform *Serenata Morisca* in the *Follies* and perhaps another solo he had made for her), one can assume that this is how she viewed him when she was leaving the fold for a possible career on Broadway.

They seem to have been friends during their early Denishawn days. According to Shawn's reminiscences, taped in 1969, Graham told him of informing her mother, when she was quite young, of her desire for a married man and announcing, "I wish to go to this man whom I love with all my heart and I want time and I want privacy and I am going to a hotel with him." Shawn was startled by her story: "The honesty of it! The decisiveness of it." He apparently had gone to her for advice about his "own personal troubles," which can be assumed had to do with his marriage and his homosexual urges (St. Denis had her affairs; he had his).

At some point in her career Graham came to believe that "Miss Ruth was a goddess when she danced. Ted was a dancer dressed as a god." Early in 1919 Shawn created *Julnar of the Sea*, a full-evening fairy-tale dance-drama based on an *Arabian Nights* tale, for the Denishawn student Lillian Powell (prior to her career as a film star and, later still, a successful television actress). He added others of his students and sent the piece out on the vaudeville circuit. Then, in 1920, while St. Denis embarked on a long concert tour with fifteen women, a tenor, and three pianists, Shawn turned to his confidante and protégée, Martha (perhaps with a little persuasion on her part), and created another full-length spectacle with a starring role for her: *Xochitl*.

Shawn drew his scenario from a long poem by José María Roa Bárcena about the legendary Toltec queen, Xochitl. A key ingredient of the story is the accidental discovery by this onetime maiden's father: he can make pulque, an intoxicating drink, from the maguey plants he cultivates. Xochitl carries a sample to Emperor Tepancaltzin and eventually becomes his wife. It's possible that Shawn also saw José Obregón's 1869 painting *El descubrimiento del pulque*, which shows the maiden and her father presenting their discovery at court. Shawn remade the varying tales about Xochitl to suit the vaudeville circuit's appetite for sex and violence, adding elaborate costumes that bared a lot of flesh. The two-act piece gave Graham a role she could sink her teeth into. She also apparently sank her teeth into Shawn when he took over the leading male role from Robert Gorham, the tall, handsome Denishawn student for whom Shawn had created it (intending to stay in the studio himself and concoct other possibly lucrative vaudeville productions).

In Shawn's *Xochitl*, the lovely virgin has to fight for her virtue when the Emperor, having sampled the interesting new beverage to excess, attempts to deflower her. Graham released onstage the inner demon that she occasionally (and not entirely apologetically) referred to in later life. Gorham never committed himself to paper about Graham's performance, but a new and inexperienced recruit, the skinny nineteen-year-old Charles Weidman from Nebraska—who, broken in by Graham, temporarily replaced Gorham in performances on the Pantages Circuit after Gorham broke his foot—also emphasized the punishment he took when Xochitl fought off the Emperor's advances.

The score for *Xochitl* was supplied by Homer Grunn, whose interest in the music of Southwest Indian tribes colored many of his compositions. The Mexican artist Francisco Cornejo designed sets and costumes that Shawn deemed to be "anthropologically and archaeologically absolutely correct." Photos of the 1922–23 production show a proscenium frame bearing Aztec-inspired designs and a huge circular shape resembling the Aztec calendar stone painted on the backdrop just above Gorham's head as he sits on the Emperor's throne. A bodyguard stands ready at his side, and six maidens with fans (Georgia Graham made her debut as a Denishawn dancer in the original cast) are divided into two groups—one on either side of the dais, in positions ranging from kneeling to standing. Martha, as Xochitl, kneels to offer a vessel of pulque while her father (Weidman) watches. Feathers figure prominently.

The first scene (dropped for the 1921 vaudeville tour) shows Xochitl's father's maguey plantation and the discovery of pulque. In the second, climactic scene, Emperor Tepancaltzin's attempted rape and Xochitl's struggles are interrupted by the return of her parent, who

has been led away by the court ladies once they've finished their dancing (which, they performed, according to one source, "completely on
the half toe" and in flattened patterns resembling reliefs). Now, knife
raised, he rushes in to defend his daughter's honor, no matter the cost.
Xochitl, having acquired, in close combat, a taste for the handsome
Emperor, pleads with her father to drop the weapon. The grateful,
smitten, and suddenly sober ruler asks her to marry him. General
rejoicing.

This can be considered Graham's first "serious" professional role,
and clearly, she played it to the hilt—first in its several appearances
as a two-act work, then on the Pantages Circuit with three performances a day on weekdays and four on weekends, then on the concert
tour Shawn secured for a smaller company of six, including himself,
plus Horst as accompanist. For the vaudeville performances, Graham
also (perhaps as the eldest and most trusted of the group of dancers)
kept the books and doled out the pay.

When *Xochitl* played in Santa Barbara in 1920, Graham told a reporter from *The Morning Press* that she adored performing in the work:
"I love this dance-drama and have every faith in it; it has brought the
joy of life to me." It also brought out her power as a performer and an
awareness of the choreographic possibilities of more savage themes.
Her success in *Xochitl* launched her into eleven new roles in the
St. Denis–Shawn repertory and a concert tour headed by Shawn that
began in Los Angeles on September 8, 1921, and ended in New York
on December 2. Family and friends could view her in a range of roles
at Santa Barbara's Potter Theatre on September 12.

Graham's early days as a performer could be considered grueling,
but they were hardly atypical. She faced one-night stands, long train
rides, grubby dressing rooms, and backstage spaces that on the vaudeville circuit might be shared with comedians, musicians, and novelty
acts. She would have been responsible for taking care of her own costumes. Makeup came from tubes of greasepaint patted down with
powder. Mascara took the form of black chunks, which had to be
melted in a spoon held over a dressing room light bulb or a lit can of
Sterno; brushed onto the lashes, it often ended in the tiny drops that

gave it its name: "beading." Also, as Jane Sherman, who joined the Denishawn company in 1925, explained all too vividly in her memoir, *Soaring*, powdered zinc, glycerin, and witch hazel had to be mixed together in large bottles to create the full-body makeup Denishawn mandated for the women (the men used a powder darker than zinc). This procedure would have been new and interesting to Graham in 1917, when she showed off her recently acquired Denishawn skills by performing a Javanese solo at a charity ball in Montecito; in addition to calling her "lithe and graceful," the writer for *The Morning Press* noted that "her makeup was remarkably true to the type of the little brown women of Java."

Such liquid disguises were not so pleasant to deal with after a show on the road, especially if the dancers had to catch a post-performance train from, say, Wichita, Kansas, to St. Joseph, Missouri, or Duluth, Minnesota, to Virginia, Minnesota. To keep the show moving along quickly, the company women often had to apply the brown makeup for their "exotic" roles over the initial pink-and-white tint that the first part of the program called for, and, as Doris Humphrey recalled in her memoir, "Often at the end there wasn't time to remove it all, so we would board Pullman trains in dirty feet and two layers of make-up." The numbers were short and the costume changes many. In both programs featured on the 1921 cross-country concert tour, Shawn, Graham, Weidman, Betty May, and Dorothea Bowen dashed through an array of roles that spanned cultures and continents. From September in Los Angeles to December in New York, Graham may have appeared in more than ten different costumes at each performance. She wore a pretty dress for *Capriccio* and *Pastorale* (the three women dancing to Scarlatti) in Program 1 and something basic for a solo simply called *Dance*. For *Juba* (to music by Nathaniel Dett titled after the famous nineteenth-century Black minstrel), she wore an Aunt Jemima bandanna and an apron, but at least there was no time for blackface. Shawn later described this trio as "a light comedy number with Martha as an old mammy, Betty May and Dorothea as pickaninnies."

As the "victim" in Shawn's setting of Chopin's "Revolutionary Étude," Graham donned a tattered dress over the "fleshings"—strappy, flesh-colored silk jersey leotards—that the women constructed themselves and wore beneath all their costumes. She could have made do with one basic outfit for both her dances in *Spanish Suite*, maybe adding a shawl for the *Malagueña* with Shawn. Or perhaps she changed out of her *Valse Aragonaise* dress while Shawn performed his *Tango*. Maybe there was an intermission before the *Oriental and Barbaric Suite*, since the Javanese number with which she opened that group of dances followed on the heels of *Malagueña*. Then, after Shawn's *Siam*, she danced two back-to-back solos, *Orientale* and *Serenata Morisca*, surely not in exactly the same costume. Both programs ended with all five dancers costumed for *Xochitl* (Weidman played the heroine's father, and only two maidens served Shawn, the Emperor).

Bowen had an even more strenuous time than Graham, going from *Juba* into two solos and then into *Revolutionary Étude*. Horst would have played the piano between certain numbers, if needed (although that's not noted in the programs). There could have been more than one intermission. But any way you consider it, a program of twenty-six dances erupts from a backstage madhouse.

Not all the dances ventured into exotic domains. *Capriccio*, *Pastorale*, *Dance*, and *Revolutionary Étude* were what Shawn and St. Denis called "music visualizations." St. Denis had seen Isadora Duncan dance in London in 1908, and possibly again in November 1917, when they both performed in San Francisco; she was struck—not entirely favorably—by the way Duncan allied herself with the expressive world of a musical selection as well as with its rhythms, dancing as herself in the landscape of great music. St. Denis, wishing to branch out from the exotic roles she had been performing for almost ten years, became interested in approaching musical structure in a more precise way.

In this, she had assistance, in addition to Horst's knowledgeable contributions. The Denishawn School had opened with a faculty member, Marion Kappes, who had studied at the Dalcroze Institute in Hellerau, outside of Dresden. She presumably passed on the system of education that the composer and musician Émile Jaques-Dalcroze (1865–1950) had developed—a system that turned the body into a silent musical instrument, "playing along" with what the student heard.

Anyone taking classes in Dalcroze Eurhythmics and other techniques of his learned how to mirror in movement the music's rhythm proper, phrase lengths, pitch, texture, and style.

St. Denis, however, credited Duncan, rather than Dalcroze, with turning her toward a choreographic embodying of music, and she created a solo to piano music by Chopin in December 1917, a month after the San Francisco appearances by both women. It's worth noting, however, that Humphrey, St. Denis's assistant, as well as a featured dancer on tours she undertook without Shawn, had absorbed Dalcroze techniques from her Oak Park, Illinois, dance teacher, Mary Wood Hinman; Hinman, like Kappes, had studied in Hellerau.

Shawn approached "music visualizations" in his own way. *Revolutionary Étude*, set to Chopin's fiery work for piano, was a revision of St. Denis's patriotic 1917 *The Spirit of Democracy*, set to the same music. Always interested in reminding audiences of the spiritual aspects of dance, he also took the somewhat daring move of opening both programs on his group's 1921 tour with *Church Service in Dance* before moving on to more glamorous material. He choreographed the "Doxology" as a solo for himself, and Graham undertook the "Andante Religioso." Keene Abbott of the *Omaha World-Herald* wrote of Graham, "Through all the program, she does nothing more impressive than her solo dance in the church service."

This critic was clearly smitten. Early in the review he divined something important about Graham: "The dancing of Martha Graham has a quality of aloofness that is almost eerie in its fascination." But he went on to rhapsodize along more sentimental lines: "It has something impalpable, a vision of lovely lines that flow into lines ever more lovely. With the dark curves of hair down either side of her face, she recalls the beautiful women Dante Gabriel Rossetti put on canvas." The *Pioneer Press* of St. Paul, Minnesota, noted, "Miss Graham exhibits several stunning solos. Her bodily movements are supplemented by the interpretive effect of a handsome and expressive face and much that she does can stand alone." The critic for *The Austin American*, listing his favorite part of the program, the *Oriental and Barbaric Suite*, included Graham's Javanese solo among those that "will stand out, like the electric signs on Broadway, in the memories of those who thrilled to them."

The three-month 1921 tour ended with an engagement at the Apollo Theater in New York on December 2. Dates that failed to materialize had stranded the cash-strapped company in Norman, Texas, and Shawn's Aunt Kate, who had married wealth, had to send him $2,000 to transport the ensemble, costumes, and scenery to New York. This was fortunate, since the impresario Daniel Mayer had attended the Apollo performance and offered to book Shawn's group for a ten-day concert tour of Virginia and the Carolinas, plus a six-week vaudeville engagement in England and three U.S. concert tours, the first of which would run from October 2, 1922, to April 21, 1923. Mayer had one request: Could Miss St. Denis rejoin her husband for these dates? She, somewhat reluctantly, could.

Between December 1921 and April 1922, while waiting for a ten-day southern tour to start, Shawn established a temporary school in New York, with Graham as his assistant. The studio and his living quarters occupied the many-windowed top floor of the Chatsworth, on the southwest corner of Seventy-Second Street and Riverside Drive. (Ever enterprising, he then established a Denishawn School in a brownstone on West Twenty-Eighth Street and left the management of it to the capable Delsartian Katharane Edson when the company went on the road. Later, Denishawn classes were also offered in Carnegie Hall's Studio 61.)

It may have been in early 1922 that Graham, along with Shawn, Weidman, Marjorie Peterson, and Lillian Powell, appeared in as many as ten short experimental silent films to test a new process. The conductor of the orchestra that played for the filming was visible in the finished product. When the films were sent out to theaters, the local orchestra could follow his baton. These movies have apparently vanished.

The ensuing tour itself cannot have been easy for Graham. St. Denis took over her role in the duet *Malagueña* and in the full-length *Xochitl* (where she proved to be a far less tigerish heroine than the dancer for whom the piece had been created). During the season at the

London Coliseum in May and June and at the Hippodromes in Manchester and Bristol, Graham regained her role in *Spanish Suite*, but she had to join May, Bowen, and Betty Horst as one of the Emperor's handmaidens in *Xochitl*.

A difficult situation of a more personal nature also bedeviled her during the British engagement. Over the course of the 1921 tour, she and Horst, the company's invaluable musical director, conductor, and pianist, had become lovers. Late in life, he described the beginning of their relationship. In October, during the company's two-day stint in Omaha, Graham knocked on the door of his hotel room. "So she came in and sat down. I was arranging music. Pretty soon she stretched out her arms to me. She wanted me to come over and kiss her. All through the rest of the tour we were a couple. That started seventeen years of life together."

In spite of this romance, Horst waived his fee in order to get Shawn and St. Denis to take his wife, Betty, to England and give her a small part or two, because she was interested in traveling to Europe; perhaps he wanted to test the strength of his new relationship. However, when Betty took a brief side trip to Paris, Martha and Louis, at loose ends in Manchester, went together to look at Tanagra figures in the museum there, prefiguring both her 1926 solo *Tanagra* and his later role as her mentor.

Horst was ten years her senior, rumpled, potbellied, and no beauty, yet attractive to women and an accomplished musician and composer with knowledge of—and interest in—all the arts. Unlike Graham, he was unflappable, used to wading through the various mishaps and catastrophes that beset a performer's life. He could conduct a musical ensemble from the piano, and when accompanying dance classes, he kept a detective story on the music rack to have it handy when the action lagged. He showed no interest in divorcing Betty. Having left Denishawn after the influenza she caught during the 1918 pandemic developed into tuberculosis, she subsequently opened a Denishawn School in San Francisco, and Louis regularly sent her money.

The weeks in England were Graham's final stint in vaudeville. The tuppenny printed program for the London engagement positioned the Denishawn segment (the "art" offering, given twice a day) as seventh of twelve numbers. The sixth item, a rendition of a Rachmaninoff prelude (played by Horst?), prepared the audience for culture, but the Denishawn dances were followed by a trained horse act ("May Wirth with Philo, the World's Greatest Riding Comedian and Company"). Philo nibbled at Graham's shawl while both were waiting in the wings. The *Dancing Times* of July 1922 gives a description in its fashion column that reveals to those who've seen only black-and-white photos of Denishawn just how radical its color schemes were: "Talking about colours, it is amazing the shades that 'go' and look lovely together. Martha Graham, of the Denishawn Company, wore a brilliant orange mantilla over a dress of vivid magenta and green, when she danced the Malaguena with Ted Shawn at the Coliseum. The colour scheme was very daring, but the shades formed a beautiful ensemble."

St. Denis relinquished her role in *Xochitl* for the ensuing 1922–23 concert tour of the United States, but Graham again had to cede her part in Shawn's Spanish duet to her idol. There is no reason to suppose she resented having to do this. She can't have been happy, but neither can she have been unaware of the business end of things. In stipulating that Shawn and St. Denis join forces again, Mayer acknowledged that the latter had drawing power that none of the younger women dancers could command.

Graham's last season with Denishawn came after five East Coast performances in April 1923 in a program somewhat different from the one the company had been touring with, the only known one from those years that featured the three most important choreographers Denishawn had spawned. Doris Humphrey appeared in two numbers, one of them her own solo, *Scarf Dance*; Charles Weidman appeared in one; and Graham in four (not counting full-company works that all three may have participated in). As she had done in London, Graham danced one of the four maidens in St. Denis and Humphrey's *Soaring* (set to Schumann's piece of the same name). In London, Weidman had assumed Humphrey's role as the central figure who danced beneath the immense China silk scarf that four nymphs in tunics made to balloon overhead; on this short tour, Lenore Scheffer took the lead.

The impact of these appearances on Graham's career was immediate. John Murray Anderson attended one of the two Town Hall performances in New York. A Renaissance man in terms of the theater, he had produced, directed, and written the first edition of *The Greenwich Village Follies* in 1919 and had been involved in every subsequent iteration of the revue. Struck by Graham's performing, he asked her to appear as a featured dancer in the fifth edition of the *Follies*. For whatever reason—Shawn and Graham's friend Agnes de Mille supposed it was the frustrating state of her relationship with Horst, as well as the need to help support her mother—Martha said yes.

—3—

DANCING ON BROADWAY, BECOMING A TEACHER

INITIALLY CALLED *GREENWICH VILLAGE NIGHTS*, the annual revue marking Martha Graham's Broadway debut had begun life in 1919 at the five-hundred-seat Greenwich Village Theatre on the northwest corner of Sheridan Square, where Seventh Avenue and Christopher and West Fourth streets intersect. The Winter Garden on Broadway at Fiftieth Street—where the revue's fifth edition racked up 140 performances between September 20, 1923, and June 15, 1924—seated 1,498 and boasted a much-larger stage. Initially, beyond its opening number, "The Paint Box"—in which ten women represented the colors in an artist's paint box and another ten his "inspirations"—that season's *Follies* made few references to the Village as a downtown haven for New York City's artists and freethinkers. The special curtain designed by the New York School painter Reginald Marsh depicted Greenwich Village in earlier days. Over the show's run, during which numbers were dropped, added, and moved around, more references to the downtown bohemian enclave appeared.

In addition to relinquishing her role in *Xochitl* to her little sister, Georgia, Graham also gave up the constant traveling and strenuous performing that a Denishawn tour entailed. The pay on Broadway may also have been better than anything Denishawn could muster, and, as mentioned, she was regularly sending money to her mother. The year 1923 was the one in which Actors' Equity fought for and achieved a union contract (although only eighty percent of the performers in any given production were required to be members). It's not known whether Graham joined Equity, but she was reportedly paid $350 a week.

A revue opening in New York in 1923 had to be competitive. *Earl Carroll's Vanities*, *The Ziegfeld Follies*, and *George White's Scandals* all presented new editions in the 1923–24 Broadway season. Although *The Greenwich Village Follies* had a lot in common with vaudeville in its mélange of skits, comedy duos, and musical numbers, it was more tasteful and offered more "artistic" acts, in addition to providing plenty to laugh about and plenty to please the eye. The anonymous opening-night review in *The New York Times* concluded with a note about the chorus: "large, beautiful and generally underdressed."

Dancing in the *Follies* may not be considered an upward step in Graham's career, but the experience could provide lessons of many sorts to one as intellectually alert and as avid for discoveries about performance as she was at thirty. Too, during her first fall season in the revue she was able to see Eleonora Duse's matinees at the Century Theatre and be impressed by the eloquence with which the actress could imbue the simplest of gestures. Perhaps her schedule also permitted her a glimpse of the Moscow Art Theatre, led by Konstantin Stanislavsky, in three Chekhov plays. In addition, it allowed visits to museums and gallery shows.

Graham had a special, not-too-demanding niche in the *Follies*; the two offerings in which she was featured were built on dance styles she had already mastered. In "A Spanish Fiesta," she performed Shawn's *Serenata Morisca*. He did not receive program credit; perhaps the solo was Martha's going-away present. The suite opened, somewhat perplexingly, with "The Birthday of the Infanta," in which Marion Dabney, the singer Josephine Adair, and an ensemble attempted to bring a Velázquez painting to life (presumably with a nod to Oscar Wilde's play of the same title). Graham's solo was the third of four ensuing

Spanish numbers. The well-known brother-and-sister team of Eduardo and Elisa Cansino performed "Gypsy Dance and Bolero," "Hota [sic]," and "Torero," possibly joined by their brothers, Paco and Angel, for the first and last (but not by Eduardo's five-year-old daughter, who grew up to become Rita Hayworth).

By October 29, The Greenwich Village Follies had been somewhat pared down, and only the Cansinos' opening number and Serenata Morisca remained of the "Spanish Fiesta." The show's length had been an issue all along. Alexander Woollcott's opening-night review in the New York Herald was subtitled "Opulent and Beautiful Scenes and Unusual Dancing Featured in Overlong Production," and he wrote, "The most amusing and by all odds the best looking review [sic] which these eyes have ever beheld under the Winter Garden's roof is the new 'Greenwich Village Follies,' which was still raging in the small moments of yesterday morning."

Graham's most important appearance was as the tragic heroine of "Kama's Garden," an elaborate oriental fantasy devised by John Murray Anderson. As in any number termed a "ballet ballad," narrators provided the story while songs further expressed feelings and dancers provided atmosphere and feasted the eye. In this lyric tragedy, a dancer (Graham) also brought the tale to dramatic life. She must have felt right at home in this fictitious India. Shawn had romanced St. Denis in their 1915 dance-drama The Garden of Kama (he portrayed the god of love and she a high-caste maiden he craved). Given that Shawn, in a 1969 interview, recalled that he "made" two solos for Graham to perform in the Follies, this one, too, may have been pulled out of the Denishawn archive, although Michio Ito was credited in the program with "arranging" the "East Indian Dances" for Kama's Garden. Since Ito, already an acclaimed performer of his own solos, was Japanese by birth and had studied eurhythmics at the Dalcroze Institute in Hellerau, it may be supposed that he created a theatrical, but not very authentic, vision of India.

The ambiance of Anderson's creation and the lyrics of the songs featured in it would have been familiar to Graham and to many in the

Winter Garden audience. In 1901, Adela Florence Nicolson, the daughter of a British officer stationed in India and the wife of another, published a book of poems, *The Garden of Kama*, under the pseudonym of Laurence Hope. The American edition was titled *India's Love Lyrics*. Readers who had devoured the earlier *Rubáiyát of Omar Khayyám* translated by Edward Fitzgerald were drawn to these romantic evocations of India. Four of the poems gained even more popularity when Amy Woodforde-Finden set them to music. Three of these were sung in the exotic tale of love and death that unfolded on the Winter Garden stage.

A promptbook for the show gives a somewhat sketchy account of *Kama's Garden* and doesn't specify at what point and how Graham performed her solo. While singers probe the drama's emotions, two Storytellers (a man and a woman) explicate the plot as it develops in an elaborate set featuring a temple. The Dancing Girl once enjoyed a day and a night of love with the Maharajah Zaharudin, in whose court she is employed. She, in turn, is adored by a Toiler in the Garden, where a White Peacock (played by a woman) parades and other dancers enter with baskets of rose petals, forming pleasing patterns. It is the Maharajah's wedding day, and the new Maharanee has arrived. But although Zaharudin has forgotten the Dancing Girl, she has not forgotten him. After the wedding, one of the Storytellers describes in words written by Anderson and Irving Caesar what Graham presumably had to enact: "And as her lord lingers for a moment upon the upper terraces of the Garden, Radha the Dancing Girl runs to him and throws herself at his feet. She would burn for a thousand years if her lord would but her adore / Be tortured, slain in unheard of ways if he pitied the pain she bore."

The song lyrics by "Laurence Hope" are more eloquent than the narrators' speeches written by Anderson in imitation of their style. Gregory Safranic as the enamored Toiler sang two of them, "The Temple Bells" and, later, "Kashmiri Song," with its famous opening line, "Pale hands I loved beside the Shalimar."

According to the promptbook, as the female singer begins the reprise of "Less Than the Dust," two curtains close behind her, leaving her on the forestage to move the audience with the second and final verse:

> Since I, my Lord, am nothing unto thee,
> See here my sword, I make it clean and bright
> Love's last reward, Death comes to me tonight
> Farewell, Zahirudin, Zahirudin.

A penciled note in the promptbook indicates that after the word "Farewell," all illumination but the footlights should go out. In the score (written in 3/4 time), the singer's two calls to her former lover are prolonged in rising and falling notes. Had Graham, too, been onstage, the orchestra's final measures would have left the Dancing Girl time to sink into her final darkness. Tempting though it is to picture Graham, spectral in the footlights, despairing and determined as she wields her surely gleaming blade, she recalled late in her life that Radha killed herself immediately after running up the flight of stairs to her faithless erstwhile lover. This would probably have occurred just after the leading female singer's initial rendition of "Less Than the Dust" and the Storyteller's words:

> Just as the dawn of love was breaking
> Across the weary world of grey
> Fate, blindly cruel and havoc-making
> Stepped in and carried love away.

It is also tempting to imagine *Kama's Garden* sowing at least a few seeds that blossomed in the profoundly etched suicides and deaths that Graham choreographed for herself many years later.

This sad drama was followed in *The Greenwich Village Follies* by Buster West and John West's "specialty act" entitled "Two Sailors."

The promptbook, which is not dated, also indicates a costume for Graham to wear in "Moonlight Kisses," although in the opening-night program for the *Follies*, she's not listed among those appearing in this elaborate number. Part of "Moonlight Kisses" involved a procession of "Dream Lovers" famed in history and literature, from Pelléas and Mélisande to Madame de Pompadour and Louis XV. By October 29, however, the preceding comedic kisses, part of the number revolving around various male movie stars ("My mother says I should be psychoanalyzed by Freud. My idea of heaven is a kiss from Harold Lloyd") had been dropped, and the Dream Lovers sequence merged with something more in tune with its romantic vision. True Lovers sang; so did the Spirit of the Stars (a man) and the Spirit of the Moon (a woman). Martha Graham (listed first) performed a Scarf Dance. In her memoir, *Blood Memory* (published in 1991, the year of her death), Graham recalled, "I danced in floating yellow chiffon, very Loïe Fuller, while the great lovers of history . . . paraded across a moonlit bridge." Whether Larry Ceballos, responsible for the bulk of the show's choreography, engineered this dance or whether Graham echoed Denishawn music visualizations in her own way is a matter of speculation. By December 10, only the parade remained in the frequently shifting *Follies*.

The morning after the opening night in New York, a *Journal* review was accompanied by a sketch of Graham in *Serenata Morisca*, captioned "MARTHA GRAHAM, Who Can Be More Indian Than a Native." Another review, presumably referring to *The Garden of Kama*, called her "a remarkably gifted pantomimic dancer whose work recalls the exotic quality of Ruth St. Denis." Critical opinion of the show varied. Some journalists praised the comedic sections; another found it "weakest in its humor." An unidentified *New York Times* reviewer sighed that "the Kama episode is one of those legend affairs, performed to a recitative accompaniment, and it is just about as dull a ten minutes as anybody could ask for," while the *Journal of Commerce* critic thought that "no more pictorially beautiful, poetically perfect, nor scenically superb conception has ever illuminated a Broadway revue than John Murray Anderson's effective stage adaptation of a tragic episode from Laurence Hope's 'India Love Lyrics,' under the title of 'Kama's Garden.' It is a rare gem of stage-craft and artistry, and is by far the most resplendent jewel in that brilliant setting."

The fifth edition of *The Greenwich Village Follies* closed in June 1924, and Graham took a summer job teaching at Mariarden, a theater camp in Peterborough, New Hampshire, two miles from the Mac-Dowell Colony; it had been founded by the well-to-do socialite Marie Currier on ninety-two pastoral acres. "Camp" may not be the right word to describe it. Among its forty buildings were studios, a small indoor theater, and an amphitheater in the woods. Graham was no stranger to Mariarden. After the Denishawn company had returned from its engagements in England in 1922, Shawn, St. Denis, and their dancers had repaired to Peterborough to teach at Mrs. Currier's establishment for nine weeks. The faculty that first summer was notable. Richard Bennett staged plays and acted in them, and his wife, Adrienne (née Morrison), taught drama. The youngest of their three daughters, then twelve and not yet known by multitudes as the screen star Joan Bennett, accompanied them. Tony Sarg and his puppet theater were in residence. According to Shawn, he left Graham in New York to carry on the Denishawn School while he commuted to teach at Mariarden on weekends and in the city on weekdays. So Graham may or may not have been among the 1922 Denishawners and students artfully posed in their black leotards on the stepped outdoor stage (among them, Humphrey, Weidman, Louise Brooks, and Georgia Graham). Surely, if Graham had been there when Nickolas Muray posed his shots, she would have been prominently placed. However, Graham is very much in evidence in at least one, maybe two photos taken that year. She's shown on the lawn, clad mostly in a fringed Spanish shawl, tangoing in front of a small ensemble of maidens and musicians with Rich Currier—the son of Marie and her husband, the lawyer Guy Currier—perhaps in preparation for a recital. That shawl could be the costume for the Javanese solo Shawn had made for her in 1921; she's kneeling and leaning back, hands extended toward Shawn, who is balancing in a Lord Shiva pose. The photo is labeled "Oriental Group."

Graham and Horst were also at Mariarden—Graham as Shawn's

assistant—in 1923, the summer before she went into the *Follies*. Shawn had to scold her for praising free love in front of the supposedly innocent young dancers. It's unclear whether she was in the work St. Denis choreographed for the outdoor stage that year. As Shawn described it, St. Denis had up to that point done more inspiring than leading classes at Mariarden, but in 1923 "she began to teach, and she did the one big production on the stage that summer, which was a Cupid and Psyche based on the famous legend, and with Charles Weidman as Cupid with a curly wig and pink tarleton wings, and a pink tunic. I was sort of relegated to just being in one of the minor scenes." More memorable than the event is the story that Shawn's dresser made him a garland to disguise the dividing line between bare flesh and tights; evidently not a country boy, he had harvested poison ivy.

When Graham came again to Mariarden after her first season in the *Follies*, her doing so occasioned a split between Shawn and his successful protégée that may have begun to set her on a new course. Mrs. Currier had not asked Shawn back, but had gone directly to Graham, whom she could pay well, but less well than Shawn. He was appalled that Martha would accept the job, given all he had done for her. He had, after all, been training her to teach Denishawn material. There is some evidence that he had also asked her for the $500 that Denishawn alumni setting up as teachers paid in order to use the Denishawn name and classwork, and she refused. He remembered in later years that his rebuke "also made Martha very mad, and I think affected the whole history of modern dance. Because she flared up, that famous cobralike hiss, and reared back and said, 'I will never again teach anything I ever got from Denishawn! I will create all of my own material from now on.'"

When Graham returned to the *Follies* for the 1924–25 season, it was with the understanding that her Denishawn years were over. In accord with the usual practice, while a new edition of the *Follies* opened on Broadway, the previous one went on the road. A program for the fifth edition's performance at one of Sylvester Z. Poli's chain of theaters scattered among northeast cities indicates that the Cansinos had left the show by then. Graham continued to perform *Serenata*

Morisca in "Spanish Fiesta," and Alberto De Lima and Marita danced "Copa del Olvido Tango." *Garden of Kama* continued to be one of the show's more "artistic" acts.

Encouraged by Louis Horst, Martha was ready for a change. So was he. The third Denishawn tour organized by Daniel Mayer had been especially grueling, and as Horst later admitted, "I wasn't in sympathy anymore with their Oriental spectacles. I didn't mind the music visualizations, but I had just had my fill." To the dismay of St. Denis and Shawn, the musical director they thought irreplaceable declined to go with the company on its 1925–26 tour of the Far East. They hadn't invited Graham (according to her, they wanted the company to consist of fairer-haired Americans, and one who could be mistaken for Asian would be out of place). But Horst had other reasons for leaving Denishawn. The charms of Orientalism had worn off, and he wanted to study music composition in Vienna, with an idea to being something more than a skilled accompanist and music director par excellence. He sailed for Europe aboard the *Bremen* in May 1925. And as he delicately put it in a letter to his biographer, Janet Mansfield Soares, "Martha and I had a little tiff in those days . . . and I wanted to get away from under her too much."

Could one have just a "little tiff" with the woman who was reputed in two separate anecdotes to yank a telephone from the wall when angered? The conflicts must have been more difficult to solve. Graham's talk of free love at Mariarden was no ruse; she certainly had affairs, one of which, according to Agnes de Mille, devastated Horst. Martha may have wished that Louis would divorce his wife, Betty, but there's no indication that she wanted to marry him.

Like him, she wanted to tap into her own creative resources, to discover how *she* danced, rather than how she interpreted the choreography of others. To accomplish this, she needed a job—and not one that required her to be onstage every night. Fortuitously, John Murray Anderson asked her to teach in the new theater school that he and Robert Milton were opening in November 1925 on East Fifty-Eighth Street in Manhattan, and Rouben Mamoulian, director of the new School of Dance and Dramatic Action at the Eastman School of

Music in Rochester, New York, wanted her on the faculty. She accepted both invitations.

After freeing herself from the *Follies*, Martha paid her annual summer visit to her mother, encountering a changed Santa Barbara (an earthquake, 6.8 on the Richter scale, had severely damaged much of the city in late June). She had the remaining hot months to explore New York City's cultural riches, acclimate herself to life without Horst (whom she expected to be in Europe for a year), and prepare for the teaching positions awaiting her. They presented dissimilar challenges and offered different rewards.

In November 1922, during Denishawn's first Mayer tour, the company had performed in Rochester's Eastman Theatre only two months after the monumental Mead, McKim, and White edifice had opened; perhaps some people associated with the Eastman School, of which it was a part, remembered Graham from *Xochitl*. It was not until 1923, however, that the noted Russian tenor and opera director Vladimir Rosing joined the faculty of this institution (created in 1921 within the University of Rochester) and persuaded George Eastman, the school's founder and principal funder, to create an opera department and to hire Mamoulian to run it. The Russian-born Armenian theater director in turn persuaded Eastman that the institution should include the School of Dance and Dramatic Action. He may have seen Graham in *The Greenwich Village Follies*, or met her in New York theater circles. Evidently she impressed him.

The Eastman faculty Graham joined in the fall of 1925 was, by and large, a youthful one. The composer Howard Hanson, the school's director, had not yet turned thirty. The English composer Eugene Goossens—leader of the Rochester Philharmonic Orchestra and the American Opera Company (founded at Eastman), as well as Eastman's teacher of conducting—was thirty-one. So was Graham. Goossens's assistant, Otto Luening, was twenty-five, Mamoulian twenty-eight, and Rosing thirty-five. They all had ambitious ideas. Rosing was interested in the power of expressive gesture and wanted to cultivate a more natural style for opera singers. Mamoulian, who at this point had directed one play in London (a success), wished, like Rosing, to promulgate the realistic acting techniques of Konstantin Stanislavsky; in addition, he was interested in merging theater, dance, and music. (He already had his eyes on Broadway—where he would direct his first American hit, *Porgy*, in 1927; possibly at Eastman, he also began to think about a movie career, which would take off in 1929 with his first feature film, *Applause*.) Graham had a bevy of students—mostly female—on whom to work out her ideas and a studio in which to experiment.

Up to this point, any dancing in the school's classes and performances had been done by ballet students trained by Enid Knapp, who had studied and appeared onstage in New York. Mamoulian's decision to hire Graham and Esther Gustafson in Knapp's place was a smart one. As Don McDonagh pointed out in his biography of Graham, Mamoulian was covering the two currently prominent styles of non-ballet dancing for the concert stage. Gustafson, who had performed at the Eastman Theatre's grand opening in 1922, was an "interpretive" dancer in the Isadora Duncan mode; Graham was versed in Denishawn Orientalism, with her sights trained on developing a more individual style, and, via *The Greenwich Village Follies*, she had gained further knowledge of theater.

The job had drawbacks. As Graham discovered, George Eastman's plan for the school he had created in collaboration with the university's president, Dr. Rush Rhees, harnessed her nascent talent for choreography in ways that left her less time to experiment than she might have wished. The mandate for the theater involved Eastman's two major interests, music and film, and he co-opted drama and dance in their service.

As a young man crazy about photography, Eastman (1854–1932) had invented an improved photographic emulsion and a better method of applying it to glass plates. The company he founded in Rochester also created the first filmstrip and, in 1888, a handheld camera: the Kodak (a name he invented, liking, he said, its brevity, ease of pronunciation, and lack of associations). His love of music had developed alongside the fortune he amassed. He employed a personal organist, who played every morning during his 7:30 breakfast (softly, since those meals were often an occasion for conferences). The organist and George Eastman's personal string quartet, plus various guest artists, performed at Wednesday and Sunday evening musicales in the Eastman mansion.

One of Eastman's objectives in incorporating into the school a 3,300-seat theater—whose building and organization he not only enabled but supervised—was to make music a more vital part of civic life in Rochester. "In this consummated whole / Rochester shall find a soul," exulted the poem by the university professor John Rothwell Slater that was read at the theater's inauguration.

Eastman—a taciturn, financially astute man who had pulled himself up by the bootstraps—knew what he wanted and what he did not want. He decided that at least one evening a week at the theater would be devoted to symphonic music and opera. However, aware of the public's interest in movies, he came up with a cost-efficient plan for most of the remaining days, a plan that would unite Eastman Kodak's interests in the developing motion picture industry with his educational zest in regard to music. The Eastman Theatre would rival the major movie palaces in New York City by presenting film showings (three to five a day), preceded by an orchestral overture and whatever the faculty could come up with in the way of dances, dramatic scenes, and musical performances. Those citizens eager to see the latest in silent movies might, Eastman reasoned, develop a taste for music, which would swell attendance at the classical music evenings.

This meant that during Graham's time at Eastman she had to concoct dances in haste, collaborating with Mamoulian and others involved in devising these entertainments. Her schedule demanded stamina and careful planning. She taught full-time in Rochester from the last two weeks of September through October 1925, and, after her other job with the Anderson-Milton School in New York City began in November, she taught at Eastman three days every other week through June 1926.

Martha made an instant impression on the Rochester students.

Thelma Biracree, who was to become a member of her first small ensemble, remembered thinking that this was a face "different from any face I'd ever seen. It was something you'd never forget once you'd seen it. The black hair. The white skin. The large eyes. The very bright lipstick." This apparition met them wearing gloves and a little hat with a brim. "She was charming. She spoke very softly to us. I think she was as nervous as we were."

Nervous or not, Graham appeared to teach her class in a long red kimono slit up the sides. She took the students in hand and worked them hard, combining barre exercises (not strictly balletic ones), Denishawn hand-me-downs, basic traveling steps—walking, running, jumping, leaping, and, according to Biracree, "lots of tension things," some of them performed sitting on the floor. This last was a practice that Charles Weidman thought she had picked up from the Swedish dancer-choreographer Ronny Johansson, whom Horst admired (Johansson had accompanied a class Martha taught at the Denishawn School on West Twenty-Eighth Street and would work with her again).

The charismatic new teacher at Eastman also taught the female students how to make "fleshings"—that all-purpose Denishawn underwear for costumes. Take a tube of white Italian silk, make a few crucial cuts, pin it at the shoulders and crotch with safety pins, fit it along the sides, stitch it up, and dip it in tea. Graham also conveyed the message that dance was a profession to which one was called—a summons to be answered by the truly gifted. Later, she put it more baldly: "Learning how to dance is not a parlor game."

Graham used the best of her pupils in numbers she contributed to the forty-five-minute presentations that accompanied the films. Fortunately, each of the onstage offerings had to be short; Eastman was a stickler about timing. Graham and Gustafson—who had been hired before Graham and headed the dance department—worked together on two numbers. One of these accompanied the movie that showed during the week of October 18 through 24 and the other the feature scheduled for November 8 through 14. No one has described how the Graham-Gustafson collaboration operated, especially since the first number, *A Pompeian Afternoon* (featuring The Lady of the Garden,

Youths of the Garden, and Dancers of the Garden), lasted only five minutes, and the second, *A Serenade in Porcelain* (which Mamoulian staged), only four. Apparently the live entertainment wasn't keyed to the accompanying film's atmosphere; *A Pompeian Afternoon* embellished *Little Annie Rooney* starring Mary Pickford. No further joint ventures for Graham and Gustafson ensued. Biracree dismissed the latter with, "I don't think she had an original thought in her head."

Graham coped. She taught *Serenata Morisca* to Biracree, added three other dancers to swell the scene, and billed it as "A Moorish Dance." She provided the dance numbers for such Mamoulian productions as *Pictures in Melody* and *A Forest Episode*, arranged a waltz for his *May Time in Kew*, and contributed a gavotte to his *Then and Now* (subtitled *How Times Have Changed Since Grandfather's Day*). She created "Dance of the French Dolls" for the identical Hurwitz twins to perform in his *A Dream in a Wax Museum*.

There were, however, loftier experiments at Eastman. In January 1926 the school announced a production based on Maurice Maeterlinck's three-act play *Sister Beatrice*, set in the fourteenth century, as a "Rhythmic Drama to Music: A New Form of Theatrical Art Conceived and Developed by Rouben Mamoulian." Paul Horgan made a new "rhythmic prose" translation of the French text. Luening's score for organ, chorus, and contralto solo developed in tandem with rehearsals. Biracree, Evelyn Sabin, and Betty Macdonald—all three of whom were to participate in Graham's New York debut as a choreographer— were featured in the cast, perhaps coached by Martha. And according to Luening, she supervised the Japanese movements and costumes (along with a Mr. Cheba) for the newly established Rochester American Opera Company's production of *Madame Butterfly*.

Graham's first appearance in connection with the school that John Murray Anderson and Robert Milton opened in a handsome four-story edifice at 128–130 East Fifty-Eighth Street was onstage at the institution's November 1925 inaugural performance. She danced. So did her friend and *Greenwich Village Follies* colleague Michio Ito (also tapped for the faculty). The actress Eva Le Gallienne was involved (exactly how, one wonders) with two others in a fencing demonstration. Noël Coward played the piano and sang.

Anderson and Milton had different priorities from those of the Eastman School. To women between sixteen and twenty-four years old and men between eighteen and twenty-five, their theater school offered classes in drama, opéra comique, and musical comedy; scenic and costume design; playwriting; pageantry; stage direction; stage management; motion picture acting; voice and diction; and dramatic interpretation. There was an "expert camera consultant" on the faculty as well as a fencing master and a physical trainer. According to a flyer for the school, Graham gave dance classes in the Dramatic Course and was one of three instructors teaching what was billed as "All Types of Stage Dancing" in the Musical Comedy Course. In the latter, presumably, she drew not only on what she knew but on what she had observed.

The two junior divisions each got two hours a week of dance for the first four weeks of the term, then one hour for the next fourteen weeks. Students in the senior divisions received one hour a week. Teaching classes in two schools 333 miles apart and taking overnight train trips every other week involved endurance on Graham's part; a gradually evolving vision of what she wanted to achieve spurred her on.

Fortunately, she was not alone in defining and pursuing her goal. Louis Horst had returned to New York much sooner than planned. Graham met the slow boat on which he arrived from Europe on October 21, 1925—in time to play the piano for her classes at Anderson-Milton.

He had been studying at Vienna's Academy of Music and the Performing Arts with Dr. Richard Stöhr, a composer, theorist, and professor of harmony and counterpoint. Horst had written some piano pieces while there and had fraternized with Stöhr, who, like him, believed in the importance of dance in the development of music. He had filled his belly with Sacher tortes and other rich Austrian foods and his head with strong images painted by such Expressionist artists as Emil Nolde. He may have seen the brooding statues of Ernst

Barlach that later influenced Graham when Barlach's work was exhibited in New York. He had attended concerts and opera performances. There were dancers to admire—or not (he wrote to Ruth St. Denis that he found Lucy Kieselhausen's dancing "a bit heavy," like her name). Rosalia Chladek was teaching in the Dalcroze school outside the city. And there was Mary Wigman to think about and read about. The profoundly personal and expressive solos that the leading exponent of *Ausdruckstanz* created for herself owed little to the styles in which Martha had been immersed. Louis brought photos and writings about her home to his lover.

In the end, he left Vienna, he said, because when he told Stöhr that the composer Erik Satie had just died, the professor's response was "Who's Satie?" A musical circle that couldn't see beyond Beethoven, Brahms, and Bruckner began to seem stuffy to Horst. Also, he missed Martha, and discovered that his love of working hand in glove with dance was even stronger than he had thought.

That said, he didn't handle Graham with gloves on. Accounts abound of him scolding her out of her doubts and doldrums, straight-talking to her about her budding choreographic efforts, snorting when she got too lofty. She, in turn, treated him to the occasional temper flare-up and threw what came to hand (in those cases, he slapped her the way one would a hysterical child). He was, she later said, "always giving me a good shove." Once, when he told her that one of her dances was bad and he'd have nothing to do with it, she attempted pathos: "Oh Louie, you're killing my soul!" His response, as reported by Graham in an interview: "'If it is going to die, it's best it die now.'" "So-o," Graham continued, laughing, "I got on my hind legs and did this dance again." "I was her whetstone," Horst noted. "I gave her form and discipline, because she was a wild one. I was the tail to her kite."

They didn't actually live together. She had a long, narrow studio at 46 East Ninth Street; one cramped corner served for sleeping and eating. A little later, she rented a larger place one block uptown. He based himself midtown in various residential hotels, then in a Carnegie Hall studio, then in a Greenwich Village apartment nearer to Martha. But they were always together. They went to look at modern paintings at the Whitney Museum on Eighth Street and frequented galleries. They bought art books at the Gotham Book Mart on West Forty-Fifth Street, run by their friend Frances Steloff (where Graham is said to have occasionally helped out during the Christmas rush by applying a helpful finger to anchor a gift-wrap bow). Martha accompanied Louis to baseball games. When she was angry, or too wound up, she went to a movie alone and joined him for dinner afterward. And he could make her laugh. Nina Fonaroff, who joined the company in 1937 and not long after became Horst's companion, recalled a ditty Louis on occasion sang to Martha:

> Her teeth stick out
> And her mouth caves in
> But she's a grand old girl
> For the shape she's in.

"And then Martha would say, 'Oh, Luigi.'"

With Graham's career in mind, Horst delved into music by such contemporary composers as Hindemith and Bartók, and by others less well known, like the Spanish composer Federico Mompou—serenading Graham with them on her studio piano. In a 1959 interview, he explained to Jeanette Schlottmann Roosevelt that during the months when Graham commuted between Rochester and New York City, "She began to develop some of her own dance materials. She'd get the idea for a dance, and I'd look for music, or I'd bring music and she'd get an idea . . . We could see the way things were going. Our music was becoming more dissonant."

Whatever was firing up Graham's mind, muscles, and sinews, she still had one foot in the Denishawn aesthetic and mystique. Martha Hill, who was later to join Graham's company, studied at Anderson-Milton in 1926. Decades later, she recounted this classroom experience. Graham "was teaching some of the East Indian movements out of Denishawn, and making a little dance study where we were lotus flowers. She was sitting in a sari. She used to sit on a little platform to teach. And she was saying, 'We are all women, we are lotus flowers, ready to open to the sun.' And from the piano came this great big male belly laugh, like, *Come on!* It was Louis."

Eighteen-year-old Bette Davis had a somewhat different memory of Graham's classes at Anderson-Milton. Davis had been at Mariarden in 1925, the summer that Graham was replaced by Roshanara (née Olive Craddock). Roshanara had lived and studied in India as a child but, judging from photos and reviews, performed "Indian" solos very like those of St. Denis (if not downright imitations). In her *The Lonely Life*, Davis wrote that Graham "was all tension—lightning! Her burning dedication gave her spare body the power of ten men. If Roshanara was a mystic curve, Miss Graham was a straight line—a divining rod. Both were great, and both were aware of the universal. But Miss Graham was the true modern." Davis had already learned that dance could help an actress convey emotion. "Now I was taught a syntax with which to articulate the subtleties fully. [Graham] would with a single thrust of her weight convey anguish. Then in an anchored lift that made her ten feet tall, she became all joy . . . There was no end, once the body was disciplined."

Louis began to urge Martha toward a concert in New York.

EMBARKING ON A CHOREOGRAPHIC CAREER

WORKING TOWARD HER DEBUT as a concert choreographer, Graham at thirty-two manifested the focused energy of a tiger stalking a potential meal. While commuting between two teaching jobs hundreds of miles apart, she choreographed four dances for her eager trio, Thelma Biracree, Betty Macdonald, and Evelyn Sabin; three more in which she appeared with the young women; and eleven solos for herself. Even considering that most of the eighteen dances composed for her New York debut were short, the undertaking was formidable. Graham also devised all but two of the costumes, cut and fitted them, and, with the help of the girls and others, sewed them. She became expert at scouting out fabric that sold on Orchard Street for nineteen cents a yard.

She and Horst between them had three steady jobs, but little money. The producers Morris Green and A. L. Jones, who were connected with *The Greenwich Village Follies*, let them have the Forty-Eighth Street Theatre on April 18 at cost. That date falling on a Sunday, the comedy currently running there, *Puppy Love*, could not be performed (with luck, those who enforced the "blue laws" that deemed Sunday a day of rest didn't always catch a one-night-only recital, although it helped if the word "sacred" appeared in the publicity). Frances Steloff borrowed $1,000 and gave it to Graham. The three neophytes from Rochester were brought to the city a week before the performance and put up at the Marlton Hotel on Eighth Street, where many actors and writers stayed over the years, and they were occasionally fed. Salaries weren't mentioned, which was fine with them: "We would have paid her!"

In her *Blood Memory*, Graham stated that everything in this first concert and a few thereafter came from Denishawn. She may have been exaggerating slightly, but certainly most of the short dances on the program displayed her Denishawn heritage in one way or another. Eastern art was the source for *A Study in Lacquer*, as it had been for St. Denis's gorgeously draped living sculpture *Kuan Yin* (1919). Graham's *Three Gopi Maidens* may have resonated with St. Denis's *Three Apsaras* (1922), in which Graham had performed, as well as with a dance staged by Shawn at Denishawn in 1917 on a program that presented pupils of the California school; it was listed as "The dance of Krishna (Mr. Shawn) and the Gopis." In 1919, not long before Shawn created *Xochitl*, he had choreographed a solo for himself to the first of Erik Satie's *Trois Gnossiennes*, modeling his flesh-baring costume in muscular two-dimensional poses inspired by ancient Cretan friezes. Onstage at the Forty-Eighth Street Theatre, Evelyn, Betty, and Thelma pressing themselves into similar (if more "feminine") stances—profiled, on tiptoe, their knees bent—in the first sections ("Gnossienne" and "Frieze") of Graham's own *Trois Gnossiennes*. A photo by Soichi Sunami shows them bewigged, clad in filmy, pleated tunics that only partly cover their "fleshings," each wielding two circular garlands—nymphs caught in a ritual dance.

But the Denishawn influence didn't manifest itself only in derivative subject matter. The theories of François Delsarte that Graham had absorbed at Denishawn helped her delineate character and mood in solos based on such artworks as *From a XII-Century Tapestry* (later *A Florentine Madonna*) and *Portrait—After Beltrán-Masses* (later *Gypsy Portrait*). The Spanish painter Federico Beltrán Masses had exhibited his shadow-eyed, red-lipped, often reclining beauties at the Wildenstein Gallery in 1924, and Graham had evidently been impressed. Delsarte tactics could also make comedy more pungent. Despite the limpid sweetness of Claude Debussy's Prelude, no. 8, "The Maid with the Flaxen Hair," it's difficult to imagine that Graham, sporting a wig with two excessively long blond pigtails, could have been anything but ironic in the solo she titled after the music.

In two simple and lovely "music visualizations" made in 1922, St. Denis had danced to a Brahms's waltz and Franz Liszt's "Liebesträum." Some of the pieces that Martha premiered at the Forty-Eighth Street Theatre were likewise set to Romantic music: *Novelette* (Schumann), *Tanze* (Schubert), and *Intermezzo* (Brahms). However, she also ventured into the more contemporary musical territory Horst had been exploring on her behalf: pieces by Rachmaninoff, Ravel, Scriabin, and Satie, plus Horst's "Masques for Piano." (Horst contributed two additional musical numbers to the April 18 concert in order to give the dancers time to change costumes and breathe—one was his setting of poems by four contemporary poets sung by "a lady in a sweeping blue gown against a mahogany piano.")

In a 1968 interview with Don McDonagh, Graham dismissed her early works as "Childish things . . . so childish . . . horrible . . . dreadful . . ." George Beiswanger, a philosopher and dance critic, looking back in 1941 on the dances Graham made between 1926 and 1929, was more generous. He spoke of her onstage presence as projecting an "indefinable but unmistakable aura of dance magic—that emanation of power to which, for want of a better term, we give the name genius." Still, he tempered his retrospective praise with what seems to have been a wise assessment: "All this in programs that were part vestigial, part tentative and part downright floundering."

Nevertheless, Graham's debut as a choreographer garnered considerable praise in newspapers and magazines. Spectators who were fans of Denishawn or recalled her as the exotic featured player in *The Greenwich Village Follies* would not have expected to see dances that could be called radical. Although her colleagues from Anderson-Milton and the Eastman School who attended the concert might have had inklings of her originality, they also counted on seeing her explore further what she already knew, albeit with some added novelties and an array of new roles for herself. Dance aficionados bought tickets costing $1.10, $2.20, or $3.30 and filled the Forty-Eighth Street Theatre, enabling Graham to repay Steloff's loan and reap a small profit.

Two dances from the April 18 program were—at least in retrospect—seen as portending new stylistic developments. Both were set to piano pieces by Alexander Scriabin. Horst later remembered *Désir* as "flaming," adding, "and some of her emotional things came out of it." He also thought it more introspective than others of her 1926 dances. Beiswanger agreed, finding it the first dance of hers to emerge from "an inner compulsion." A critic reviewing the group's May 27 concert in Rochester called the solo "strikingly poignant" and "a thing made eloquent by Miss Graham's ability to make every muscle, every movement of arm and hand, count for emotional meaning."

In *Danse Languide*, three women, Sabin, Macdonald, and Biracree, wore long, narrow gowns of a supple fabric, with full, gathered, winglike sleeves; headbands of a darker color trailed their ends along the floor. In spite of its Art Nouveau curves and drooping bodies, it was, according to Bessie Schönberg, who danced in the piece later, "in no way really romantic. It was quite cool. It had a lot to do with . . . moving slowly from position to position . . . *Languide* was legato, simple but not stark." It was, she thought, "much more remote" than Doris Humphrey's lovely 1928 *Air for the G String* (set to J. S. Bach's piece of the same name), whose extra-long gowns might possibly have been influenced by *Languide*'s costumes, but suggested a ceremonious sisterhood and hinted at religious exaltation.

"Moving slowly from position to position . . ." Schönberg saw what seems to have been characteristic of many of Graham's first dances. The choreographer was already beginning to prune away excess movements and to avoid embellished transitions from one image to the next. Nor did she cover much ground onstage. Perhaps because what she was doing was unlike both ballet and the fast-stepping numbers of vaudeville, descriptions of her by writers of the day seem to suggest that she was focused on bringing a sequence of poses to fluid life, like the more inspired exponents of "statue-posing" in the previous century. A critic for *The Dance Magazine* wrote that she presents a series of pictures that fire the imagination and make a hundred stories for every gesture. Shall we say her dances are motion pictures for the sophisticated—motion pictures without the banality of subtitles and the sugary narrative of the movie theatre?

Martha Graham seems to have been moulded for such portraiture in motion, for she is in appearance a maiden after Rossetti, slender, unearthly and exotically graceful. Her talent is for making pictures. This compensates to some extent for her lack of power and virtuosity.

Another writer characterizes her art as one of "mime and posture" and writes of her "plastic qualities"—summoning up images of graceful malleability and the "plastiques" taught at Denishawn, in which dancers arranged themselves into sculptural designs.

More than ten daily papers kept New Yorkers abreast of the news—political, social, and artistic—and even though few journalists were knowledgeable about dance, you catch glimpses of these early Graham works through their reviews, as well as from photographs. You learn, for instance, that *The Marionette Show* (to music by Graham's Rochester colleague Eugene Goossens) was "a symbolic piece, portraying a tragic love triangle, enacted with jerky, puppet-like motions." In one photo of the trio from Rochester, Macdonald wears a high, pointed cap and a dark cape over a short dress; kneeling, she plays a mandolin. Biracree is apparently dancing dreamily to the tune. Hers is the most extraordinary of the costumes—a tutu that has migrated upward or a Pierrot collar fluffed out of control. Made of at least three tiers of big, filmy white ruffles, it is fastened around her neck and extends down to her thighs. Her head appears through its opening like the center of a large peony. On the other side of her, Sabin, looking slantily at the other two, is poised on tiptoe. She wears a domed cap and a short dress with what could be two big, dark pompons down the front of it, and she brandishes a still larger, more ragged dark object that could be an immense flower.

In a second photo, Biracree lies supine, apparently dead, while Macdonald, holding up the mandolin, walks away, looking back at her. Sabin follows Macdonald, but droops back to gaze regretfully down at the figure on the floor. At a 1927 performance, the audience liked *The Marionette Show* enough to request an encore.

One of the most enduring lessons Graham had absorbed from watching St. Denis was the way in which costumes and props could be used, not just to indicate a particular character, but to enhance or inhibit motion and to symbolize emotional states. When at the end of Graham's great 1947 *Night Journey*, Jocasta slips off her gown to reveal a simple sheath, she is not only preparing her neck for the rope she holds up but also divesting herself of all that she believed she knew about herself. The central Joan of Arc in *Seraphic Dialogue* (1955) reappears for her apotheosis clad in a gown of gold.

In 1926, of course, Graham's aims were more decorative than symbolic, and audiences and critics took note of the theatrically stunning and mobile costumes she utilized. *The Dance Magazine*'s critic described her in *A Study in Lacquer* as being "clad in a heavy gold kimono, making patterns with her body against a screen of brilliant lacquer." A photo further reveals that the kimono was long enough to trail behind her and puddle around her feet. A fashion editor at *The Bookman* wrote effusively of the array of rich fabrics that "come to life in her expert hands," adding that *Danse Rococo* "was done in a pair of green mules, a feat any woman knows is equaled only by a tightrope Charleston, that amazing stunt seen at the recent circus in Madison Square Garden."

Bonnie Bird, who saw Graham perform *Tanagra* in Seattle in 1930, remembered that "her shawl was made of a very soft, lightweight pure silk, 'glove silk' as it was called, which had a certain amount of stretch. She threw it into space so that it went out at a right angle to her body and then, with the speed of lightning, she pulled it back before it fell so that it lay across her hand. It was a breathtaking gesture requiring great skill." Three years earlier, Robert Bell of *The Washington Post* wrote, "She dances in a tight skirt that flares at her ankles into a long ruffling train. She does not touch her hands to the train, only her feet control it, yet it dances too. It seems to repeat and give emphasis to the motive of the dance." This same critic waxed eloquent about Graham in her Debussy solo *The Moth* (*La Soirée Dans Grenade*) when it premiered in November 1926):

> As the woman like a white moth seeking the light stalks the streets of Granada, it is a veil she handles to perfection. The veil clings to her body, loving it, she and it find protection in each other—her hands seem to call to it and it comes flying. For a moment it is submissive; then the dancer wearies of the veil and it drops quivering from her hands [?] to her feet, and the woman stands without it, proud and free.

Horst was extremely supportive of Graham's earliest dances, but once she had, with his encouragement, ventured into modernism and a more Spartan style, he looked back on many of them disapprovingly. Could *The Moth* be the dance that he later referred to as "something sad and scarfy"?

Graham was on her way. The day after her debut concert, she was interviewed for *The New York Telegram*. She was not, however, asked about her art. The article was titled "The Leading Question—'Why Is a Fat Lady?' Martha Graham, Premier Danseuse, Gives the Answer." Graham tells her interviewer that overeating and underexercising are less potent in producing fat than "the narrow-mindedness which limits a housewife's interest to the confines of her home and kitchen." In the wake of Isadora and Miss Ruth, Graham reached for a more exalted recipe for weight management: "The woman whose mind is alert to the currents of the universe, to the world happenings of the day, who responds to beauty in all forms, who finds time to read poetry and listen to good music, will never fear to face the scales, whether she plays tennis or golf or not."

On May 27, Graham, who was finishing her teaching year at Eastman, gave a full concert in the school's Kilbourn Hall. She not only repeated some of the dances from the Forty-Eighth Street Theatre performance but also added four new ones. Three of these were noteworthy in that she used men in them—her last concert choreography for the male body until 1938. Three of her Eastman students (Robert Ross, Harold Kolb, and Harold Conkling) appeared in *Bas Relief,* no doubt posing in two-dimensional muscularity in the Denishawn manner. These men, plus Henry Riebeselle and one woman, Jean Hurwitz, joined her and her three acolytes in a suite set to incidental music from Christoph Willibald Gluck's opera *Alceste.* And Hurwitz, Kolb, and Ross were added to Graham's *Scène Javanaise,* performed to a score Horst had written for Graham while in Vienna.

The Eastman concert was memorable for another reason: three weeks before the performance, the Kodak Research Laboratories decided to use a dance of Graham's as a test subject for a color movie process that Robert Smith had developed. For both the silent film and the Kilbourn Hall performance, Graham fleshed out her *Three Gopi Maidens,* embedding it in a new framework and calling the result *The Flute of Krishna.* Eastman's skilled designer, Norman Edwards, created a set that gave Orientalism a children's-book clarity. Horst located additional music by Cyril Scott (possibly also from his *Indian Suite*). Ross played the amorous Krishna, Evelyn Sabin became his Radha, and Susanne Vacanti joined Biracree and Macdonald as one of "Three Apsaras." Graham told Lydia Barton of *Stage and Screen* that the film was being made by people who knew how the camera operates in regard to motion: "There must be no sudden movement of any kind—nothing remotely resembling ballet, because it is a story, first of all, and as all life is dance, it is so shown."

Much, thinks the article's author, "may be proved by this experiment. Someone, sometime, is certain to perfect color photography."

The film process used for *Flute of Krishna* involved printing a blue-green image on one side of the film and a red-orange one on the other. The resulting silent film was discovered in the Eastman Kodak archives and reprinted to make its 16 frames per second conform to the 24-frames-per-second standard. Except for a black-and-white film clip of Graham performing a few moments of her *Tanagra* in a garden, *Flute of Krishna* is the sole record of her early choreography.

The style of the film is very much of its time. Ross, turbaned and made up as the Blue God (although looking more green than blue), affects amorous, yearning gestures that might have been inspired by Rudolph Valentino. He plays his flute to entice three sari-clad women to come down the partially hidden staircase and dance with him. Actually *for* him; he spends most of the time sitting or lounging to gaze at them, rising periodically to chase them around—all of which they flirtatiously enjoy. Anyone wishing a crash course in the handling of drapery would do well to study this film. As the beguiling maidens playfully flee his attentions or take simple, soft-footed steps around the tiered platform and up and down its steps, they transform their costumes in endlessly inventive ways: they loosen their saris one rhythmic tug at a time, so that the fabric trails behind them when they pose and arch backward. They swirl it up and cover their heads with it, revealing the slender pantaloons they wear beneath it. As they flee Krishna, they hold it out in ways that make it billow. They turn, and it spirals around them. Finally, they detach the fabric completely from their waistbands and again put it over their heads—this time letting the ends of the material drape over their bent arms, which they hold decoratively out to their sides.

Sabin, who arrives after Biracree, Macdonald, and Vacanti finish their enticing dance, is lovely—slender and very flexible. She also seems to fall naturally into those S-shaped curves so prominent in St. Denis's dancing. Standing beside Ross, she inclines her head shyly toward him even as she pulls away, and her hips sway nearer to him for counterbalance. Arching backward, twisting and turning while holding a curved branch of flowers with both hands, she is a study in teasing ambivalence. She slides to the floor—perhaps grieving that he has left her to chase the others as they run up the staircase and disappear—but he swiftly returns and lifts her into an embrace as the lights go out. St. Denis would surely have been charmed, yet those who subsequently paid attention to Graham's career could discern her developing skill at providing a drama through dance rhythms and arrangements in space.

On September 25, after a summer that also included performances at Mariarden (with a new duet for Sabin and Macdonald to music by

Chopin) as well as at the Eastman School, Graham was able to write to Sabin's father that Daniel Mayer's office was speaking of handling the three New York concerts she had apparently already secured. She will be opening her own studio, she tells him, as well as continuing to teach at the Anderson-Milton School (she, like Mamoulian, had decided against another year in Rochester). A Miss Beardsley, who had initially managed the New York Denishawn School and is slated to manage the new studio, has "splendid social connections" and will try to arrange private engagements and ones at clubs.

The purpose of this gracious and tactfully written letter was to sound Stewart Sabin out about his daughter's future. Does he wish her to enter a field other than dance? Graham hopes not. She very much wants eighteen-year-old Evelyn to continue to work with her, allowing herself perhaps to exaggerate a little to that end: "She is exquisite—and has the greatest gift of any young dancer I know or have ever known." Graham must have already secured scholarships for her girls at Anderson-Milton, for she tells Mr. Sabin that the faculty member Michio Ito has used Evelyn in a dance of his and thinks highly of her. The sculptor Harriet Whitney Frishmuth has invited the girl to pose for one of her small bronzes of dancers. Apparently Mr. Sabin has suggested that keeping an eye on young girls turned loose in the big city will be a burden to Graham. "Never," she declares. "I do truly want to do what is best for Evelyn—but unless you deem it in your heart wise, please do not take her away. I love them more than I can say." Perhaps a similar letter was sent to Betty Macdonald's parents, but Thelma Biracree had left the trio to teach in Rochester and choreograph for Eastman productions. Rosina Savelli, a student at Anderson-Milton, replaced her. In the 1970s, Graham described the adoring girls in her first trio as "pretty little things and smart as traps," but in 1926 she knew their worth.

The year in which Graham made her debut as a choreographer was a fertile one for both established artists and emerging ones in many fields. D. H. Lawrence published *The Plumed Serpent* and Ernest

Hemingway *The Sun Also Rises*. Arthur Waley's translation of Lady Murasaki's *The Tale of Genji* introduced English-speaking readers to the customs of eleventh-century Japan. Those who, like Graham, prowled the cramped quarters of the Gotham Book Mart could lay their hands on new novels by Sinclair Lewis, Edna Ferber, and Louis Bromfield, among an array of others. Or selections of poetry by Vachel Lindsay, Robert Bridges, Archibald MacLeish, and Amy Lowell.

Puccini's posthumous opera, *Turandot*, received its American premiere, and something close to 260 plays and musicals lit up Broadway during the 1926–27 season (some of them for only a few nights). *Abie's Irish Rose* (an Irish-Jewish romance) was still running, having racked up more than a thousand performances. So were *The Green Hat*, the Pulitzer Prize–winning *Craig's Wife*, *Rain*, *Shuffle Along*, and an array of winsome operettas by Sigmund Romberg and Victor Herbert. New shows opening in 1926 ranged from Anita Loos's *Gentlemen Prefer Blondes* to Patrick Kearney's dramatization of Theodore Dreiser's *An American Tragedy*.

An unusual number of major European dramas were presented that season by the newly established Theater Guild and by Eva Le Gallienne's Civic Repertory Theatre. Graham and Horst could have taken in Henrik Ibsen's *Ghosts*, *The Master Builder*, and *John Gabriel Borkman*; Chekhov's *The Three Sisters* et al.; and a dramatization of Dostoyevski's *The Brothers Karamazov*. The Habima Theatre brought *The Dybbuk*.

Manhattan itself was expanding, making its borders more porous to visitors. The Holland Tunnel, the first to cross the Hudson, was ninety-five percent completed by the end of 1926. The plans for the George Washington Bridge were approved, and construction began in 1927. Funds were appropriated to extend the two existing subway lines, and the city received bids for its mission to connect Manhattan and Queens by a new line that made the crossing between boroughs at Fifty-Third Street.

Graham's repertory was expanding too, as were her ideas and her reputation. Able to accept engagements as a soloist, with Horst at the piano, as well as performing with her three young protégées and employing one or two additional musicians when necessary, she wedged herself firmly into the array of "serious" female solo performers who appeared in the wake of Duncan, St. Denis, and Loïe Fuller—three who had clambered out of variety shows and vaudeville to ally dancing with important music or poetry or philosophical-religious speculations. In Germany, Mary Wigman was the finest of many performers who sculpted styles for themselves based on what suited their temperaments and bodies. Frank Thiess's 1927 *Der Tanz als Kunstwerk* brought a number of German choreographer-soloists into prominence for those who, like Horst, knew German: Lucy Kieselhausen (the possessor of his aforementioned heavy name and body), the exotic Sent Mahesa, the satirical Valeska Gert, the elfin Niddy Impekoven, Gret Palucca, and Yvonne Georgi, among others. In America, Agnes de Mille was beginning to create and perform a series of danced portraits, and Angna Enters built vignettes that fell somewhere between mime and dance. Enters, to whom Graham was sometimes compared, chose to portray many women from art history and religious iconography—as Graham was beginning to do—and she too was praised for her ability to create pictures that moved. All these high-minded dancers were, in one respect, like the wire walkers and rope dancers and skirt dancers and contortionists who continued to flourish; they devised their own onstage personas and made up their own "routines."

As Graham's career took wing—artistically if not financially—her solo portraits began gradually to diverge from those of St. Denis. For her concert at the Klaw Theatre in November 1926, she ventured outside Denishawn's Asian and Spanish milieus to create *Baal Shem (Two Pictures of Chassidic Life)* to music by Ernst Bloch. The three girls performed "Simchas Torah (Rejoicing)," and Martha, with a shawl over her head, performed "Vidui (Contrition)." To "Old French Airs," she danced *From Heloise to Abelard.* A review of her October 1927 New York performance noted, "To Ravel, she was a wistful peasant girl on a holiday. In yellow dress and red handkerchief, she was far gayer and more smiling than she usually allows herself to be on the stage."

She also experimented with a dramatic layering of characters. In her 1927 *Lucrezia,* she conflated the notorious member of the Borgia family and her supposed incestuous doings with her father, Pope Alexander VI, with another seductive daughter. A quote in the program read, "As Salome, Lucrezia did dance before the pope, her father," although there's no indication that Graham removed any part of her rich, full-skirted, and sleeved satin gown.

When St. Denis reached for spiritual subject matter, she looked to cultures whose gods were adept at dancing. Graham turned instead to the Christian iconography that had been part of her growing up—beginning with *From a XII-Century Tapestry* to music by Rachmaninoff (retitled *A Florentine Madonna* and then, for her group's February 1927 concert at the Guild Theatre, re-costumed and called simply *Madonna*). At that same performance, her three-part solo *Peasant Sketches* ended with "In the Church" (music by Tchaikovsky). Sabin, Macdonald, and Savelli performed *Danza Degli Angeli* (music by Ermanno Wolf-Ferrari) in the 1926 summer concert at the Eastman School and *Spires* at New York's Little Theatre in October 1927 to a Bach chorale. Graham could still enchant her audiences with her 1926 *Three Poems of the East* and the visions promised by its subtitles of the music that Horst wrote for her: "On listening to a flute by moonlight," "She like a dancer puts her broidered garments on," and "In measure while the gnats of music whir the little amber-colored dancers move" (the second from the Rig-Veda, the last from Arthur Addington Symonds's poem "Javanese Dancers"). However, *Three Poems*, with its poetic allusions to Chinese, Indian, and Javanese culture, was the only "oriental" number in the performances Graham and her trio gave in January, February, October, and December 1927. She set dances to music by such Post-Romantic composers as Scriabin and Satie and by her contemporaries, Hindemith and Honegger. *Fragilité*, *Lugubre*, and *Poème Ailé* joined *Désir* and *Danse Languide* to form a Scriabin suite, *Five Poems*. Photos by Soichi Sunami show Martha in *Fragilité* turning slightly away from the camera and curling her body protectively inward, eyelids lowered, as she gathers up the front of the long, diaphanous ruffled skirt that trails behind her. In *Poème Ailé*, she wears long, winglike sleeves.

Deeper, darker ideas about dance were gradually shaping her

choreographic choices. The critic who found her October 1927 program "certainly one of the finest she has given up to date" also offered some cavils on behalf of the audience:

> Miss Graham tends to begin far away from realism and some find it hard to follow the processes of refinement to which she subjects her themes. Then, too, her mood is characteristically somber and becomes depressing to those who are not sensitive to the fine rhythmic emphasis that gives even her tragic numbers a song-like quality.
>
> The exotic character portrayals for which Miss Graham has been famous reappeared last night after more or less of an absence. The audience was definitely pleased.
>
> An artist is to be admired for refusing to be a slave of the first success, but there is always danger in developing a more mature style of losing the spontaneity of the first fine frenzy. Miss Graham proved last night that she was in no danger of becoming a rarified spectre of her former self. She has developed an original style in movement, rhythm and costuming and is rapidly adding the force and abandon.

At that October concert, among the five new dances was one that surprised the devotees she had acquired and dismayed some viewers with its angularity and thrust. It was titled *Danse* after the last part of Arthur Honegger's *Trois Pièces*. The Honegger music lasted a bit more than two minutes, and Horst found it "a helluva thing to play." In rapid 6/8 time, the pianist attacks with abrupt, repeating chords that seem to approach a destination. You can imagine them accompanying a cinematic cavalry charge. Punched-out melodies emerge above this, quavering and tangling. The tension between this dense motion and Graham's passionate constraint must have been astonishing. "To Honegger's mad music," wrote *The Dance Magazine*'s critic, "she was significant as a typical product of modern industry—a downtrodden, agonized soul, trying to free itself from the tremendous power that was crushing it to earth." The writer called this solo the highlight of the program. Later, Graham renamed it *Revolt*.

Coincidentally, she confirmed her mission to rebel against an inherited aesthetic one month and three days after Isadora Duncan, a great rebel of the preceding generation, died when her long scarf became entangled in a wheel of the car in which she was about to ride down a street in Nice. Whether by chance or partly in homage, *Fragilité*, *Lugubre*, and *Poeme Ailé* were set to the first three delicate little piano pieces of Scriabin's *Quatre Morceaux*, op. 51. Among Duncan's own last works, created in 1923 during her years in Russia, were three eloquent, weighted, and very spare solos that she danced to Scriabin études.

Earlier in 1927 Graham had confided some of her developing ideas to another interviewer for *The Dance Magazine*. Throwing on a "mandarin coat" over what the writer mistook for a bathing suit, she sat on a low coach in the anteroom of the Carnegie Hall studio that she was using for rehearsals and the classes she had begun to teach, and she spoke of a process of reduction and simplification that echoed some of the ideas of forward-looking architects and designers.

When the reporter queried Graham's rationale for using a sarabande from Christoph Willibald Gluck's *Alceste* (a sarabande in a Greek tragedy—was that not an anachronism?), Graham shot back, "But it will not be a sarabande . . . It will be the shadow of the sarabande—the spirit that lies beneath the formal patterns of the old dance." Nor was it was possible, she averred, to "duplicate the Oriental dance. We can only duplicate—in our way—the feeling of that dance—its spirit, its shadow." She assures the apparently doubtful interviewer that, no, she would not discard her Eastern dances, "but as with the sarabande, the figures must be reinterpreted; they must be reduced to their essence."

Years later she was to define abstraction in relation to her scenic collaborator, the sculptor Isamu Noguchi. His work was abstract, she said, in the sense that orange juice is an abstraction of an orange. She was already, in this early interview, saying, "Out of emotion comes form." And, speaking of expressive design, "There are certain eternal symbols we use. Love, for instance, is expressed through circular motions; religious feeling in spirals."

Graham, with Horst's guidance and her own theatrical instincts, filtered her new, "modern" material into her performances judiciously, accompanying them with old favorites that she deemed still acceptable, as well as lighter new views of contemporary life. At her Little Theatre concert on April 22, 1928, she balanced *Immigrant* and *Poems of 1917* with *Fragments* ("Tragedy," "Comedy") and *Trouvères* ("The Return of Spring," "Complaint," and "A Song, Frank and Gay). Ernestine Stodelle recalled that in "Tragedy," Graham, "clad in sculptured folds of bright red jersey . . . moved slowly with a sense of profound resignation." She mentioned the flute's melodic line and intermittent strokes on a gong. In "Comedy," Martha was "a tightly wound spring of perpetual motion. Staccato runs, sudden stops, abrupt kicks in bas-relief profile called Pan to mind." Horst noted that *Trouvères* was "very cute" and that "Martha can be 'medieval' marvelously."

Immigrant's two sections were titled "Steerage" and "Strike." It's not clear how Graham connected them. The music was two selections from Josip Slavenski's "Aus dem Balkan" suite.

Poems of 1917, set to Leo Ornstein's music of the same title, also had two parts: "Song Behind the Lines" and "Dance of Death." Clearly, Graham was acting on her resolution to pare dances down to their essence, which made them possibly more static. Critics from two publications compared these two new works to sculpture: John Martin, the *New York Times*'s new dance critic, wrote of *Poems of 1917*'s two parts, "In feeling they suggest modern reproductions of ancient wood sculptures, and are deeply moving by their very sparseness." (Horst mentioned that the costumes—or one of them—was made of heavy rubber and hardly moved.) *The Dance Magazine* critic Nickolas Muray wrote that his first impression of *Immigrant* "was that of a Bavarian wood carving of peasant figures with stiff black shawls and skirts that remained almost motionless during the dance, save for the curious hard folds which accentuated the inarticulateness of the immigrant. The *Strike* was in a gray drab one-piece dress—drab and gray like the life of the proletariat."

A photo by Soichi Sunami, identified as being of Graham in the "Steerage" section of *Immigrant*, contradicts Muray's mention of black shawls but reinforces the impression of blockiness. This European girl bound for America stands with her feet planted slightly apart, her arms hanging stiffly. Her remarkable dark dress barely seems to have folds; it stands out from her indeed wooden figure like a bell, its sleeves falling into points; over it she wears an immaculate, starchy white headdress. She looks like a doll representing a Flemish peasant.

Among those who welcomed Graham's forays into the precincts of modernism and those who preferred her "oriental" solos, there seemed to be none who doubted her skills as a performer. She was, wrote the critic for *Musical America*, "more than a dancer . . . She is well versed in mime. The success of her portrayals depending to a great extent upon the tragedy one saw in her eye or the pallor that lay on her forehead or the scintillating humor at the corner of her lips."

In his long, thoughtful review in *The Washington Post*, Robert Bell mentioned an "austere, mystic calm" that he associated with Eastern philosophy and identified her as

> one of those artists that are not imitative but who believes that in her own being are all the potential qualities of all emotions and characterizations, This personality of hers is thoughtful and this therefore colors all her work. She sees things clearly but in a detached manner as if she is watching from afar.

In this prescient review, Bell was glimpsing and attempting to articulate what would become a crucial element of Graham's style as a performer and a choreographer. She fully inhabited whatever character she presented on the stage, yet by various devices also identified herself as an observer—one who pondered her actions and reenacted her memories.

— 5 —

TAKING ON NEW YORK, MODERNISM, AND NIETZSCHE

URING THE LATE 1920s, Graham and other independent choreographers struggling to present their work in New York or
on out-of-town engagements may have been rivals, but none
of them could yet afford to be isolationists. Willy-nilly, Louis Horst—
while devoted to advancing Graham's career—became a liaison among
these artists: the dance accompanist every choreographer wanted to
hire. He played for Michio Ito's classes at the Anderson-Milton
School, and Ito was among the many artists, such as Ronny Johansson, whom he rushed around town to accommodate whenever they
presented their choreography. Horst had a considerable knowledge of
music, in particular the work of contemporary composers, many of
whose names were not yet familiar in this small, defensive, hardscrab-
ble dance community. He could recruit other musicians, such as the
flautist Hugo Bergamesco and the violinist Winthrop Sargeant (later
The New Yorker music critic and Graham's brother-in-law). He could
also conduct a small orchestra from the piano and, in a pinch, take on
some of the duties of a stage manager.

When Adolph Bolm had expected to bring his Ballet Intime and
an orchestra to perform upstate under the auspices of the Cornell
Dramatic Club but had encountered unforeseen problems on tour,
Horst helped him to put together a substitute program of twenty solos

and duets featuring Bolm; the Ballet Intime ballerina Ruth Page; Vera Mirova, a Russian ballet dancer who specialized in dances she had studied in Asia; two of Bolm's best students; and Martha Graham. Martha would have been glad to participate; she wrote years later of Bolm—a former member of Diaghilev's Ballets Russes, a colleague at the Neighborhood Playhouse, and an artist whom she loved and with whom she felt a kinship: "He was fearless in experiment and did not protect himself, and he was ruthless where mediocrity was concerned."

As might have been expected, Horst also accompanied performances by Doris Humphrey and Charles Weidman, whose careers he had followed since their early days together in Denishawn. It was he who urged them to leave the Denishawn fold (they no longer performed with Shawn and St. Denis, but were teaching at the organization's New York studio after the company's return from its Far East tour in November 1926). During a weekend visit to Doris and Charles at a summer place Denishawn had acquired in Westport, Connecticut, Louis and Martha further advanced the argument for that pair's defection. Humphrey, honoring St. Denis, still had doubts about striking out on her own, although in June 1927 she wrote disapprovingly to her parents that "the Shawns, I'm ashamed to say, are jealous of Martha . . . They think that Martha should mention Denishawn on her programs, and in her interviews—and that is the fly in the jam. She considers that she has broken away from everything they do, and is individual."

A few days later, on June 7, Humphrey reappraised her perception of Graham, with whom she had had little contact during their separate Denishawn touring schedules. Mentioning to her family that Graham had worked "so hard to keep her studio going," she wrote, "I liked her a lot—seeing her after such a long absence I get a fresh impression as of a new person," and she provided an astute portrait of Martha: "Of course, she's extremely artificial—not silly, I mean but like a hothouse flower that grows best in a hot, moist climate, intensely feminine, not a flaming obvious flower—but a night-blooming thing with a faint, exotic perfume." Doris noted that Louis, however,

was "the same old bundle of contradictions. He believes in equality &
freedom of the sexes, but dies of jealousy and says no man can love a
woman who is unfaithful to him. He believes there is no happiness in
love, and that art is the only fun that lasts, and in the next breath says
that a half hour with the one you love is the greatest ecstasy."

Graham was proud enough of her students (the members of her
trio among them) to want to coach some of them in her solos for a
program at the Anderson-Milton School on August 27, 1927, and to
show them off to colleagues.* However, she went through what Humphrey, in a letter to her mother, termed "the usual Graham emotional
pyrotechnics, being afraid to invite us, and fighting with Louis about
it, telling us we couldn't come—and changing her mind, ending by
calling at the studio twice and telephoning three times to be sure we
were coming." Doubtless Doris and Charles showed up.

While Horst was playing the piano for what he later recalled as "an
electric men's convention" in Atlantic City in 1926 (one of the various
entertainments that John Murray Anderson devised), he met Helen
Tamiris, who was appearing as the Goddess of Light, immobilized in
a costume made of glass that he estimated weighed "about a thousand
pounds." Graham came down from Rochester to go to Atlantic City
with him. (Tamiris had spent time dancing in the Metropolitan Opera Ballet and contemplated venturing into modernism.) In June of
that year, at Pennsylvania's Longwood Gardens, "Mlle Tamiris" appeared in a Divertissement, while Graham performed three solos near
the conclusion of the lengthy program Anderson had devised. Horst
and Graham talked her into doing a solo concert, and in 1927 Horst,
Tamiris, and Elsa Findlay, who taught Dalcroze Eurhythmics in a
Carnegie Hall studio, brought young John Martin to Graham's studio, and together all five of them went down to *The New York Times*
and asked the paper to please make him its full-time dance critic.

---

* Evelyn Sabin performed *Maid with the Flaxen Hair*, Rosina Savelli took on *Gypsy
Portrait*, and Betty Macdonald danced *Intermezzo*. Graham gave *Novelette* to
Ethel Rudy, *Tunisia—A Courtyard* to Ray Moses (afterward Lillian Ray), and *Valse
Caprice* to Louise Gotto.

(Martin got the job only weeks after the *New York Herald Tribune* made the music writer Mary Watkins its dance critic.)

When the German Expressionist Harald Kreutzberg and his partner Tilly Losch gave a concert in New York in 1928 during the time they were performing in Max Reinhardt's production of *The Miracle*, Horst accompanied them too, and they rehearsed in Graham's Carnegie Hall studio (Graham sat and watched them, which unnerved Losch). When Kreutzberg returned the following year with Yvonne Georgi, the two were slated to appear at the Hudson Theatre on January 20, the same evening that Graham planned to present her solo program at the Booth. To their mutual advantage, she prudently moved her performance to the matinee slot. She must also have sensed that the German dancers' choreographic interests were close to her own.

Certainly German dance was in the news. Graham herself, when interviewed at Eastman about *Flute of Krishna* in 1926, mentioned a student production she was thinking of staging—one in which the dancers would move without musical accompaniment "as is being done a great deal now in Germany." Horst wrote about the dance scene in Germany for *The Dance Magazine*. The Austrian dancer-choreographer Hans Wiener (later Jan Veen), who had trained in Germany with Mary Wigman, Émile Jaques-Dalcroze, and Rudolf Laban, settled in the United States in 1928. The young José Limón decided to be a dancer after seeing the power, manly dignity, and brooding thoughts that Kreutzberg could convey. Still, it's odd that John Martin, in his first review for the *Times*, would write that the program Graham presented on February 12, 1928, was "said to be in the nature of a farewell to Miss Graham's familiar style of dancing before she goes over to the new German technique." (One wonders who his informant was and what he deemed her "familiar style" in a repertory so varied in subject matter.)

Struggling and intermittently rivalrous choreographers also at times found themselves sharing the stage. Even before Graham and Horst left the Anderson-Milton School in 1928 to teach at the Neighborhood Playhouse School of the Theatre and at the Carnegie Hall studio that Graham rented, she, along with other New York dancers and dancemakers, was willing to appear in the ambitious music-driven productions masterminded by the Neighborhood Playhouse founder Irene Lewisohn, who, with her sister, Alice, recruited orchestras, scenic designers, faculty members, and willing dancers around town. Just before Humphrey and Weidman finally broke with Denishawn in June 1928 and were working to maintain their own fledgling company, they had found the Misses Lewisohns' music dramas "a dignified way of earning a little money."

In the three programs (May 4, 5, and 6 of that year) at the Manhattan Opera House, the Cleveland Orchestra under Nikolai Sokoloff played Ernst Bloch's *Israel* Symphony, with its full chorus; Claude Debussy's *Nuages* and *Fêtes*; and Alexander Borodin's *On the Steppes of Central Asia* and dances from his opera *Prince Igor*. The sculptor Jo Davidson designed the scenery. Irene Lewisohn was credited with the "stage direction and dramatic composition." This last means that she dreamed up scenarios to fit the music, then turned the various choreographers loose in the studio while she watched them and gave directions and suggestions. Soloists like Graham devised their own movements.

Anyone knowing the later careers of the dancers who participated might be startled by the diversity of the cast and the roles they were asked to play. Graham was one of four Mourning Women bearing candles in the Bloch symphony. Michio Ito played one of the Men of the Priestly Order. Esther Junger danced among the Other Suppliants. Benjamin Zemach (formerly of Tel Aviv's Habima Theatre) played a Mystic, listening for the voice of the Messiah.

In the Borodin setting, Weidman, Ito, Zemach, and the up-and-coming young Japanese dancer Yeichi Nimura were among the six tribesmen of the Khan, who were given such names in the program as Ascar and Sartach. Weidman was Buri. The dressing room chatter must have been illuminating.

Neighborhood Playhouse students, such as Anna Sokolow and Sophie Maslow, appeared in the Debussy pieces alongside Ronny Johansson and Graham, their teacher. In *Nuages*, Graham danced as a

Passing Cloud Form, and, according to Zemach, he, as a Storm Cloud battled with Ito, as a Fawn-like Creature, for her favors.

Graham was singled out by the *New Republic* critic Stark Young for her dancing in *Nuages*. He called her phrases of movement beautiful and "beautifully composed," although he missed the breath of life in each musical phrase. Ito bored him: "It took only Mr. Zemach's first pose to wipe Mr. Ito from the dramatic composition."

Zemach captivated Graham as well. She had seen him in the production of *The Dybbuk* that the Habima Theatre brought to New York, and according to him, he took her dance classes. They had a brief affair and remained friends (whether Horst was aware of this is unknown). Decades later, Zemach revealed to Francis Mason, who was assembling a book of interviews about Graham, that Martha had told him that "in the past [Louis] had been untrue to her, and how she left him" (his faulty memory or Graham's deviousness may account for this). He also said, "Martha told me that when the creative state came upon her, she felt like a wind was behind her back. She couldn't talk about it to anybody."

During the first half of 1929, Graham's career showed increased activity of a more stable kind. The week before the program that she presented on her January 20 matinee at the Booth Theatre, she and her trio performed at the MacDowell Club of New York City dinner in honor of Elizabeth Sprague Coolidge. On January 24 she appeared alone at the Bennett School in Millbrook, New York, and gave another recital at Smith College on February 18.

Among the five new works in her solo concert was one that startled many spectators and displeased others. She called it *Dance*. Like the earlier *Danse* (which she had renamed *Revolt*),* it was set to a thorny work by Arthur Honegger. To emphasize the artistic statement she was making and the irony of the title, Graham included a program

---

* It is not always possible to guess what Graham's early dances were like by their titles. In a second recital that she gave at the Booth Theatre on March 3, 1929, Mary Watkins noted in her *New York Herald Tribune* review that *Resurrection* had originally been called *The Avenger*, which Watkins thought would have suited it better.

note—with a phrase drawn from Friedrich Nietzsche: "strong, free, joyous, action."

Bessie Schönberg remembered that Graham performed *Dance* wearing a short red dress slit up one side, with one sleeve longer than the other (another observer recalled a "long-sleeved, tightly fitted red chiffon-velvet dress"). She had placed herself on a small platform, from which she never budged. Schönberg also recollected Martha Hill saying that Graham looked as if "she dared anyone to move her feet." All her movements—pulsating on her strong legs, twisting against her stance, recoiling, thrusting—took place between her shoulders and her knees. Strong, yes. Free, evidently not yet. Joyous? If so, she kept it under wraps.

In appending a quote from Nietzsche to the program for *Dance*, Graham not only announced a new direction in her work—creating a virtual manifesto to remain almost immobile rather than continuing to cultivate exotic portraits—but also acknowledged the influence of certain philosophers on her thinking about dance. In this she was not alone among dance artists.

Anyone rooting around in the reading lists of Isadora Duncan, Ruth St. Denis, Ted Shawn, Doris Humphrey, and Martha Graham will discover that three names stand out among writers the choreographers admired and plumbed for ideas: Havelock Ellis, Arthur Schopenhauer, and Friedrich Nietzsche.

Isadora devoured Schopenhauer's *The World as Will and Representation*—and "don't forget," she wrote in a parenthetical aside to her pupils when they toured America in 1918–19, "that [Nietzsche's] *The Birth of Tragedy* and *The Spirit of Music* are my Bible, and with these to guide you, and the greatest music, you may go far." Shawn and St. Denis were thrilled to meet with Ellis—Shawn several times—during Denishawn's London appearances; both had been intrigued by the essays found in his *Psychology of Sex* and were shortly to be impressed by his *The Dance of Life* (1923). During a rare vacation in 1931, Doris Humphrey wrote to her mother, "I have been feeding on Havelock Ellis and Nietzsche, the two most inspiring people I know of." In a 1928 interview, Martha Graham did not hesitate to credit her influences:

"I owe all that I am to a study of Nietzsche and Schopenhauer." Horst, who was able to read these philosophers in the original German, had introduced Graham to their ideas.

What drew two generations of dancers to these particular thinkers? At the most basic level, the choreographers were responding to a cultural climate that treated dance as nothing more than agreeable—and sometimes titillating—entertainment, but also sought to put it on a par with soul-stirring, thought-provoking works of art, theater, and music. How inspiring it must have been for St. Denis and Shawn to have Ellis reinforce their fascination with the dancing gods of Indian religion and to declare that "the art of dancing stands at the source of all the arts that express themselves first in the human person." He put it on an equal footing with "building" (i.e., architecture), which, to him, had spawned the visual arts. In Ellis's *The Dance of Life*, the chapter titled "The Art of Dance" comes first, preceding "The Art of Thinking." This physician and psychologist considered dancing to be "the loftiest, the most moving, the most beautiful of the arts, because it is no mere translation or abstraction from life; it is life itself. It is the only art, as Rahel Varnhagen said, of which we ourselves are the stuff." And his "ourselves" included the empathic spectators. For dancers trying to leave the vaudeville stages behind, such thoughts could be an affirmation and a challenge.

In the same way, Schopenhauer's argument that music transcended all the other arts found favor with late nineteenth-century and early twentieth-century composers. Music, he wrote, did not copy the aspects of the material world that he termed Ideas, but copied the Will itself, as a blind and purposeless striving—not expressing an individual's joy or pain, but joy or pain as things in themselves. Choreographers seeking a kind of passionate abstraction could, as Graham began to do, ally themselves with these ideas and redefine them for dance. For her, Schopenhauer's discussion of the distinctions between the sublime and the beautiful in art was stimulating, as she and Horst came to decry prettiness and embrace darker subject matter. When asked (in that above-mentioned 1928 interview) who took her Carnegie Hall classes, she spoke of the shopgirls and secretaries who "come with all sorts of conventional notions of prettiness, graceful posturing, and what not. My first task is to teach them to admire strength—the gestures that are evocative of the only true beauty. I try to show them that ugliness may be actually beautiful, if it cries out with the voice of power."

Nietzsche presented choreographers with an even more uplifting gift: a nimble philosopher-god. In *Thus Spake Zarathustra*, Nietzsche (who himself suffered from bouts of debilitating ill-health) exalted strength and well-being as well as dedication. Zarathustra, the dancing god, "one who loveth leaps and side-leaps," descended to walk among men, offering what could be construed by ambitious choreographers as encouragement. "I tell you, one must still have chaos in one to give birth to a dancing star." For Nietzsche, dance could serve as a metaphor for ambitious and enlightened thinking. He decried absolutists as ones with "heavy feet and sultry hearts; they do not know how to dance." His imprecations are as fervent as they are merry: "Lift up your hearts, my brethren, high, higher. And do not forget your legs! Lift up also your legs, ye good dancers, and better still, if ye stand upon your heads!"

For Duncan, Nietzsche's greatest gift came via his *Birth of Tragedy from the Spirit of Music*; she was struck by his extolling of the primacy of the Chorus in the earliest forms of Greek drama. "I have never danced a solo," she wrote. "I have always been the Chorus." Alone onstage, she populated some of the great pieces of music with invisible companions, to whom she beckoned and among whom she moved. Humphrey, reading the same work, took from it ideas that she could transfer to the dancers in the group she and Weidman formed— making of the ensemble not a decorative background, but an expressive force. And for both Graham and Humphrey, the philosopher's discussion of the Apollonian and Dionysian elements and their necessary intermingling in art fueled ideas more structural than Isadora's depiction of maenads and furies. Eventually Humphrey developed a system of movement built on the opposing principals of Fall and Recovery—Dionysian inklings of instability or reckless passion pulled the dancer's body into a struggle against gravitational pull, while an

Apollonian sense of balance, form, and moderation restored its equilibrium. Graham, instead, amplified the intake and exhalation of breath into a close-knit duality that she labeled Contraction and Release. As if socked in the solar plexus, the dancer expelled air so deeply that her body became concave, pulling deeper into itself (or she might gasp—the kind of gasp so pulled in and up that the air didn't fill her lungs). The inevitable intake of breath restored the body to erectness, the dancer to a waiting Apollonian calm.

Graham inherited from Duncan and St. Denis not only a lust for reading ideas that elevated dance to a level with music and the visual arts, but a desire to speak and write about it in ways that portrayed the choreographer as a visionary thinker rather than someone who strung steps together with an intent to please a crowd. Christena L. Schlundt aptly summed up St. Denis's outpourings: "Philosophical experience as set forth by St. Denis ranged over generalized concepts. Great ideas about Beauty or Love were labeled and intoned; large ideas about the nature of the universe were dropped profoundly at tea, in a kitchen, under a tree, on the stage."

In January 1928 the MacDowell Colony of New York City offered an unusual event: dinner and a symposium titled "The Dance, Its Place in Life and Art." Twelve speakers (among them Adolph Bolm, Michio Ito, Angna Enters, and Graham) covered topics including folk dance, dance in ancient Greece, Dalcroze Eurhythmics, dance in poetry, in theater, in history, and more. Maria-Theresa, one of Duncan's six famous pupils, demonstrated "the classic dance" while her husband played the piano. Graham spoke about dance in relation to music and, thanks to Horst, could discourse eloquently on the topic.

Dance, with its Nietzsche quote and Honegger music, was the bravest new work on her January 1929 solo program; the other premieres were *Three Florentine Verses*, *Cants Magics*, *Two Variations (Country Lane, City Street)*, and *Four Insincerities (Petulance, Remorse, Politeness, Vivacity)*, the last of which gave Graham the opportunity to show her gift for satire and wit, as had the previous year's *Fragments (Tragedy, Comedy)*. In *Four Insincerities*, noted the critic Margaret Lloyd, "she began to hold inner qualities to the light." John Martin wrote approvingly that *City Street*, set to music by Alexander Gretchaninoff, "retained the same thematic characteristics" displayed in *Country Lane*," but was more inhibited. The young dancer Jane Dudley's impression of the solo, however, suggests that *Country Lane* was not inhibited at all: "Martha did a jump and landed with her feet together, and then she split in the air in a joyous jump, bavoom, bavoom, bavoom, about eight times. The curtain was down. It was wonderful."

This was the day, Sunday, January 20, when dance aficionados could see Graham in the afternoon and Kreutzberg and Georgi in the evening. Comparisons were inevitable, but certainly *Dance* outdid the Germans in starkness. Martha was venturing very carefully into territory that she understood might alienate her fans. One critic, betraying a certain confusion about what constituted Germanic dance, may have written, "Some of her latest and most interesting dances are in the German mechanistic manner," but John Martin was grateful for the presence of *Tanagra* on that program later in March and noted that it received the most applause. Its "lyrical calm," he wrote in the *Times*, "made a happy oasis in a program bristling with cerebral provocation and emotional upheaval of the sparse and direct character which is so strongly Miss Graham's." And his commentary reveals that *Dance* was not Graham's only foray into minimal movement that spring. The interest in *Danza*, set to music by Darius Milhaud, lay, thought Martin, "in its impression of dance movement where there is only the barest skeleton of such movement." He found it the least intriguing of her new pieces.

Martin was largely supportive of Graham, even though he thought that her pruning away of what the public considered to be dance went too far, and he worried that spectators who came thinking to be entertained might go away disappointed by programs that "are alive with passion and protest and are couched in a vein to frighten away somnolescence." Still, the "passion of her dances . . . nevertheless burns with the slow and deadly fire of the intellect."

Writers of the day clearly understood that Graham was attempting to lay claim to a condensed style all her own, to stimulate audiences into seeing the echo or the shadow of something full and deep. When Mary Watkins wrote in *The Dance Magazine* of the choreographer's *Adolescence* (performed in a short black dress with an outsize sheer white collar that subtly alluded to a school uniform), she called it "a masterpiece of Miss Graham's new style." A photo shows Martha sitting decorously on the floor, looking shy and vulnerable, her head bowed, her hands shielding her. She performed the piece on a small, narrowly lit platform, reaching out tentatively into the surrounding darkness.

One impetus to a further expansion of Graham's career may have come from within the dance community. In March 1928 Doris Humphrey and Charles Weidman mounted an ambitious concert with the Denishawn students they had been teaching while Shawn and St. Denis toured on the vaudeville circuit. Horst served as musician for most of the numbers on their March program at Brooklyn's Little Theatre. That concert included two remarkable group works, Humphrey's *Color Harmony* and *Grieg Concerto in A Minor*; neither showed much evidence of Denishawn style. (Horst groused about the amount of practice he had to put in to master the last movement's difficult piano part, which he played while conducting the small orchestra assembled for the Grieg work.) In *Color Harmony*, the dancers were costumed to represent the primary and secondary colors of light that, in the end, united to form an upward spiral that gave birth to a pure white beam (represented by Weidman, the only man, at its apex); the choreography throughout captured the feeling tones of the separate colors and the prismatic ways in which Humphrey could organize them. Photographs of *Grieg Concerto* show Humphrey as the solo voice represented by the piano, encouraging and leading a horde of women in short black (or dark) tunics, who fall backward on the floor or reach out to her.

If Graham was not already thinking of what she might accomplish, given the students she was presently teaching and those she would work with at the Neighborhood Playhouse, one can imagine that seeing these works would have goaded her to think about forming a company, and by the spring of 1926 she had taken that forward leap.

In 1928, bound for Santa Barbara aboard a train, Graham had written a letter to Evelyn Sabin and a similar one to Betty Macdonald, informing them that they were among the ten handpicked girls in a talented group that Alice Lewisohn and Rita Morgenthau had chosen to receive "practical training for the theater" at the Playhouse. There would be scholarships for them (the tuition was $300) and stipends of $15 a week. They would receive training in diction, voice, and dramatic expression, as well as play reading. They would study dancing with her and with Blanche Talmud,* as well as "Music as Related to the Dance—Practical Application" with Horst. They might participate in two scheduled productions and be required to learn about theater management, costumes, lights, props, et cetera.

In writing to Sabin and Macdonald, Graham may have been hedging her bets. Should maintaining a company not be feasible, she would still have her trio, and Sabin, Macdonald, and Savelli appeared as such in the momentous concert at the Booth Theatre on April 14, 1929, when Martha Graham and Group premiered *Vision of the Apocalypse*, *Moment Rustica*, *Sketches from the People*, and *Heretic*. The group was composed entirely of women drawn from Graham's classes at the Neighborhood Playhouse and in her own studio: Virginia Briton, Hortense Bunsick, Louise Creston, Irene Emery, Lillian Ray, Kitty Reese, Mary Rivoire, Sylvia Rosenstein, Ethel Rudy, Lillian Shapero, Sylvia Wasserstrom, and Ruth White. In Graham's mind, they were to represent the world.

These four new works can't have been long—even though *Vision of the Apocalypse* consisted of what the *New York Herald Tribune* critic called "sinister subdivisions" (Toil, Famine, Blasphemy, Ruthlessness,

---

* Talmud, an actress and dancer, had studied Dalcroze Eurhythmics in both Paris and New York and taught at the Playhouse beginning in the early 1920s. A photo by Arnold Genthe shows her and Graham wearing draped garments and head coverings, posed together in what appears to be a dramatic moment.

Pestilence, Mourning, Prayer, and Death). The trio appeared in three numbers, including the new *Dance Piece* to music by Hindemith, and Graham danced several solos.

However, as the *New York Telegram*'s critic wrote:

> The feature of the evening . . . was the group, and it is increasingly born in upon at least one spectator of the dance's progress that in the plastic molding of massed ensemble lies the brightest promise of this art's future eminence. Doris Humphrey has heretofore been a leader in this work, but the compositions by Miss Graham, as disclosed last night . . . have written a new page in the history of dance.

In the eleven newspaper reviews, little more was noted about *Vision of the Apocalypse*, set to Hermann Reutter's *Variations on the Bach Chorale* "Come Sweet Death." Kitty Reese played a monk, exhorting the crowd, and, according to a program note for later performances of the work, she represented "the central melody, with seven pictures paralleling the musical variations." The "Famine" sequence was praised for its "relentless march of destruction." Nor was much made clear about *Sketches from the People*, evidently a vision of society, possibly a glum one. The Russian-Jewish composer Julian Krein had written his *Eight Preludes* (of which Graham used three) at the age of thirteen. Two pianists (Horst and Dini de Remer) accompanied the concert, along with the flautist Hugo Bergamesco.

Moment Rustica found favor for Graham's "puckish humor and piquant use of the grotesque," which was "delightfully projected" by her and her dancers. In a description that was unusually detailed for those years, the anonymous *New York Telegram* reviewer identified Graham's nascent use of counterpoint in choreography, although, groping to explain something clearly not familiar to him in dance, he didn't use that term; instead he calls the new form that he believes Graham has invented "the split and multiple unit."

> Two girls on the left and two girls on the right side of the stage were balanced in a composition that included a trio of girls in the center of

the stage. As Miss Graham circled about the full circumference of the platform, the trio and the two pairs of dancers indulged in a series of dissimilar rhythms. While all were in harmony with the music, and while all three themes were idealizations of country dances, the circling figure, the left pair, the right pair, and the trio held to a characteristic decoration, unique with each unit.

That the writer found this structuring extremely novel and mentioned the "great possibilities" it opened may be attributed to his own interests (judging from his comparison of Graham's contrapuntal patterns with the harmony of orchestral parts, he could have been a music critic). He could not have known that she had composed *Moment Rustica* in silence and then adapted it to "Rustique," the second movement of Francis Poulenc's *Sonata for Piano* (four hands). However, his description reveals how intently Graham had been studying the possibilities opened up by choreographing for a group. Denishawn's music visualizations, with the assigning of groups and individuals to depict the instruments in an orchestral composition, may have provided her with some background, but clearly in *Moment Rustica*, her contrapuntal devices added to the festive effect provided by roistering peasants and what the Graham dancer Dorothy Bird described as their "laughing falls."

Heretic is the only one of these first group compositions to have survived, thanks to 1931 film footage of it that was apparently intended for Fox Movietone News, installments of which regularly accompanied feature films. The dance is terrifyingly succinct, only five minutes long and composed, according to Bessie Schönberg, in a single evening's rehearsal.

This piece, too, Graham worked out in silence while Horst looked for a suitable score. His search turned up a collection of songs put together by the singer-songwriter-playwright Théodore Botrel in 1899. The texts were drawn from a 1793 manuscript titled *Chansons de "la Fleur-de-Lys."* One can assume that the song Louis chose, "Bretons Têtus," fit an idea already fermenting in Martha's head—that of an individual defying or resisting an established order.

The musical setting of the poem by the composer Charles de Sivry consists of just ten measures in 2/4 time—no chords, just a succession of single piano notes. This structure is repeated over and over to accommodate the five verses of the poem. Horst raised the repetitions to seven, and although the words didn't figure in his score, they shaped Graham's austere drama. The text tells of an established religion, presumably Roman Catholicism, enforcing its beliefs on a Christian sect that preferred its local Breton saints.

In de Sivry's song, the clergy threatens the supposed heretics in various ways, and each time, on the sweet melody of the last two measures, the steadfast (or obstinate) Bretons counter and resist. *"Alors, nous passerons les seuils de vos chaumières: Vos Saintes et vos Saints nous vous les briserons!"* says the group in the second verse. ("Then we will cross the thresholds of your cottages and smash your saints!") *"Au pieds des arbres des clairières, Devant la Vierge nous prierons!"* respond the rebels. ("At the foot of the trees in the clearings, we will pray to the Virgin!")

Graham, wearing a long, simply cut white monk's cloth gown with kimono sleeves, uses each initial set of eight stentorian notes to stride through the space and gesture to the group. Each time, when she has finished, she is met by the same obdurate response. Wearing black caps that conceal their hair and long, slim-fitting, semitransparent black dresses over what they called "soaring suits" (in memory of those worn for the Humphrey–St. Denis *Soaring*), the dozen women stand shoulder to shoulder in a semicircle, arms folded. They use the first seven counts of the next measures to rise slowly onto the balls of their feet, and on the eighth note, they slam their heels down on the floor. "Never," wrote the dance educator Elizabeth Selden in 1935, "has 'No!' been said in a more formidable manner."

Then, in silence, the dancers move instantly and with great force into adversarial positions that differ in each of the stanzas. At one point they form two horizontal ranks of six, one row behind the other, each woman pressed against the one ahead of her; their bodies face stage right, but their heads are turned sharply to the left toward Graham—as if, recalled Bessie Schönberg, who performed as one of them, they were spitting at her over their left shoulders. In another response, six of them drop into a front-to-back line facing the audience, planting their feet wide apart, bending their knees deeply, and leaning forward, their hands braced on their thighs. The six on the other side of the stage are also lined up; facing diagonally upstage, they stand with their hips thrust forward and lean slightly back, as if in aversion. Both ranks aim hostile glares at Graham as she waits to pass between them. When they are not blockading her, they are shunning her.

After each attack, the plaintive melody sounds, and Graham wilts. Then, in silence, stiff-legged, the women take the two or three necessary steps to bring them back to their initial places, where they again fold their arms and await her next statement or entreaty. Only temporarily can she breach the wall of intolerance that they form. By the fifth repeat of the music, she is on her knees before them, arms spread. Suddenly they lunge toward her in two ranks, their arms straight up and their hands curled into partial fists. She recoils from the attack and then, almost beaten, folds her arms in and bends over until her head touches the floor.

In her final attempt to assert herself, she faces the center of the women's semicircle, her arms raised high and her hands touching, palms toward her, thumbs out; it's a gesture unlike the traditional Christian prayer, it's more like a surrender to heaven. This time, after their rebuttal, her opponents break into two opposing lines, step away from her, and then suddenly lunge back toward her again; the movement has the force of a blow. In the avenue between them Graham twists, caves in, falls slowly backward, and rolls over until she is prone, her hands reaching out along the floor. Her last utterance is to raise her head slightly and lift her hands slowly toward each other—perhaps to form fists, perhaps to pray. The oppressors refuse her again. In the song, the outcasts have the final word: "We will pray to the stars. Tear them down if you can." In *Heretic*, when the sad melody plays for the last time, the solitary rebel remains motionless, facedown, defeated.

In the black-and-white film, the women move into their architectural formations like units of a single vengeful machine. Those positions, says Schönberg, "were struck—and I mean *struck* . . . The whole thing was so biting that if you allowed for the least flicker or uncertainty or tremble or anything, the meaning would have been disrupted. It had to be hard and harder." How did they manage to change positions on a single impulse? "I think by—you know, like the army, by feel of cloth." That's how close together they were.

During what must have been a grueling day, Graham and her company performed *Heretic* for Fox's crew almost seven times. Sometimes the lighting was too dark, sometimes the cameraman moved closer; a high side view yielded little. The fifth take is the best, although the shadows created for the remaining two versions create an interesting effect. Watching Graham through them all reveals her as the fine actress she was then—simple, intense, and seemingly spontaneous. In each take, there are subtle changes of nuance in how she gears herself up for each new declamation, usually with a toss of her black hair,* as if she wants to get it out of the way. You can see how she freezes in a pose, listening for the clunk of those heels on the floor, waiting to sense the following regrouping, and then letting the strength drain out of her with the melody's plaintive fall, rise, and fall. Once, her body contracts slightly, as if she's allowing herself a sob. When she kneels before the unheeding women, her head is lifted in one take, lowered in another. Whether Graham imagined her role as a Joan of Arc before her judges, a person of conscience speaking out against the evils inherent in a bigoted society, and/or a choreographer battling against dance traditions, she made the actions real for herself and wrenching for her viewers.

What seems remarkable to those who have come through the political and social battles of the 1960s and 1970s is that in these group works, Graham made her all-female company not only stand for an entire society but also express some of the larger issues in it. And no one whose opinion is on record appears to have found that strange. Lincoln Kirstein, writing in 1937 of his resistance to her early work, noted that Graham and her group appeared to him then as "this soli-

---

* Graham brushed Vaseline into her hair before performances in order to make it glossy and to make it swing as a unit.

tary dancer, not even a girl, with her Spartan band of girls, seeming to me to press themselves into replicas of the steel woman that she was."

Offstage, however, Graham wore the gloves and hats of her day. She spoke in a voice devoid of stridency and told her company members that if they went to a party in someone's apartment, they should be sure to leave the bathroom exactly as they found it. She could on occasion huddle under the bedcovers and whimper that her latest work was a disaster, until Horst hauled her out and shook her into action. In some of her solos she could be girlish—charming or petulant. However, in the letter she wrote to Evelyn Sabin from her mother's garden in Santa Barbara in the summer of 1928, she marveled over a performer in a Japanese company she had seen. "Her discipline had made her transcend her personality, her individualism, and she became the essence of femininity, grief, play, laughter, womanly strength— She taught me a great lesson—She never entered man's field once— yet she was divinely strong." Just so, Graham at this point in her career sought the themes for her group that demanded power, the "virile" gestures that, in her mind, belonged to women as well as to men. And she got away with it.

The direction Graham's work was taking was at odds with what she was expected to do in another Neighborhood Playhouse presentation on April 26 and 27, 1929, less than two weeks after *Heretic* premiered. The "company of dancers & actors" that Irene Lewisohn had assembled was again accompanied by the Cleveland Orchestra. And again the emerging "modern dance" choreographers had to bury any rivalries they felt and use their talents in the service of ideas they would not have explored themselves. Doris Humphrey joined the Playhouse's Blanche Talmud and Ronny Johansson, as well as Felicia Sorel (the partner of Senia Gluck-Sandor and, like him, one of Jerome Robbins's early mentors) in *The White Peacock*. The four danced to Charles Griffes's tone poem, and apparently an excerpt was recited from the poem by William Sharp that had inspired the music. A possible sample:

Here, as the breath, as the soul of this beauty
Moveth in silence, and dreamlike, and slowly,
White as a snow-drift in mountain valleys . . .

Cream-white and soft as the breasts of a girl,
Moves the White Peacock, as though through the noon-tide
A dream of the moonlight were real for a moment.

Wrote Kenneth Burke in *The Dial*, "The interpretation of Charles Griffes' Tone Poem entailed awesome responsibilities as all the artists could possible do was come out and be peacocks."

Two of the five numbers were repeats from the 1928 program. This time, Humphrey joined Graham as one of the mourning women in Bloch's *Israel* Symphony, and Graham was just one "cloud form" among four in Debussy's *Nuages*. The most ambitious work on the two programs was a musico-dramatic work that Irene Lewisohn devised to illustrate Richard Strauss's *Ein Heldenleben*. Strauss had intended his fifty-minute tone poem to reflect the life of the hero of the title in terms of his character, his adversaries, his companion, his triumphs in war and in peace, and his final retirement from the world. The hero, it has been assumed, was the composer himself (Strauss was not a man given to modesty).

An actor portrayed the Hero, while Charles Weidman was his inner self, battling (according to Lewisohn's program scenario) the five men depicting "the phantoms of his mind" that blur his "vision of untrammeled power." In the third section, the Hero in both his aspects dallied with "Passing Loves" (Humphrey among them), but Graham was his Companion.

The reviews weren't good, but Graham and Weidman were praised. Horst thought their performing "unforgettably beautiful." "Not until the music rose to nobility and fervor did the true companion appear," wrote Burke in his *Dial* review. "It was at this point that Miss Graham suddenly enriched the action with her impersonation of a girl stricken with the magic of love, her struggle between terror and attraction, her flight and helpless return, her blind surrender at last." He found the scene to be "beautiful and moving to a degree, but it had not the slightest warrant in the music."

As Doris Humphrey said, none of the dancers could afford to turn down the Lewisohn sisters when Miss Irene wished to herd them into her musical dramatizations, and no doubt Graham was pleased to perform with her dancers (probably her trio) at a "Garden Dinner" given by the American Woman's Association in honor of the author Alfred S. Amer. Perhaps the dancers were also able to partake of the asparagus with hollandaise sauce, the cold duck, and other dishes that weren't likely to be their usual fare.

In a *Dance Magazine* article confusingly titled "Does Classical Dancing Pay? A Rebuttal," the writer took issue with the idea that it did not. All of Martha Graham's recitals, he claimed, had been financially successful, and her solo concert at the Booth yielded a "clear profit of $400." This, however, is unlikely to have fostered an affluent lifestyle. And at the end of June 1929, when the country's economy began the long downslide that led to the October Panic, it is perhaps fortunate that Graham and the dancers who carried out her ideas lived parsimoniously. On those ideas they dined well. In mid-June she had delivered her bold new aesthetic to the German newspaper *Der Tag*. "We aren't country people," she told the interviewer,

> and therefore we aren't sentimental and naïve. Life in the big cities wakes and teases the brain. Therefore must its art be more thoughtful, more intellectual. Life in the cities today is far from being a round, wavy line that sways and dances pleasantly into a pretty circle. Life today is nervous, sharp and zigzag, and often stops in mid-air. That is what I aim for in my dances, I do not want to run away from the struggle that is found in the present day of machines, but I want to understand it and express it artistically.

In the narrow, angled streets of New York and the pace of its workers and its factories, she, like the architects and designers of her day, had been finding new rhythms and new shapes.

6

FROM *RITE OF SPRING* TO A SEATTLE SCHOOL

WHEN MARTHA GRAHAM NOTED in 1927 that "Out of emotion comes form," she was echoing what Wassily Kandinsky had written fifteen years earlier in an essay titled "On the Problem of Form" and emphasized in italics: "*The form is the outer expression of the inner content.*" The painter also acknowledged that the inner content he mentioned would of necessity differ from one artist to another and that "the spirit of the individual artist is mirrored in the form. The form bears the stamp of the *personality.*"

The forward-looking American dance modernists of the late 1920s and 1930s were forging their own styles accordingly. And if Graham, Humphrey, Weidman, and others most often referred to themselves as dancers rather than as choreographers, the choice of words might mean not only that they were the leading performers of their own works, but that their individual bodies and desires were the material with which they labored. Their use of angularity and simple stances, as well as basic actions like breathing, walking, running, falling, and thrusting themselves into motion, affirmed basic aspects of the human body, however much they stylized these.

In this, they were akin to the architects and designers who insisted that their "materials" be treated in ways "consistent with their inherent nature." Thomas E. Hibben—expanding on Louis Sullivan's famous

1896 decree that form should follow function—wrote that form is not only "determined by function and evolved in three dimensions simultaneously," but that "the execution of this form is determined by the honest use of materials." (He also remarked that the result of the manipulation of these materials "can only be in the personal vocabulary of the creator," words that, like Kandinsky's, certainly resonated with what Graham was attempting to do.)

In stripping her dance of what she referred to as "decorative non-essentials," she was not only in lockstep with the bold new architects and designers but also in agreement with an unlikely advocate of simplicity, Robert C. Stanley, president of the International Nickel Company. "It would seem to me," he wrote, "that engineers, through their development of the Machine Age, have been important allies of the artist in emphasizing that functionalism is a basic factor in true beauty. Just as the Greek sculptors went directly to the anatomy of the human body to create their best statues, the artists of the present day are stripping off the 'gingerbread' and the general fussiness affected by their immediate predecessors."

A key word in these debates and manifestos was "streamlined." It proposed a conjunction of simplicity, functionalism, and beauty. Away with decorative embellishments, tassels and draperies, carved moldings, and mansions whose stonework summoned up Gothic cathedrals. The top of the Chrysler Building, when it was unveiled in 1930, could be thought to compromise the sleek modernity of its main structure by providing gargoyles modeled after the hood ornament on Plymouth automobiles. The Machine Age—if society didn't allow itself to be enslaved by it—made some aspects of life easier. Wrote the authors of *The New Interior Decoration: An Introduction to Its Principles, and International Survey of Its Methods*, "The best inspiration for the architect is to be found in the streamline of an automobile, the scientific curves of a liner, the geometrically ordained forms of an aeroplane. Those who are imperceptive of the beauty of these may have eyes, but cannot use them."

That final admonishment could also be applied to audiences who quailed before the powerful and uncompromising austerity of the emerging modern dance. And if streamlining art expressed the image of the speed that characterized contemporary life, it also suited an economy-minded nation heading into a devastating Depression and artists bent on stripping onstage emotion to its bones. "There is beginning to be manifest an economy of gesture in the dance," wrote Graham, "an intensity and integrity of mood, a simplified external means, and above all a concentration on 'the Stuff' of dance, which is movement—divinely significant."

January 8, 1930. The curtain at Maxine Elliott's Theatre opens on a figure sitting on a small bench, quite close to the front of the stage. Her feet are planted wide apart. When she sways stiffly on her pedestal, her shoulders, knees, and elbows create small peaks in the tube of lavender stretch jersey that covers her from the top of her head to her ankles. Only her feet, her hands, and her face are immediately visible, although you occasionally glimpse her throat and the top of the garment that she wears under the shroud. The music, Zoltan Kodaly's Piano Piece, no. 2, op. 3, ripples along, asking its questions quietly at first, later hammering out chords.

This is Martha Graham's *Lamentation*.

A black-and-white film made in the early 1930s shows her in a more nuanced, less emotionally obvious performance than those given in later years by dancers in her company. When she suddenly turns her head sharply to the right, it's as if she had heard a familiar step and was looking to see if the death she mourned could be a mistake; you might think for a moment of John Millington's Synge's play *Riders to the Sea* and the wives and daughters of fishermen reported lost in a storm at sea.

As she tilts joltingly from side to side—pulling away from stability, from balance—or leans back, raising one bent leg, its foot clubbed, and stretching her clasped hands high, her gestures strain against the fabric that encases her, the skin of her grief, creating folds and creases. Her rocking has the force of a whiplash, an aversion from what she would rather not confront. Only once does she stand briefly. Sometimes she lifts her palms, as if pleading to God. Her face is a mask, but when she swings her body around, you think of keening, and at one point she slows down that circular path and yields for a few seconds—bending to the right, her face turned to the floor.

The fabric not only is symbolic of the grief that shrouds her but also lends itself to metaphor. When she pushes wide the opening in the material with her forearms and gazes toward the audience, she seems be looking out from a dark cave. When she sheathes her hands in the edges of it and brings them to her mouth, you imagine a muffled cry. At another moment she clasps her hands together and slowly plunges her arms straight down in front of her, between her thighs, creating a deep pool in the resisting fabric. Once, when she lifts the top of the tube high, her head vanishes, and she becomes briefly inanimate—a totem figure. Her final gesture is to reach up with one hand, grasp the edge of the material, pull it over her head, and bow slowly down to touch the floor in an immense, conclusive sigh.

For all its theatricality, *Lamentation* is private—an anguish repressed, the performer's face a mask. It lasts about three minutes. In it, she is both a woman lamenting and the embodiment of sorrow. Something of the same impassioned objectivity and a kind of primitivism mark the works of the German artists Käthe Kollwitz and Ernst Barlach that had impressed both her and Horst. The kinship is strongest between *Lamentation* and Barlach's small bronze statue titled *Russian Beggar Woman* (1907); faceless, she sits bent over, wearing a hooded garment that stretches into folds between her legs and conceals almost everything but her pleading hand.

In later years Graham often told a story about the impact of *Lamentation*. A woman came to her dressing room after a performance and said that she had recently lost a son to death, but had been unable to cry. This dance, said the woman, had allowed her, finally, to weep.

Lamentation premiered on the third night of a very ambitious season in the Thirty-Ninth Street theater named after its owner, the actress Maxine Elliott, who had leased it to the Schubert brothers' organization. Helen Tamiris, buoyed up by Horst, had managed to get Martha Graham and Group and the Humphrey-Weidman Company to join her in renting the theater for a week; a modest list of sponsors helped out. The title, Dance Repertory Theatre, optimistically suggested future collaborations, and invitations went out for an afternoon event on New Year's Day honoring the four choreographers' vision and enterprise; the eminent theater critic John Mason Brown delivered a lecture titled "The Place of Dance in the Modern Theatre."

Negotiations among the choreographers, however, had not been easy, despite their mutual desire to bring the new dance to a wider public. Writing to her mother of her worries about the legal and technical aspects of the venture, Humphrey remarked, "I haven't much faith in Martha Graham; she is a snake if ever there was one." Still, she, Graham, and Weidman—linked by their past with Denishawn, their common aesthetic goals, and their reliance on Horst—continued to admire one another. José Limón recalled a restaurant dinner in the early 1930s, when he was a young member of the Humphrey-Weidman Company. He and his two bosses were joined by Graham and Horst. Martha (whom he had met only once and who terrified him) told Doris that she had been moved to tears by her performing. Trust was another matter. Their young dancers enjoyed the rivalry, according to Limón, and fanned its occasional sparks into mutually satisfying flames.

Contentious egos notwithstanding, the *New York Times* review of the joint program that opened the season on January 5 was headlined "New Dance Theatre Scores a Success," and the subtitle underlined that with "Performance Witnessed by the Most Brilliant Audience Since [dancer] Argentina Debut." The choreographers shared additional programs on the Saturday, January 11, matinee and the closing performance on the twelfth. Humphrey and Weidman appeared with their dancers on January 6 and 9, Tamiris on January 7 and 10, and Graham and her company were featured on the eighth and the evening of the eleventh. Taken together, the four introduced not only adventurous dance but contemporary and near-contemporary music that might have been unfamiliar to many in the audience.

Graham had been ill, and Horst was too downed by flu to play at the final performance (the *Times* reported that it took four musicians to replace him). Also the equitably arranged joint programs were marathons for the audience. On January 5 Graham offered six works, of which only one, *Heretic*, featured her group; Tamiris performed five solos; and Humphrey and Weidman presented five dances, ranging from his Denishawn-flavored solo *Japanese Actor* to one of her most recent group pieces, *Life of the Bee* (1929). The program started late, and John Martin noted in his review that the audience had been there for two hours when the first of the Humphrey-Weidman selections began.

It's no wonder Graham had been under the weather. Five of the works on her January 8 performance were premieres. In addition to *Lamentation*, she danced two new solos: *Two Chants* ("Futility" and "Ecstatic Song") to Ernst Krenek's Piano Sonata, no. 2, op. 59; and *Harlequinade* ("Pessimist" and "Optimist"), set to Ernst Toch's Klavierstücke, op. 32. She did not appear in *Prelude to a Dance*, which used Honegger's Counterpoint No. 1 for Piano, but she led an augmented company of sixteen women in *Project in Movement for a Divine Comedy*, which was performed in silence.

The absence of a musical score was not entirely innovative. Humphrey's 1928 *Water Study*, which was presented on two of the programs, featured an ensemble of women who created illusions of cresting and breaking waves to no accompaniment beyond the soft sound of their feet and their breathing, and *Life of the Bee* was danced to the sounds provided by Horst and Pauline Lawrence (former Denishawn dancer, accompanist, and close friend of Doris's) humming on combs wrapped in tissue paper. Humphrey's new *Drama of Motion* also had no musical score. Richard Hammond, writing in *Modern Music*, called *Project in Movement for a Divine Comedy* "a beautiful choreographic poem"; the only other record of it seems to be a *Times* review—"Martha Graham Gives Delightful Dance"—of the shared January 11 program: she moved "with exquisite dignity against a background of two lines of dancers doing a simple pattern." The piece disappeared from Graham's repertory after the season. The critic G.N.W. of the *New York Telegram* announced that she outshone the other three choreographers.

Certainly the public and the critics had their favorites and warmed to the possibilities of comparison. One writer spoke of "the robust, four square methods of Tamiris following upon Miss Graham's illusive insinuations" (three of Tamiris's notable *Negro Spirituals* may have given birth to this view). There was little doubt, however, that all the choreographers profited by the exposure. Offering three shared programs and making tickets available on a subscription basis broadened the perspective of audience members who perhaps knew only one of the four artists (if that). Spectators encountered some of the choreographers' boldest experiments to date, as well as more easy-to-grasp pieces, such as Graham's *Harlequinade*. Margaret Lloyd's review in the *Christian Science Monitor* of a later performance of this two-part solo makes vividly evident how captivating Graham could be when she wished. Focusing on Graham's prop, a red handkerchief, Lloyd writes:

> The Pessimist waves the kerchief dolorously, holds it as if to staunch tears, lays it on the ground and surveys it in isolation, then with an ineffable touch that is Graham's own, hauls it up with a weary motion that transforms it into a heavy knapsack and carries it like a great burden across her back. The sense of weight, the pulling muscles are irony made plastic. For the Optimist, the kerchief becomes a gay, insouciant knot in her girdle or flutters recklessly to denote the frivolity of a flibbertigibbet's gullible belief in easy happiness. Here, perhaps, Miss Graham's rare smile is slightly wry.

Years later, however, Bessie Schönberg recalled an aspect of Graham's style in this solo that indicates it was no easy crowd-pleaser:

> Martha was as simple as a tragedienne as she was simple as a comedienne. They were very stark statements. She made the dance a little

wooden, cutting off body movements which didn't have to end. That
cutting off was not from your shoulders. It was from deep inside . . .
In retrospect this stark style seems to me to have been Martha's way
out of romanticism that she could no longer adhere to or believe
in . . . To us today it could look a little too wooden perhaps. But it was
never lifeless because she used the entire body. Peel down, peel down,
peel down. You never finished a gesture. It stopped.

If further evidence is needed to prove how shrewdly Graham
tested the waters before she became a full-fledged modernist, the
Dance Repertory Theatre's first season provided it. On the three
shared programs and the two devoted to Graham's work, *Lamentation*, which outlived almost all the sixty-eight dances she had created
so far, was given only once.

Days after Dance Repertory Theatre's final performance, Graham
and her original three-woman group set out for three dates down
south, beginning at the Springer Opera House in Columbus, Georgia, on January 16 and moving on to the Tuskegee Institute in Ala-
bama on January 18 and then Gulf Park College, Mississippi. Her
solo *Immigrant* was the only "tough" work on the program. The ensuing New York State appearances for Martha Graham and Group at
junior high school auditoriums in Watertown and Amsterdam, New
York, under Daniel Mayer's management, indicate that she had decided she could not sustain both her trio and a twelve-member company when touring. She bravely took all four of her new group works
to these New York dates, but only ten dancers accompanied her, so
some modifications must have been made in the choreography and
casting. Louise Creston, Ethel Rudy, and Irene Emery replaced Sabin,
Macdonald, and Savelli in the 1927 *Spires* (as they had at Maxine
Elliott's Theatre, perhaps in preparation for the upstate engagements);
although the original trio performed *Danse Languide* on one of the
programs at Maxine Elliott's Theatre, after the southern tour, they no
longer appeared with Graham.

The *Columbus Enquirer-Sun* headlined its rave review "Dancers
Thrill Audiences," but it's clear that dances like Graham's were not an

easy sell. A review in the Amsterdam *Recorder* presented the audience's possible responses very smartly:

> If her dance technique was in part non-understandable to those who saw her, her program was nevertheless intensely interesting, except perhaps to the few who immediately reject that which they are unable to at once analyze. In many of the dances it was impossible not to catch the thought underlying the dance form. Miss Graham employs fluidity and rigidity in what is often striking contrast. Her means of expression is highly individual. It has truly been said of her that "because she paints so skillfully with movement, she creates dance where literally there is none." Her courage is also shown in her successful attempts to portray the abstract in rhythm.

"Where literally there is none . . ." To many people, dancing meant lively movements of the feet in time to music. It was inevitable that they would be bewildered by the nascent modern dance, with its emphasis on gestures of the whole body.

Graham returned from these adventures in time to take up her teaching at the Neighborhood Playhouse and prepare for the third presentation organized by Irene Lewisohn—this one celebrating the Playhouse's fifteenth anniversary. The February 20, 21, and 22 performances at the Mecca Temple (now City Center) on Fifty-Fifth Street again featured the Cleveland Orchestra under Nikolai Sokoloff, and Harold Bauer played the piano in the dramatic visualization of Charles Loeffler's *Pagan Poem (After Virgil)*, op. 14, for orchestra, piano, English horn, and three trumpets obbligati. There was innovation this time. The entire audience sat in the balconies while the orchestra occupied the main floor of the theater, unseen by many of the spectators.

The program explained that the stage action and dances expressed the sentiments of Virgil's Eighth Eclogue, in which Daphnis, the god of pastoral poetry, has forsaken the countryside for the city; his love, a sorceress (interpreted by Lewisohn as "his creative inspiration"), casts spells to bring him home. Graham and Weidman enacted the aspirational aura that Miss Irene's scenario promoted; it involved, eventually, "the understanding and control of the physical and spiritual—the welding of the human and the divine." Blanche Talmud was also featured, and an ensemble of six Neighborhood Playhouse students who were members of Graham's company (Rose Cohen, Betty Macdonald, Kitty Reese, Bessie Schönberg, Anna Sokolow, and Joan Woodruff).

Music critic Richard L. Stokes's review in *The Evening World* conveys, however sardonically, some images of *Pagan Poem*, mentioning "a pyramid of stairs, at the base of which Martha Graham, with bare feet planted wide apart, sat in a scarlet dress and directed into the distance a haggard and formidable scowl." Oscar Thompson of the *New York Post* felt that the staircase indicated the levels of understanding that the poet-hero, Weidman, must climb. And he could do so after his duet with Graham and the general rejoicing that followed. Bessie Schönberg, who was in *Pagan Poem*, has a different memory of it: while members of the cast were carrying Weidman up some of the steps, he told them dirty stories, and they tried to restrain themselves from shaking with laughter.

Weidman was also featured in *La Procession Nocturne* (Symphonic Poem after Nicolas Lenau's "Faust"), op. 6, by Henri Rabaud, along with Talmud and five men (pros like John Glenn and Charles Laskey were joined by a new Neighborhood Playhouse recruit, Henry Fonda). Zemach, motionless, played the statue of a saint. The jazz-influenced music by Werner Janssen for *New Year's Eve in New York* had received its premiere by the Rochester Symphony Orchestra the previous year. For the Manhattan performance, Horst played the piano part, and the assistant stage manager was Jean Rosenthal, later to become Graham's master lighting designer. In this offering, sailors and sluts populated Times Square in numbers titled "On the Street" and "In the Dance Halls, the Shows, and Nightclubs." Weidman, ever versatile, appeared in this work too, partnering two women in four duets. The acidic Stokes lauded a number by Talmud and Zemach as "a brilliant satire on the fox-trot."

Graham closed *New Year's Eve in New York* as the Figure in a Skyscraper, "a composite expression of the desires, hopes, aspirations that have found asylum in Manhattan" (how she managed all this is unclear; Schönberg's memory is that "the lights would go on behind the scrim and here would be little Martha throwing herself around in that tower—throwing herself around is probably the only description"). The program noted that she appeared courtesy of her manager, Frances Hawkins, which conveyed a new stage in her career and added a certain cachet to her participation.

Brooks Atkinson of the *Times* found the dramatic aspects of the program "undeveloped in the foregrounding of dance and music," while Mary Watkins of the *Herald Tribune* thought that the "modern dance styles" were not "in sympathy with the music." The prevailing turbulence and rich textures of Loeffler's *Pagan Poem* were at odds with the spare musical structures Horst had provided or discovered for Graham's recent works.

In this eventful year Graham secured two more out-of-town dates—a solo performance at the Arts Club of Chicago on February 28 and a performance at Bennett College by Martha Graham and Group on March 29, as well as one at New York City's Washington Irving High School, where dance concerts were often hosted during the 1930s. She was also, in early spring, preparing for a performance that turned out to be a milestone in her career and an influence on her subsequent work. On April 11, 12, and 22, 1930, she danced the central role of the Chosen Maiden in three fully staged performances of Igor Stravinsky's *The Rite of Spring*—the first to be seen by the American public.

In 1913, Parisians who flocked to Serge Diaghilev's Ballets Russes had come to expect Russian fairy tales, commedia dell'arte charmers, and seductive tales of love and death in a fabled Orient. On May 29, when Vaslav Nijinsky's ballet *Le Sacre du Printemps* and Stravinsky's score were presented for the first time, those spectators were in for a shock. Nijinsky, the great dancer, had already puzzled them with his first forays into choreography. His 1912 *L'Après midi d'un faune* unrolled in two dimensions, like a Greek frieze come to life, and he, a great jumper, jumped exactly once. His *Jeux*, which premiered on

May 15, 2013, took place beside a contemporary tennis court, hinted at a ménage à trois, and required Ludmilla Schollar and Tamara Karsavina (the latter one of the company's major ballerinas) to assume awkward stances that exasperated them and hurt their necks. These ballets, however, did not cause the kind of uproar provoked by *Le Sacre du Printemps* at its first night. Oh, *mon Dieu!* The frightful dissonances in Igor Stravinsky's music! The pounding chords! The stamping, turned-in feet of the dancers! The lumpish costumes of Nicholas Roerich! Primitivism was acceptable in some of the paintings of the day, but in a *ballet?* Those who loved *Sacre* and those who hated it duked it out loudly while the dancers and musicians soldiered on.

In 1920, Léonide Massine, another dancer whom Diaghilev had turned into a choreographer, approached Stravinsky's score and made a new ballet. It followed the same basic scenario outlined by the music: a strenuous midwinter ritual results in the sacrifice of a virgin; in order that spring may come, she must dance herself to death. Seven years after Nijinsky's premiere, Diaghilev's audiences were better prepared for modernism in ballet, and Massine's *Sacre* gave them enough identifiable ballet steps to keep them in their seats. His work, too, met with mixed reactions. Stravinsky evidently preferred it to Nijinsky's, declaring in an interview that "the choreographic construction of Nijinsky was one of great plastic beauty but subjected to the tyranny of the bar," while Massine had constructed phrases that arched over several bars. The critic André Levinson, however, did not care for the new *Sacre*; Massine had avoided pointing up the narrative elements in favor of stressing group architecture (something in which the choreographer was deeply interested). The program for the 1920 performances at the Théâtre des Champs-Elysées describes the work as "a spectacle of pagan Russia. The work is in two parts and involves no subject. It is choreography freely constructed on the music." The statement is a curious one. A ballet that ends with a strenuous solo, after which the fallen soloist is lifted high, as if on a bier, surely conveys a drama within this "spectacle."

It was this version, or something close to it, that Massine, who had taken detailed notes, staged in New York in 1930. Always committed to introducing new music to the American public, Leopold Stokow-ski, the conductor of the Philadelphia Orchestra, assembled a provoc-ative program to be presented with the support of the League of Composers. *Le Sacre du Printemps* was preceded by the first American production of Arnold Schoenberg's *Die Glückliche Hand*, a "Drama with Music" in four scenes, directed by Rouben Mamoulian, Gra-ham's colleague from the Eastman School, and featuring Doris Hum-phrey and Charles Weidman.

Graham was Stokowski's choice to play the Chosen Maiden in *Sacre*. He and the ballet's original designer, Nicholas Roerich, had seen at the Roerich Museum in New York one of the demonstrations that she prepared for potential bookers. According to Agnes de Mille, Stokowski's wife, Evangeline, who took Graham's classes in the East Ninth Street studio, engineered this meeting. Eleven women from Martha's group or her classes also joined the cast of Massine's cre-ation. Two men and two women were drawn from the Humphrey-Weidman Company. Others of the thirty-nine dancers came from various places, although probably not from the Roxy, where Massine had been directing the ballet company and appearing onstage himself; those dancers were involved in four shows a day and five on Sundays.

Time and tolerant memories have polished the creative relation-ship between Graham and Massine to a nice gloss. In decades-later interviews and memoirs, they praised each other and the experience. It was left mainly to the dancers to note the conflicts that cropped up in rehearsals. Certainly it cannot have been easy for Graham—prestigious as the enterprise was—to have "her" girls watch her rehearse material choreographed by another and take directions from him. She even had to dance briefly among the ensemble of women in order to emerge suddenly and startlingly from the group. Unlike Maria Pilz in Nijin-sky's *Sacre* or Lydia Sokolova in Massine's 1920 version, Graham was not simply a dancer in the company presenting the work; she was her-self a choreographer of consequence. Bessie Schönberg remembered that when Massine visited Graham's studio to observe her dancers and explain his artistic vision of the revival, he announced, "'And when I have worked with the company, Miss Graham, I will teach you your dance.' Silence. Then Graham rose, walked out of the room, and slammed the door. Poor Mr. Massine looked as if to ask, 'What have I done?'"

Eleanor King of the Humphrey-Weidman contingent paints a picture of Graham during the monthslong rehearsals in the Dalton School's gymnasium, sitting "in a corner, shawl over her head," waiting for her entrance while watching Massine—who was at the same time choreographing ballets for Radio City Music Hall—work with the chorus of youths and maidens, and never dancing full out until the final rehearsals. The Graham dancer Anna Sokolow, on the other hand, remarked that Martha "might have held back because she wanted to see what we were doing and how we were reacting to Massine's direction. Remember, what a big experience it was for us modern dancers to have a Russian ballet artist come in, introduce us to another world, introduce us to Stravinsky."

A photo shows Graham, like the rest of the cast, clad in one of Roerich's striking costumes for the 1913 *Sacre*, barefoot and wearing a circlet of flowers in her hair. Her arguments over wigs (she refused to wear one) and shoes with lace-up leggings (no to that) are understandable. Of course, none of the other dancers—many of whom found Massine charming and very agreeable to work for—were privy to all that went on between him and Graham in rehearsals for her momentous solo. The two may have found some kind of rapport. Once, when he appeared for a private rehearsal with her, dressed, as was she, in black, he remarked, according to Graham, "We look enough alike to be brother and sister." One can imagine them side by side, gazing into the mirror, studying their similar bony faces and dark, deep-set eyes. Graham later said that she learned faithfully every step that Massine taught her, but, with his approval, she adjusted certain things that seemed balletic and made the solo her own.

The conflicting memories of the Massine-Graham saga may never be sorted out, but clearly tensions existed, and Graham undoubtedly displayed some temperament. In one rehearsal session, recalled King, Massine suggested that Graham might be feeling unwell and asked if she would like Anita Bay—who played the role of the Old Woman and understudied Graham—to dance her part in the rehearsal. No, Miss Graham would definitely not like that. According to Richard Hammond, who (along with Humphrey, Weidman, and Graham) was on the board of the League of Composers, he and Stokowski, as the performance dates became closer, made an appointment to go to the Roxy and see if Tamara Geva, the principal ballerina, might be a suitable replacement for the recalcitrant Graham. Hammond cannily advised that Martha should learn of their visit, and that information had the desired effect. Graham herself later remarked that Massine at one point asked her to resign, saying that Stokowski had recommended this; she went to the conductor, who strenuously denied the allegation.

Despite the conflicts, Graham admitted in 1977 that dancing in *The Rite of Spring* had been a "great turning point" in her life. "*Sacre* is a ritual. When I danced it in 1930, I was so immersed in the ritual and the sacrifice of the Chosen One that I believed in it . . . I think the Chosen One is the artist. The principal thing is that it has to do with the artist as his own doom-maker; he composes himself to death."

In 1987, four of the dancers who'd been involved in the 1930 *Rite* took part in a panel assembled at the New York Public Library for the Performing Arts for a Dance Critics Association mini-conference titled "*The Rite of Spring* at Seventy-Five." Schönberg, in the end, did not perform in *Rite*; to do so would have violated the terms of her Neighborhood Playhouse scholarship. The other Graham dancers on the panel, Anna Sokolow and Lily Mehlman Rady, were not so conscientious. Eleanor King joined them onstage for the panel.

What emerged from their conversation is borne out by a silent film of a rehearsal of Massine's 1958 reconstruction of *Sacre* for the La Scala Ballet. You can see in the film what the eighty-year-old King described—and demonstrated—at the conference: "In the 'Harbingers of Spring' section, we were sitting [on the floor] with our feet in front of us. Then came a tremendous battering in the music, and we were plucking grain and threshing it. The men behind us were doing great big slashing movements, as if they were axing trees. Then everything was repeated . . . And then there was a unison section where we all did this leaping and bowing, repeated that over and over again."

She also described what she remembered as twenty-one gallops at the end of the ballet's first half, "Dance of the Earth." Interestingly, King alluded to the movements with the women seated and the men standing as being "Navaho-style things," and apparently Stokowski had advised Massine to head out west and see some Native American dancing. Rady recalled a sequence, also visible in the film, in which the women are carried about sitting on the men's shoulders (this stuck in her memory principally because of the stifled giggles that erupted when, during one performance, her partner "thought it would be great fun to goose the boy in front of him)."

Although Massine used the word "primitive" to convey to the dancers the look he wanted, his *Rite* seems to have been less stylized than Nijinsky's, with more links to Russian folk dances. King, having seen Millicent Hodson and Kenneth Archer's 1987 reconstruction of Nijinsky's *Sacre* for the Joffrey Ballet, thought that Massine's choreography was simpler and more "open" in its phrasing, despite its many repetitions. In her autobiography, she recalled a sequence in which six groups of dancers moved in contrapuntal figure-eight circles:

> My set, stamping along, began with eight beats of elbow thrusts, then nine to fifteen progressive gallops with arms curvetting in the air; sixteen to twenty-one counts on the knees, clapping the hands, swinging the arms from side to side. Each group started on a different beat.

In the film, the shuddering, shoulder-to-shoulder group of dancers, splitting in half and pulsing toward and away from the center of the stage, opened and closed the formation like an accordion. The pinwheel pattern in which they circled the stage, their feet shuffling (this just before the "Sacred Dance"), gave the stage a sense of order within congestion, of mounting purpose. When invited to play the Chosen Maiden, Graham had been tactfully told by Stokowski that he sensed she was not ready to choreograph for such a large ensemble, and she confirmed that belief. Watching Massine's assuredness in orchestrating a mob, she would have learned a great deal.

In the recording made by Stokowski and the Philadelphia Orchestra in 1930, Stravinsky's music has a driving force that blazes its way with less regard for the inner voices than can be heard in, for example, a later recording with Eugene Ormandy leading the same orchestra. Massine's choreography reflects that impetus. Stokowski, according to King, often attended rehearsals, recommending adjustments to the costumes, moving in to help a dancer animate a gesture fully, and—with Massine looking on—making a few adjustments in the spatial designs. Often flamboyant, he conducted the first rehearsal in Philadelphia's Metropolitan Opera House from a saddle perched on a sawhorse, his feet in the stirrups.

One can imagine the excitement generated by a spectacle unknown to most who attended one of the three performances. Some people may have been introduced to the music through a 1922 performance of it (the first in America), as well as a 1929 radio broadcast by Stokowski and the Philadelphia Orchestra. Also in 1929, recordings were made under the baton of Pierre Monteux and of Stravinsky himself. However, other spectators may not have been prepared for what the music critic Alex Ross has called "the quadruple shock . . . in the form of harmony, rhythm, image, and movement" that arrived in the "Augurs of Spring" section and the "crunching discord" that announces it. Or for what another critic has described in another section of the score as "great crunching, snarling chords from the brass and thundering thumps from the timpani." The 1930 performances of the ballet for which the music had been written—in Philadelphia on April 11 and at New York's Metropolitan Opera House at Broadway and Thirty-Ninth Street on April 22 and 23—were then in every way epochal, as was Graham's performance.

An imaginative critic wrote of her solo, "Martha Graham, The Chosen One, leaps with both arms and legs windmilling in front of her like a prehistoric bird whose wings try to raise the body." She went into "a delirious spin, the feet almost on the points striking the ground like daggers." Dancers in the cast recall that Graham had first to stand for more than five minutes—motionless, near the front of the stage, with the ensemble ratcheting up the ritual behind her. That summer, when she was teaching at the Cornish School in Seattle and trying to induce ballet-trained students to be more aware of what was happening in their bodies, she told them of that long stillness in *The Rite of Spring*. Sokolova, as Nijinsky's doomed heroine, had written that she held her position by staring at an exit light; Graham instead "thought about trying to hear things, to see things, to make all her senses very aware . . . and to be moving inside her skin the whole time" before exploding into her solo. And the way observers and participants tell of that moment, it was indeed an explosion.

Although the La Scala film shows the Chosen One early on, leaping to one side and then falling back, leaping again and falling back numerous times without moving from her spot, the women on the 1987 panel all remembered Graham mainly as just jumping many, many times—a revelation to them, since at that time jumps and leaps weren't stressed in her dance classes or her choreography (with the exception of *Country Lane*, as described by Jane Dudley in the previous chapter). In some of these jumps, she bent her knees and lifted her feet behind her. Schönberg: "She was in the air practically all the time. There were complete splits in the air—not, of course, with her toes pointed, but with her heels pointed and her hands at an angle. Her leaps were like little screams in the air; they were like little yells. It was frenetic, extraordinary, and deeply moving. Deeply moving." The panel also remembered her circling the stage with leaps. In the 1958 film, the Chosen One travels the course with a strenuous repeating sequence of a turning leap (the kind dubbed a "barrel turn" by dancers), a spin, and a drop into a squat to touch the earth—out of which she has to recover quickly in order to spring into the leap again. It's soon after this that she collapses and four men lift her high—two of them seated on the shoulders of the other two.

The impact of *Rite of Spring*, second on the program, overwhelmed Schoenberg's *Die Glückliche Hand*, which was composed around the same time and had not yet been heard in America. In this grim, semi-autobiographical tale of an artist, with its Freudian undertones, a Chimera (the actor Olin Howland) represents the primal, self-devouring ego of the Man; an artist (the baritone Ivan Ivantzoff) sang the role.

The superficial and successful Stranger (Charles Weidman) twice lures away the Woman (Doris Humphrey), who represents inspiration. The Man's single brilliant stroke with a hammer produces a diadem but destroys the anvil. He ends alone, bitter and dissatisfied, with the Chimera crouching beside him. Dancers John Glenn and Charles Laskey played Two Workmen, and seventeen singers from the Curtis Institute (five more than Schönberg required) formed the Chorus, whose *sprechstimme* queried and scolded the downcast hero from the outset ("Once again you fix your longing on the unattainable. Once again you give yourself up to the sirens of your thoughts"). Robert Edmond Jones was apparently not able to duplicate all the elaborate lighting and color schemes that Schönberg—inspired by Kandinsky's writings on the emotional connotations of color—had desired.

You can see how Stravinsky, Massine, Graham, and a horde of dancers might have wiped this more introspective work from the audiences' minds and, incidentally, introduced Graham to musicgoing spectators who might not have encountered her before.

When Graham arrived in Seattle in mid-June to teach in the Cornish School for ten weeks, she brought with her the residue of ideas and feelings that *The Rite of Spring* experience had ignited. Bonnie Bird, one of her new students, remembered that "Martha showed us movement phrases from this dance. It was a demanding solo . . . full of leaps and jumping splits and very difficult movement sequences." Bird had the mistaken impression that Graham had choreographed it herself. Dorothy Bird (the two girls were not related) recalled in her memoir, *Bird's Eye View*, Graham's words about the lessons she gleaned from performing in Massine's work. That above-mentioned notion of motion in stillness was an important part of the speech with which Graham introduced herself and Horst to the Cornish students. (Horst would be there for the first five weeks, after which he and his dachshund, Max, a gift from Martha, headed for Steamboat Springs, Colorado, where from 1928 through 1933 he was the musical director at the arts camp Perry-Mansfield.)

In that speech, Graham announced that she and Horst were to be called "Martha" and "Louis" and that much of the classroom work would be focused on preparing the students to be members of the all-female Chorus for a production of Aeschylus's *Seven Against Thebes*, the grim tale about the besieged city. Thebes is saved, but the two sons of Oedipus, as predicted, meet as enemies and slay each other. At the Cornish School, there was no time for anything but highly concentrated work. "Here in this class," Graham told the students, "I will teach you how to command the stage without your even making a move. But first you must forget everything you learned before."

In 1914, Nellie Cornish, a would-be pianist and a piano teacher, had founded the school that bore her name, and in 1921 she moved it into a new building high up on Seattle's Capitol Hill, where many of the city's wealthiest had built mansions. Cornish herself lived in a sunny apartment in this Spanish-style building and had gradually turned a music school into a college where all the arts could be studied. The students called her "Miss Aunt Nellie," a name bestowed by her little niece (who'd been told to be more formal when at the school). When Martha and Louis arrived, ballet had already been replaced in the curriculum by modern dance; Michio Ito taught there in 1929, and Ronny Johansson, recommended by Graham, preceded her in the early summer of 1930.

Nevertheless, to the Cornish dance students, Graham was a revelation. Off with the ballet slippers! Forget about turning out the feet. They were to place those feet parallel to each other and three inches apart and imagine them as railroad tracks crossing the American plains. But throughout the classwork—the exercises done sitting on the floor, the falls and balances executed while standing in one spot, and the walks, runs, and leaps across bright white studios with skylights that let in sun and clouds—"Martha" was molding the young West Coast girls into the powerful, intense figures she deemed necessary for an ancient Greek tragedy, even though, in the end, only five of them would be in the interludes that she was to contribute to the production.

Perhaps drawing on the kind of strategies she had devised for working with actors at both the Anderson-Milton School and the Neighborhood Playhouse, she brought the Cornish students up to snuff, not just through rigorous training but via metaphors and semi-improvisational strategies—making them aware of how their muscles and bones meshed, of how their skin reacted to the air. "Feel as if you have whiskers that enable you to judge your body's width as you move through a narrow place"—that's one of the many images Dorothy Bird absorbed and remembered. "Feel as if your arms are covered with huge, strong feathers, like the wings of an eagle, longing to spread out and take flight. Feel that you are a snake moving secretly, ever so subtly, inside your skin." However, Graham was not in favor of imitating nature. Instructions like these were followed by, "Absorb these images. Compress them and store the concentrated essence of the image in the notebook of your mind."

The enthralled students were to imagine a fiercely observant third eye in the hollow at the base of their necks. They practiced closing their eyes and listening intently for sounds. They felt the floor against their bare feet or with the palms of their hands; they used it as a spring-board. And how hard they worked—sometimes in pairs, pushing and pulling against each other, first with contact, then with inches of air between their pressing hands. They practiced stamping with full force and then, with the same force, stopping the foot before it touched the floor; they clapped their hands, then tried halting them shy of hitting each other. Mechanically, they generated the sounds of crying or laughing, until these actions overcame their bodies and they were heaving with sobs or rolling around the floor mirthfully. Then they *thought* about how these emotions affected the body.

Graham also told them to envision dancing as verbs and adverbs—action words. She turned the swinging movements that figured in German modern dance into something akin to hurling a weapon or releasing a slingshot. When teaching the students a difficult lunge that had to be performed with their feet in a single line across one of the studio's boards, she told them that they should imagine their forward thrust having the power to split a rock; Dorothy Bird, Bonnie Bird, and two other students walked uphill from the school to

Volunteer Park, found a likely boulder, and aimed lunge after lunge at it, to no avail. Martha commended them for having understood what was required. At the end of the long days, they massaged their aching muscles.

She also spoke to them of Greek art and drama. Like Isadora, she considered the *Winged Victory* in the Louvre, despite its missing head and arms, to incarnate the woman she wanted her dancers to emulate—strong, bold, open-chested, thrusting themselves into action.

Nellie Cornish noted in her autobiography that Jean Mercier, the director of *Seven Against Thebes*, didn't allow Graham to collaborate with him on the production (presumably she meant on the movements of the Chorus), but one review and various recollections suggest that the interludes Graham contributed were memorable. Reviewing the first of three performances, the critic for *The Seattle Times*—after praising the opening play on the program, Molière's *The Jealousy of le Barbouillé*—wrote approvingly of Mercier's groupings of the actors, the speaking chorus in *Seven Against Thebes*, and the "uniform and rhythmic grace" with which they moved, but he devoted as much space to Graham's contribution. Viewers, he wrote "will be fascinated by some unusual dance creations by Martha Graham. These weird interludes are interpreted admirably by Bonnie Bird, Bethene Miller, Dorothy Bird, Grace Cornell, and Nelle Fisher. Miss Cornell's work is outstanding." And "the Cornish Players have outdone even themselves in interpreting the unusual in drama."

The theater at the Cornish School was (and is) not huge. The eleven rows in the narrow, steeply sloping audience space contain between 130 and 140 seats; a balcony holds five more rows. The five chosen dancers made their striking entrance down one of the side aisles, a living frieze against its wooden wall, pressing themselves in slow motion through the two-dimensional positions that Graham had been working on for weeks. With her, they had dyed yards of cheesecloth in hues of terra-cotta, red, and sand; then, in a process familiar to Isadora Duncan's followers, they had twisted the wet fabric into bundles and baked them in a slow oven to approximate the pleats familiar from Greek statues and Fortuny gowns. It's not clear how many interludes Graham choreographed for the play. Dorothy Bird mentions "Dance of Grief" and what she dubbed "Circle of Pain" (which may or may not have been the same section).

At the end of her stint at Cornish, Graham invited Dorothy Bird and Grace Cornell to come to New York and join her company. Bonnie Bird would come as soon as she finished high school. Graham herself headed south to Santa Barbara to see her mother (since 1927, Mrs. Homer Duffy). Such trips could be both healing and irritating, as she had explained in a letter to Evelyn Sabin two years earlier:

> I haven't yet gotten over the thrill of waking up to a day full of sunshine—little fragrant breezes and birds—There are many mocking birds near—Then there is a glass Chinese wind bell on the porch and it makes the most delightful tinkling little sounds. It is stirring now. Where I am lying I can see two silvery old olive trees—from the old ones at the mission . . . I lie out here hours at a time doing nothing, except listening to life—and I have gained a peace and strength. All I want to do, however, is to be quiet. Its [*sic*] been an amazing experience.

She also admitted that "it has been difficult to fit into a home life with its unending routine of meals and beds to make etc." (Her mother, she reported, was, at the moment, preserving fruit.) Participation in this domesticity and living at close quarters with others would, she reported, "kill me—and I should quickly grow old."

Having had her respite and fulfilled her family obligations, she met Horst in Albuquerque after his work at Perry-Mansfield was done. In that high desert country barricaded to the east by the Sangre de Cristo Mountains, they sought out the Indigenous cultures they had glimpsed on at least one previous visit. According to Horst's diary, they visited three pueblos within thirty miles of Albuquerque—Isleta, San Felipe, and Santa Domingo—after which they drove to Santa Fe for the annual fiesta, where they saw dances at the Armory, then made their way to Taos. Their time in New Mexico proved to be yet another fertile one in what had already been a very fruitful year.

7

PRIMITIVE MYSTERIES AND THE BIRTH OF MODERN DANCE

IN LATE 1930 the theater critic Oliver M. Sayler assembled a book that he titled *Revolt in the Arts*. It began with his own 169-page essay, after which thirty-six artists and others representing their various fields responded to the topic he had thrown down like a gauntlet: the creation, production, and dissemination of art in a time of change brought about, in large part, by machines. Among the writers was Martha Graham, her essay sandwiched between "Nature, Teacher of the Dance" by Isadora Duncan's sister, Elizabeth, and "Toward an American Ballet" by the theater designer Robert Edmond Jones. Graham's title: "Seeking an American Art of the Dance."

Sayler's book provides a glimpse of worries not unlike those that beset twentieth-century prognosticators in regard to the internet. He and the selected writers turned their thoughts toward the Machine Age (always capitalized, perhaps to convey its clanking-into-the-future power) and how it might affect the arts, both usefully and harmfully. Would radio broadcasts and phonograph records lead to the demise of symphony orchestra concerts and staged opera? Might "a sort of Ford plant for the reproduction of sculpture" develop someday, and would that have a damaging effect on sculptors' careers? Would the trend toward speed in many aspects of life tarnish writers who had to conform to the pithy brevity demanded by tabloid editors who assumed readers' attention spans to be shrinking? Lillian Gish laments the invention of sound films as a whole: the ongoing development of the silent film, she felt, had been "cut short by the intrusion of spoken dialogue and by the consequent throwback of the cinema toward the theater." She is sure that some of the camera's mobility will diminish and the expressive gestures (at which she and other screen actors excelled) would be lost; the camera would stay in a fixed position and people would talk at each other.

Yet contributors as dissimilar as the poet Hart Crane, the composer George Gershwin, and Sayler himself gladly faced the inevitability of new subject matter, new sounds, new forms, and new rhythms. The designer Paul T. Frankl put it briskly in his 1930 book, *Form and Re-Form*: "We are no longer preoccupied with our past. We are piercing the future."

And Graham? She was not the only contributor to Sayler's book to dodge the machine issue (for the time being anyway) and speak up for an art that would reflect America—its Indigenous cultures, its melting-pot values, its ideals of freedom and innovation—but she was among the most fervent. And the most bent on piercing the future. She did not mince words when she spoke about "borrowed forms." A paragraph in her essay begins with this statement: "Fatuous in our adoration of all things European, we gazed longingly at the fruits of a tired culture, while Europe smiled and reached past us to help itself to the wine of our land; its monstrous vital rhythms, crude, glowing colors, dynamic economy of gesture, and that divine awkwardness which is ever a part of what is vital, fresh and masculine in the arts." (Certainly, in her repeated use of words like "virile" and "masculine" in relation to the work she made for herself and her company of women, she was appropriating the right to strength and assertiveness in her art and to a seriousness that brooked no condescension.)

In her essay, Graham characterized the "Negro dance" as a "dance toward freedom, a dance to forgetfulness, often Dionysiac in its abandon and the raw splendor of its rhythm." The American Indian dancer, on the other hand, was "for awareness of life, complete relationship with that world in which he finds himself; it is a dance for power, a rhythm of integration."

She was deeply drawn to the dances she had seen in the Southwest in the summer of 1930—to their connections to ritual, their simple clarity, and the dancers' stamping acknowledgment of the earth. "I arrived when they were dancing," she wrote to a friend after seeing a performance in the Santo Domingo Pueblo.

> I heard their voices and I rounded the corner of an adobe house in a narrow street, to enter the plaza—and saw them—one hundred men in a straight line—dancing and chanting . . . The chanting was low, deep, intense. The faces of the men pure and fanatical and beautiful as gods. They danced in perfect unison—for no one . . . [N]othing I have ever seen or dreamed of equaled that great communal dance ritual in earnestness, intensity, faith in the eternal recurrence of natural phenomena—such savage ruthless awareness of life.

Two of the new works Graham contributed to the second season of Dance Repertory Theatre in February 1931, *Two Primitive Canticles* and *Primitive Mysteries* (unarguably her first masterpiece), showed that she had absorbed and transformed not only the dancing she had seen but also the feel of the high desert's open spaces, the angular patterns on Native rugs, and the daily life of the Indians she and Horst had seen in the pueblos.

One pueblo ritual that may have influenced the structure of *Primitive Mysteries* was Los Matachines, a dance that Graham could have seen during the Santa Fe Fiesta she attended in 1930—a fiesta in which it is performed today and has been for years. It was also performed that summer in Bernalillo and in the pueblos of Cochiti and Santo Domingo as well as in villages in the mountains east of Albuquerque.

Scholars have debated at length the origins of the ancient Matachines, but its many variants in Mexico and the western United States blend Indian beliefs and Catholicism in striking ways. Men of the pueblo (often twelve of them) face each other in two parallel lines—

stamping, hopping, turning, sometimes to the music of a violin and a guitar, sometimes to a flute and percussion. Their costumes feature headdresses that resemble backless bishops' miters with streamers falling from them, while heavily fringed scarves partially mask their faces. One of the four featured performers weaving among them or passing between their lines—sometimes enacting fragmentary scenarios—is La Malinche, a little girl, often wearing the sort of white dress she might wear at her First Communion. The name is that of the young Aztec woman who acted as an interpreter for the explorer (and her lover) Hernando Cortés during the Spanish conquest of Mexico, but the chosen girl more likely represents the Virgin Mary, since the dance often celebrates the Virgin of Guadalupe.

To go from participating in the Stravinsky-Massine *Sacre du Printemps* to seeing this ritual performance—in which a maiden is chosen to honor the Virgin and ensure the health of the community—would have been a spirit-stirring, brain-heating experience for Graham. And in terms of themes, the three sections of *Primitive Mysteries*—"Hymn to the Virgin," "Crucifixus," and "Hosanna"—show a striking correspondence to three core sections of the Matachines: "La Paseado de la Malinche," "La Cruz (the Cross)," and "Juvilo (Jubilee)."

Late in her life, Graham said of *Primitive Mysteries*, "It is a participation in a rite of initiation. The dancers are not worshipping, they are celebrating the figure [of the Virgin Mary] through one of themselves." Dancers in the 1964 reconstruction learned from Graham that "the metaphor was that you were all the virgin. You are these young women. It's a town which re-enacts this ritual every year, Next year, maybe one of you will be the virgin."

By using the word "primitive" in the title, Graham further abstracted the dance from specific Indian influences. Its Catholicism, as with others of her dances relating to Christian iconography, also draws on her childhood memories of attending Mass in Alleghany, Pennsylvania, with her childhood nurse, Lizzie, or visiting the Santa Barbara Mission when she was a teenager. It can't have escaped her that the image of a charismatic leader with twelve devoted followers linked her and her company to a more famous spiritual model.

As Marcia B. Siegel wrote after seeing a film of the 1964 revival of *Primitive Mysteries*, "It is not a dance you go to in order to be entertained—satisfied, yes, uplifted, mystified, moved. It is a terse, severely disciplined dance, not a kinesthetic joyride. Everything is brought to a certain pitch and then immediately modified." The clarity and formality of the images are almost shocking. For each of the work's three sections, the women and their leader enter in silence; in silence they regroup and in silence they exit when the section is done. After a charged pause of a few seconds, while the audience stares at the empty landscape of the stage—the plaza of a virtual town—the women process back into sight to perform the next part. Arlene Croce, writing of a still later revival of the piece, described its choreography as "a few incisive strokes on a shadowless plain, organized to music by Louis Horst that sounds like a singing bone."

This may be the first dance in which Graham allowed—encouraged—the audience to perceive shifting meanings in the austerely elegant designs she created. Sometimes the central figure seems to lead the others; sometimes they succor her and guard her. Although you can perceive her as the Virgin Mother and as the Mater Dolorosa taking upon herself the sufferings of her son, she is also the village girl *representing* these images, and as all these, she is both venerated and supported by the celebrants who escort her on and off the stage and encircle her at the end of each part. Neither she nor the women she moves among express overt emotion. They are as solemn as church statues. Yet the positions they strike, their rhythms, and their redesigned iconic gestures resonate with feeling. And as Siegel has pointed out, members of this female community need no male priest to interpret their actions or intercede in them.

The dancers entering from stage left for "Hymn to the Virgin" wear long, plainly cut dark blue dresses. Their hair is twisted into a bun and netted. A thirteenth dancer was played by Graham in 1931 and by Yuriko (Kikuchi)* in the 1964 revival approved by Graham. In the black-and-white film, Yuriko looks almost like a bride. Her long,

---

* Yuriko Kikuchi used only her first name when dancing or choreographing.

full white organdy gown, with its layered, petal-like sleeves, was inspired, Graham later said, by the eventful sight of a night-blooming cereus in her mother's garden. Dorothy Bird, a member of the original cast, watched how, in a single session and with Dorothy's help, Martha constructed the costume on her own body out of two large squares of white organza, pinning, folding, cutting, and basting these with extraordinary skill. (When the teenage Martha was taking sewing classes at the Santa Barbara High School—at a time when many women still made their own clothes—she could not have imagined the creative asset that skill would become.)

The dancers with whom the Virgin enters form a three-sided box around her. In the extreme tension of its rhythm, the performers' ceremonious walk is like nothing seen entering a New Mexico pueblo; neither is it much like anything that the 1931 spectators were likely to have encountered in a dance performance. In silence, the women thrust out a foot, heel first, sharply propel their weight onto it, then bring the other foot to join it before they step out again. They hold their arms and bodies still; only that striding foot and the motion of their skirts reveal their action. In their deliberateness and blocky strength, they resemble the clay *santos* Graham and Horst had observed in pueblo churches and bought in village markets, now set in motion.

Horst's music for flute, oboe, and piano (created after the choreography was completed) begins only after the women are in place onstage. The four women in the upstage line sit down to watch the first sequence in a formalized depiction of a casual position—their feet wide apart, their arms clasped around their bent knees. To a jaunty tune for the woodwinds, the woman in white hurries back and forth between the other two groups with little pattering steps, clasping her hands in prayer. When she reaches a group, the four women in it stop their springy, back-and-forth walking and, with her, form a tableau to three or four piano chords. When Yuriko danced the leading role, Martha told her that in each of the Virgin's forays, the clusters of women were summoning her to them; she was not the instigator of these little visits. The images imprinted on your eyes as "Hymn to the

Virgin" unrolls are as clear as line drawings: once, four women bow, straight-backed, when she reaches them; once, four support her when she leans sideways like a toppling statue. On another visit to a group, she turns and, lifting one leg, swoons backward; the women's arms are ready.

Some of the poses the Virgin creates with her quartets of followers suggest iconic Christian imagery. Women, shoulder to shoulder and leaning forward, create a cradle with their forearms and rock it for her affirmation. Another time, their splayed fingers form a halo around her. In still another encounter, two women crouch and two stand, their bent elbows pointing toward her, framing her like a living retable. But this is a joyful hymn; four celebrants, holding hands, circle her with springy steps.

In a subsequent passage, she seems to offer benediction to her flock. Eight of the women kneel in two lines leading away from the audience; as she walks forward down the aisle between them, she blesses each woman—now favoring one on this side, now one on the other. Those on her right bend deeply sideways, as if to place one slightly cupped hand beneath her feet; those on her left stay slightly more upright when they reach out to her. When she has finished, she backs quickly down the line between them, reaching out to bend each pair over, like a teacher prompting her students or a herder shooing her flock into the pattern she has in mind.

The final circle of this section could allude indirectly to the circle Graham had traveled in *The Rite of Spring*. The woman in white sits meditatively at its center, her palms lifted to receive blessings from above. To stentorian five-count measures, the others begin stalking forward along the circumference of the ring, then turn and walk backward, clasping their hands behind them. Gradually, the phrase builds in length and variety to include—as in *The Rite of Spring*—a slight spring into a squat to touch the floor, with a jump straight upward after it. In turn, each set of three women adds these moves, then each six, then all twelve. The tempo accelerates until, on chords that sound like an "amen," they bow low to the Virgin in the center, regroup, and exit in silence at the same deliberate pace with which they had entered.

When they reappear again for the "Crucifixus," two women flank the Virgin, and the remaining ten are divided into three groups. Once in place, they begin trudging back and forth to weighted piano chords, above which the woodwinds sing out plaintive, sustained tones. The women's hands rest on their shoulders and their elbows point forward. When they walk backward, constantly gazing upward, their bodies cave in and they lift their knees high.

The Virgin moves very little in this section. As if transfixed, she stands near the back of the stage with her cupped hands formally shielding her eyes (or her mouth), but touching neither. Each dancer in the pair on either side of her points a finger upward, as if toward the invisible Cross. Their raised arms frame her, creating a peaked roof like that of a shrine or a church doorway. The other women, after a time, congregate at one side of the stage; there they wait, each with her head turned away from the trio, one hand, fingers open, pressed to her brow in an acknowledgment of the crown of thorns. All this time, the Virgin and her two attendants have been moving toward the audience by increments so small that it takes the spectator some time to realize that they are traveling. The music stops, and the Virgin steps forward, opens her arms to form a larger cross, and stares upward, her body sinking slightly, as if ready to receive a heavy load—the devout spectator-participant as the bereaved mother who has walked the long distance to the foot of the Cross. The condensation of a complex and bloody event into this one moment is heart-stopping. And what follows is almost frightening.

The women, now crouching, feed, one by one, into a large circle around the Virgin, who remains frozen. Each celebrant, as she rises and joins, throws one arm forward to launch herself into a huge gulp of a leap (in Graham classes and rehearsals over the years, this leap has acquired a nickname, "the buffalo"). Eventually the ten women—their bodies leaning forward almost parallel to the floor, their arms clasped behind them—are leaping over and over with no preparatory steps between the airborne ones. They are not aiming to leave the ground as much as to belabor it. The pace around the circle accelerates until they are running in an orderly stampede. They stop on a dime. So does the music. As the group bows and reorganizes itself to exit, the two women moving upstage stop, twist back for a moment, and gaze behind them and upward. Just so, the Crucifixion. Then all thirteen women walk slowly, firmly, out of sight.

Only twelve enter for the "Hosanna," the Virgin preceded by one woman, the other ten divided in half. Their entry in silence is as gravely ceremonious as it was at the beginning of *Primitive Mysteries*, but as soon as a lively tune begins, the women step buoyantly back and forth, divided into rows on either side of the stage's center, where the seated Virgin and her attendant (Mary Rivoire in the 1931 cast) enact a series of tableaux. In one of these, the acolyte/companion leans perilously back, and the seated Virgin reaches up to catch her and lay her across her lap. Another time, the Virgin, now standing, bends the other woman backward and gazes down at her. This woman's penultimate act is to stand behind the seated Virgin, raise her own hands, fingers spread, and bring them firmly down to crown her leader's head. The others have continued to move in their groups, with many stopped moments. They form lines, a circle. Four fall on their faces in homage. They kneel and crouch. Often, in the pauses, they lean back, hinging at the knee, gazing upward, and opening their arms to form a cross.

In a few succinct, time-fragmented moments, you can visualize the Deposition from the Cross, the Rising from the Tomb, the Assumption of the Virgin, and the ensuing rejoicing.

Primitive Mysteries, which precipitated a long-lasting ovation at its premiere, had entailed many months of rehearsals. To get the processional walks in perfect synchrony, the women of the group practiced moving in threes and fours, their arms pinned to their sides and the knuckles of their cupped hands pressing those of the person next to them. Dorothy Bird recalled a rehearsal during which Graham laid a broom handle across the shoulders of one trio to keep its members in line. When the dancers went to Jones Beach for recreation, they practiced in the surf so they could remember the oppositional pressure of the tide when they walked onstage.

You would never know, however, from watching this dance in its reconstructed form that its launch onto the stage in 1931 was preceded by a rehearsal that lasted into the morning hours and included displays of panic and rage on Graham's part (she, it is said, spent the night in her dressing room, which is understandable; final rehearsals for the Dance Repertory Theatre's performances might begin after the preceding night's show). As she was to do many times in future years, she decided at almost the last minute that the women's costumes were not right, sent helpers down to Orchard Street to buy different fabric, and set the dancers to sewing. A botched moment in the rehearsal induced her to rage and retreat to her dressing room—a painful form of therapy—after which, thanks to Horst, she emerged and work resumed. The dancers knew her angers to be like cloudbursts: she was refreshed; they could stop shaking.

The 1964 revival has been the benchmark for subsequent performances of *Primitive Mysteries*, although it may not exactly duplicate performances of it in the 1930s. The work was reassembled through the input of every one of the early dancers who could be found, plus a tiny film clip of one of them doing a few movements, written descriptions, and Barbara Morgan's remarkable 1940 photographs. Horst had died in January 1964, and the work was staged that summer as part of a memorial concert during the American Dance Festival at Connecticut College, where he had taught for many years. He and Graham had not been close for some time, but she mourned him fiercely.

The dancers of the 1960s were not the sturdy, forthright women of the 1930s; they were lighter, slimmer, more flexible. They were awed by the force and speed of the women now in their fifties and sixties who came to work with them. One among the young cast, Jean Nuchtern, said that she imagined that Ethel Butler (by then a doyenne of dance in Washington, D.C.) "could lift up a truck with no problem." Graham had been in Israel during the early stages of the reconstruction and participated reluctantly only after the piece was being rehearsed under Sophie Maslow's direction—demanding, for instance, that a white ruffle be added to the hems of the women's dresses, acting as a kind of wake, accenting the force of their entering walk. She also decided that in the "Crucifixus," when the women walked with their hands on their shoulders, they should bring their elbows together in order to create more strain across their backs and, as a consequence, more intensity. Graham could inspire the dancers when she talked to them about the atmosphere of a rite in which any girl could have been its focus, or the origin of the desired hairstyle. However, in her grief, she was drinking heavily, and for much of the time she watched an occasional rehearsal balefully from the sidelines or screamed at everyone.

One member of that 1960s cast, Marcia Lerner (later Hofer), captured something of what the original dancers must have felt, albeit from a different perspective: "The desire to be noticed as an individual, so integral a part of the usual performing situation, had no place in this experience . . . We were so closely attuned as a group that during our final rehearsal when Graham lashed out at us in a rage which no doubt had more to do with her anxiety about the performances than any provocation on our part, all twelve of us burst into tears, as though some common reflex had been set off."

In 1931 John Martin of the *Times* dubbed *Primitive Mysteries* a work of "major importance." His review points up again, with fine understanding, the aesthetic that Graham had set herself to define: "It is composed with the utmost economy of means, though it is never meager. Like all of Miss Graham's compositions, it suggests rather than expresses the fullness of its emotional background."

The edition of Dance Repertory Theatre at the Craig Theatre from February 1 through 8, 1931, was structured slightly differently from the one in 1930. Each of the five choreographers involved—Graham, Humphrey, Weidman, Tamiris, and Agnes de Mille—headlined a mixed bill. In addition, Martha Graham and Dance Group, the Humphrey-Weidman Company, and Tamiris (now also with a group of her own) were each allotted a single program consisting of only their own works. The mixed bills were by their nature stressful. For instance, on the February 6 program, Graham, the headliner, opened the evening with five dances, including the second performance of

Primitive Mysteries (at the third, a matinee, group member Lillian Shapero took her role); after an intermission, three works by Tamiris and three by de Mille were interspersed, with Humphrey's *Water Study* shoehorned in between them.

During the Dance Repertory season, Humphrey premiered a major work too—one also inspired by a religious practice. *The Shakers (Dances of the Chosen)* deployed the men and women of the Humphrey-Weidman Company in fervent movements that split the stage in half and brought out the inherent tensions that lay beneath the devout surface of a celibate community.

Apparently neither Humphrey nor Graham admired Tamiris's contributions. It was Humphrey's opinion, expressed in a letter to her mother, that Tamiris was "a grand girl but a bad dancer." (As "choreographer" was not a label the season's participants often used during those years, one can assume that Humphrey's assessment was aimed at Tamiris's work rather than at her performing ability.)

The February 2 program belonged exclusively to Graham and consisted of twelve works, of which five were premieres. The new group work in addition to *Primitive Mysteries* was *Bacchanale*, although only six of the women performed it, with Graham as their leader. With the help of the League of Composers, the score had been commissioned from Wallingford Riegger. Dorothy Bird, who danced in it, recalled that the movement theme was tilting: "Not just tilting; but tilting with wild abandon that led inevitably into tilting falls . . . The rhapsodic moment was the arch in the body when the tilt became a fall." John Martin wrote perceptively in the *Times* that the dance was "a suggestion of the Dionysiac rites rather than an attempt to visualize their complete abandon, and its effect is one of complete delight." *Bacchanale* evidently pleased the audience mightily. At its first showing, it had to be encored.

Both *Two Primitive Canticles* and *Dolorosa* were solos set to music by Heitor Villa-Lobos. Graham had gleaned more images and ideas from her visit to the American Southwest than she could express in *Primitive Mysteries*, and the mixture of Indigenous culture with elements of Christianity fueled these dances, which were, wrote Martin, "both stark in their simplicity and as clear as crystal in their design and purpose." Barbara Morgan's photos of Graham in *Two Primitive Canticles* ("Ave" and "Salve") make it clear that her legs must have moved only minimally. She wears a long-sleeved, narrowly cut sheath of a dress; the fabric is dark, with a few bold, widely spaced white stripes running down it. One might imagine it made of woven material that she bought in New Mexico.

The music for *Rhapsodics* ("Song," "Interlude," "Dance") was by Béla Bartók, and, according to Martin, amply demonstrated what its title implied. Oddly, the Craig Theatre program lists it as a dance that Graham performed with members of her group, while subsequent mentions indicate that it was a solo.

Two pianists (Horst and Dini de Remer) played most of the music, assisted by flautist Hugo Bergamesco and oboe player William Sergeant. *Heretic* brought the evening to a powerful if somber conclusion.

The Dance Repertory Theatre's ambitious plans came to an end after this second season, and the choreographers again went their separate ways, freed from wranglings over the business aspects of the enterprise and comparisons by the critics and the public that may have rankled.

While preparing for this last joint season, Graham had been able to lay to rest one particular doubt that had been haunting her, given the many times the words "German dance" and the name Mary Wigman were mentioned as influencing the American dancers. By the time *Primitive Mysteries* premiered in February, Graham had seen Wigman perform her solo program. The powerful exponent of German *ausdruckstanz* (or "expression dance") had arrived in New York in November 1930 to begin a solo tour of the country. The leading dancers in New York were present at the party that Edith J. R. Isaacs, the editor of *Theatre Arts Monthly*, gave to welcome her. Graham joined de Mille and La Argentina in sitting around a table with Wigman.

A member of Graham's group who sat next to Martha at Wigman's New York debut said that Martha gripped the young woman's hand tightly throughout the first dance, maybe longer. Afterward, she sighed in relief; she had been frightened, she confessed, that

Wigman's work would resemble hers more closely, and she found that not to be true. Fixing on a particular movement of the German choreographer, she declared it to be "a gesture of empire," presumably, therefore, not threatening the uniqueness of American dance.

It was undoubtedly trying for her that the impresario Sol Hurok had mapped out a well-paying United States tour for Wigman and that a school bearing her name and headed by one of her dancers, Hanya Holm, would be established in New York City before the end of 1931. Graham also discovered that she would now often be compared to the visitor, at times to her detriment. By 1932, one drama critic not enthralled by Wigman was ready to write that American dance in general and Graham in particular had been "overwhelmed by the gray Germanic wave."

Graham, prudently, decided to show a generous spirit and to clarify the territory she had staked out. When an interviewer insisted on an opinion of her supposed rival, she announced: "Mary Wigman, through her greatness as a person and as a dancer, has given us all an added courage. The comparison of the dances, I am afraid, between Mary Wigman and myself must be left to others. The modern dance in America, however, was firmly grounded in its own way before Mary Wigman came to this country."

John Martin's reviews of Graham during the Dance Repertory Theatre's season introduce an aspect of her work that may not have been evident to him before; either that, or the physical virtuosity her work demanded had reached a new level. Some of the movements of the group in *Bacchanale*, he thought, "would almost seem impossible of performance by the human body." And *Rhapsodics* (its third section in particular) "contains some extraordinary choreography which few dancers besides Miss Graham could compass."

Her physical skills and choices were developing to suit her themes and the times she lived in. And her deeply devoted dancers, willy-nilly, gladly wracked their bodies in her service. During the early years of Martha Graham and Group, her classes developed side by side with

her choreographic ideas. If she wanted her dancers to be able to maintain their bodies in a single straight line from their knees to the tops
of their heads while bending at those knees in order to lean backward
at a perilous slant, that's what they worked on, over and over. Did she
plan on incorporating jumps into a dance? Then, in class, jump they
did. And jumped and jumped. Some of her exercises were extremely
difficult. Jane Dudley recalled struggling with a move that began with
the dancer in a squat; she then stretched one leg out in front of her
and, holding it there, slowly rose to a standing position on one leg;
after this, with her weight still on one leg, she lowered herself to her
original position and repeated the move on the other leg (it helped,
said Dudley, if one had elastic Achilles tendons like Martha).

The modern dancers of the 1930s went barefoot—not to suggest
the oneness with nature that had motivated Isadora Duncan, but the
better to sense the floor; their movements both acknowledged the pull
of gravity and strove against it. The basic structure of the classes that
trained them was similar to that of a present-day class in Graham
technique: stretches and other exercises done while sitting, kneeling,
or lying on the floor; exercises performed while standing in one spot;
passages of walking, running, turning, and leaping that carried the
dancer across the studio floor; and finally a series of falls. Certain sequences might be executed with the aid of a barre, but Graham disci-
ples' forceful swings and thrusts of the hips bore little relationship to
ballet. A difficult stance that Dorothy Bird recalled from Graham's
classes at the Cornish School—the one in which the dancers set their
feet parallel to each other, one directly in front of the other, as if the
performer had been about to walk a line and been frozen between
steps—had to be maintained while she twisted her body to the right,
say, while maintaining her gaze forward. Turnout of the legs and spiraling (as opposed to twisting) in the body slid into the classwork
when Graham began to experiment with movements—especially certain falls—that would have been impossible to accomplish without
these ballet hand-me-downs.

The exercises to prime the body for what Martin christened "The
Modern Dance"—whether these appeared in classes taught by Gra-

ham, Humphrey, Weidman, or others—were often performed in a series of diminishing time sequences. In a sample 1930s Graham class that Bonnie Bird re-created in New York in 1981, she had the students fall slowly backward to the floor in four moderately timed counts, impelled by a sharp contraction in the solar plexus that Bird likened to an emphatic "NO!" as if the breath had been punched out of the body; once on the floor, they rolled sideways into an arched "release" and rose to the starting position in four additional counts. The fall and rise were then performed with two counts to fall and two to rise, then with one count to fall and one to rise. Finally, said Bird—at the time a robust sixty-something—those Graham dancers of the 1930s fell and rose again on a single count; then she did exactly that.

In the emerging modern dance classes the pianist improvised to suit the dancing (often playing just a sparse march of single notes), thus facilitating structures like the above as well as dance exercises that began short and simple and grew in length and complexity with each repetition.

Whether Graham was teaching her company members, beginners, or actors at the Neighborhood Playhouse, she made some of the same demands. She often accompanied these strenuous ordeals, however, with images that could help model the shape and stimulate the impetus of a movement. She asked her dancers to think of the floor as a drumhead—a surface from which to rebound. She wanted them to sense the center of their bodies as a whip handle impelling their limbs to lash out. She asked them to sense that they had fox ears, pricked to every sound, or to feel like a snake balancing on the end of its tail. (They may well have felt like this last when attempting to unfurl from a huddled sitting position until they were balanced on their tailbones—their uplifted straight legs and their torsos forming a V, with no hands on the floor to support them.)

The system of Contraction and Release that was so crucial to the development and identity of Graham's style has certain basic elements in common with the polarity of Fall and Recovery that supported Doris Humphrey's technique, although Humphrey's could more eloquently engender lyricism. In choreography by both women, movement sprang up in the struggle between dualities, and both systems emphasized breath—Humphrey's lingering in the suspended moment before being undone by gravity; Graham's contraction as a harsh expelling of breath and caving in of the body, followed by a restorative inhalation and expansion. However, lest Graham's falls suggested negativity or defeat rather than the high moral purpose behind her art and the optimism that got people through the Depression, she wrote, "My dancers fall *so they may rise*" (emphasis hers). And, perhaps weary of hearing "angularity" applied, sometimes crankily, to describe her more adventurous works, her manager, Frances Hawkins (prompted by Martha), endeavored to reimagine geometry: "This angularity is only apparent, not actual; it appears because her movements are arrested and one sees only the segment of a circle instead of the completed curve; the climax must take place in the mind of the audience."

In addition, the styles and techniques that Graham and her peers developed were not only about the physical motions. Just as in Humphrey's *Water Study*, dancers arching and bending forward in graduated ranks turned the motion of the entire stage into one huge wave cresting and breaking, the "walls" of women in Graham's *Heretic* epitomized the barriers erected by prejudice.

In the spring of 1931, Graham reluctantly agreed to participate in several educational events that John Martin was presenting in the oval basement auditorium of the New School for Social Research on West Twelfth Street. Struggling not to crash into one another in a space that had not been designed with dance in mind, her group performed classwork and excerpts from the repertory (the fact that, at one of these events, after almost no rehearsal, Graham entrusted Dorothy Bird with her own part in *Heretic* attests to her discomfort with Martin's series).

The New School lecture-demonstrations may well have expanded the audience for Graham's work, but they also inadvertently exacerbated the simmering conflict between ballet and modern dance. During the question-and-answer period at one of these presentations, a man in the audience began to question Graham's ideas about dance, carrying his objections into outright hectoring. Some of his negative opinions centered on what could be considered "natural" in dance. Apparently he misunderstood her contention that, for example, one raised one's arm (or a Graham dancer did) as if by a lever that rotated the shoulder back and down (or, in some cases, used the shoulder to impel a rippling motion). The man made his disdain evident by exaggerated demonstrations. See? Unnatural! Graham fought back. She also, evidently, expressed a dislike of ballets that attempted to show Grecian dance. Only when Martin, attempting to calm the two down, addressed the spectator by name did she realize that her opponent was the eminent Russian choreographer Mikhail Fokine, who in 1912 had created the "Grecian" ballet *Daphnis and Chloe* for Serge Diaghilev's Ballets Russes.

That Fokine—who had defined for himself what was natural in dance, in contrast to the nineteenth-century ballet tradition in which he had been trained in St. Petersburg—should find Graham's style unnatural and unattractive is no surprise. Although in his own ballets he had been innovative in flouting many aspect of classicism, he had already spoken publicly of his distaste for Mary Wigman's solo work ("Ugly girl makes ugly movements onstage while ugly mother tells ugly brother to make ugly sounds on drum"). Graham apologized for an insulting remark she had made, but Fokine refused forgiveness. Words he wrote about the encounter in New York's Russian-language newspaper, *Novoye Russkoye Slovo*, were translated and quoted in Victor Dandré's 1932 biography of his wife, Anna Pavlova; and they appeared again in an issue of *The Literary Digest* later that year with a battle-cry title: "The Old and the New in Dance at Odds." Fokine had found all that he saw that evening at the New School to be "ugly in form and hateful in content." Graham's style of dance, like that of Wigman, expressed only "strain as much as you can." His descriptions of Graham's group seethed with anger and incomprehension: "The young women lay, sat, walked on flat feet and . . . that was all. Their arms either hung down helplessly or stuck out with the elbows up. Their chests were continually thrust forward or suddenly allowed to fall in." Those who found Graham's work "difficult" or "not dance," had an outspoken ally. Interestingly, the editor at *The Literary Digest* chose to accompany the article with a photo of the young Fokine and his wife, Vera Fokina—he in a Grecian tunic, she in a chiton—during their days with the Ballets Russes; the two were captured by the camera in angular and aggressive friezelike two-dimensional poses, while the caption ironically reads "The Dance Is the 'Expression of Happiness'" (this last being one of the statements Fokine used at the New School to define the true mission of dance).

Shortly after this encounter, Graham's background in theater and her present involvement in it at the Neighborhood Playhouse, along with her skills as a choreographer and charisma as a performer, brought her an invitation to participate in a production of Sophocles's *Electra* that starred the actress Blanche Yurka as the death-driven daughter of Agamemnon and Clytemnestra (the first of several dramatic presentations during the 1930s that involved Graham). Billed as "The Dancer," Graham choreographed three isolated solos for herself (to music composed by Horst) in the scaled-down version of the play, which was shown in Boston on Wednesday, May 18, before its official premiere the following week as part of a theater festival at the University of Michigan in Ann Arbor (where Graham also gave two solo concerts).

Sophocles's choral odes were eliminated, much to some critics' disappointment, and five new characters were introduced to deliver lines that the Chorus usually addresses to the principal actors. Graham created an Invocation, which she performed before the play began—a "sort of fury dance" that heralded the entrance of Clytemnestra, and (after an intermission) a lament over the burial urn containing the ashes of Electra's brother, Orestes. She also appeared onstage at the end, whipping on the final tragic moments of the play.

Her participation in *Electra* fed ideas into a radical new solo that she presented in December 1931. She and Horst had attended the first performance of Aaron Copland's *Piano Variations* in a concert sponsored by the League of Composers. With Louis's encouragement, she decided to choreograph a solo to that knotty score. The composer (thirty years old at the time) later told an interviewer of being astonished "when Miss Graham told me she intended to use the composition for dance treatment. Surely only an artist with a close affinity for my work could have visualized dance material in so rhythmically complex and aesthetically abstruse a composition."

Copland's work lasts ten minutes, or longer, depending on the pianist. Few dance soloists of the day were prepared to dominate the stage for that amount of time, accustomed as they were to presenting short vignettes that depicted a character or mood. Copland told Graham that she was not to cut his music, and she agreed to tackle the entire composition. Dancing to what one music critic has termed "a defiant howl of a piece" for that amount of time amounted to an ordeal (that Horst could play it with the required power attests to skills that went far beyond those demanded of most dance accompanists).

Piano Variations consists of a theme; twenty variations, all but the last of which are short (ten measures is a typical length); and a coda. The music's harsh staccato passages suited the bleak years of the early 1930s. The single declamatory notes, dropping in pitch to announce the theme and create a minor third, are followed by emphatic, pounced-upon chords, as if to jolt the listener into alertness and warn of difficulties ahead. The music is above all percussive, even in its lighter moments. It conveys a sense of argumentation—matters with which to wrestle. Vertical note clusters chafe in dissonances that have no intention of resolving in conventional consonances. Gradually the variations build in terms of density, the end of each often igniting the one following it, with or without a marked pause. The eleventh variation is almost unique for its delicacy and pensiveness; the fourteenth through the seventeenth stagger both rhythmically and in terms of pitch. By the last variation, the music has built to a fury, which continues into the coda, insisting with strong stacks of notes and repeated rhythmic motifs until it finally diminishes, exhausted.

Copland's irregular meters and the music's assertiveness and wildness spoke to Graham of ancient rituals. She called her solo *Dithyrambic*. Viewed retrospectively, it can be seen as presaging her later works—such as *Errand into the Maze, Night Journey, Cave of the Heart,* and *Clytemnestra*—just as the choric dithyramb of ancient Greece, celebrating Dionysus, the lusty, goat-footed god of wine, prefigured the tragedies of Aeschylus.

It is known that at some climactic moment in the dance, Graham fell back and rose repeatedly, as if in god-struck ecstasy, and that somehow this process moved her through space. "Orgiastic abandon" is how Martin described her performance, lauding it in his *New York Times* review as "a dance that extends the theories of modernism to lengths heretofore unknown on the concert stage." He needed, he felt, to see it more than once, since it was "so long and indescribably sparse." It was also noted by more than one writer that the choreography for *Dithyrambic* seemed a development of what Graham had created in *Rhapsodics*.

Dithyrambic made its New York debut on a program that Louis Horst later recalled as a "Russian benefit" (adding, "we were all pink in those days"). Graham opened the evening with another work new to New York; *Incantation*, set to music by Heitor Villa-Lobos, was identified in the program as "A primitive evocation of natural forces by means of dance." *Serenade*, however, reminded viewers that, although in it she presented an unmistakable image of Pierrot, she was "needless to say . . . a Pierrot who wears his rue with a difference." The solo was defined as "a charming and witty trifle, which does not neglect the melancholy of the subject nor its romantic origin."

Yet references to Greek tradition aside, *Dithyrambic*, like Copland's *Piano Variations*, announced itself as contemporary in ways that shocked some spectators and moved at least one writer to spout poetic allusions to the prevalent Machine Age images: "Miss Graham wrought a dance pattern that suggested the sound of rivets on steel, the beat of a city's traffic, toil and strife and turmoil, a subway train flashing through a hidden darkness, the mellow light of a skyscraper reaching to the stars."

8

CREATING DANCES FOR PLAYS

D ANCERS WORKING WITH GRAHAM during the early 1930s were used to scrimping and penny-pinching, despite the $15-a-week stipend received by those fortunate enough to be on scholarship at the Neighborhood Playhouse and the intermittent $10 that Graham paid for a performance out of the box office receipts. The Playhouse, however, had strictures about scholarship recipients tiring themselves out with additional projects, even if they had time to seek out what jobs could be found in a city coping with the Depression. Some dancers modeled for classes at the Art Students League on Fifty-Seventh Street; others waited on tables. Three could share an apartment; one could maybe rent a room in someone else's apartment. The two girls from the Cornish School, Bonnie and Dorothy Bird, got a little money for cleaning the studio and walking Graham and Horst's his-and-hers dachshunds, Max and Mädl (and eventually their off-spring, Alla), and cleaning up after the little dogs (they had notoriously weak bladders).

Martha's girls, bound together by their devotion to her, managed, in one way or another, to get by in a city gripped by austerity, and they knew the strategies involved in getting enough to eat. You could pocket the excess rolls and butter if asked out to dinner. You could live on oatmeal and cottage cheese. (Alcoholic beverages were, of course,

all but unthinkable to a cash-poor, hardworking dancer in these wan-
ing days of Prohibition, unless escorted to speakeasies by a man of
means.) In 1930, two days after eighteen-year-old Dorothy Bird arrived in New York from Seattle to work with Graham, Martha walked
her to the Horn & Hardart Automat on Fifty-Seventh Street (handy
to the Neighborhood Playhouse and the Carnegie Hall studio where
Dorothy would be taking Graham's classes) and showed her how to
get a breakfast of juice, toast, and coffee by putting nickels in the correct little glass-fronted doors. Total cost: fifteen cents. The dancers
were used to the sight of people queuing up at food pantries or beg-
ging on the streets. Bessie Schönberg, who lived in International
House on Riverside Drive above West 123rd Street, usually traveled
by subway to and from the Neighborhood Playhouse on East Fifty-
Sixth Street; she loved the double-decker bus ride with the river view,
but that cost ten cents, the subway five.

As the Depression lingered on, the city's unions included dance
groups made up of laborers, such as one formed at the Needle Trades
Workers Union, and groups such as Nature Friends, one of three companies run by the ardent communist Edith Segal. The New Dance
Group offered affordable after-work classes. Ten of these groups united
under the umbrella of the Workers Dance League, with its incendiary
slogan, "Dance Is a Weapon in the Revolutionary Class Struggle." By
1932, Anna Sokolow had formed her own Theater Union Dance
Group, and her Graham colleagues Sophie Maslow and Lily Mehlman joined her in orienting choreography to political and social goals,
drafting other Graham students and company members to perform
with them. However—young, strong, and fierce—they never missed a
single one of Martha's classes and rehearsals, and she repaid their dedication as best she could.

When five dancers who'd been in Graham's group in the early
1930s were brought together in a panel at the New School for Social
Research in 1994, they glowed at the remembered luxury of the short
tours they went on during those lean years and the minimal pay they
received. *Then* they ate, oh yes! A sponsoring woman's club or university organization might have been surprised at how quickly the dancers

scarfed up whatever might have been provided at a post-performance reception.

Their New York days were long. Because Graham taught classes to working girls seeking exercise and artistic vision when they finished their daily jobs, her company began their daily class around 8:00 p.m. and rehearsed after that—sometimes past midnight. All were summoned to rehearse, even though, on some nights, they did more sitting around than dancing (Martha frequently hit a roadblock in her creativity). Too, 1931 had been a lean year for them in terms of performances. Martha Graham and Group had only two New York engagements in the spring following the Dance Repertory season—a single date on a series held at Washington Irving High School in March and an appearance at the Guild Theatre in April. On March 18 the Century Club in Pennsylvania presented Graham in a solo concert, and in late May and June she was rehearsing and performing in *Electra*. The program on which *Dithyrambic* premiered took place at the Martin Beck in December.

The year 1932 turned out to be better for her, in good part because of her manager. Years later, Lincoln Kirstein wrote admiringly of Frances Hawkins, who had served him well too: "The daughter of a distinguished labor lawyer in Denver, she had absconded from Bryn Mawr to perform for several seasons in vaudeville in a acrobatic adagio act. There was little about vaudeville she didn't know; American vaudeville was at once her preparatory school and postgraduate course in theatrical administration."

Frances Hawkins (who at one point shared an apartment with Graham) eventually secured four New York performances for Graham and the group or for Graham as soloist in the early winter and spring and one in November, plus more than a dozen engagements in cities that included Washington, D.C., Boston, and Philadelphia during the first half of the year and again in November.

The young Graham dancers who had been granted Neighborhood Playhouse scholarships had more than enough to do. For instance, a program presented for two afternoons and evenings in June showed off its gifted students in a number of areas. Among those whom Laura Elliott had coached in drama were Dorothy Bird presenting a speech from Ferenc Molnár's *Liliom* and Georgia Graham giving one from Rudolf Besier's *The Barretts of Wimpole Street*. After Graham's students displayed their technical prowess, those taking Horst's Pre-Classic Forms class offered their own compositions.

At the Neighborhood Playhouse, Horst developed the two courses that he would teach until the year of his death—the later iterations taking place at the Juilliard School of Music. Bypassing the nineteenth-century compositions that he thought too emotional and heavily orchestrated, he began working with music of the Baroque era—pieces that were meant to accompany or suggest dancing. The students in his Pre-Classic Forms class didn't attempt to learn the actual steps of such social dances as the courante, gigue, sarabande, pavane, and gavotte; they mastered the musical structure and the ambiance without attempting to impersonate the court ladies who might have performed such dances. Those dancers who took his Modern Forms class absorbed the pieces of contemporary music that he played for them on the piano and came back with solo studies labeled, for example, as "Archaic" or "Primitive."

In the wake of *Primitive Mysteries*, Graham had begun to refer to certain of her dances as parts of a "Primitive Cycle." Her 1931 solos *Dolorosa* and *Two Primitive Canticles* (now simply known as *Two Canticles* and identified in programs as "Primitive seeking wed to ecclesiastical ritual") were followed by *Incantation* ("A primitive evocation of natural forces by means of dance"). In February 1932 *Ceremonials* ("Virgil Interlude," "Song of Vengeance," "Interlude," and "Sacred Formula")—a group work led by Graham and featuring Lillian Shapero and Mary Rivoire (the latter one of Graham's most cherished dancers)—also earned a subtitle with "primitive" in it, despite its allusion to Virgil, the Roman author of *The Aeneid* and Dante's guide through the Underworld. At this time, the term "primitive" had not yet been tarnished by the air of condescension that ultimately came to hang over it, and one may imagine that Graham linked these dances in primitivism not just to give them the status of belonging to an opus dominated by *Primitive Mysteries*, but to universalize and dignify their cultural aspect. Audiences, in other words, should not expect to see tribal dances around a hypothetical campfire.

A welcome honor, with money attached to it, came Graham's way during that 1932 February season. Early in the previous year, when she had been feeling pinched economically, she had written a letter to Henry Allen Moe, the head of the John Simon Guggenheim Memorial Foundation, saying in the course of it, "I need help badly." Perhaps spurred on by Mary Wigman's forthcoming American tour—indeed goaded by it—she had applied to the Guggenheim for funding that would enable her and Horst to travel to Europe, where they would live for seven weeks and perform there "to get European recognition." Her manager, Frances Hawkins, Martha tells Mr. Moe, is sure that dates would materialize. She supplies a projected budget and requests $1,800.

To bolster her reputation, Graham submitted the names of twenty-seven prominent people who might be willing to recommend her for a fellowship. Moe and his associates were surely impressed that of the twenty-seven, twenty-one responded by the December deadline: conductors, composers, writers, educators, and others. Predictably, they waxed eloquent on her behalf. Leopold Stokowski said that he considered her "one of the greatest dancers not only of America but of the world" and bolstered his opinion by listing the many countries whose dances he had seen. Henry Cowell, who composed works for numerous modern dancers, linked Doris Humphrey and Graham as twin leaders in American dance, but acknowledged the latter to be "the only dancer in America whom I could truly recommend for a fellowship."

The grant, if approved, would be the first Guggenheim awarded to someone in the field of dance, and those writing in support of Graham had been asked to justify supporting such a radical step. Most of them tackled this question fervently as well. Wallingford Riegger, a composer who had worked with Graham, wrote that the kind of dances she made and performed constituted a "creative art on a par with the drama, music and sculpture." The musician/composer/conductor Carlos Salzedo thought her "one of the greatest creative artists of the day—along any line."

However, Graham's friend Edith J. R. Isaacs of *Theatre Arts Monthly* raised what could have been an oblique cavil in her otherwise enthusiastic letter: "I do not think our dancers should be sent abroad to study with foreign teachers. We must create our own systems and our own expression."

Anyone reading some of Moe's correspondence with Graham can sense that he was increasingly impressed and charmed by her and very much wanted to see her receive a fellowship; still, he and those at the Guggenheim considering her application may have taken note of Isaacs's remarks. On February 19, 1932, Moe wrote Graham a letter implying that the trip to Europe was not a project worthy of the foundation's support and asking if she could rethink her request. Four days later, she replied with a touching honesty. She had wanted to become acquainted with what was going on in European dance, but hadn't thought that project in itself to be an appropriate Guggenheim one. Now she sees, she says, that seeking funding for a hoped-for European tour was inappropriate. After offering her vision for dance in her own country, she amends her proposal: "To me the answer to the dancer on this side of the Atlantic is to turn to the land itself; to find what we are before we can dance what we are." Therefore, her new plan would be to travel with Horst to Mexico, specifically the Yucatán, to study the dance culture there in relation to what she had seen in New Mexico. She closes by offering Moe or anyone else at the foundation tickets to her recital at the Guild Theatre on February 28.

Moe responded with alacrity. Two days before that performance, he wrote telling her that she had a grant of $800 for studying "the native dances of Mexico and Yucatan" during four months of the upcoming summer. That spring, a writer, present at a tea that La Argentina gave in her stateroom aboard the *Île de France* before the ship set sail for Europe, overheard a conversation between the hostess and one of her guests, Martha Graham. In her "charming French," the great Spanish dancer reinforced Martha's plan, announcing that America had dances of its own and "American dancers did not need to use those of older lands."

In June, Martha and Louis embarked for Mexico on the *Morro Castle*.

They did not, however, stay away for the full four months. On August 6, Graham wrote to Moe from New Mexico, where she had the day before seen a Corn Dance at Santo Domingo. What prompted the early return? She confessed to being terrified on first arriving in Mexico—to the point of feeling ill. The land she called "dangerous" and "insatiable" might, she sensed, either swallow her up or tear her apart. She had not expected to feel a culture shock that affected her both physically and spiritually.

Yes, she explained, she had recovered enough to attend a fiesta in Puebla, but not much dancing was taking place in the summer heat. The composer Carlos Chávez had shown her a film of Native dances, and in the villages she visited, musicians had played for her. She talked dance with the minister of education, saw enough old-fashioned "art" dance to dismay her, and heard interesting music by Silvestre Revueltas and Higinio Ruvalcaba, as well as by Chávez himself. And photographs show her not only climbing the many steps of the Pyramid of the Sun in the ancient ruined compound of Teotihuacán, but kneeling on its small, flat summit, her arms lifted to the sky and an exultant smile on her face.

She assured the sympathetic Mr. Moe that the experience had been salutary, causing new questions and ideas to blossom in her mind. She did not offer him details about the violence that had alarmed her. It's possible that the three earthquakes that tore at the west coast of the country in July helped to unsettle the atmosphere. Too, the conflicts between the Catholic Church and the powerful Revolutionary Party were coming to a head in decisions on the government's part to make public schools nonsectarian and to close many churches (of the two hundred some churches in Mexico City, only twenty-five were permitted to hold services). The inevitable resentment simmering among Catholics may have been palpable, especially in the larger cities.

One might question, however, whether Graham was exaggerating a bit about the violence in Mexico or whether she had ever seriously considered spending four months in a country whose language and customs were foreign to her, especially with her two early-November tour dates for the company in Worcester, Massachusetts, and Philadelphia and a Sunday concert on November 20 at the Guild Theatre. Horst had duties to fulfill at Perry-Mansfield that summer, and Graham expected to visit Santa Barbara as usual and perhaps meet him in New Mexico in September. Following those rest periods, her schedule would be strenuous, and her creative mind was already at work.

For the New York performance she prepared five new solos and a group dance. Seventeen-year-old Bonnie Bird, who had finally graduated from the Cornish School and joined Dorothy Bird in New York to work with Graham and Horst at the Neighborhood Playhouse, wrote letters home that aimed to help her mother "see" those dances. Of *Prelude*, she said, "To this tumultuous flood of Chavez's chaotic music, Martha moved quickly, lightly, almost unconcernedly catching the changing tempi in amazingly dexterous foot rhythms. It was a frank, joyous greeting that finished as simply and startlingly as it began." Of *Dance Songs* (to music by Imre Weisshaus):

> It is an ingenious and exciting work. Of its four exquisitely danced solos, *Ceremonials* was like a sacred rite in which the earth, giver of great fruitfulness, was blessed. It was a sensitive and extremely stirring dance. *Morning Song* was full of exuberance and the joy of living, conveying the feeling of a clear, bright Indian morning. *Satyric Festival Song* was accomplished in the impudent, slightly mad style that is one of Martha's best, and *Song of Rapture* was serious and not at all in the usual sense of rapture. Formal in the beginning, it built logically to a beautifully controlled ecstasy that finished with simplicity.

Graham's style in this last work, thought Bird, had become "more positively lyric and pervaded by a great sense of clear, wakeful stillness."

John Martin noted that the Weisshaus score accompanied *Ceremonials'* four dances with "a single musical line. Sometimes a baritone sings alone, sometimes a drum punctuated his song and sometimes a flute carries the burden of the music." The program as a whole required a flute, oboe, cello, clarinet, and an assistant pianist for Horst.

Satyric Festival Song, which Graham subsequently detached from the other three sections, comes alive in photographs taken at a later date by Barbara Morgan. The dancer wears a long sheath of a dress with bold horizontal stripes. Her loose hair flying up, her jutting hips, her arms angling at elbows and wrists bespeak the impudence that Bird noted, along with Graham's eye for archaic Greek art. The title also suggests a play on words: alter a single letter and "satyric" becomes "satiric." (Martin found it "a ludicrous piece of grotesque buffoonerie.")

Graham's growing interest in the myths, drama, and art of Greece could also have produced the group piece entitled *Chorus of Youths—Companions*. Dorothy Bird's mother had to know that her daughter found it to be

> an exquisite thing for which Louis has written superb music. The dance is quite delicate and sensitive in mood, reminiscent of *Adolescence*, which we saw in Seattle. For me, it is one of the loveliest things Martha has done in this vein, despite the fact that she does not feel it is such a fine thing herself. She dressed the girls in white skirts, with solid bright red or blue tops with kerchiefs—almost like middy tops. Dorothy was very beautiful and danced extremely well. Everyone commented on her handsome blondness.

Buried in this excited account is a revealing point. Once the heat of creation was over and a new dance had been presented to the public—slightly obscured in Graham's mind by the intense pressure and irritating details that usually accompanied such occasions—she sat back and scrutinized what she had done. She did not shy away from self-criticism, and the opinions of others—if worthy of consideration—weighed in. Reviewers frequently addressed her revisions in their writing. Maybe a new costume altered the impression of a solo. Perhaps a group work had been tightened and strengthened. The dance first written about in a next-day review may not, therefore, be exactly the same dance seen weeks, months, or years later.

Graham surely needed those summer weeks of relaxation in Santa Barbara, given how full her schedule could become. She may well have had to read the New York comments on her November 20 concert the following day while on a train to Greensboro, North Carolina, where that night she performed ten solos with one intermission and Horst played two piano pieces to give her time to breathe and change costumes; two days later, they repeated the program at Randolph-Macon College in Ashland, Virginia.

Another project began almost immediately. One involved the actress Katharine Cornell, who had seen *Primitive Mysteries* and other dances in 1931 and become deeply impressed by Graham's work—attending her performances, offering financial assistance and friendship. Cornell had established scholarships at the Neighborhood Playhouse and may initially have heard about Graham through the Neighborhood Playhouse's Laura Elliott, who had coached Cornell in voice and diction, or through Edith J. R. Isaacs, who adored bringing together artists for whom she thought communicating would prove beneficial. Cornell and her husband, the director Guthrie McClintic, invited Graham to assist them on the movement aspects on a new production.

The year 1931 marked a turning point in Cornell's own career. At thirty-eight (a year younger than Graham), she was no pretty ingénue, but a tall, strongly built woman with a large-featured face that carried to the top balcony. She and McClintic formed their own production company and staged *The Barretts of Wimpole Street*, which was a considerable cut above three other plays in which she had recently starred. Stark Young, writing in *Theatre Arts Monthly*, had decried two of the offending works (Michael Arlen's long-running *The Green Hat* and Somerset Maugham's *The Letter*) for their "vulgar plausibility" and labeled the third, *Dishonored Lady* by Edward Sheldon and Margaret Ayer Barnes, "appalling." To Brooks Atkinson of the *Times*, remarking on Cornell's performance in Rudolf Besier's play as the poet Elizabeth Barrett Browning (playing opposite Brian Aherne as Robert Browning), "the disciplined fury that she has been squandering on catch-penny plays becomes the vibrant beauty of finely wrought character."

Cornell and McClintic's choice of a second production was more unusual, and for this one they needed Graham's assistance. Cornell had commissioned Thornton Wilder to translate into English André Obey's *Le Viol de Lucrèce*, a play based on Shakespeare's long narrative poem *The Rape of Lucrece*. Wisely, the actress did not choose to make her Shakespearean debut playing Cleopatra or any other well-known Shakespearian heroine. In *The Rape of Lucrece*, an unidentified narrator recounts the background and the action, with quotes enclosing the words spoken (primarily) by the two principal characters. Lucrece is the virtuous wife of a Roman general, one of whose officers, Tarquin, confronts her when he knows she is alone, rapes her, and demands her silence. Should she refuse his attentions, he will kill both her and a handsome household slave and lay them together as proof of her wantonness (and his own unimpeachable morals). In the end, she summons her husband, tells him and his companions what occurred, and commits suicide on the spot.

Obey's play required a large cast—sixteen characters listed, plus additional servants, soldiers, and citizens. Few of these had lines to speak. Two elaborately masked narrators (played by Blanche Yurka and Robert Loraine) explain the plot and the feelings behind the actions. Only at the end of the first act, the rape scene, does Lucrece open her mouth (to implore, argue, and rage against her attacker); Tarquin (portrayed by Cornell's *Barretts of Wimpole Street* costar, Brian Aherne) disappears after their encounter.

There was a spare, much-praised set by Robert Edmond Jones, and musical interludes by Deems Taylor led into each scene, but given the structure of the play, much of the tale had to conveyed by pantomime and silent acting. The performers mimed imaginary props. Tarquin sneaked to Lucrece's chamber through what the actor, hiding now and then behind a pillar, had to convey to be many rooms and corridors. It is easy to see why Cornell and McClintic wanted to have Martha Graham beside them devising useful strategies and suggesting movement ideas, and she went from her two southern recitals to Cleveland, where *Lucrece* had its first tryout on November 29. According to Agnes de Mille, Cornell and McClintic paid Graham $500, which would have been extremely helpful in that lean year.

When *Lucrece* opened in New York's Belasco Theatre on December 20, 1932, the program included the information that "Miss Cornell and Mr. McClintic gratefully acknowledge Miss Martha Graham's valuable assistance in this production." Six days later, a drawing of Cornell appeared on the cover of *Time* magazine.

Cornell must also have been happy to read the following words in *The New York Times*: "The high, white tones of her voice, the deep grace of her submission, the horror that burns in her eyes and the pride that never surrenders to despair disclose her as a tragic actress who can touch greatness and sustain greatness by the sublimity of her spirit."

Although the critics praised the actors in *Lucrece*, they deprecated the literary quality of the script. Wilder, who had yet to write his Pulitzer Prize–winning plays *Our Town* and *The Skin of Our Teeth*, was not—for all his writerly talents and his command of French—an ideal playwright to translate into English Obey's play and what of Shakespeare's poem had sifted into it. "Stilted" was one of the words critics used to describe the result. Cornell later thought that everyone involved had loved the production too much, and she didn't think the rape scene came off well. In her autobiography she wrote, "I agreed with one of the critics who said that we looked like a couple of Vassar girls having a pillow fight. I'm convinced now that the only way to do it is as they did it in Paris—with two dancers." Despite the brevity of the New York run (four weeks), *Lucrece* established Cornell as an artist willing to take risks. Like her friend Martha.

Before *Lucrece* opened in New York, Graham was taking what turned out to be a different, less elitist sort of risk with a project that had signs of bringing in some money for her, Horst, and her dancers. Samuel "Roxy" Rothafel was opening an immense new variety theater in New York. Radio City Music Hall boasted a ballet company of eighty dancers, headed by Patricia Bowman and directed by Florence Rogge, plus forty-eight "Roxyettes" set in motion by Russell Markert. The December 27, 1932, opening was conceived as a gala spectacle to astound the potential six thousand ticket holders. The Sixth Avenue elevated railroad had its Fiftieth Street station painted silver for the event.

Did Rothafel remember Graham from her Denishawn days, when

Shawn devised prologues for the entrepreneur's Los Angeles movie theater? Maybe. He remarked publicly that he considered her the greatest dancer in the world and gave her and her company members a tour of the new theater. The program was a preposterous surfeit of high art, low comedy, and acrobatic feats. Graham, increasingly interested in Greek matters, devised for her company *Choric Dance for an Antique Greek Tragedy* to music composed by Horst. Of the evening's sixteen numbers, this was the fifteenth. Preceding it were performances by the Music Hall's two resident dance companies (Harald Kreutzberg created *The Angel of Fate: A Dramatic Dance Scene* for the ballet company, pillaging his own repertory for material). Fraülein Vera Schwartz of the Berlin State Opera sang a song from Johann Strauss's *Wiener Blut* and appeared in several excerpts from the opera *Carmen*. The Wallendas did their aerial act, and the Kikutas from Japan lay down and balanced objects and each other on their feet in their "Oriental Sisley Act." Ray Bolger tapped. So did the three Berry Brothers. The vaudevillian "Doc" Rockwell performed two of his comic sketches impersonating a member of the medical profession. Those spectators who stayed past midnight saw a finale that featured some of the groups and individuals who had already performed (including the members of the Tuskegee Choir and the Roxyettes), as well as a few newcomers (Weber and Fields, tenor Jan Peerce).

If the performance was a five-hour marathon, imagine the dress rehearsal (a two-days, two-nights affair). Think of the "Contour Curtain," touted as the "first of its kind in the world" and operated by thirteen motors. Picture the revolving stage that could hold three hundred people and a horse or two. Much could go wrong, as one Graham dancer made very clear:

> The stage floor was still moving as I got to my place. Through a sliver of light coming from below I could see scores of performers and a horse from *Carmen*, the previous act, still walking around. They were on the lowered upstage section of the stage, while we performed on the downstage area. I had to lie on my back, feet toward the audience, exactly where two interlocking blades of the stage came together and

I could feel the restless floor underneath me just beginning to settle. It was a terrifying experience.

Louis Horst was conducting. At the drum roll we sat up in second position, a rather startling effect; you didn't see us, and then you did, but not in what would be called "a ladylike position" even though we wore skirts. We filled the whole width of the stage with our dancing, but hardly 20 feet of its depth. Only a cloth curtain masked the huge drop onto the set below, making us very nervous when we had to move backwards upstage.

The second night was fraught with mishaps for Horst. The orchestra pit began to rise, unaccountably. A violinist too near the edge had his instrument's fingerboard sliced off. The percussionist—exhausted from the interminable final rehearsals—fell asleep, and the big drumroll—a cue for the dancers—never materialized. A sportswriter gave Graham's company a good review. "He especially loved Martha's dances," said Bonnie Bird, "because the girls galloped over the stage at such a fantastic pace."

John Martin was not enamored, but he lauded Graham for her heroic effort to fill the vast space not only with her group but with her small self: "She ran furiously, she leaped, she extended herself to fit the stage at her disposal with a composition worthy of its dimensions. Yet with all the exhibition of what for her amounted almost to bravura, she managed to keep pure the savage force, the archaic splendor of heroic emotion upon which she based her dance." He couldn't help wishing that the whole production had been given to her so that she might stage "the hypothetical Greek tragedy of which this dance was but a choric fragment." (More than a decade later, beginning with her *Cave of the Heart*, he was to see her create that tragedy.)

Not many spectators got a chance to see what Graham had devised; the evening's program was reduced bit by bit. Her presentation lasted less than a week (Rothafel had had a heart attack, so perhaps others made the decision). She and members of the group went to the theater every night and sat there—determined to be paid in full, whether or not they were allowed to perform. One former company member,

Martha Hill, recalled, "We diehards made a point of calling the box office to place a ticket order for a theater party. I'd ask when the group would be performing. To the answer, 'Martha Graham isn't on the schedule,' in protest I said, 'Graham isn't on? Well then, cancel!'"

In an article headlined "Roxy Slips," the *New Haven Register* reported, "It took exactly one week for the much-publicized Radio City Music Hall in Rockefeller Center to recant its original vaudeville policy and become just another movie house next to the Sixth Avenue L, where you can ride in glory to smoke cigarettes on the mezzanine and watch the pantomime of the pseudo General Yen drinking bitter tea."* The live spectacle was reduced to a lavish appetizer, as it was in Rothafel's other theaters.

Graham refused to think of the whole experience as an entirely bitter one. Never one to let a dance that had involved weeks of rehearsal—and whose subject interested her—slide into darkness, she pulled a solo for herself out of *Tragic Patterns: Three Choric Dances for an Antique Greek Tragedy* for a February 1933 performance in New Jersey; and for the company's May 4 performance at the Guild Theatre, she reworked and expanded the piece into *Tragic Patterns*— adding "Chorus for Maenads" and "Chorus for Suppliants" to the "Chorus for Furies" that had made its debut at Radio City Music Hall.

Throughout the 1930s, Graham's association with the Neighborhood Playhouse led to connections with playwrights, directors, and actors—many of the latter having come to Broadway from classes in which she worked their bodies into expressive instruments. Imagine how shaken up a young actress's dreams of glory might have been when Martha asked her and several other girls in her class to recite the speech that Hecuba delivered after the fall of Troy in Euripides' play named after her, at the same time rolling slowly down the flight of four stairs leading from the stage to the auditorium floor. She had one student actor recite Hamlet's "To be or not to be" bending over the one leg that he had lifted onto the studio barre. In both cases, the effort yielded

---

* The writer is referring to the Frank Capra movie *The Bitter Tea of General Yen*, which, on January 3, 1933, became the first film to play at Radio City Music Hall.

excellent results. She also kept up with her former students—attending their plays and films and occasionally offering sage bits of advice.

Not only did procuring money to maintain her company figure in Graham's acceptance of the occasional theater job during the 1930s; perhaps, too, she thought that being associated with a successful play could bring new audiences to her dance performances. There can be no doubt that she gleaned something from each experience outside the rigorous and profoundly idiosyncratic works she created for her company, even if she learned that there were some projects she would prefer never to undertake again.

One such project came her way in January 1933, undoubtedly accompanied by a sizable fee: she was to direct and choreograph *Six Miracle Plays* in preparation for February performances. According to Bonnie Bird, Graham was "roped into [it] against her will." Under the rubric of the Stage Alliance, two artists, Natalie Hays Hammond and Alice Laughlin, had set out to produce Hammond's selections of excerpts from six plays dating from the time between the eleventh and the fifteenth centuries, and one, *The Miraculous Birth and the Midwives*, drawn from William Hone's *Ancient Mysteries Described, Especially the English Miracle Plays*, an examination of unpublished texts in the British Museum. The women (Laughlin not yet thirty years old and Hammond thirty-eight) had met while traveling through the Near East. They shared—or came to share—an interest in medieval art in all its forms. Both had been born wealthy; Hammond's father had struck oil out west and Laughlin's was a Pittsburgh steel man (who may or may not have been familiar with the Graham family). Hammond designed the costumes, with careful references to medieval colors and patterns; Laughlin provided simple sets, including a three-level one to indicate Hell, Earth, and Heaven in the fifteenth-century morality play *The Magdalen*. They rented the Guild Theatre for two Sundays, February 5 and 12, and Graham set to work.

In each play, the text was spoken by narrators while others danced or mimed the events. The distinguished Danish actor Paul Leyssac spoke the words of the French plays: *Les Trois Rois*, *Les Trois Maries*, and *The Magdalen*. John O'Shaughnessy delivered the texts of the English plays, and the well-known actress Alma Kruger (then in her sixties) added her voice to *The Magdalen* and to *The Lamentation of the Virgin Mary*, which Graham performed as a solo.

Many of the dancers Graham recruited had worked with her before on one project or another—among them John Glenn, William Matons, and Kenneth Bostock from the Humphrey-Weidman camp (Bostock and John Harrington had also been at Seattle's Cornish School). Four of Graham's steadfast girls (Joan Woodruff, Lillian Shapero, Dorothy Bird, and Mary Rivoire) were in the cast, as was her sister Georgia. She herself appeared as the Virgin in four of the six playlets.

Three of these were structured as plays within plays. In *La Nativité*, as enacted in a cathedral at midnight on Christmas Eve, five deacons, garbed in their ceremonial robes, played the shepherds while bishops took the roles of midwives. *The Miraculous Birth and the Midwives* took place in a Franciscan monastery, with the performers portraying the monks who played minor characters. In *Les Trois Maries*, an Easter drama, the relevant roles were undertaken by cast members costumed as monks and nuns.

Most of the performers played multiple parts. Georgia Graham, Bird, and Rivoire came to the tomb of Jesus as Mary Magdalen, Mary Salome, and Mary Jacobee in *Les Trois Maries*. Shapero played a Child Angel in that, as well as Envy in *The Magdalen*, while Bird played Lechery and Rivoire undertook Wrath.

This was not Graham's first foray into playing the Virgin Mary, nor was it her first venture into the naivete and simplicity of woodblock prints and illustrations in medieval manuscripts. She staged the scenes with groupings and poses and telling movements designed to bring the spoken texts to life. Reticence must have determined the depiction of at least one scene. Salome and Zelome, the two monks-as-midwives, have been summoned by Joseph to attend to Mary. When these "midwives" arrive, Jesus has already been born, and yet, asserts Mary, she is still a virgin. Zelome does a quick examination and determines that this is the case. When doubtful Salome reaches for Mary's garment, her hand becomes paralyzed. An angel intervenes; Salome apologizes and is healed.

Graham did not have an easy time of it. Some of the costumes, for instance, were so elaborate that they both inhibited and concealed the performers' movements, and there may have been other obstacles. Bonnie Bird wrote to her mother that "Martha hates directing plays, but she is being very good about it . . . Poor darling, she is so tired of contending with stubborn people when she wants to do her own work."

The overlap of scenes featuring the miraculous birth and the links between the various characters named Mary may have been somewhat confusing to audiences. The critics showed off their erudition in regard to the texts, and the principal dance writers who usually championed Graham—Martin of the *Times* and Mary Watkins of the *New York Herald Tribune*—while lauding aspects of her performance, found much to criticize. Still, John Mason Brown of the *New York Post* wrote that in visual terms, the production was "possessed of a kind of loveliness that is all but unknown in our culture." Graham's dress in three graduated shades of pink, her crimson cloak, and a light shining on her, as if from a cathedral window, charmed viewers. The brown-and-white habits of the early Franciscans were striking. Only Stark Young, the theater critic of *The New Republic*, writing several weeks after the second performance, provided details of the staging. Pointing out Graham's "remarkable" inventions in terms of gestures and groupings in *The Miraculous Birth and the Midwives* and *Les Trois Maries*, he went on to say,

> Sometimes they were motifs—the Virgin after the doubts and the miracle, laying her cheek against St. Joseph's palm, or the shepherds breaking into a dance as they moved toward her, or the monk-midwives kneeling whenever the angel passed, circling around the group with the Virgin and child—in these and many other motifs the invention was of a sweetness and imagination for which words can only be silly.

Young also praised the "gentle honesty and tenderness" of the performers and their lack of showiness. He did, however, share one cavil with Martin: during the middle section of *The Lamentation of the Virgin*, Graham mimed the spoken words too closely.

What she accomplished—or hadn't been able to accomplish—in *Six Miracle Plays* may have led her to accept a less prestigious but also challenging theatrical assignment—devising movement within a rather unusual play, as well as dance interludes between scenes that would augment the feelings expressed in the text. The play, *Iron Flowers* by Cecil Lewis, was performed for a week in June at the Westchester County Center in White Plains, and Paul Creston provided music for the dances. It's not clear whether Creston got Graham involved in the project (his wife, Louise Creston, danced in her company) or whether Graham was given the job and proposed him as a composer.

The dancers she supplied—Mary Rivoire, Anna Sokolow, Sophie Maslow, Ailes Gilmour, and Louise Creston—were onstage in all the spoken scenes. In this tale, of a young woman in love with a married man who finds her feelings for him gradually eclipsed by her moral sense, two additional dancers could be seen as versions of the leading characters played by Gale Sondergaard and John Bukler. (One wonders how this early experience of doubling characters may have fed into her later works, such as the 1955 *Seraphic Dialogue*, with its several aspects of Joan of Arc.) The dancers were Jerome Andrews (then in the Radio City Music Hall chorus and at some point a student of Graham's) and Vera Milcinovic, a Croatian dancer who performed under the name of Tashamira.

The device of dance interludes related to the plot of a play could be traced back to Molière's *comédies-ballets* of the seventeeth century, but to the White Plains audiences and critics, the experience was a novel one to be marveled over, argued about, and questioned. The director, Herbert Biberman, who was married to Sondergaard, had prepared them for what he promised would be "an adventure in the theatre." (By 1936 they had both immigrated to Hollywood.)

It was May before Graham and her dancers had another Broadway performance, but earlier in the spring—in addition to preparing new dances and rehearsing and revising old ones—she and Horst took her solos to theaters as near as Newark and as distant as Detroit, and the group appeared with her at Bennington College in Vermont (where Martha Hill was teaching, where the students and faculty turned out, and reviewers, predictably, raved), as well as in New York City at Columbia University and at Washington Irving High School. In April, Graham lectured in Springfield, along with several other speakers on dance.

In addition to *Tragic Patterns*, the May concert at the Guild Theatre featured two new solos for Graham: *Elegiac*, set to Paul Hindemith's Music for Unaccompanied Clarinet, and *Ekstasis*, for which Lehman Engel provided music. The image of *Ekstasis* can be evoked more strongly than that of *Elegiac* through Barbara Morgan's photographs of it and the extraordinary costume Graham devised. The long tube of the sleeveless dress that she wore was made of a coarsely knitted thread that could, nevertheless, become translucent enough to reveal the shape of her legs when she stretched them the modest foot or so apart that it permitted. A two-finger-thick roll of the same material circled her neck, and another girdled her body just beneath her breasts. The effect in the photos is that of a statue dug from Mycenaean soil that evokes a living, breathing celebrant of an ecstatic rite. Martin acknowledged that with *Ekstasis*, Graham had "moved into a new field" and "touched a new level of achievement."

In responding to *Tragic Patterns*, the *Times* critic echoed his earlier prescient remarks about a possible mythic drama in Graham's future: "The whole suite has tremendous force behind it and a theatrical quality that suggests what Miss Graham might do with the production of an entire Greek tragedy."

Her work was not always received enthusiastically or written about favorably. At one of her recitals in the South, Horst's piano solos were applauded more vigorously than was her dancing. The Detroit critics wrote uncomprehending and denunciatory reviews. Worse, in the January 1933 issue of *Dance Culture*, four people appraised her, two of them anonymous. Of those who signed their articles, Oliver Sayler presented an opinionated but fair-minded view of Graham's artistic development, but Lucile Marsh was harsh, disappointed that the woman she had considered a "first-rate artist" had gone astray, her creative "spark snuffed out" due in part to the attention she had received. ("Selfish adoration, insincere ravings, biased criticism, stupid imitators can do this to an artist."). And even more severe: "Today she is an introspective craftsman mulling over esoteric forms, repeating sterile devices with the intellectual absorption of a mathematician. Simplicity has become a formula, a pose; drabness an obsession."

It is not reported how much crockery Graham broke upon reading this or how long it took Horst to pry her out from under her bedclothes and get her back to work.

She may have had more practical issues to worry about. Although neither she nor Horst managed to save much money, a banking crisis had been simmering. As 1932 ended, more than thirteen million Americans were unemployed. Banks across the country had been in a perilous condition for some months, aggravated by people alarmed enough to withdraw their savings when banks declared unexpected three-day "holidays." By early 1933, more than nine thousand banks had failed. To stem this, on March 6, 1933, the new president of the United States, Franklin Delano Roosevelt, closed all the nation's banks for seven days, during which time Congress passed the Emergency Banking Act and the economy pulled itself out of catastrophe.

Sometime during the spring of 1933—presumably after the recovery—Graham's mother (perhaps with her husband) paid a visit to New York. Bonnie Bird found her to be "a darling—old-fashioned, very wise, gentle, homey and unlike Martha, whom she worries about. I doubt if she can see Martha as a great person. When Martha dances, Mrs. Duffy worries about her tiredness. Typical mother."

And Graham persevered, and her dancers managed to eat. Also, that spring, she moved her classes and rehearsals to a long, relatively narrow studio at 66 Fifth Avenue, just south of Twelfth Street, where she would remain for almost twenty years.

In November, Cornell and McClintic called on her again. They were planning to embark on a strenuous twenty-nine-week tour of American cities, presenting three plays in rotation: *The Barretts of Wim-*

pole Street, George Bernard Shaw's *Candida*, and *Romeo and Juliet*. Cornell had evidently taken seriously the remark with which John Martin had ended his review of *Lucrece*: "By every sign, she is the actress Shakespeare needs in the current theatre."

Basil Rathbone played leads in all three plays, and a promising eighteen-year-old actor, Orson Welles, was cast in three roles: Elizabeth Barrett's brother Octavius, Marchbanks to Cornell's Candida, and Mercutio. Graham choreographed dances for the Capulet's ball in Shakespeare's tragedy, as well as other incidental dances, and worked on movement for the scene in Juliet's tomb and possibly on the duel between Mercutio and Tybalt. When the company traveled to Buffalo, Cornell's hometown, for the final rehearsals and first performances, Martha went along.

Her skills as a costume designer also came in handy. The gown Juliet was supposed to wear for the balcony scene proved, in Cornell's view, to be "completely out of key." The actress recalled that on the play's opening day, Graham went out and bought "some soft white nun's veiling, and made me a flowing, classic robe which was beautiful and right . . . When I got to the theatre at half past seven I found her still in my dressing-room, sweeping up threads. I was very touched, but that is Martha's way." When the long tour ended and *Romeo and Juliet* opened in New York at the Belasco on December 20, 1934, the designer, Jo Mielziner, copied Graham's contribution. For its Broadway run, McClintic rethought the entire production, again calling on Graham to tune up the dances and other movement aspects of the production.

It is tempting to imagine Graham's influence on the production when you read words written by the critics. Cornell may have been in her late thirties, but her Juliet was "an eager child, rushing toward love with arms stretched out." And: This Juliet "moves gracefully and lightly; it is endlessly haunting in its pictorial qualities."

Graham was always fascinated by compelling performers and interested in what she might learn from them. In later years she recalled how much she had admired Edith Evans, the great British actress, who played (not for the first time in her career) Juliet's nurse in the

Cornell-McClintic Broadway production. (Evans, she said, had reminded her of Lizzie, who had been so important to her as she was growing up.) "I went up to her during a quiet moment of rehearsal and said, 'Would you mind if I asked you one thing. From what point did you take the characterization of the Nurse, or is this too much to ask?' 'Oh, no,' she said. 'I will tell you the exact line. It is "I think it best you married with the County."'" How practical! Had Juliet married Paris, as had been planned, her nursling might have had a longer and simpler (if stodgier) life.

December 5, 1933, brought rejoicing to much of the population of the United States, with Congress's ratification of the Twenty-First Amendment, which repealed the Eighteenth and ended Prohibition's thirteen-year reign (and the hegemony of New York City's tens of thousands of speakeasies). Graham and Horst, who had no thought of producing offspring, had always shown special fondness for the Bird girls, who were far from their respective homes in the state of Washington; the two saw their first Wagnerian opera, shepherded to the Metropolitan by Martha and Louis. In December, recalled Bonnie, "Martha suddenly got the idea of taking us to some new tap room to have our first real cocktail . . . She laughed when Louis said, 'Well now, maybe our daughters are a bit young.' But she promised to take care. You would think we were still in rompers." Wine and beer had been freed from the ban earlier, and in any case, wine might have been the drink offered when the two young dancers were taken out to dinner by Louis and Martha during the Christmas season and gathered again at Martha's on New Year's Eve, on which occasion Martha read aloud to them from a book of Navaho legends.

As 1934 approached, a timely project for modern dance was already brewing in a small woman's college in Bennington, Vermont—one that would bring Graham, Humphrey, Weidman, and Hanya Holm out of summer-hot New York to teach and eventually to create new works. And Graham would soon turn her mind to other American legends, drawing her inspiration less from the country's Indigenous inhabitants than from its hardy pioneering settlers.

─9─

SUMMERING IN BENNINGTON, FORGING *FRONTIER*

L OOK AT THESE DANCERS! In still photographs and grainy film clips from the 1930s, they move like athletes but with the fervor of Dionysian revelers. They're leaping over an immense green lawn that butts against a low rock wall and then seems to fall away into nothingness. Beyond it are the Green Mountains of Vermont and above them a sky with cumulus clouds. In some of the images, the women (the dancers are almost all women) wear white outfits with cap sleeves and short wraparound skirts; they can add a longer skirt and be practically dressed up. Often they wear no-nonsense trunks and knitted tops, their bare midriffs showing the muscles needed to do what they do. They can drop from the air into a semi-split with a speed that shocks you, even on film.

You can identify some of them. Here's a film clip of young José Limón with two other male dancers; they're springing into the air—one leg bent in front, one bent in back—without moving from their spot. It's a leap that goes nowhere but up. Here's a woman in a skimpy top and a long, flared skirt that swirls around her as she races and bounds across the grass. Here's a female Graham dancer on her knees, executing what is still, eight decades later, called the "exercise on 6"; in profile to the camera, she arches and contracts, her powerful thighs supporting the swing of her action through the six moves.

Compared with the dancers of later generations, these lusty women and the few men among them look a bit rough around the edges; they appear to care less about perfectly pointed feet and beautifully sculptured positions than about impetus and a zest for movement. They are skilled and disciplined, yet—captured off the stage and under the sky—they present an image of dance that is both natural and spontaneous.

Then there are the snapshots. Martha Graham raises one leg in front of her, while her dancers, wearing identical white dresses, sit watching on the grass behind her, reinforcing her authority as their leader. Graham and Doris Humphrey sit side by side on some outdoor steps, looking intently at something we can't see. Graham, Humphrey, Charles Weidman, and Louis Horst have been captured sitting around a breakfast table, looking companionable; Weidman is laughing.

These archival images were taken at Bennington School of the Dance in summers between 1934 and 1938. Or in 1939, when the school was temporarily moved to Mills College in Oakland, California. In those years, student dancers and teachers of dance were exposed to the American choreographer-teachers who were deemed "The Big Four" of modern dance: Graham, Humphrey, Weidman, and Hanya Holm. During their appointed summer weeks on the campus, the choreographers also presented their dances and labored on new ones. In addition to fees, they received food and housing in pastoral surroundings—no small asset in America's Depression years. The musicians who accompanied their classes or the composers they were working with were also happy to spend time on the campus. Said one of them, "Bennington was the first time we had all eaten regularly for a long time."

Bennington College itself had been in existence for only two years. That it opened at all in 1932, one of the darkest years of the Depression, had been a triumph of reason and compromise over extravagance. Robert Devore Leigh, the first president of Bennington, and his board had had to scale down what they had planned in the 1920s. The original site was no longer available, and ambitious plans for a Gothic structure remained on paper. A new property, 140 donated acres of an existing farm on a plateau in North Bennington, came with buildings (such as barns and a chicken coop) that could be repurposed into offices, studios, and classrooms. New structures—big white clapboard houses—fit both the New England landscape and the college's innovations in terms of progressive education. Leigh might have been speaking of modern dance itself when he used the words "simplicity, directness, and relation to function" in speaking of the institution's atmosphere as well as of its role in educating young women. The land that had produced crops and dairy products was to yield creativity, independent thinking, and strong bodies.

Leigh's wife had heard of Martha Graham; Graham in turn recommended Martha Hill to devise and head a dance program at Bennington. Hill, a former student of hers and a dancer who had performed with her group, had become an experienced teacher. Already teaching graduate students in New York University's School of Physical Education, Hill split her weekdays between the two institutions. Bessie Schönberg—sidelined by an injury from continuing to perform with Graham—was her assistant. Unlike colleges that offered dance classes in their physical education departments (if at all), Bennington was to offer dance as a coequal of the other arts.

It was in part the need for economy and stringency during the Depression years that fostered a haven for professional dance companies on the Vermont campus; Bennington's administrative and maintenance staffs needed to be paid year-round. How to bring in money during the summers? Create an innovative program. Mary Josephine Shelly of Columbia Teachers College in New York became its administrative director (she and Hill had met as students at the Kellogg School of Physical Education in Battle Creek, Michigan).

The students who attended the six-week summer course at Bennington submerged themselves in dance—one might even say wallowed in it. They were offered graded classes in modern dance technique with Hill and/or Schönberg. They studied teaching methods with Hill. Faculty in the college's theater department instructed them in aspects of stage production. Advanced pupils could take Hill's composition class and study Music and Dance with Bennington's Gregory

Tucker. John Martin boned up on dance history and kept, in his words, "one step ahead of the class" he taught several times a week. Louis Horst taught Music Related to Movement the first year and in later years gave his Pre-Classic Forms and Modern Forms classes.

The major draw, of course, were the guest choreographers—Graham, Humphrey, Weidman, and Holm—teaching their dance techniques in overlapping two-week sessions. All but Holm performed works from their repertories in the theater housed on the top floor of the Commons building, while Holm (who had not yet founded her company) presented her students in a demonstration of the technique based on what she had learned in Dresden as a member of Mary Wigman's company and was developing at the Wigman School in New York. One hundred and three students enrolled that first summer at Bennington—all women; the youngest was fifteen, the oldest was forty-nine. Sixty-eight of them were teachers (mainly in college physical education departments) who had the good fortune to be on salaries all year.

Diversity was promoted as an attraction—at least within limits. Wrote Leigh in the *Bennington College Bulletin*'s February issue, "The modern dance, in common with the other arts of this period, is a diversified rather than a single style. At the same time, it possesses certain identifying characteristics which are common to all of its significant forms." The summer experience was a heady one. Exposing the students to the major figures of modern dance encouraged them to compare and evaluate the ideas these choreographer-teachers espoused and the works they presented onstage. They learned about the relation of music to dance and listened to the invited artists and scholars who gave concerts and lectures.

At Bennington, Graham and her colleagues had a place to work out new ideas and draft new dances. Also, in addition to providing training for the students and income for the artists, those summers fostered a growing public awareness of modern dance nationwide through those would-be dancers and established dance teachers who came from all over the United States to take the classes, see the performances, and hear the lectures. Many people who had never seen Martha Graham and her colleagues began to know her name.

The leaders of the Bennington School of the Dance were also aware of an inevitable downside: a crammed-in exposure to the various aesthetics could result in an inspired, but not always fully nourished, crop of physical education and dance teachers who would pass on to their students in schools and colleges around the nation what they had managed to learn in a few weeks (fortunately, more than a few appeared for several summers). One critic, mentioning the gains of the plan (dancers could eat, audiences would grow), brought out what he considered the less inspiring aspect of the Bennington summers: "The endless chains of pupils turned teachers in order to teach more pupils to be teachers." Yet some education, all agreed, was better than none.

Another way of arousing interest in modern dance had preceded the first Bennington summer and further spread its credos. In February 1934 Louis Horst recruited a select bunch of writers and—from his apartment—published the first edition of his monthly *Dance Observer.* Graham's dancers often assisted his helpers in circulating it. At twelve sheets, it was a modest publication, usually consisting of an article that raised ideas and theories about dance and/or music, plus reviews of performances. His timing was excellent, and not just for recruitment purposes. Bennington attendees and their students back home could swell its modest circulation, spreading ideas about modern dance in colleges across the country and stimulating those colleges to host performances of such talked-about choreographer-dancers as Graham.

Martha Graham and Group hadn't garnered much income during the first part of 1934 ($10 per performance was the usual fee for the dancers, and Graham plowed much of what she earned into fabric for costumes and other necessities). Nevertheless, they had a busy spring: a solo concert for Graham at the Guild Theatre on Sunday, February 18, and one for her and the company a week later; a March performance in Toronto by Graham and seven of her dancers (she offered to lend a tweed coat to Bonnie Bird so that the West Coast girl could better weather the northern cold); the performance at the Alvin in April, as well as one in the dance-supportive Washington Irving High School's auditorium; and a lecture-demonstration at one of John Martin's evenings at the New School. In addition, the Graham studio hosted two March concerts and another in April featuring work by company members. Graham and Horst also did a teaching stint at Sarah Lawrence College in Bronxville, where she met Joseph Campbell—whose writings on myth were to influence her considerably—and the student Jean Erdman, who four years later would marry Campbell and join Graham's company.

By summer, Graham needed a rest, and her Bennington weeks were only part of an unusually bucolic summer. The munificent Edith J. R. Isaacs rented a small cottage for her in Pound Ridge, New York. Dorothy and Bonnie Bird were taken along, and when not at Bennington, Horst joined the three of them. They procured a car for $75—a 1928 Model A Ford convertible that they nicknamed "Tookie the Tin Chicken"—and, with Bonnie at the wheel, they tooled around Westchester County and beyond, visiting Edgard Varèse and his wife on a rented houseboat and dropping in on Alexander Calder to investigate the possibility of his constructing sculptural objects for a dance Graham had in mind for the summer of 1935.*

With two tiny loft bedrooms for Martha and Louis and scant floor space in the small living room with its central fireplace, the girls slept on the equally small porch. Each morning, Bonnie and Dorothy did their floor exercises while Martha had her bath; then they repaired to the little foyer to do exercises standing in place, while she took over the living room. Graham was used to eating out at low-priced restaurants, and although she appreciated good food, she was not much of a cook. She did, claimed Dorothy, teach them how to make "a sensational pot roast," although Martha's recipe for "Italian style" green beans suggests more wit than culinary sophistication: take some partially cooked beans and pour olive oil over them.

---

* She and Louis had seen Calder's exhibit at the Pierre Matisse Gallery in Manhattan earlier in the year.

Graham's mother and stepfather drove east for a visit that involved a tour around New England after the summer session at the college was over. The two young dancers gave up their beds and slept elsewhere for the week, and Bonnie revised her formerly sympathetic portrait of Mrs. Duffy; now she found her "a difficult person who was continually dissatisfied," while Mr. Duffy came across as "a fussy Rotarian type, stubborn and loquacious." "They can be very sweet when they try," she added, "which is wrong because people should not have to try."

In a 1959 symposium at Connecticut College's American Dance Festival, Louis Horst, José Limón, Pauline Lawrence Limón, Bessie Schönberg, and Norman and Ruth Lloyd, who had been at Bennington during its first summer sessions, made it clear that when the work of the day was done, they hadn't always repaired exhausted to their beds. "Oh those first-year parties," recalled Norman Lloyd. There was, the symposium's participants agreed, a gathering in somebody's quarters every night. This wasn't New York City; proximity made socializing easy.

And the end of Prohibition seven months earlier could still be celebrated, and although Bennington was dry, well-stocked Hoosick Falls, New York, was just west of the state line. As Bessie Schönberg later reminded her colleagues, some of them, especially the teaching assistants like her, were younger than many of those they were teaching. "At 12 o'clock," said Norman Lloyd, meaning midnight, "the faculty would start running across the campus—jumping and screaming—to the horror of the students."

Events taking place far beyond Vermont were also to influence American dance in the 1930s in ways both political and artistic. The United States was not the only country to experience economic hardships. In March 1933 Adolf Hitler had become chancellor of Germany, his party elevated into power by the Depression's faltering economies as well as by the discontent that had been smoldering since the Armistice that ended World War I. Anti-Semitism grew rapidly in this climate. In April, Jewish businesses in Germany were boycotted, and in short order, a law forbidding Jews to hold positions in civic or state institutions went into effect. In August 1934, Hitler became führer as well as chancellor.

As Germany promoted nationalism and the preeminence of Aryan ancestry and embarked on its policy of *lebensraum*—expanding its power to take space beyond its present borders—American artists of the 1930s began to think more aggressively about qualities that defined their own country: its history, its democratic government, its open spaces and hardy pioneers, its conflicts between free thinking and intolerance, its optimism in the face of defeat.

Graham began her contribution to Virginia Stewart's *Modern Dance*, a compilation of vanguard choreographers' credos, with these blazing words: "To the American dancer I say: 'Know our country.' When its vitality, its freshness, its overabundant youth and vigor, its contrasts of plenitude and barrenness are made manifest in movement on the stage, we begin to see the American dance." Now was not the time to copy European ballet or "oriental" styles, she announced, continuing her argument: "An American dance is not a series of steps. It is more, infinitely more. It is a characteristic time beat, a different speed, and accent, sharp, clear, staccato. We know the American expression; we see the American gesture. Of things American the American dance must be made."

Two works that Graham premiered early in 1934 emphasized the power of her dancers in ways that affirmed this "American" image. In *Celebration*, to a score by Horst for trumpet and drums, there were fourteen women, divided into subgroups. Wearing identical dresses in deep blue and black, they jumped and jumped and jumped and jumped (a hundred times, one of them was sure), with only a brief seated section to power them up again. Barbara Morgan's later photographs of this piece show performers in the air, arrow-straight from head to pointed toes, the floor their springboard. The company dancer Frieda Flier remembered that they barely bent their knees to propel their takeoffs.

According to Bonnie Bird, more than a hundred people were

turned away from New York's Guild Theatre, where the program also featured a new trio for Dorothy Bird, Sophie Maslow, and Anna Sokolow, who wore floaty dresses and danced to music by Henry Cowell. Titled *Four Casual Developments*, the piece both countered and supported the athleticism of *Celebration* by satirizing the gentility expected of Victorian maidens.

Intégrales also involved the dancers in artful endurance tests. Created by Graham for an April concert at the Alvin Theatre, the piece was made possible by the Pan-American Association of Composers. Edgard Varèse's 1925 composition *Intégrales* was performed by eleven members of the Pan-American Symphony Orchestra on wind and brass instruments while four others handled seventeen different percussion elements. To this dense, dissonant score, the dancers also jumped many times. And ran and leaped. The work began with Graham atop a "mountain" constructed out of huddled dancers. Her first move was to step from one woman's back to another's until she reached the floor; her final undertaking was to encounter a clump of women again and climb up to stand triumphant atop them. Graham provided a subtitle of her own that suggested primality: *Shapes of Ancestral Wonder*. The sold-out performance, which included *Four Casual Developments*, *Primitive Mysteries*, and two of Graham's solos, *Two Primitive Canticles* and *Frenetic Rhythms*, may have attracted more than the usual dance audience, and spectators stood and cheered.

During the first Bennington summer, Graham was gestating a new group dance, for which Horst would compose a score. If *Celebration* and *Intégrales* conveyed images of buoyant and hardy young American women creating a tribe of their own, *American Provincials* inaugurated Graham's interest in choreographing dances that more directly conveyed aspects of the history of the nation. The theme of *American Provincials* was similar to that of *Heretic*, but it was clearly linked to the puritanical New England of Nathaniel Hawthorne's *The Scarlet Letter*. Graham—wearing a long, dark full-skirted gown with a broad white stripe down its front from neckline to below the waist—performed the first section, "Act of Piety," capturing, thought John

Martin, "the essence of the ferocious Puritan tradition." In "Act of Judgment," the women of the cast—who had been standing in judgment, barely visible, at the sides of the stage—took over the space as a malignant mob as soon as she walked away and left it. "Act of Piety" was not exactly what its title implied. Graham had lowered the costume's waistline to her hips, which accentuated their motion as, slack-bodied and lewd with her belly protruding, she advanced toward the audience. One critic referred to the atmosphere of *American Provincials* in such terms as "grim gauntness" and "remorseless rhythms." It was thought by some, but never clarified, that *American Provincials* tended slightly more toward theater, while *Heretic* told its vengeful story solely through pared-down dance. Although the full two-part piece was warmly received, it had a short performance history. Graham, however, included *Act of Piety* (minus the watching crowd) on a number of subsequent programs.

In the spring of 1935 she ventured into territory that was both personal and even more recognizably "American." The solo *Frontier* premiered in April as the first part of a suite called *Perspectives*. (The second part, *Marching Song*, in which she led Dorothy Bird, Sophie Maslow, and May O'Donnell to music by Lehman Engel, vanished almost immediately.)

For the first time, she commissioned a set. The American-born, half-Japanese sculptor Isamu Noguchi had never designed one before, but he had met Graham through Michio Ito in 1928. In 1929, the handsome twenty-five-year-old had a studio near hers in Greenwich Village and earned a living turning out bronze portrait busts. He made one of her. That year, his half sister, Ailes Gilmour, had gone straight from high school to study at the Neighborhood Playhouse (she danced with Martha Graham and Group in 1931–32). Noguchi understood the sparseness intrinsic to Graham's choreography, and his design for *Frontier* determined much about the choreography.

A single portion of a two-log fence sitting upstage center became Graham's home base, but it was not a barrier, and she never went behind it. The other part of Noguchi's decor was more abstract. A

V created by two thick white ropes anchored its point directly behind the fence while its ends stretched out and forward to the top corners of the proscenium arch, "thereby," wrote Noguchi, "cutting the stage space in a perspective delineation so that the whole area in that void seemed to jump out at the audience. I realized then that the sense of vastness could be accomplished through such simple means, by the placement and proportion of things, by the lighting, by the use to which these are put in the dance." His "ropes," like the costumes the dancers were used to sewing, demanded exacting handiwork; five dancers braided one hundred feet of cheesecloth to create them. To a viewer in the theater, the set suggests not just a vanishing perspective but an expanding one, and Graham's gaze took in a space that extended far beyond the actual boundaries her movements defined. Her original costume—innovative as always—was a long, full dress in a heavy pinkish-beige fabric, with something close to batwing sleeves of a lighter shade. In photographs, she looks almost as if she were wearing a short, open-fronted jacket over her dress, but that is an illusion. Her long hair is folded under and held away from her face by a white bandeau.

Frontier has been performed by a number of dancers in Graham's company over the years—most often excellently. But a black-and-white film (originally silent) made between 1936 and 1939 of the choreographer herself dancing the solo is a revelation. Standing in front of the fence, resting her hands on it, she stares forward, as if she is taking in an immensity of space. When she steps widely from side to side without traveling from her spot, she seems to be raring to go, yet needing to size up the landscape. She's comfortable with this fence, lifts one leg to rest on its top rail, and pulses up and down on the other leg. You might imagine her riding a horse, except that she goes nowhere in terms of actual territory. She lies back and lazes briefly along the fence, then sits back up, her arms folded around her bent knee. It's the stance of a woman settling into her home, daring anyone to move her.

At one point during this sequence she turns her head sharply from side to side, staring into the wings of the stage. She also lifts a hand, angled sharply at the knuckles, her fingers pressed together, and gazes skyward or bends to touch the ground. And, in that early film, she is still looking to her right when she suddenly tears herself away from the fence and begins to advance toward the audience. In the split second that Graham's gaze lingers in that direction, she (subtly, amazingly) gives you the sense of a woman newly alone—perhaps a husband is away at war—who is testing both her freedom and her necessary strength. When she sits on the floor and alternates splitting her legs apart and opening her arms, she might be metaphorically clearing a path and opening herself to the surrounding space.

Louis Horst's score for trumpet, flute, clarinet, bass clarinet, piano, and percussion begins with a stirring call to action by the two highest instruments, their summons almost shrill. Although their voices can mingle together softly, their stauncher rhythms suggest a bygone fife-and-drum band accompanying marching soldiers. It is to the drum alone that the woman begins to travel forward, hopping on one leg, swinging her other leg to the side and raising one arm, as if to hail the territory before her. Several times throughout the solo she travels this path and then makes the same step carry her backward toward the fence; the last time she does it, she no longer stares at the horizon; both her legs are bent in the air, and her head, arms, and body swing with the pleasure of cavorting in this way.

She repeatedly traces her almost militant forward-and-back path with a similar step—one that strides rather than jumps. Again she tosses one leg to the side as she advances, but in Graham's filmed performance, although her leg flies equally high each of the four times she does this, the action is not as mechanical as the drumbeats that accompany it; the effect is of a woman taking in increasingly deep and exhilarated breaths.

It is also in exhilaration that she embarks twice on a curving path, tipping her body forward as she kicks up one leg behind her. Once, she clasps both hands behind her back when she does this; the second time, one bent arm hovers near her brow. This woman, so dedicated to carving out her path, has suddenly had an another attack of girlish glee.

Her other path is one of right angles—an almost complete square. She delineates it always facing front, her arms at her sides, her feet taking swift little tiptoe steps, like a sewing machine stitching her world together. Forward, sideways, back, sideways. The next time she does this, she folds her arms in front of her; Graham executes this straightforwardly, without sentimentality, but the image could suggest that she is rocking an infant (some dancers in subsequent performances have dramatized this).

In the end, she is back on her fence, surveying the scene, and after she reaches out one arm as if to gather in her horizon, she folds her hand into a fist and settles it firmly down on her bent knee: the artist as pioneer—staking out her territory, reveling in her independence, and keeping her eyes on a vision of what she might accomplish.

Lincoln Kirstein, the young founder, with George Balanchine, of the company that would eventually become the New York City Ballet, hadn't always understood or appreciated Graham's predominant starkness, but he linked *Frontier* to "[Walt] Whitman's unrealized dream" and honored her for creating "a kind of candid, sweeping, and wind-worn liberty for her individual expression." In Leopold Stokowski's words, "Miss Graham steps from the American scene into lucid abstraction where one can feel one's own mind pushing against the horizon of its limitations and expanding in a new and altogether stimulating manner. The frontier she dances becomes any and all frontiers, physical or mental—due to this remarkable power of Miss Graham to portray the universal through the particular."

When Graham repeated *Frontier* on a program the following November, the audience tried hard to get her to repeat it (she wisely declined).

Looking back from the vantage point of Graham's works in the 1940s and her innovative approaches to narrative in dances that drew on Greek myth and drama, such as *Cave of the Heart*, *Errand into the Maze*, and *Night Journey*, it is interesting to contemplate the possible influence of discoveries she made during her intermittent forays into theater—even though she had undertaken these forays primarily to pull in a little income to sustain her own choreography and also, possibly, to keep her name before the theatergoing public. In late 1934, one of her jobs—a minuet in the play *Valley Forge*—may have contributed obliquely to her delvings into Americana. During March 1935, when she was preparing *Frontier* and the other part of *Perspectives* and rehearsing older works for her April concerts (as well as teaching classes at the Neighborhood Playhouse and in her own studio), she accepted a more demanding theater job—the most overtly political stage presentation in which she involved herself.

In choreographing movement for Archibald MacLeish's verse play *Panic*, she might also have drawn on knowledge she gleaned from working on *Seven Against Thebes* at the Cornish School and performing and choreographing material in Blanche Yurka's *Electra*. *Panic* was structured as a Greek tragedy, although its subject was a burning issue in contemporary America: the greed and ignorance that led to the disasters of the 1929 panic and the ensuing Depression. Actors playing various types of citizens opened the piece. Nine additional performers were cast as the unemployed. Five bankers argued and sounded off in the second scene, with the greatly gifted young Orson Welles (taking time away from his role as Mercutio in the Cornell-McClintic *Romeo and Juliet*) playing a much older Wall Street mogul (modeled, it is said, on J. P. Morgan)—a King Lear of sorts, arrogant and willful and, when ruined, sick with self-knowledge and primed for suicide. Graham was in charge of a chorus of ten men and thirteen women; these performers commented on the action in gestures, but unlike the chorus of classic Greek drama, they didn't speak. As for the other actors in street scenes, the author made clear in his preface to the printed play that "the attempt to use the crowd as an actor has resulted in a chorus speaking, not with the single voice of the Greek chorus, but with the many voices of the American crowd." His blank verse had the rhythms of contemporary speech—rhythms he felt to be "nervous, not muscular; excited, not deliberate; vivid, not proud," rhythms that Graham could attack or simmer beneath.

John Houseman had rented the Imperial Theatre for the final ten days of rehearsal. In his memoir he wrote that during that period, its stage "was mostly occupied by Martha Graham, her chorus, her metronome and her incredible energy. Actors who worked with her during those exhausting three weeks still talk with awe of the disciplined fervor and the rigid perfectionism with which she drove them—with charley horses and screaming tendons—through the slow, angular ballet that grew before our eyes out of the moods and rhythms of MacLeish's unrelenting three-beat lines."

All this effort culminated, as planned, in only three performances (on March 14, 15, and 16, with the show on the sixteenth featuring a post-performance discussion put together by the fiercely left-wing paper *New Theatre*). The critic Stark Young thought that Graham's "arrangement of the crowd groups" was the best thing in *Panic*, but it was a far-left critic who most revealingly described her approach: "Although the poet successfully carries across the footlights a nervous, staccato urban rhythm, the dancer slows down the figures and masses of the chorus into a Grecian frieze." The reviewer didn't care for Graham's approach, but it's evident that the slowed-down crowd movements—set against the single agitated voices and news headlines that the chorus watched blinking into life on an overhead screen at the back of the stage—helped to convey the paralyzing nightmare that the Crash precipitated.

Panic was produced by means of a $3,500 loan (almost a third of it from MacLeish) and lost all of it. Jo Mielziner designed the set for free and let it be known that the Imperial Theatre's stage was "so full of dust that all we had to do was light it up and magic happened." By special arrangement with Actors' Equity, the performers were guaranteed a fee for only one of the three performances and nothing for rehearsals. It is not known how much Graham was paid, nor whether she put the money to immediate use or salted it away for future production costs.

The play, thought its producer in hindsight, appeared onstage a little too late. The former stockbrokers he had come across selling apples were no longer so evident on New York streets, and the ticket prices he set for those three nights at the Imperial were high for the straitened times: $5.50.

Working with a large cast for *Panic* may have helped Graham shape her ideas for her 1935 project at Bennington that summer. American choreographers were aware of Rudolf Laban's "movement choirs," which, in his and others' hands, had proliferated in Germany and Austria. The performing groups, usually composed of amateurs, stressed architectural patterns that presented, on the positive side, an image of a harmonious, cooperative society and, on the negative side, a police state in which submissive hordes followed the decrees of a hidden dictator. In planning the Bennington School of the Dance, Martha Hill had decided that beginning in its second year, the four choreographers would take turns being in residence for the entire six-week summer session, and each would be given a chance to augment his or her company with dancers chosen by audition. Graham was handed the first of these ventures, categorized as Workshops. In 1936, Humphrey would get a chance to create a "big" dance; in 1937, Holm would take her turn; in 1938, Weidman would get his opportunity. The usual Bennington courses went on around these daily rehearsals.

Graham created *Panorama* for her twelve company members plus twenty-four additional women. With this mass, she hoped to achieve a synthesis of themes that are "part of the national consciousness and form an inheritance that contributes to the present." Her lengthy program note indicated that the three chosen themes were "basically American." Hence, "Theme of Dedication" concerned the Puritan fervor in which the country took root; "Imperial Theme" referred to the American South and "a people in bondage ridden by superstitions and strange fears"; and "Popular Theme" offered a vision of "awaking social consciousness in the contemporary scene." This ambitious work unfolded over forty minutes—her longest yet. Did she quail? Perhaps she did, but in private. She was also working with a substantial black and silver set, designed and erected by the Bennington College faculty member Arch Lauterer. This model of modernity featured a small raised stage set at the back of the expansive Vermont State Armory in downtown Bennington; sculpted walls and four-step structures framed it on either side. The dancers' movements flowed onto the floor of the armory; the audience sat on chairs set on bleachers and in the balcony. Twenty-five-year-old Norman Lloyd wrote the music (for Graham's usual ensemble of flute, clarinet, bass clarinet, trumpet, and drums) in fits and starts—at least one portion of it (Graham's solo) for parts of the dance that he had not yet seen; he based his composition on descriptions in one of Martha's detailed notebooks.

For the first section, Alexander Calder designed large (maybe five feet in diameter), red-and-white-striped disks made of cloth stretched over wire; these were anchored by ropes that passed over pulleys and attached to the wrists of three of the dancers, who controlled them on the small platform at the rear of the space. Graham, recalling these for *The New York Times* when Calder died in 1976, remembered having no place to rehearse with the mobiles, "so we rigged them up in the open field, stretched ropes from tree to tree, and learned to manipulate them to give the illusion of the world of fantasy that Sandy wanted." Calder also created a wooden machine that Bonnie Bird described as a "huge, jointed, scissor-like 'lightning' device." Set up high at the back of the armory, "its joints were supposed to stretch out in a sideways, jack-in-the-box-like explosion when Bonnie stepped on a lever, but in rehearsal its force was so great that she was nearly thrown off the balcony," and the unruly object was shelved.

Given that *Panorama* wasn't repeated after its sold-out Bennington premiere, it's difficult to know how these dancing mobiles could have coordinated either thematically or practically with the Puritans' founding of a new nation. Graham had envisioned them descending at different times in one sequence, revolving as they went, but they all moved at once. (By February of the next year, she—not one to give up—found another way to use mobiles in her *Horizons*.)

Course, a dance Graham had premiered in February, may have served as a template for some of the group's movement in *Panorama*. Set to a score by George Antheil, *Course* identified its eight dancers by color: three in green, two in blue, and three in red (Graham, wearing red, was the leader, and Anita Alvarez and Lily Mehlman, two of the smaller girls in the group, matched her). And in keeping with the title, they raced a great deal, human athletes trumping the Machine Age. Henry Gilfond conveys as much in a review for Horst's *Dance Observer*:

> Rarely has a dance ended so brilliantly, in such swift-moving patterns, urgently gathering energies in its momentum. The curtain moved slowly down from its moorings, the running circle stiffened its tempo, feet trip-hammered out their contagious, swifter rhythms, and the audience, caught in the pull and the pulse, the beat of the dance, found voice and shouted out its approval. Martha Graham has perhaps been more profoundly moving, but never before more exciting.

It may have been *Course* that Helen Priest Rogers (a member of the 1935 Workshop Group) was remembering when she mentioned that running in place had appeared in an earlier work of Graham's as well as in the classroom exercises. In *Panorama*, she said, groups of dancers entered in canon from the wings and walked or ran in circles, merging in one big ring and racing furiously.

Silent black-and-white footage of *Panorama*, shot in 1935, bears this out, even though it's not easy to decipher details, since the lighting was low and the women wore dark clothing, with dark wraps covering their hair. Nor is much of the space in which they're dancing visible. But, yes, they lunge—either in profile to the audience or facing them—and in those lunges they pump up and down or change feet to simulate running in place, going nowhere. You can also see three groups of runners entering in counterpoint, thrusting their arms up in V shapes, creating a patterned turbulence of curves and straight lines. They not only run counterclockwise in a huge circle around one woman (Graham?) but also rush into the center like the spokes of a wheel, retreat, and rush again to form a clump. It's not certain which section this is—perhaps the last one.

Nor is it clear which section features a quintet of women, recognizable among whom are tall Jane Dudley (who had been studying with Hanya Holm but soon joined Graham's company) and the British, ballet-trained Muriel Stuart (who was about to begin teaching at the School of American Ballet and had been advised by Lincoln Kirstein, fascinated by Graham, to study modern dance with her). These women may be performing on the small stage at the back, since they don't move from their places as they rise, one by one, to join in forming tableaux of support and determination. You see this one lift a leg to the side, another reach out to hold the lifted foot of a fallen comrade. The sequence is very designed, very orderly—individual expressions of strain counterbalancing the group. It could be part of the section that Graham devised to reflect the slaves of the Old South or other people oppressed by colonial land grabs.

Edna Ocko, a critic for the left-wing *New Theater*, wrote one of the most detailed accounts of *Panorama*. The "dignified" opening of the Puritan section, she noted, "made way for a vividly fantastic grotesquerie on hymn and prayer." She saw Graham as "interpenetrating the group and moulding it," urged on by some sort of "ecstatic self-communion." She praised the "hex dance" of Anna Sokolow and Anita Alvarez in the second section ("Imperial Theme"), as well as its "recurrent primitive theme." Graham, the imperialist, "stalks through the group, wielding a red gash of a handkerchief as symbol of the blood of the workers who alternately sway in ritual, or bow in tortured fear to the brazen and imperious Moloch demanding sacrifice at the altar." In the third section, "Popular Theme," Graham portrays "an agitator who, separate from the group—a separation which seems false—animates it to action."

Bringing up Mussolini's attack on Ethiopia, Ocko also raps Graham lightly on the knuckles about "Imperial Theme," which, she thought, needed to "show an awakening social conscience."

John Martin was impressed by *Panorama* and expected Graham

to rework it a bit and present it in New York City, but its very large cast militated against that. At Benningon, however, a third performance of Graham's program had to be added to the sold-out two, and it was estimated that a thousand people saw the work. Too, Graham could make use of her achievement: her company's souvenir program for 1936–37 called *Panorama* "the first full-length American ballet produced with American choreographer, composer and performers."

Although the 1935 Bennington Festival did not turn the Vermont town into "an American Salzburg," as one enthusiastic critic thought it might, the campus activities that summer did not maintain a narrow focus on dance, but brought forth ideas about the incendiary situation in Europe, the state of the American economy, and the role of art in society. There were discussions, exhibits, music recitals, experimental films, and lectures. Jacques Barzun spoke on "Culture and Revolution." George Beiswanger tackled "The Social Implications of the Contemporary Dance."

In addition, members of the New Dance League (formerly the Workers Dance League) came up from New York to give a concert on July 28. Among them were branching-out Graham dancers (Anna Sokolow, Sophie Maslow, Lily Mehlman, Marie Marchowsky, and Lil Liandre), who—primed by Horst's classes—were also choreographers. A number of the titles of their dances indicate yeasty social consciences. Mehlman contributed *Fatherland: a. Persecution, b. Defiance*; Marchowsky, *Agitation*; and Maslow, *Forward*.

During the 1930s, New York City spawned a number of politically ardent dance companies, such as Edith Siegel's Red Dancers. While dancing with Graham, Sokolow had created *Homage to Lenin* in 1933 for her own Dance Unit (sponsored by the American Dance League). In 1934, Maslow, a force in the New Dance Group, had choreographed *Two Songs About Lenin*. That same year, the New Dance Group, working as a New York City collective, presented in New York Miriam Blecher's *Van der Lubbe's Head*, protesting the scapegoating and beheading, on Hitler's orders, of communist leader Marinus van der Lubbe for setting on fire Germany's house of parliament, the Reichstag.

Left-wing writers might berate Graham for not expressing her political views more explicitly; *Imperial Gesture*, a solo that she premiered on her company's program at the Guild Theatre on November 11, 1935, made it clear that she was affected by the climate of outrage but thought a degree of abstraction might deepen and broaden any "message" she desired to convey—or, better, embody. When cornered by an interviewer, she definitively cut through queries about her intent in the work and the guesses as to what ruler or dictator she might be portraying: "I do not make social or political comments in my dances . . . If I had something of great social importance to say, I would say it from a lecture platform." She then set about correcting any impression that *Imperial Gesture* pointed a finger at any specific public figure: "The dance was created to demonstrate the movement of the body influenced by an imperial feeling. It may suggest to one the imperial attitudes of a duchess, an English butler, or a police sergeant. As a dance, its sole purpose lies in presenting imperial movement in the abstract." What she refrained from saying, but made evident in the dance, was that she viewed that "imperial attitude" as a destructive— and eventually self-destructive—force.

It is instructive to sift through the critical commentary attending *Imperial Gesture*. As might be expected, the *New Masses* critic created a dramatic scenario that suited his own view of imperialism. "The figure like a giant bird, stamps upon its prey and gathers more and more, until finally bulging with deformity, it collapses under the burden of gluttony." A more restrained writer thought that the solo "might be taken for a study of arrogance with an allegorical collapse for its conclusion," while another saw mainly the dancer's "magnificent struttings and posturings."

On her annual visit to Santa Barbara in September 1935, Graham told a journalist that "costumes deemed contemporary have grown out of the modern dancer's attitude toward movement, rather from attitudes and patterns in the dance." In *Imperial Gesture*, she put a remarkable costume to expressive and symbolic use. Russell Rhodes, who saw the solo at New York's Guild Theatre, described her garment as a slim black silk dress plus a brown overskirt lined with black, which she "skillfully manipulated, now in the manner of a cloak, now in the manner of a hood, the pattern of the dance suggesting majesty and military ceremonial, empty until it enveloped itself (as Miss Graham actually indicated) by enshrouding her at the close."

Whether brown, copper, or "apricot" (as one viewer described it), the deployment of the overskirt—almost a full circle, open at the front, without gathers, and said to weigh twenty-five pounds—drew on the transformative skills Graham had learned from St. Denis, but in order to reveal desires rather than to indicate a character.

Horizons, which first appeared at the Guild Theatre on two Sundays in February and March 1936, was a short-lived work, but its subtitles revealed Graham's now firm allegiance to American themes: "Migration: New Trails," "Dominion: Sanctified Power," "Building Motif: Homesteading," and "Dance of Rejoicing." The program may have provided guidelines for spectators searching for "meaning," but Graham offered no scenes depicting pioneers trudging westward or hefting logs. Again insistent on presenting herself as no storyteller, she indicated that *Horizons* was to be the first part of a suite and characterized it as "not specifically American, but abstracted from the American background."

Excited and somewhat bemused by what was a relatively new element in modern art and most certainly a novelty in dance, the New York critics gave more space to the mobiles (an art form unfamiliar to some of them) than to the choreography. This time, Graham confined Calder's constructions to three of what the program defined as "visual preludes" and explained that "the dances do not interpret the 'Mobiles,' nor do the 'Mobiles' interpret the dances. They are employed to enlarge the sense of horizon." On an empty stage, against a white or a red background, disks, balls, and other shapes—six in all—mounted on horizontal poles at various levels swung and revolved mechanically, eliciting enthusiasm, laughter, a boo or two, and hisses. The dance was deemed not Graham's greatest, and more than one critic thought that "Building Motif," with its "stationary blocks" (one of the two middle-section solos for the choreographer), seemed a variation on *Frontier*; one liked it (for the "new sentient warmth" he discerned); the other did not. The *New York Post*'s critic enjoyed himself describing "a monstrous corkscrew rotating sullenly in a frustrated attempt to prick a coy blue balloon which turned squeakily against a red background."

There is no doubting Graham's admiration for Calder's work. But there was perhaps a more strategic aspect to her desire to try something with mobiles again. Early in the month in which she premiered *Horizons*, the Pierre Matisse Gallery mounted another exhibit of the sculptor's mobiles, and in March, his work was included in two group exhibits, one at the Paul Reinhardt Galleries and the other at the Museum of Modern Art. Affiliating herself with him could attract audience members more drawn to the visual arts than dance.

Frances Hawkins, as the company's manager, secured Graham's first substantial solo tour in 1936, with the assistance of Merle Armitage, who, in addition to being a book designer and publisher, was a concert promoter. The tour began in mid-March and ended the last week of April. Eight of the approximately sixteen performances that Martha and Louis gave took place in California (four members of the Seattle Symphony joined Horst and flautist Hugo Bergamesco during the far west part of the tour). Sponsors included such organizations as the Detroit Health Education, the Carmel Music Society, and the Ladies Musical Club of Tacoma, Washington, as well as educational institutions (San José State College and Stanford University). But Graham also danced in theaters as prominent as the War Memorial Opera House in San Francisco and Los Angeles's Philharmonic Auditorium.

With a few program changes along the way, she performed ten or eleven dances per engagement, with one intermission, and gave interviews or an occasional lecture. As one might imagine, she thrilled some spectators, baffled others, and prompted some interesting reactions. In Los Angeles it was reported that there was "prolonged applause after each number and shouts of 'bravo' following certain dances, notably 'Frontier,' 'Imperial Gesture,' and 'Act of Piety.'" And in that same city, where she performed twice, she not only received a bouquet at the end of the evening; she was "showered with blossoms" before the intermission." She was, ventured one Chicago critic, "an Edith Wharton of the dance." A less enraptured but very observant San Francisco writer noted how often Graham lifted one leg (her left, as usual) high to the side—reporting that "one woman in the audience was heard to say, 'Good lord! There goes that leg again.'" A critic summed up the contradictory responses: "You find her magnificent and the woman on your right decides emphatically that she's impossible, the man to your left is cautious, and says, 'interesting.' Intriguing, superb, elemental, ugly, inspired, morbid, penetrating, mad—I heard them all used again and again." This commentator was one of the first to link Graham with avowedly powerful contemporary artists in other fields. He thought audiences needed to learn to see her dancing not in terms of "a stark costume, a powerful stance and a bewildering title but as an old art, given the expression of our age, requiring a technique as certain and telling as Mr. Dos Passos, who writes, or Mr. Picasso, who paints." She herself was pleased to be found controversial.

While on tour that spring, however, she made another kind of political statement. Three newspapers noted that she turned down an invitation from the German Ministry of Culture for her company to represent the United States in the dance festival that accompanied the 1936 Olympics in Berlin. "I would find it impossible to dance in Germany at the present time," she wrote. "So many artists whom I respect and admire have been persecuted, have been deprived of the right to work for ridiculous and unsatisfactory reasons, that I should consider it impossible to identify myself, by accepting the invitation, with the regime that has made such things possible." She also made the point that several members of the company, being Jewish, would not be welcome in Germany.

That summer, she presented no new works at what was now known as the Bennington Festival. It was Doris Humphrey's turn to create a work for an expanded company. *With My Red Fires* completed a trilogy, to music by Wallingford Riegger that included her 1935 *Theatre Piece* and *New Dance*. Unlike the city bustle and competitive fervor projected in *Theatre Piece* and the gloriously democratic harmony of *New Dance*, *With My Red Fires* had a story to tell—or rather two stories. Ostensibly the conflict was between a domineering mother and a daughter who ran off with the "wrong man," but Humphrey's matriarch, wearing an overlong skirt that she could lash like a whip, had a shuddering temper fit that spectators could have connected to some of Hitler's fanatic speeches and galvanized a mob as orderly as an army to find the lovers and drag them home. The couple's escape and optimistic final pose presaged the cooperative society of *New Dance*. This was one of the rare times when the more lyrical Humphrey could be as possessed by the demon as Graham.

Graham presented a program of her earlier dances at Bennington that summer and did her two weeks of teaching—her criticism enthralling and terrifying her students as usual. Most of them seemed to take her temperament in their stride. Said one of them, "Martha was always very intense, and if things didn't go right, she'd get very angry, and there's nothing more exciting than to see Martha Graham angry!"

In 1936, ballet also took a plunge into American subject matter, and in mid-July the newly formed Lincoln Kirstein's Ballet Caravan gave almost its first two performances as part of the Bennington Festival. The appearances were, in Kirstein's words, "no more than open dress rehearsals," for which young American choreographers had readied five small-scale ballets in six weeks.

Kirstein, having in 1933 brought George Balanchine to the United States to join him in creating an "American" ballet company, was finding himself in financial difficulties. By 1935, his American Ballet Company had been absorbed into the Metropolitan Opera, where Balanchine contributed dance to operas and presented occasional evenings of his ballets. Kirstein took some of the dancers and in 1936 founded Ballet Caravan. Stung by critics such as Martin, who pilloried Balanchine for being too "Russian" or too "Parisian," Kirstein built a repertory that featured new choreography by American dancer-choreographers Lew Christensen, Eugene Loring, and William Dollar—choreography that focused in large part on American subjects.

Kirstein had met Frances Hawkins through Graham, with whom he had become friendly, and Hawkins managed to book a forty-week tour for the new small company that was to function much like a modern dance company—performing mostly one-night stands in college auditoriums, movie houses, and the occasional civic auditorium and dancing mostly to piano accompaniment. Bennington spectators in mid-July could see five ballets, among them Loring's *Harlequin for President* and Christensen's *Pocahontas* (this last set to a score by the twenty-seven-year-old Elliott Carter). Graham saw onstage for the first time the ambitious young dancer and would-be choreographer Erick Hawkins, who'd been friendly with Kirstein during their Harvard days. As Chief Powhatan, Pocahontas's father, Hawkins would assuredly have looked dignified as well as charismatically strong and handsome. In two years, he would be dancing in Graham's company and, in short order, become her lover. By that time, he, along with Kirstein's mythologizing approach to American subject matter, would have begun to stimulate Graham to move in a new direction.

─10─

WORKING THROUGH WAR AND LOVE; ERICK ARRIVES

THE COVER FOR THE DECEMBER 1934 ISSUE of *Vanity Fair* featured a drawing by Miguel Covarrubias. To the left, the smiling, blond-ringletted burlesque star Sally Rand partially conceals her nakedness with her trademark: a huge pink ostrich-feather fan. To the right, Martha Graham, in a plain red gown, her face cadaverous and faintly green, pulls away from the stripper in angular horror. The drawing points to one of Corey Ford's "Impossible Interviews" in the body of the magazine. "Sally" begins with "Hello, Martha. Still doing the same old intellectual strip-tease?" She figures the two of them are "in the same racket . . . Just a couple of little girls trying to wriggle along." "Martha" counters with: "But my dancing is modern-classical-imaginative. If you leave anything to a customer's imagination, it's because he's near-sighted." In the end, Rand snipes, "You take the women's clubs, and I'll take the men." Martha: (Enviously) "For plenty." (Rand wrote a protesting letter to the editor. She very much admired Martha Graham, she said, and had even taken some dance classes from her.)

In the Ziegfeld Follies of 1936, the comedian Fanny Brice garbed herself in a leotard and a wraparound skirt to parody Graham in a number by Vernon Duke and Ira Gershwin called "Modernistic Moe."

The heroine's boyfriend, Moe, having modern-art aspirations, plucks her from a Broadway chorus line and turns her into an angular, rib cage–contracting Modern Dancer, who sings, dances, and, from the depths of her burgeoning social conscience, yells "Revolt!" Graham said she was a fan of Brice's and loved the imitation.

She also endured questions from the journalist Harry Salpeter, who was preparing an article about her that appeared in the February 1937 issue of *Mademoiselle*. He gets her to talk about what she might like to have that she lacks now. She'd like not having to choose between a new street dress and a costume, to have longer vacations, to cut up a bit, to stay up late. She may permit herself a glass of wine with dinner and a seat at the theater or opera. She sees Fred Astaire movies and thinks Ray Bolger and Bill Robinson are men of genius.

This attempt to humanize Graham contrasted dramatically (and was meant to) with the writer's opening view of her: "She is thin, plain, gaunt, unadorned. She talks a combination of hard-boiled sense and a mysticism in which romanticism has no art. She looks like a New England school teacher come to town on a limited dress and food budget." Salpeter notes that her dances have been described as "projections of the pioneer woman, 'stark, earth-riven, gaunt, inward-eyed,' in the manner of a Lynn Ward woodblock or a Walt Whitman poem."

The point is that putting her name before the public in these ways certainly counted for a woman who often had to borrow money from her own dancers to pay bills connected with upcoming performances.

Her name also appeared in the papers in loftier contexts. However often she insisted that her dances did not depict specific events or characters, her refusal to take her company to Berlin to perform in the 1936 Olympics was but one well-publicized indication that she had a social conscience. During the 1930s, her contribution to a number of symposia and benefit performances belied her previous image as an isolationist in her practice and as an artist unconcerned with politics. In October 1935, for instance, she performed at the Sixth Plenum Celebration of the International Workers Order. The evening began with the organization's orchestra playing the INTERNATIONAL (capitalized in the humble typed program) and moved from other musical selections into four solos by Graham; after the speeches, the Y-4 drama group enacted Clifford Odets's recent play *Waiting for Lefty* (or some of its seven scenes dealing with striking taxi drivers and their attempt to form a union).

Eleven days later she spoke on "Dance and the Theatre" at a dinner given by *New Theatre*. Among the five speakers were Graham's friend and colleague Archibald MacLeish ("Poetry and the Theatre") and Odets ("The Social Impulses in the Theatre").

After performing with her company at the Guild Theatre on two November Sunday evenings, she shared a Carnegie Hall program with Tamiris, the Humphrey-Weidman Company, and the Dance Unit of the New Dance League, headed by Anna Sokolow. In December, she and her group performed five dances alongside *A Bunt Mit a Statchke* (*Rebellion with a Strike*), a Yiddish folklore operetta; the occasion was an international celebration under the auspices of the Worker's Training School. Such appearances—whether donated or paid for—raised her profile as an artist with a conscience, a left-wing bent, and a generous heart.

The year 1936 had begun with *Horizons* and its sense of open spaces, and the spring tour to cities across the country had expanded the horizons of Graham's career and demonstrated her pride of country. But events of the summer roused her political conscience, and the year ended with *Chronicle*, which was immediately taken by many of those who saw it to be an indictment of the burgeoning of fascism and the potential for a large-scale European war.

In July of that year, the simmering conflict between the Spanish Democratic Republic (the Republicans) and the Nationalist faction that would be led by General Francisco Franco had erupted into the Spanish Civil War. Given the practical support of Italy's Benito Mussolini and, in ways more understated, the approval of Adolf Hitler, the Nationalist coup added to the perception of fascist power on the rise.

Many liberal-thinking Americans joined the International Brigade and other units fighting on the Republican side.

At its first performance at the Guild Theatre on Sunday, December 20, 1936, the three-part *Chronicle* ran for over an hour. "Dances Before Catastrophe" had two subsections, "Spectre—1914" and "Masque." "Dances After Catastrophe" was made up of "Steps in the Street" and "Tragic Holiday—In Memoriam." "Prelude to Action" concluded the suite, which was set to a score by Wallingford Riegger.*

Graham—like Doris Humphrey in *With My Red Fires* four months earlier—wore an unusually long skirt in "Spectre—1914" (any direct influence is only guesswork). This solo featured the dancer on a small, smooth, round platform with a broad attached step on either side, provided by Noguchi. In her warning evocation of World War I, the skirt of her figure-of-doom could drape over the platforms' edges to make her look taller than she was, or could be lifted and let fall like a dark, crimson-bordered cloud—or, as one writer put it, like "a red cascade."

True to habit, Graham must have reworked the dance fiercely during the week between the premiere and the group's second performance of it on December 27. John Martin found it so transformed—both in terms of steps and a new warmth and fervor on the part of the sixteen women who danced it—as to seem a new version of itself (Graham had also wisely omitted one number from the first part of the dauntingly long program).

Julien Bryan's film of "Steps in the Street"; clips shot during a 1938 performance by Chicago's camera-toting critic Ann Barzel; and Barbara Morgan's photographs enabled a 1988 revival by former Graham dancer Yuriko [Kikuchi], with input from Martha as well as from such Graham company members as Sophie Maslow, who had danced in the 1936 premiere.

This section of *Chronicle* is striking in its simplicity, its strength,

---

* When "Steps in the Street" was revived in 1989, Riegger's score could not be found, and the choreography was (ironically) fitted to a later orchestrated version of parts of his score for her rival Humphrey's *With My Red Fires*, with Graham's opening walks performed in silence.

and its fervor. As it begins, the women, one by one, enter and leave the stage walking backward, their bodies falling slightly away from the direction from which they came. No step flows into the next; each footfall on the individual straight or curving paths stops with a sudden jolt before the next one starts. Yet, clearly, these people are wandering.

A leader (May O'Donnell in 1936) summons them to return, standing on one leg and dropping the other repeatedly against it like a drumstick, lifting herself slightly into the air as she does so. When the women reenter, it is with huge jumps that sometimes propel them across the stage. They jump facing the audience; one leg, scything out to the side, is straight while the other is bent, and their arms copy that pattern. Over the course of the dance, these women in long white dresses repeat their feats of elevation many, many times, with no steps linking them; the landing from one jump sets off the next. Performed rhythmically and in squadrons, the movement comes to suggest an aggravated march. Or a flight.

Chronicle's underlying theme for the group is that of people on the move, of people feeding into formations; their every movement is as strong as a shout. Members of this all-woman squadron also stalk, heel first, across the stage on a long, diagonal path, each woman holding her arms in one of several iconic positions (this march may actually be part of the section entitled "Prelude to Action"). They plunge forward with one bent leg lifted behind them and one arm knifing down.

Graham was interested in counterpoint during these years—more so than in her later dance dramas. At one point, while most of the women are either jumping or—lined up along at the back of the stage—lowering themselves to their knees (rising, kneeling, rising, kneeling . . .), three other women sit on the floor and several times wrench their bent arms forcefully down in front of them, elbows first, hands balled into fists; they look as if they're yanking a shade down between themselves and what they will themselves not to see. This they intersperse with twisting away from their upright posture, as if struck.

In a passage that is repeated at the end of "Steps in the Street," the women slowly and stiffly cross the back of the stage in two parallel lines, gazing upward and holding both arms straight out in front of them. In between these lines, O'Donnell walks haltingly backward in the same direction. Because she is leaning back on a slant, the impression is that they are forcing her along, mowing her down, yet when they have left the stage, she is still there.

The left-wing critics of the 1930s plunged enthusiastically and approvingly into interpretation. A writer for *The New Masses* wonders if the color scheme of *Chronicle*—red, black, and white—refers to the colors of "Imperial Germany of 1914 and the Third Reich." The term "imperialist" and its variants looms large: In "Spectre—1914," the "red cascade of the skirt" conveys the "the brutalization of imperialist conflict." In "Tragic Holiday," the "charlatan attempts to mask the memory of imperialist conflict." "Masque," in which Graham "alternately controls and is controlled by unpredictable group movements," shows the "hypocritical face of imperialism." Even the critic of Horst's *Dance Observer* couldn't entirely refrain from a degree of interpretation. Of Graham's red-and-black costume, "designed so that its deployment is part of the action," he noted that "the colors suggest blood and desolation, rivers of blood which are spread at the whim of an impersonally mad figure which sits playing with the destiny of nations. In *Masque*, a similar figure is shown treading the staid traditional measures of society's dance, unnoticed among the conservative members." Elsewhere, the writer stated that the group moved in a pavane (rather than a sarabande), while Graham was part of the design but "rhythmically at variance with them."

This last writer offers clues to what now-lost sections of the dance may have looked like and conveyed. Noguchi's platform was again center stage, and the critic interprets "Tragic Holiday"—performed, in part, by a group of dancers center stage near and on the platform—as a comment on nationalism and "orgiastic indulgence in celebration" at the tombs of the war dead: "Here the action slows down and is confined to the action between the main figure and the sympathetic celebrants who indulge in sorrow by proxy. The patterns and gestures are satiric, not as ruthless as satire can be, but evident in their intention."

Graham, wearing a black-and-white costume for this section, turned a square black gauze flag into a mourning veil. The writer goes on to say that in the final "Prelude to Action," the design "piles movement on movement, beginning upper-stage left, until the whole group, integrated, solid, continues in unison toward one point, counterpoint resolved into a definite, cohesive solidarity, continuing, as does the earlier section, to the fall of the curtain."

With her titles and subtitles Graham evidently wanted to assist those who found her dances "difficult," even as she insisted that she was not creating specific stories. Perhaps, too, Frances Hawkins, Horst, or others she trusted had advised her to clarify her intentions. By the time of her group's New York performance at the Guild in March 1937, she had added bits of information about *Chronicle* to the program: "Spectre—1914" was now clarified by "Drums—Red Shroud—Lament"; "Masque" was followed by the words "Idolatry of Tradition"; "Devastation—Exile" modified "Steps in the Street"; and "Prelude to Action" made itself clearer with "Unity—Pledge to the Future." Yet the introduction to the dance printed in the March 2 program contained this warning: "'Chronicle' does not attempt to show the actualities of war; rather does it, by evoking war's images, set forth the fateful prelude to war, portray the devastation of spirit which it leaves in its wake, and suggest an answer." Narrative may have been luring Graham on, but she was still holding back—perhaps not yet certain how she might shape it in her own way.

Graham's habit of turning a critical eye on her work once it premiered landed severely on *Chronicle*. She was also undoubtedly galled by John Martin's application of the terms "dryness" and "overformalism" and "too long" (the final section). Since her December "season" consisted of two Sunday-evening programs, she had a week to reconsider, and Martin could then pronounce that at its second performance, *Chronicle* was so transformed that it amounted to a new version of itself. In addition to some cutting, he found that the "passionate performance" made the difference: "A kind of heroic elevation of spirit emanated from Miss Graham's personal performance and diffused itself throughout the whole work." The following spring, he mentioned that *Chronicle* had been even further altered: Graham's own role in "Prelude to Action" had been reworked in both mood and choreography, and she was onstage throughout it. The result? "What was formerly scarcely more than a well-wrought theme with variations has taken on the character of a lively work of art."

The same month that *Chronicle* premiered, Graham was invited by Eleanor Roosevelt to dine at the White House on February 26, 1937, and perform in the evening's "musicale" afterward. Her courageous stance in turning down the invitation to the Berlin Olympics, as well as her growing reputation as a socially aware artist, may have garnered her that honor (the fact that Graham dancer Rita Morgenthau's brother-in-law, Secretary of the Treasury Henry Morgenthau, Jr., was being honored that night also helped secure her the invitation). She danced *Frontier* and *Imperial Gesture*, with *Harlequinade* for leavening. Eleanor Roosevelt, chatting with Graham after the performance, wrote in her syndicated column, "My Day," of the "tremendous" amount of daily labor and devotion Graham's career involved. Newspaper readers in forty-eight cities learned that Miss Graham was "probably the most modern expression of the dance we have." The chat between Graham and the country's First Lady apparently continued after the evening's entertainment. Martha had not wanted to dine before performing, and Mrs. Roosevelt walked her into the White House kitchen afterward and rustled up something for her to eat.

In June 1937, Graham's life and work took another turn. She had had a grueling spring: two New York concerts at the Guild Theatre; another tour with her group (fifteen performances between March 12 and the end of April); and a May concert at the Guild. Out in California, Merle Armitage, the theater promoter and designer of stunning books, was putting together a collection of essays by and about her and had asked Carlus Dyer, a gifted young art student, to provide a drawing to head each one.

Dyer had been working as a painter with the Los Angeles branch of the Works Progress Administration, which Armitage headed. He had been recommended for the job by Ramiel McGehee, who had been a foreign correspondent for the *Los Angeles Times*, studied Buddhism intensively, and, for a time, tutored the young emperor of Japan in English. (Call it fate that McGehee knew Ruth St. Denis and had met Horst and Graham during their Denishawn days, and that Dyer, when a precocious twelve-year-old, had read the writings by Nietzsche and Schopenhauer that Graham and Horst so valued.)

In preparation, Dyer set out for New York to watch Graham work with her dancers in the studio at 66 Fifth Avenue. Horst, who was living a couple of blocks farther downtown at the Hotel Brevoort, secured an affordable room there for Carlus, who occasionally ate with Louis and Martha after the workday was over, often at Horst's favorite restaurant, the Blue Ribbon on West Forty-Fourth Street, with its robust German cooking. The three of them went up to Harlem; he and Martha danced together while Louis nursed a beer and watched.

Horst wasn't in the best of health at the time, and his personal relationship with Graham was fraying. Before long, Dyer was in love, and in later life he recounted the tale of his first night alone with Martha, still able to picture the "long, white, loose-fitting gown, a red sash holding it about her waist" that she had changed into for the evening. And how, after washing the dinner dishes, they sat on pillows on the fire escape outside her apartment window and talked for a long time, how they kissed, how they made love in her narrow bed. She was forty-three; he was nineteen.

Graham was no prude, yet her upbringing had left ineradicable traces. She would not brook coarseness or vulgarity from the girls in her company in that era, when no lady—and she considered herself one—went out into the street without a hat and gloves. Bessie Schönberg said that Martha instructed the members of her group that if they were invited to a party in a "nice" house or apartment, they should be sure to leave the bathroom exactly as they found it. No splashes, no splatters, no badly folded hand towels.

Graham also made a distinction between a purely sexual liaison and the love that could include sex. Just as she constantly and eloquently defined the art that she admired (and the art that she made) as a discipline that could uplift and refine both mind and spirit, so she tended to speak of a love affair in exalted terms, as if to do so would elevate its physical aspect and turn what some might consider baser instincts into elemental processes in tune with the universe. And in her letters to Dyer (as read aloud by him decades later during an interview with Francis Mason for a book that Mason was preparing) she assures him that their union is enriching her as a woman and an artist.

When Dyer returned to California in late June, Graham wrote him that she had gone to Brentano's bookstore and purchased Suzuki's *Essays in Zen Buddhism* and Claude Bragdon's *Delphic Woman* and *The Kybalion*. Lincoln Kirstein had sent her a new translation of *The Ten Principal Upanishads*, and on the summer solstice, she sends her "beloved" these words: "When lovers realize their deep desire, one for the other, that sundered god . . . for realization through unity shows . . . the path to divinity . . . When lovers . . . petition, in a spirit of all humbleness . . . 'What wilt thou have us do?' . . . Who knows but that they may be vouchsafed some answer wonderful and new?" (The ellipses are Dyer's, as he strove to read the passages he was allowing Mason to hear.)

In her two Bennington concerts on July 30 and 31, *Immediate Tragedy* closed the first half of her program of ten solos. Graham subtitled it *Dance of Dedication* and implied to Dyer that he was as much the recipient of her tribute as the events and heroes that prompted the dance, although she talked to her dancers about *Immediate Tragedy* and the Spanish Civil War heroine Dolores Ibárruri, known as La Pasionara, one of the Communist deputies in Spain's Republican parliament. Ibárruri, who coined the battle cry "*No Pasarán!*" to hold back the enemy, might have found a kindred spirit in Martha Graham, on her knees and striking the floor again and again.

The ongoing struggle in Spain arrived at the newspapers daily via cable. In June, Pablo Picasso completed his massive black, white, and gray painting *Guernica*, inspired by the two-hour German bombing of the Basque village of Guernica in the month of April—a favor from Hitler to Franco.

The music for *Immediate Tragedy* embodied a different example of tragedy and courage. In 1936, its composer, Henry Cowell, had been convicted on a morals charge as a result of his having had sexual congress with a seventeen-year-old man. He was currently serving four years in San Quentin, where he led the prison band and continued to write music. Graham and Horst had visited him there to discuss the new solo in terms of what she envisioned.

When the score for the dance arrived at Bennington, Norman Lloyd and Horst had never seen anything like it. Unable to be present at rehearsals and knowing the choreography's atmosphere, tempo, and meter, but not the exact timing of each section, Cowell had constructed an "elastic form," spare in its sonorities. He wrote two basic phrases for oboe and clarinet and provided these in a range of measure lengths, from which Lloyd could choose whichever fit the given passage of choreography. If a phrase of movement needed eight measures, Cowell's score had one ready and waiting; overlaps could be managed. So thoroughly had the composer anticipated the choreographer's needs that producing the final score took Lloyd only about an hour. John Martin praised Cowell's "deeply poignant music with its persistent phrase . . . couched in the measure of the sarabande."

José Limón, at Bennington with the Humphrey-Weidman Company, was effusive in his later memoir: *Immediate Tragedy* was the "apogee of all her works. For me it was a supreme experience, if not *the* supreme experience of dance." Martin raved in *The New York Times* about it in terms that Graham could appreciate. "Lest there may be something of the suggestion of 'propaganda' or of mere timeliness about a theme deriving from the Spanish War, let it be said at once that this will be a moving dance long after the tragic situation in Spain has been brought to a conclusion, for it has completely universalized its material."

Lincoln Kirstein—who not only was friends with Graham but,

willy-nilly, had rethought his initial repelled response to her "wiry concentration, her awkward, jarring idiosyncrasies and stammering activity"—called *Immediate Tragedy* a "keystone masterpiece of the same powerful wave-length as the concatenation of energies operating throughout the world today." His Ballet Caravan had performed for a second time at the Bennington Festival just the week before, again opening the one-night-only program with Lew Christensen's classical *Encounter* but offering another Americana ballet: Eugene Loring's *Yankee Clipper* to a score by Paul Bowles. Erick Hawkins, who danced in Loring's work, also presented his first piece of choreography on that July 24 evening: *Showpiece (Ballet Workout in One Act)*, intended to display the individual qualities of the dancers. Graham saw it and went backstage to compliment him on it. When it was later presented in New York, Graham saw it again.

After her July 30 and 31 performances of ten solos in the armory, including another new (and promptly discarded) one titled *Opening Dance*, Martha wrote to Dyer, again addressing him as "Beloved" and telling him that she was "deep in joy" and that "the one new dance to the Cowell music is good enough to be a gift to you, I think. People say it as a point of departure. That I seem to be re-born. They say I have not danced like these two performances for years. One man said to Dorothy Bird—'Does Martha have someone? She must to dance like that.'"

Graham's teaching schedule at Bennington ended on August 14, but she had undoubtedly seen—either in final rehearsals or at its August 13 premiere—Hanya Holm's *Trend*, the "big" piece of the summer, that is, the one involving the student dancers in the Workshop. Twenty-two women augmented her group of eleven. The titles of some of its subsections—"Our Daily Bread," "Satiety," "The Effete," "Lucre Lunacy," "He, the Great"—give the sense of a social conscience at work. *Trend* highlighted the increasing interest by modern dance choreographers in a theatricality that also took into account their commitment to austerity. Holm later wrote that her subject "demanded a departure from the usual abstract symbolic handling of dance themes. Dance action was required rather than dance abstraction . . . The three-dimensional significance of space also demanded the architectural handling of light, as well as the rhythm and volume of color—in lights, costumes and the covering of the setting, the floor cloth and the cyclorama." (Arch Lauterer was involved, along with Gerard Gentile, in creating various above-the-floor spaces within the armory.)

Given the harrowing political climate of the times, numerous modern dancers weighed in with works ranging from unabashed agit-prop to less obvious references to unions that united workers, corporate greed that threatened them, and the fascist regime led by a dictator who saw himself as a conquistador. Charles Weidman's ambitious *Quest*, which also premiered at Bennington in 1937, presented an image of a traveling artist—enticed by a foreign dictatorship to present his work—consulting his inner self and, finally, realizing he cannot live in an ivory tower, returning home, and calling his colleagues to action. Anna Sokolow had already put to excellent use the skills she'd developed as Horst's assistant in his Neighborhood Playhouse composition classes. While still dancing in Graham's company, she created for her own group, Dance Unit, such works as *Anti-War Trilogy* (1933), *Inquisition '36* (1936), and *Façade—Esposizione Italiana* (1937), as well as less unequivocally political ones.

Both Sokolow's 1935 *Strange American Funeral* and Miriam Blecher's *Van der Lubbe's Head* (1934) had used spoken poetry onstage. The dramatic poem by Michael Gold that accompanied Sokolow's work told of an overworked toiler in Braddock, Pennsylvania's steel mill who died when he fell into a vat of molten steel. The text crucial to Blecher's work for the New Dance Group documented a man scapegoated in Germany for the fire set in the Reichstag in 1933. It is possible that such works, in addition to the Americana repertory of Ballet Caravan, set Graham thinking. As she developed her next major piece, *American Document*, she laid out a spoken text.

In the meantime, exhausted from the tour and the ensuing classes, rehearsals, and performances, she was persuaded to travel to California by Armitage, who subsidized the trip. Martha needed a rest after Bennington, he thought, and she could work in peace on the essay she was contributing to his book, *Martha Graham: The Early Years*. Ensconced in a house near Ramiel McGehee's in Redondo Beach, she stayed for a month—breathing the sea air, writing every morning, having long daily talks with McGehee about Zen Buddhism, and reveling in her intimacy with Dyer during the meals and nights they shared. According to Dyer, after her talks with McGehee, she "would spend the late afternoons alone in meditation or otherwise working upon a koan or other subjects related to her study with [him]."

Graham's ecstatic relationship with Dyer continued in letters and meetings over the year and a half, and their friendship lasted much longer. In April 1938 she wrote to him that he and McGehee turned out to be two people "who would bring me to re-birth." Graced by Dyer's drawings and numerous photographs, the book Armitage designed was published in November 1937. Eight people (Lincoln Kirstein, Evangeline Stokowski, Wallingford Riegger, Edith J. R. Isaacs, Roy Hargrove, James Johnson Sweeney, George Antheil, and Louis Danz) contributed new essays about Graham's work. Previous writings by John Martin, Margaret Lloyd, and Stark Young were included. Armitage provided a preface, and Graham's brother-in-law Winthrop Sargeant put together a career summary. Horst, to whom the book was dedicated, helped choose telling extracts from Graham's many definitions of her aims and her ideas of what dance should be. Only a thousand copies were printed and distributed. The word "genius" made numerous appearances in it, and the composer Antheil ended his contribution by placing her "in the greatest tradition of Stravinsky, Picasso, Brancusi, Dali, Ernst, Cocteau, Breton, Aragon, Wigman, and herself!" Some forty years later, when the book was reprinted, Graham wrote a new introduction in which she said that she had been "stunned and shaken and forced to think many things I might never have thought of." It seemed, she said, "to be about someone else whom I did not know at all."

Two new works presented during Martha Graham and Group's two performances at the Guild Theatre in December showed her poised to change from creating indirect condemnations of the events of the

Spanish Civil War to hailing the American spirit, its heritage, and the nature of democracy, all of which might be considered as a counterstatement to the rise of fascism in Europe.

Her solo *Deep Song*, like *Immediate Tragedy*, was set to a score by Henry Cowell.* As in her 1930 *Lamentation*, Graham anchored herself to a small bench. Perhaps "anchored" is a misleading word. However, although she didn't, like the woman of *Lamentation*, remain sitting on the bench, it drew her close in more complex ways. As Barbara Morgan's photos reveal, the bench became an insecure refuge—to fall from, crouch over, collapse onto, and huddle beneath; from it Graham could venture with large, imploring, or denunciatory movements, and to it she could return.

In a 1938 review for *The Christian Science Monitor*, Margaret Lloyd describes in symbolic terms the long dress Graham wore: "A hint of Spanish feeling in red touches leaves the gray and black costume related to all people, as Spain's passion is related to the world." Graham would have approved of that statement's universalizing impact. When she and her company appeared at the Los Angeles Philharmonic Auditorium in a series produced by Merle Armitage, a program note assured spectators that "'Deep Song' is not meant to be an exact picture of a Spanish woman but presents the torture of mind and body experienced in common by all people who react to such suffering as the Spanish people have found." Audiences unfamiliar with dance and at a loss might try to find stories where none were intended. Martha would have none of that—for the time being, at least. Her other premiere, *American Lyric*, a group work to a score by Alex North (Anna Sokolow's lover at the time), presented an optimistic view of open spaces and the spirit that conquered them. Graham, Sokolow, and May O'Donnell led the fourteen women of the ensemble. Lloyd's re-

---

* Cowell wrote the score around the time he was composing the music for *Immediate Tragedy* and titled it *Cante Hondo* after the flamenco song form *cante jondo*. The music for both ballets was lost, and when Graham was persuaded to reconstruct the dance in 1988 (with the help of Morgan's photographs and the memories of former dancers), Cowell's *Sinister Resonance* was used to accompany it. In 2003, the score for *Cante Hondo* was found behind a desk at the office of the Martha Graham Dance Company, but not put to use.

view said only that it "brought a stirring program to a stirring close." And so, Graham used it to accomplish that for a year or two more.

Whether any of the movement material in it found its way into her next project, *American Document*, is moot, but the difference between "lyric" and "document" reveals the differences between the two dances. Graham had been reading *In the American Grain* (1933), essays by William Carlos Williams that dealt in part with the voyagers who discovered the American continent and the men, such as George Washington, Benjamin Franklin, and Abraham Lincoln, who shaped its destiny. And at some point she realized that the dance she began to work on in the spring of 1938 would need words as well as dancing if it was to make its points clear.

In June 1938, when Erick Hawkins arrived at Graham's Fifth Avenue studio, she and her company were already working on *American Document*. The first half of the year had been moderately busy; they had performed on a modern dance evening that brought together Holm, Humphrey, Weidman, Tamiris, Ruth St. Denis, and others; appeared at the Hippodrome in an event to raise money for victims of the Spanish Civil War; and had a small tour. They had also performed a short new group piece in Flushing Meadows, in an event to announce the opening in New York a year later of the 1939 World's Fair.

Hawkins had enrolled in Martha's annual intensive June Course. As a budding choreographer, he also watched *American Document* rehearsals. (According to Graham's friend Agnes de Mille, so, often, did Kirstein.) Hawkins may have been as surprised as the company members were during the work session when Martha announced, "Erick and I come in here." She had evidently already considered adding a man to her group, but José Limón, when she approached him, had no wish to desert the Humphrey-Weidman Company, his lover (Weidman), and the woman, Doris Humphrey, whom he considered a genius and a beauty.

The universality and commonality that Graham insistently emphasized when she spoke of her dances' subject matter relaxed their hold on her. Some months after *American Document* premiered at Bennington and before its New York presentation at Carnegie Hall, she told Marcia Minor of *The Daily Worker* that she wanted the audience to "feel no obscurity or doubt at any time about what is happening on the stage. This dance is supposed to bring back to its full meaning what has largely become meaningless in America through familiarity. I refer to such a word as democracy that reminds us of rights we have but may not avail ourselves of. As the line goes in the script of the dance, 'We forget too much.'"

Graham assembled the text with assistance from Francis Fergusson, who headed Bennington's drama department, although he later said that he gave her only very minimal advice as to structure. The *American Document* scenario—published (with stage directions) in a 1942 issue of *Theatre Arts* magazine—takes its style from poems of the day that call in clarion tones for a true democracy, such as Langston Hughes's 1938 "Let America Be America Again," which includes these lines:

> *Say, who are you that mumbles in the dark?*
> *And who are you that draws your veil across the stars?*
>
> I am the poor white, fooled and pushed apart,
> I am the Negro bearing slavery's scars.
> I am the red man driven from the land,
> I am the immigrant clutching the hope I seek—
> And finding only the same old stupid plan
> Of dog eat dog, of mighty crush the weak.

Carl Sandburg's masterly book-length poem *The People, Yes* (1936) employs similar repetitive strategies to trumpet his ideas across divides:

> The people is the grand canyon of humanity
>   and many many miles across.
> The people is pandora's box, humpty dumpty,
>   a clock of doom and an avalanche when it
>   turns loose.

> The people rest on land and weather, on time
>   and the changing winds.
> The people have come far and can look back
>   and say, "We will go farther yet."

In *American Document*'s fourth part, "Emancipation Episode," the dancers enter gradually as Sandburg's following lines are recited:

> One state has mountains.
> One state has no mountains.
> One state has sea.
> One state has no sea . . .
> More than one state had slaves.
> Now, no state has slaves.
> Now every state has one deep word.
> Here it comes:
> Emancipation!

The last dancer took her place for "Emancipation" after "More than one state had slaves." And when they finished dancing, a passage from Lincoln's "Proclamation of Amnesty and Reconstruction" was read onstage.

Like Sandburg, Graham asked many questions. Among the most persistent: "What is an American?"

In dealing with the country's Puritan origins, the displacement of Native tribes, slavery, and the present imperfect democracy, Graham was obliquely directing a defiant statement at the rise of fascism: in March 1938, Germany annexed Austria (the *Anschluss*) and had other conquests in mind; in October it would begin taking over Czechoslovakia. But the choreographer's subject was primarily the ongoing struggle for a true democracy within the United States—a society without racial and religious prejudices—its people united not just for ethical and moral reasons but for protection against potential enemies without and within. Biblically derived words that had been spoken by Patrick Henry in 1799 in his last public speech were to provide World War II with one of its mottos: "United we stand, divided we fall."

Given the breadth of her subject matter, Graham had to find a structure that would bear its multifaceted narrative. She chose the minstrel show. Contemporary dance historians find this perplexing, given the form's explicit racism: predominantly white performers in blackface, dancing, singing, and performing comedic skits in which the "Negro" characters were often portrayed as stupid and lazy. Given that the year after *American Document* premiered, Al Jolson starred in the movie *Swanee River*, playing a blackface performer, one can assume that the image wasn't taboo at the time, nor did it become so for two more decades.

In any case, Graham used minstrelsy only as a framework that could support serious material within the vaudevillean structure of unrelated acts. She also borrowed its terms. *American Document* began with "Entrance—Walk Around" to introduce the performers, and "walk-arounds" stitched some of the ensuing sections together. Part V was called "The After Piece: Crossfire—Cakewalk." In minstrelsy, "Crossfire" applied to rapid-fire comic questions and answers, but could in this case define both counterpoint and crisscrossing groups (and, by implication, victims caught between two warring factions). The cakewalk referred to may have had that dance's thrusting kicks, but hardly its high-stepping exuberance. Two small, sprightly Graham dancers, Anita Alvarez and Thelma Babitz, as the End Figures, stood in for minstrelsy's Mr. Tambo and Mr. Bones, named for the instruments those performers played (tambourine and knucklebones) and known as the End Men because of their placement in the usual minstrel show's semicircle of chairs. These details were, of course, never mentioned in the dance, but Alvarez and Babitz—both small—frequently worked together, zooming across the stage or cartwheeling through the action. The actor Houseley Stevenson, Jr., was billed as the Actor as Interloctor, the master of ceremonies who knitted the minstrel show together, and it was he who recited *American Document*'s text. Ray Green's music for piano and percussion provided the fanfares and snare-drum rolls needed, but on a modest scale; and in "Part I: Declaration," Alvarez and Babitz beat their feet against the floor while Stevenson began with the stirring, "We hold these truths to be self-evident . . ." from the Declaration of Independence. At the same time, four dancers opened curtains at the back to form four doorways, and the rest of the cast entered, always stopping when the Interlocutor spoke a line.

Graham wanted the audience to see her dancers as themselves—taking on roles rather than *becoming* characters. The Interloctor's opening speech, delivered after all the performers had entered in the "Walkaround" and bowed to the audience one by one, made her intention clear:

> Ladies and Gentlemen, good evening.
> This is a theatre.
> The place is here in the United States of America.
> The time is now—tonight.
> The characters are:
> The dance group, led by Sophie,
> You, the audience,
> The Interlocutor—I am the Interlocutor,
> And Erick and Martha.

"Part II: Indian Episode" had two sections. The first, "Native Figure," was a solo for Graham. Stevenson named the Indian tribes like drumbeats—"Mississippi, Susquehanna, Monongahela, Pottawattamie . . ."—while Graham walked into place wearing a long, narrow gown, her hair tied back at the nape of her neck, a blanket over one shoulder. In Barbara Morgan's photographs, she is severe, dignified, quiet. At the end of the piece she is kneeling, and the other women enter and replace her in that position. While they are crouched, Stevenson reads extracts from the eloquent speech that Red Jacket delivered at a council of chiefs of the Six Nations in 1805; the words were addressed to a young missionary who planned on converting the tribes to Christianity. The gist of this courteously delivered but firm statement—which began with "Listen to what we say"—was "No, thank you." In the second section, the dancers, led by May O'Donnell, rose to perform "Lament for the Land."

"Part III: Puritan Episode" caused the most comment. Neither Martha's "girls" nor the spectators had ever seen her dance with a male partner. The text begins,

> A wooden boat grates on the new shore
> Guns in the Indian wilderness.
> A stiff-necked generation claims the land,
> Claims the Lord,
> Denying the tender creature.

Graham and Hawkins entered together, and as they danced, the Interlocutor interpolated lines from one of Jonathan Edwards's fire-and-brimstone sermons and subtly related ones from the biblical Song of Songs. For instance, Edwards's "Death comes hissing like a fiery dragon with the sting on the mouth of it" is followed Solomon's "Let him kiss me with the kisses of his mouth, For thy love is better than wine."

The few filmed fragments that exist show the same few moves repeated over and over for the camera. Graham both clings to Hawkins and pulls away from him, and he lifts and rocks her over and over into low leaps that look as if she's being pitched over a barrier and recovered. They leap around each other. In a photograph by Morgan of the two taken during an outdoor rehearsal at Bennington, they stand pressed together; both have their hands raised overhead, although not touching, and she has lain her cheek against his bare chest. For those who knew Martha and her earlier work, her submissiveness was almost shocking. Jean Erdman, who joined her company early in 1938, felt that *American Document* lured Graham into movement that was more spiraling, more three-dimensional, more yielding.

"Part IV: Emancipation Episode" consisted of a group dance and a more militant duet for Graham and Hawkins. Part V was performed by three women: O'Donnell, Jane Dudley, and Sophie Maslow. The

Interlocutor stated the year, 1938, and announced, "Listen to what we say, / We are three women." A photo by Morgan captured the three whirling, their bodies bending, their hair flying. At *American Document*'s first performance, they exited as Hawkins entered and stayed, while the drum beat faster. He danced as both "one man" and "one million men."

Stevenson then intoned his last list:

"America! Name me the word that is courage.
America! Name me the word that is justice.
America! Name me the word that is power.
America! Name me the word that is freedom.
America! Name me the word that is faith.
Here is that word—Democracy!

And that government of the people, by the people, for the people shall not perish from the earth."

Apparently, at that first Bennington performance, Hawkins was alone onstage at the end. Graham tightened and altered the piece before its New York performance and added a group reprise before Stevenson wished the audience good night and they all bowed and exited.

One critic found things to admire about it and things to like less well, but he thought it to be "an experiment of immeasurable significance" for modern dance. There were other equivocaters, but Lincoln Kirstein raved about it in *The Nation*: "The whole piece was so nobly framed, so flawlessly executed, that every other work, new or old, offered at the Bennington Festival seemed by comparison puerile, unprofessional, or academic" (so much for Doris Humphrey's masterly *Passacaglia* and *Variations and Conclusion* from *New Dance*, Hanya Holm's *Dance of Work and Play* and *Dance Sonata*, as well as Charles Weidman's *Opus 51*, which shared billing with *American Document*'s two performances).

Kirstein went on to elevate *American Document*: "Graham's work had the sober, frank sincerity of a Thanksgiving hymn heard in the open air. Its surface finish resembled some useful Shaker wood-turning. Its exalted plasticity of formal movement was as proud and objective as a New Bedford whaler's figurehead." He used the word "miraculous" about the fusion of speech, dance, and ideas.

Other critics praised, equivocated, or damned. John Martin insightfully called the piece "as successful a combination as any that has yet been made, partly no doubt because the lines themselves are the very essence of Miss Graham's personal style and rhythm." Margaret Lloyd, writing later, noted that "the stripped clean, poetic words said all there was to say, so that the movement served chiefly as illustrations." The dance critic Walter Terry found Graham's view of America "bloodless, characterless, humorless," while in *Modern Music*, Edwin Denby was troubled by "the monotony of equal thrusts, the unrelaxed determination." For Joseph Arnold Kaye from *Dance*, the duet between Graham and Hawkins had "beauty and power such as the modern dance has heretofore not known"; to Lloyd, it "administered a new kind of shock . . . not so much for its eroticism as for its lack of taste."

Months later, the young Merce Cunningham wrote to Bonnie Bird, who had been his teacher at the Cornish School, about seeing *American Document* for the first time. He thought it "undoubtedly the most exciting, breathtaking piece of dance one could hope to see in this era. I have seen it [in] performance and rehearsal maybe a dozen times and it still takes my breath away, and as for Martha, to see her is to wonder why other humans attempt to walk!"

As usual, Graham reworked *American Document* before its New York premiere, and the group performed the whole work on selected tours as well as sections from it on programs containing other works. Its revival in 1944 may have been ill-judged; in June, Allied forces crossed the English Channel to land in Normandy, and after D-Day, World War II entered its last, exhausted days. America's looming theme was a gradual return to "normalcy" rather than a hopeful invocation of its past history's triumphs and disgraces. In any case, by then,

Graham had moved on. Although Hawkins continued to work in Ballet Caravan into 1939, after that, he would no longer be listed as part of Graham's "Apprentice Group." As a full-fledged company member and soon to be her lover, his presence in her life gradually altered the way she constructed her dances and the roles she created for herself.

—11—

ENTER THE MEN

ON OCTOBER 12, 1938, three days after *American Document* was performed in Carnegie Hall, Graham sent a telegram to Erick Hawkins c/o Ballet Caravan:

I WANT TO TELL YOU AGAIN HOW HAPPY I WAS DANCING WITH YOU AND HOW BEAUTIFULLY I FELT YOU DANCED SOME DAY THE TRUTH CAN BE KNOWN ABOUT MR MARTIN I HOPE DO NOT LET HIM TOUCH YOUR DANCING OR YOUR FAITH IN YOURSELF BEST WISHES=MARTHA.

Hawkins must have been depressed by John Martin's *New York Times* review of *American Document*, which wrote of his performance: "with so little experience in movement of this sort he is unable to give it conviction." The telegram was the first, but not the last, message with which Graham strove to build up the self-confidence and soothe the ruffled ego of the man who became her partner.

The advent of Hawkins in Graham's life was so significant that it would not be entirely amiss to hark back to her long-ago loving letter to Ted Shawn, and to label her working years prior to meeting Hawkins "B.E." and the next dozen that followed as "A.E." Starting in

1938, he would unsettle, stimulate, and assist her in ways that affected her company, her subject matter, her movement style, and her life.

Fifteen years her junior, tall and muscular, with outstanding cheekbones and a strong nose, Hawkins had settled on his career relatively late in life. Growing up in Trinidad, Colorado, a mining town along the eastern flank of the Sangre de Cristo Mountains, he saw and admired the dances of nearby Indian tribes, but at no point during his youth would studying dance have been an option.

In time, Martha would come to know something about his parents, his four sisters, and his high school years after the family moved to Kansas City, Missouri. There, his father, whom he characterized as "an inventor," was employed at the Bauer Machine Works Company. (Years later, his much older sister Fern, to whom he was very close, characterized the family's years in Missouri as "ghastly.") Martha would also discover how his time spent studying Greek civilization and other topics at Harvard would shape his thinking.

Like José Limón, he had set his mind on a dance career after seeing the German dancer-choreographer Harald Kreutzberg and his partner Yvonne Georgi perform in New York in 1929; and during the early 1930s he went to Europe to study with Kreutzberg. In January 1934, when George Balanchine and Lincoln Kirstein opened the School of American Ballet in New York, Hawkins was among the first thirty-two students. When the select group of what became known as the American Ballet Company gave its first performance that June—on a platform erected at the White Plains estate of the banker Felix Warburg, the new organization's president—Hawkins was onstage in the premiere of Balanchine's *Serenade*. As one of four men who enter for the final "Elegie," he helped lift the leading ballerina and slowly bear her along a diagonal path toward a shaft of light.

He and Lincoln Kirstein had met at Harvard, both graduating in 1930, and it may have been Kirstein who eventually steered him toward Graham, since his ballet technique was not on a par with that of Lew Christensen and Charles Laskey, the most experienced men in the American Ballet Company. Balanchine evidently didn't think much of him, and Kirstein, on December 10, 1934, wrote in his diary that Hawkins was "unfit as yet for the stage," although on a car ride earlier that year, Vladimir Dimitriev—the former singer who had accompanied Balanchine's first small ensemble out of Russia and was now the School of American Ballet's administrator—surprised Kirstein by naming Hawkins as one of the four most talented dancers in the evolving company, after Annabelle Lyon, Laskey, and Gisella Caccialanza. Watching Hawkins some months later in the advanced class at the School of American Ballet, Kirstein thought that he "kept up very well, much better than for example Agnes de Mille."

Kirstein's opinion of Hawkins, like many of his opinions, seemed to change with the weather. After the dress rehearsal of Balanchine's *Mozartiana*, which was performed in the White Plains program on June 9, 1934 (a day before *Serenade* made its debut), Kirstein told his diary that Hawkins (who was not in *Mozartiana*) was "sweet & very enthusiastic & inspired." In November, however, he was "hard-headed, thick & even dumb." During the dress parade of costumes for the December 6 performance at Hartford's Wadsworth Atheneum, he wrote that Hawkins was "slightly uppity & fractious I thought, as if at any [point] he might soar off into a mania of self-importance however it may be concealed now." And at the school's Christmas party (at which Balanchine did "an elaborate & funny imitation of [dance monologist] Angna Enters"), Hawkins, said Kirstein, "was mad with love of life and dangerous to get in the way of it." It was reported that in the dressing room before the company's New York debut on March 1, 1935—as the American Ballet Company—Erick wouldn't joke with the boys but liked touching the girls' legs.

Later in 1935, the financially stressed American Ballet, headed by Balanchine, became the Metropolitan Opera's resident ensemble, and Kirstein, with Balanchine's blessing, shunted some of the dancers the following year into a new company he called the Ballet Caravan (later American Ballet Caravan). On friendly terms with Kirstein, Graham watched the progress of this new, America-eager company.

As the dance historian Lynn Garafola has pointed out, during its brief performing life (1936–39), Ballet Caravan functioned very much like a modern dance company; it was small in size (initially a dozen dancers) and bent on forging an American identity for ballet—in part, perhaps, because John Martin of *The New York Times* had characterized Balanchine as having "found in the musical comedy field a more fitting outlet for his particular talents than those loftier fields with which he has been chiefly associated heretofore." Kirstein contributed essays to Louis Horst's modern-dance-oriented *Dance Observer* rather than to a major newspaper. Too, Frances Hawkins, while still Martha Graham's booking agent, procured New York performances for Ballet Caravan at institutions associated with modern dance—not just Bennington College, but the 92nd Street YMHA, Washington Irving High School, and the New School for Social Research. In the last week of December 1939 she produced an eight-performance season featuring her clients: three programs apiece for Martha Graham and Group and American Ballet Caravan, plus one each for Carmelita Maracci and the Korean dancer Sai Shoki, both in Los Angeles.

Erick Hawkins did not appear in Balanchine's *Serenade* when it was first performed in New York, and it's not certain whether what Kirstein enigmatically termed "Erick's failure"—in Eugene Loring's *Alma Mater* at Ballet Caravan's performance in Hartford, Connecticut, on December 6, 1934—led to his being dropped from the cast of that ballet, although he later appeared in Loring's 1938 *Billy the Kid*, as well as in both Christensen's 1939 *Pocahontas* and his *Filling Station*. It is clear, however, that Hawkins was being encouraged to choreograph—also that Kirstein had found another use for the ambitious young dancer. On January 24, 1935, he noted in his diary that from 1:30 to 3:00 he had been given his first private ballet class by Hawkins: "Started basically at the beginning. Extremely hard for me although I didn't feel tired afterward & learned a lot in a way I [couldn't] do in any other, Eric [*sic*] a fine teacher." By February his feet hurt when he gets up in the morning, but he keeps at it; his subsequent entries are pitted with references to lessons with Hawkins. The writerly and intellectual side of him craved to understand, however imperfectly, just what the dancers that he and Balanchine had brought together dealt with every day.

One could wish to have been a fly on the wall to watch one of these sessions. Kirstein, a well-heeled, twenty-seven-year-old ballet-smitten impresario trying to hold his lean body erect and muscle his long, untrained legs into fifth position, while a twenty-five-year-old member of the company he founded and helped finance puts him through his paces. On March 2, he is able to say, "Improving some."

Kirstein's diary entries also reveal Balanchine's responses to Graham's work and hers to his. The two men saw a performance by Martha Graham and Group in February 1935. According to Kirstein, Balanchine thought her talent was superior to that of Léonide Massine; he had the impression (not entirely correct) that of all the contemporary European choreographers, she had seen only the works of Mary Wigman—certainly not the modernist constructions by Kasian Goleizovsky or Vaslav Nijinsky that were familiar to him. Kirstein thought that all the running the women did in Graham's *Course* was "effective" and *Celebration* was "also OK." He didn't care for any of the music. As for Balanchine, reported Kirstein, he "liked [Graham's] body and her hair & would like to baise her" ("baise" being the *au courant* slang for something much more intimate).

Kirstein was prepared to be generous to Graham—at least in a limited way. He thought that perhaps she could "do something for us," providing she could work with Balanchine; in fact he suggested as much to their joint manager Frances Hawkins—"but not using her group because that w[oul]d merely mean an invitation to use 1/3 of our program." Graham, in turn, was interested in Balanchine's work (although Louis Horst, according to Kirstein, hated what he saw in March 1935, and someone else reported that the Graham company's left-wing rebel Anna Sokolow—an emerging choreographer herself—did too). Graham, wrote Kirstein, "thinks the turns are unnecessary & the costumes embarrass the girls."

Hawkins's diary, letters written to him by his sister Fern, and the letters Graham sent to him (every one of which he saved) attest to how smitten she was with him, as well as how much she admired him, bolstered his ego, and gave him tactful artistic advice. (No letters that he wrote to her during the 1930s survive, and beginning late in 1939, the two were so often together that few were exchanged.)

However, in a letter she sent him from California after her three-week teaching stint there in 1939 (the summer that the Bennington School of the Dance temporarily moved to Mills College in Oakland), she makes it clear that they have become lovers and that their physical connection is not to be taken lightly: "The reason people grow old is that they do not worship sex as the great immortality—and because they do not know it is to be practiced deeply with concentration and simple delight. It is like air to be breathed and food to be eaten." She has been reading the poem by Emily Dickinson that begins "Come slowly, Eden!" and writes it out for him, all the way through the last verse:

> Rowing in Eden!
> Ah! The sea!
> Might I but moor
> Tonight in thee!

She is also, however, down-to-earth and frequently humorous with her lover. On one of her westbound trips, she writes him that a "sweet little girl from Brooklyn" had come upon her washing her face in the train's dressing room, "looking like a cross between a monkey and a peeled onion."

Already worrying about the effect of their affair on Horst, still her invaluable music director and accompanist, she hoped to join Hawkins in "Indian country" in early September, but writes instead, "I dare not go into any of that country if Louis is still there without letting him know—and to stay on after he left might complicate . . ." She trails off.

As always, her work is topmost in her mind. Thinking back on *American Document*, she writes, "I wish I could make it so much better—particularly the last—also let us try to tighten the Puritan a little, make it a little more hard—more truly beautiful with a hard flaming whiteness—not forget the tenderness—make it more so. I cannot explain—but I know what it is. I think sometimes it was tender because we knew it was tender—now it must be tender with a kind of hard deep pain at its root."

Because her letters are rarely dated, it is difficult to be certain of their sequence, but it is clear from the beginning that Hawkins was both insecure about his talent and quick to take offense. He finally told her, for instance, that she had hurt his feelings in the way she worked with him on *American Document*, and she explained her reasons patiently and at length: "I was trying to make you feel free. I was not trying to 'break through' simply to make you dance well with me. That I can truly and honestly say." Perhaps, she added, she was wrong, and she went on to speak of the differences between ballet and the aims of modern dance.

Since he was still performing and touring with Ballet Caravan and working on his own choreography, she answered some of his letters with what sounds like remarkable insight (and in what may, for him, have been daunting detail). He is planning a duet for Christensen and Caccialanza (partners offstage as well), both of whom Graham is sure "will be lovely in it." He shouldn't worry, she says, that its subject matter is too close to that of Fokine's *Spectre de la rose*, a duet for a dreaming girl and the spirit of the rose she carried at the evening's party. However,

If you should feel that it is you might reverse the order and have her enter. I realize that would not be so dramatic or as good from a dancing viewpoint—theatrically speaking. Also it would mean changing the idea to be his dream of her—in a lull in battle—or in a dug-out. Then it would be the man's piece essentially. It would mean he danced alone when there was battle in the air—when battle cleared she reappears and he dances with her in variations of passionate and tender mood. Then, of course, it is man alternating between war and love—a kind of mad round. Then it finally would be "Soldier's Fate" or "Fate of a Soldier."

I do not say these things to confuse you. I like your idea. I feel, perhaps, it could be deepened into a "War Classic" or "Classic of a Soldier" not as a title. It might be quite terribly moving at times—if she entered on her points each time in complete silence or sound as like a little drum sound made by her points—as a contrast to the drums of war—the drums of the heart—a man made to dance in different ways by two kinds of drums—the drums of war and the drums of her foot fall—within it all is re-evaluated—their meeting—broken—their first embrace—broken—their farewell—broken. Etc—etc.

Now I have probably been a devil and upset you. I hope not, Erick. Whatever way it comes, keep it as you plan, concise—clear "the rhythm of the spirit in gestures of living things."

But Graham was eager to let Erick know how much she admired his performing. So, writing to him from San Francisco about Limón's solo suite, *Danzas Mexicanas*, which had premiered at Mills College, she reassures him that José "is marvelous in movement—but that is not enough—Something is burned out of him—it would seem—He is a shadow—not alive—He has energy, beauty of movement—tragic line—but he is a shell." She goes on to tell him that the San Francisco sculptor Raimondo Puccinelli "thinks you are magnificent—feels there is no comparison between you and José!—& I agree." The Ballet Caravan dancers, she tells him, especially Christensen, have spoken highly of his performance in *American Document*. She's "very happy about that because he [Christensen] is such a beautiful dancer himself."

After attending two performances of the recently reorganized Ballet Russe de Monte Carlo under Léonide Massine's direction, she writes him that the more she saw, for example, of Serge Lifar's ballet about Icarus and his ill-advised flight, "the more I know you American bred men have a sweep—a loose beauty—a virility—they do not possess." In Balanchine's *Apollo*, Ballet Caravan's Christensen "filled the stage. In 'Icare,' Lifar did not. He danced well but he leaves me untouched. He is petulant, He has no inner power, That is a sin. 'Icare' was childish—and he was vain. I have seen enough 'drops' and 'scenic pieces' for some time to come."

Interestingly, she finds *St. Francis* by Massine, with whom she had so mildly wrangled during rehearsals for his *Rite of Spring* almost ten years earlier, "very beautiful and very moving . . . There was organization on Massine's part that resulted in movement—passionate, ecstatic and simple but not simple at all. It possessed the grave 'beyond technic' [*sic*] quality of great dancing."

After Graham's "hard three weeks" at Mills College, she wrote to Hawkins that she had decided to augment a new work she was planning to premiere in December: "You know I spoke to you of the Ringmaster—that will be it—I know—so we will begin. It will be satire."

The dance to which she referred was *Every Soul Is a Circus*. It would be introduced to New Yorkers during the Graham company's performances at the St. James Theatre during Frances Hawkins's "Holiday Dance Festival" (December 26–31, 1939). It astonished New York's dance aficionados: Martha Graham being funny, Martha Graham allowing herself to be dominated by a man. People didn't just giggle; belly laughs rang out. Martha Graham, in fact, was happy and in love, but as giddy as her onstage persona was, the dance she had described as a satire could be taken as a cautionary tale for any strong woman artist deep in an affair of the heart.

The dance also brought Graham to a reconsideration of her onstage persona. The supple, occasionally flirtatious femininity of some of her 1920s solos returned as an element of movement dialogue between herself and a male dancer and also presented a more complex image of the female body in order to encompass indecision or uncertainty. Over the next few years those changes would extend to the women dancers who stayed with her, and the men she added to her company would take over the strong, stalwart style that she had demanded of her women.

Graham had drawn her new work's title from a verse in a poem by

Vachel Lindsay that had implications beyond Lindsay's 1928 phantas-magorical, politically tinged visions of acrobats and trained animals:

> Every soul is a circus
> Every mind is a tent
> Every heart is a sawdust ring
> Where the circling race is spent.

Only five of her "girls," labeled as "Arenic Performers," appeared in its cast: Nelle Fisher (the principal one), Ethel Butler, Frieda Flier, Sophie Maslow, and Marjorie Mazia. In addition to Graham as Empress of the Arena and Hawkins as the Ringmaster, Jean Erdman appeared as the Ideal Spectator, and a second man, billed as Mercier Cunningham, made his debut with the company as the Acrobat. Coming from Seattle's Cornish School, where he had studied acting, plus dance with former Grahamite Bonnie Bird, the twenty-year-old Cunningham had enrolled in the summer dance program at Mills and had been solicited by Humphrey and Weidman as well as by Graham. Graham invited him to come see her if and when he might be in New York, but she professed to be surprised when he actually showed up on her doorstep (so to speak). Years later, he recalled thinking, "Lady, you don't know me very well."

You have to imagine Paul Nordhoff's score when watching a silent black-and-white record film of *Every Soul Is a Circus* (made in the early 1940s), nor can you be sure of the original color of the ingenious costumes (attributed to Edythe Gilfond but surely imagined by Graham). You can postulate that the arena is—in part anyway—that of the Empress's own mind, and, inevitably, she is the heroine of the story. Prancing like trained ponies, the five women and Cunningham bring in, move, and remove the props and pieces that constitute Philip Stapp's set, sometimes entering and exiting through a small curtained doorway between two simulated theater boxes, in one of which sits the Ideal Spectator—changing hats or covering her head with veils as she watches (or avoids watching) the "performance." You can also perhaps envision her in this mostly stationary role as the Empress's alter ego.

Her onetime sudden appearance, popping up from out of sight, her head covered with a black veil, perhaps prophesies danger.

This is a circus in which tricks are announced with fanfare but, absurdly, come to nothing much (although that doesn't stop the Ringmaster from taking bows after them). You can envision Graham—self-satirizing though her role in the story may be—musing over how much power this man can wield over her and how much she's prepared to yield. Perhaps, in part, she also represents herself as the choreographer, debating her ideas and restlessly flogging herself into creation.

We are to imagine that the circus has not yet begun when the curtain rises. Graham reclines on padded bench and practices an annunciatory gesture toward the portal. She lies back and flips a hand to suggest that she's splashing water on her face; she smacks her buttocks rhythmically against the bench three times and later does the same with her elbows. Uneasy lies the head that wears the crown. Or the performer who waits for the show to commence.

She freezes when the Ringmaster marches in (possibly the first time she used this device of immobility, of temporary erasure, that later became a crucial ingredient in her dance dramas). Hawkins is very virile in his first solo—jumping straight up, swinging his legs around, spinning, and stepping for brief, suspended moments onto the low circular stool that also resembles a wooden cage for a very small animal. His bearing and his shifting gaze suggest both arrogance and dedication to his task.

In their first duet, "Training Ring," the Empress, rising from her bench, both defers to him and outfoxes him. He cracks his whip (a slender, flexible stick). She deliberates (who me? move where?) and shakes her head demurely. He indicates that she should circle him, but she finishes by going the "wrong" way, then sits and, briefly but meaningfully, strokes the whip he brandishes above her. When they exit to prepare for the show, the Ideal Spectator enters and tries out a few of the moves from the Ringmaster's warm-up before taking her seat in the ringside box.

At his command, two of the women grasp what has appeared to be a slim vertical pole dividing the stage in half. They separate its attachments into two ribbons that they drape and attach offstage to create the pitch of a tent. Graham, now wearing a full, ingeniously shaped, boldly striped cloak over her dress, arrives to perform "The Show Begins: Star Turn." Holding the ends of a cord that's tied around her left ankle, acting as her own puppeteer, she yanks her leg this way and that, slides into a split, twitches her shoulders, and, for a fleeting moment, pretends that the rope is the string of a viol and plucks it. She also gallops about the arena and jumps, legs bent, looking like a butterfly as the cape billows out.

This circus not only alludes to animal trainers and curveting horses; it makes use of the well-known magic-act tricks (a cloth is whipped away; behold! a rabbit!). But Graham's disappearing acts are endearingly flawed, like a child's efforts at magic tricks. When she mounts the little platform (now set adjacent to the main exit) and Cunningham holds a small curtain in front of her, we can see her legs perfectly well as she "vanishes." Before long, Hawkins conjures her up again from behind the small curtain, whisking it impressively away.

Now with a sleeveless black overdress over her gown (in the box, Erdman puts a veil over her head), she warms up for a stunt with Cunningham. He kneels, and she pushes him backward; he bounces right back up, like one of those inflatable toys you can't keep down. She enjoys doing that, but Hawkins keeps picking her up and carrying her away. Although the two men collaborate in lifting her and carrying her along between them, the result is a tug-of-war for her attention.

On one of his entrances Cunningham holds a horizontal stick in front of him, and the four Arenic Performers, yoked to it by ropes, prance and turn within those limits. He shows off his jumps. However, other of his presentations fizzle out almost before they begin—for instance, his poses and moves with the delectable leading Arenic Performer and their very temporary disappearing act under a large translucent veil that three women have thrown over the pair. In a later number he will jump and twiddle his feet together in the air, Nelle Fisher (Nina Fonaroff in the film) will copy his moves, and while others come and go, the two will demonstrate what they obviously see as an accomplishment: holding the pole in front of them horizontally, they each drape one leg over it and stand there for a while swinging it gently from side to side.

What makes the askew stunts funnier is that, although they have the timing of a big deal, the performers don't smile or look as if they intend to please the audience. Most of their encounters map the relationships among them rather than theirs with us. One duet between the Empress of the Arena and the Ringmaster is telling—a conjugal relationship condensed into a scant number of minutes. The two indulge in a quick game of patty-cake, after which she takes his arm for what looks like a stroll by a companionable couple, except that she dips down into a squat every other step, and he doesn't notice. They step out in a tango, their joined hands stuck out to the sides. He clasps her from behind and makes her tilt from side to side. She ensconces herself on the floor, he lies down stiffly with his head in her lap, and she rocks him. They sit, knees bent, facing each other, then hold hands and lean back; thus evenly braced, they slowly rise together. Later, he holds one of her hands and rotates while she runs and hops around him to keep from being twisted up. In the end, she sits in the middle of the seesaw on which they have earlier attained equilibrium. He pushes on one end to make it go up and down a couple of times, then gives her a look and a "so, is this it?" gesture and exits. She follows.

The final scene features a large fake flower, enigmatic in its symbolism. Graham, in white again (after what has amounted to a parade of costumes), lightly whacks Hawkins's buttocks with it to get his attention and persuades him to sit beside her on her bench. They pass the blossom back and forth, she gazing questioningly at him. Cunningham prances in to repeat the little game of kneeling and being pushed back by her. And soon, as she dithers about, he picks up the flower, passes it to her as he races by, then grabs it back. She chases after him but stops with a jolt as she comes up beside Hawkins, whose waiting arm she then takes to resume their decorous walk, until he, on the platform, holding her hand, again makes her run and hop around him.

In the end, she hunkers down on the bench, her face in her hands, then falls forward onto it, her feet scrabbling against the floor. The show is over. Up in the box, Erdman, the Spectator, lifts the black veil off her head and dons her hat. Passing across the stage, she appears aghast to see Graham, sitting up and lying back down over and over, lashing her long black hair back and forth. Hawkins meanwhile ushers the bevy of women-horses out the curtained entry without a backward glance. Alone onstage, the Empress of this charged arena falls onto her face on the bench and lies there inert as the curtain falls.

Perhaps only in retrospect can one find inklings in *Every Soul Is a Circus* of Graham's feelings about how this new relationship with Hawkins meshes with her role as the head of a company and the creative force behind it. Most critics saw the piece as simply a bright, surprising comedy that, on a later tour, generated enthusiastic applause among Chicago spectators. Those who had not seen some of Graham's earlier frisky solos were thrilled to see her as a skilled comedian.

Claudia Cassidy, writing for Chicago's *Journal of Commerce*, saw something deeper:

> Here Miss Graham mimes the sawdust ring of a silly woman's soul and in that mime she combines her unique beauty of movements with Beatrice Lillie's hilarious understatement and Chaplin's poignant diffidence. On the surface she is slapstick, superficial, concrete; below that comic patina lies a depth of observation, projected by the profound abstractions of a great dancer.

To the composer/critic David Diamond,

> The circus she creates is one of silly behavior and ridiculous situations, its theme, the desire of woman to be the apex of a triangle, the beloved of a duet, who, as the spectator of her own actions, becomes the destroyer of experiences necessary to her essential dignity and integrity. It represents the fullest consummation of Miss Graham's

conceptions. She has unified her entire dance vocabulary into a simple and direct theatrical means of projection and communication. The perfection of her technique, the warmth of personality make this performance a piece of the most poignant clowning seen in the dance.

At least two writers dubbed *Every Soul Is a Circus* a masterpiece, and it stayed in Graham's company's repertory for eight years, a sure-fire closer to any program.

The advent of Cunningham had added a new dimension. In *Every Soul Is a Circus*, you sense her trying him out, seeing how he will fit in. As the Acrobat, he's hardly acrobatic in the traditional sense, but she made use of his wonderful lightness, his unstrained buoyancy in leaps, his long neck, and his animal alertness. Still, although she reaches adoringly for him at one point, she doesn't then, or in later dances, cast him as her lover. His roles are more androgynous: the Christ figure in *El Penitente*; March, the harbinger of Spring and, possibly, a childhood playmate in *Letter to the World*; Pegasus, the Winged Horse, in *Punch and the Judy*; the "Poetic Beloved" in *Deaths and Entrances*; and the Revivalist in *Appalachian Spring*. She also made use of his acting training by having him take over the Interlocutor's role in *American Document* on later tours and perform as Yankee, an orator, in her short-lived 1942 *Land Be Bright*.

Every Soul Is a Circus can be thought of as a transitional piece in Graham's creative voyage into theatrical storytelling. Like the very different *American Document*, it was a collection of thematically linked vignettes—acts in a show. The 1939 work linked these within the span of a day's rehearsal and performance, yet Graham was already trying to discover new ways to deal with narrative beside the conventional one of a single plot moving through introduction, conflict, rising action, climax, denouement. Over the next five years she proceeded to build her structures on the religious rituals of the American Southwest (*El Penitente*), selected poems by Emily Dickinson (*Letter to the World*), a puppet show (*Punch and the Judy*), biography (*Deaths and Entrances*), and a wedding ceremony (*Appalachian Spring*). None of the works, however, would use those forms in traditional ways.

Graham's offstage life in the months of 1939 before she began work on *Every Soul Is a Circus* says something about how wholeheartedly she had reconciled herself to the paid activities and publicizing that might help her sustain a company. She gives lectures, including an hour-long one at the three-day First American Congress for Aesthetics at the University of Scranton. She gives interviews. Seven newspapers syndicated (via UPS) a January 22 article titled "Noted Dance Artist Approves of Shag and Hop of Jitterbugs" in which Graham reports how much she admired the looseness and suppleness of the men in a Madison Square Garden dance contest. The jaunty strut of the Lambeth Walk, she says "doesn't fit the vitality of this Nation like tap dancing and the Shag." She singles out Fred Astaire and Paul Draper for praise. (This in advance of her company's fourth United States tour.) A few days later, the *New York Post* photographs her at the emporium of I. J. Fox, trying on a fur coat and a snappy little hat while the furrier, Fox himself, watches. She plugs the coat, and the paper mentions her company's performance later in the month in a series in the McMillan Theater at Columbia University that also features Trudi Schoop, Angna Enters, Lotte Goslar, and others.

At various times throughout the year, a photograph of her accompanies articles about the Yale Puppeteers' touring revue, *It's a Small World*. The image, syndicated in sixty-two papers, is of Graham in her costume for *Frontier* posing with a gaunt-faced puppet dressed just like her (the puppet figures in a number called "Tremors on Toid Avenue"). In one photo of her and her double, they're shaking hands. Few of her modern dance colleagues received—or were willing to agree to—that kind of publicity. It helped build her company's touring schedule, and vice versa. In the spring of 1939, her company had averaged two performances a week on its six-week tour, with Hawkins managing to weave his appearances around his commitments to Ballet Caravan. Twenty-five hundred people attended a performance at Chicago's Civic Opera House. During the long 1940 spring tour—with both *American Document* and *Every Soul Is a Circus* on the program, along with *Frontier* and Graham's new stars-and-stripes solo, *Columbiad*—the performances averaged four per week.

By then Hawkins had left Kirstein's company and given up his apartment to share Graham's at 29 West Twelfth Street, handy to her 66 Fifth Avenue studio. And with her, he traveled to Bennington in the summer of 1940, where—surely on her recommendation—he would present a solo concert featuring three solos he had choreographed and would also continue to rehearse the two pieces she would premiere there in August: *El Penitente* and *Letter to the World*.

Graham was not the only one shifting artistic focus. The Bennington School of the Dance had returned to Vermont a changed entity now called the Bennington School of the Arts. Economy may have been a factor. No longer would visual artists and musicians work mainly to assist choreographers during the six-week session, although it was possible for students immersed in the Dance Division, the Drama Division, the Music Division, or the Theatre Design Division to take a course or two in another of the four. Dance, as might be expected, still accounted for eighty-three percent of the college's tuition income.

Graham was the only one of the Big Four to be in residence and show work during the festival that followed the school's sessions. Although Holm taught an advanced Master Course in Dance for chosen students, her technique—and that of Graham, Humphrey, and Weidman—was taught by a member of each company (and Graham technique was also taught by Ethel Butler). Martha Hill, Bessie Schönberg, and Louis Horst continued to teach their usual courses. Two firsts: Hawkins taught a ballet class for advanced students, and Helen Priest (later Rogers) introduced a course in Dance Notation. Lincoln Kirstein was a visiting lecturer.

The escalating war in Europe made the Bennington Armory unavailable for performances. Students, apprentices, and fellows presented their plays, scenes from plays, choreography, and music compositions in weekly "Workshops" in the college theater or, in the case of the music concerts occurring during the festival, in the Recreation Center. The relatively small upstairs theater was well suited to Hawkins's solos: *Liberty Tree—A Set of Four Dances* (music by Ralph Gilbert, who accompanied the classes in Graham Technique); *Insubstantial Pageant—A Dance of Experience* (music by Lehman Engel); and *Yankee Bluebritches—A Vermont Fantasy* (music by Hunter Johnson). Carlus Dyer, Graham's onetime lover, provided sets for the first two, and his wife, the artist Charlotte Trowbridge, designed those for the third. Graham would have had trouble fitting *El Penitente*—a trio for herself, Hawkins, and Cunningham—into such a setting. For this, she'd drawn on a Christian tradition of self-flagellation (for centuries outlawed by the Roman Catholic Church), as adopted by the Mexican and American Indian Christians she and Horst had seen in New Mexico, with which Hawkins may also have been familiar. Lashing themselves as they walked in a procession, the peninitents took upon themselves the punishment Christ endured before his crucifixion.

Graham structured *El Penitente* as a play within a play. The three performers march onto the stage like celebrants entering a town plaza, and at the end of the story they've come to tell, they join in a lusty little dance. Their props and other accoutrements lie in the floor at the back of the stage. An early program note likened them to the minstrels arriving in a medieval town to enact a mystery play. Hawkins becomes the Penitent, whipping his bare back with a ragged belt that looks as if it's made of horsehair. Cunningham plays the Christ figure. In the first performances he wore a long, belted tunic over white pants, with a headpiece first resembling a crown of thorns and later a gilded palm-leaf fanning out behind his head like a sunburst or an aura; later, when Isamu Noguchi redesigned the decor, he put Cunningham in priestly black and covered his face with a large, highly stylized mask that evoked the bleached cow skulls that might be found in a desert. Graham, wearing the ruffle-edged white dress that Gilfond stitched for her, played three Marys: Virgin, Magdalen, and Mater Dolorosa.

Everything about the style of the piece asks us to believe that these three extraordinarily skilled professionals are devout amateurs—a little clumsy, their props perhaps homemade—and their audience the unseen members of their community. Horst's simple score for flute or piccolo, oboe, clarinet, violin, and piano conveys a sense of open spaces, and its melodies evoke Mexican tunes; a taut, high-pitched drum mimics those of the New Mexican tribes. The "play" evolves in little scenes, and a piece of fabric, attached to the large wooden cruciform shape wielded by the Christ figure, serves to conceal the performers when necessary. The Penitent whips himself, contracting under the force of blows that the music emphasizes with sharp chords. He sidles along on his knees, then circles the stage with a springy, tiptoe step that has the uneven rhythm of a gallop, his close-together feet striking the floor. His ordeal ends when he holds the belt away from himself and falls onto it.

When Graham appears from behind the fabric as the Virgin, she brings her niche with her: no molded church hollow, but a piece of sky-blue fabric hanging from the arched frame that she holds. Within it, she moves with a certain innocent wonder—an earthy young woman, not an iconic figure. When she lifts a leg to the side or bends it behind her, she doesn't employ a dancerly turnout and her feet are flexed. Her scurrying runs and low hops bring her to hover occasionally over the Penitent. She looks as if she's checking to see that he's all right. The Christ figure advances, raises the Penitent to his knees, and admonishes (or praises) him with some jumps and oratorical thwacks of one foot against the floor. The Penitent, finally upright, falls into his Savior's arms.

The middle scene is one to cheer up the onlookers. Graham, a big pink fabric flower sitting on her head, its attached pink veil falling behind her, is now the temptress. Billed as Mary Magdalen but acting more like Eve, she teases the Penitent with an unrealistically large, two-dimensional apple, exploiting the theme of hitting the floor with the ball of one foot while lying on her side like an odalisque. In this rustic duet the Penitent follows her around like a dog being lured by a bone. He's so innocent that when he touches the hip she juts out for him, he springs back as if he's just laid his hand on a hot stove. When Christ discovers the "sin," he succinctly and rhythmically slaps the kneeling Penitent lightly on both cheeks, as if admonishing a naughty schoolboy, and then jumps over and over to knock the message home.

The transition between these scenes allows the audience to watch the performers prepare for the next stage of the ritual, but at other times the transformation comes as something of a surprise. The pile of wood turns out to be a small, collapsible cart—the "death cart." The Penitent, the lash tied around his chest and his head covered by a black hood, crawls along dragging it while Graham, almost entirely covered by a black sheet, travels on tiptoe within it. This cart and its burden, says the program, represent his sins. The Christ figure travels along behind the two, and in one of the dance's most touching images, he lets part of his curtain slide down (via cord and an invisible pulley) to allow us to see, for seconds at a time, his sympathy and his encouragement, while Horst's music becomes sweetly hymnlike.

The music becomes heavier in rhythm and tone during the journey to the crucifixion. The wooden prop is bare now; Christ lays it over the Penitent's shoulders, and he trudges slowly along under its weight. Graham designed this slow progress as almost two-dimensional, like a church frieze showing the Way of the Cross. Mary, now the mother, with a black shawl over her head, walks bent over and close to him, her steps in time with his. She wipes the sweat from his face and tries, if she can, to take part of his burdened weight on herself. Several times, Christ briefly lifts the cross from him, as a respite. All this time, the sense that they are traveling along a road persists, even though the procession barely moves across the stage.

And then, without fanfare, he is "dead" and the play is over; the participants tidy up the props, Cunningham removes his robe and headdress, and, to sprightly music, the three performers engage in an invented folk dance—kicking out their feet, hopping, taking twisty little steps and low leaps, slapping their hips and lifting their arms. Their last move is to link arms and sidle toward the audience, as if ready to take a bow now that they feel nearer to God and ready to celebrate.

El Penitente shared the Bennington program with a far more ambitious new work that, according to the critics who made the trip to Vermont, was not fully fledged and much too long. By the time *Letter to the World* received its first New York performance, in January 1941, it had undergone serious surgery and acquired a new set by Arch Lauterer to suit the larger stage of the Mansfield Theatre. Most influential in shaping the work was a casting change. At Bennington, excerpts from approximately thirty of Emily Dickinson's poems were spoken by the actress Margaret Meredith, who wore a period costume and delivered her lines from a chair; the Graham dancer Jean Erdman described her as "a lady in white with curls."

Perhaps Graham had a reason for recruiting Meredith. The actor Houseley Stevenson, Jr., had fitted himself neatly into the role of the Interlocutor in *American Document*, and words mattered when one was choreographing a dance inspired by a poet. But, as she came to see, the role of an announcer for a high-toned, patriotic series of scenes differed from that of a stand-in for Emily Dickinson reciting words that were intimate with the dancing. The catalyst for change was an injury to Meredith, at which point Graham asked Erdman to stand in for the actress while *Letter* was being revised. Erdman, gutsy and outspoken, asked instead to audition for the role: "Don't ask me . . . me, a dancer, [to] sub for an actress who couldn't move." By the time *Letter to the World* made its New York debut, Erdman and Graham had become twinned aspects of Dickinson, described in the program as "One Who Dances" and "One Who Speaks." That this speaker was a dancer too made all the difference.

Graham had added three men to her company (George Hall, David Campbell, and David Zellmer), and their advent enabled new choreographic considerations. She gathered the poetry into several main themes: childhood, youth, nature, love, death. But the images conjured up by these impinge on one another, pass through, or wait on the sidelines. There is no single narrative on which audiences can fix-ate. Emily, who at one point appears dead, returns to life, as if she has only been imagining her demise.

In a program note on the dance six years later, Graham tried to discourage spectators from interpreting the dance as a biography of Dickinson: "The action is built on the legend rather than the facts of her life; and the scene is laid in the shadow world of her imagination, rather than in the real world of Amherst where she lived." Except for the doomful figure termed the Ancestress, who exemplifies the rigid-ity of religion, each of the female characters, the note says, represents an aspect of Dickinson at various periods of her life, while the men are "extensions" of the character identified as Lover, who represents "her gesture toward happiness." True happiness would be found in her work. However it's not only Dickinson's words that drive the choreog-raphy; in addition to steeping herself in the poems, Graham read bi-ographies of the poet, and the images in *Letter to the World* do evoke—however fleetingly—the world in which the poet lived and those who peopled it.

Although the two artists lived in different decades (Dickinson died in her family home in Amherst, Massachusetts, in 1886, eight years before Graham was born), ideas about women's roles and strict Protestant observance affected the upbringing of both. They both, too, became irreverent about organized religion later in their lives. You can understand the choreographer cherishing the poet who writes, "The Bible is an antique Volume / Written by faded men / At the suggestion of Holy Spectres." Graham, in opposition to estab-lished dance forms, was bold in shaping an original way of expressing herself onstage. Dickinson, although admiring of the poetry of Keats and the Brownings, wrote in her own ideosyncratic way and without thought of publication.

Graham had created her dance language through a process of stripping away excess in order to create strong, direct movement. Dickinson spoke a franker, plainer language than did most poets of her generation. Glorying in her garden flowers and the birds that flew about in them, she personified these or addressed poems to them and to other less tangible visitors, yet without romanticizing her subjects. What other nineteenth-century poet, enamored of nature, could have said of the grass that it "so little has to do"?

In a number of other ways, however, the two artists were not at all alike. When, beginning in 1862, Thomas Wentworth Higginson, Dickinson's mentor, informal editor, and epistolary friend, finally met her—after they had been corresponding for eight years—he found her just as she had described herself to him: "[I am] small, like the wren; and my hair is bold, like the chestnut bur; and my eyes, like the sherry in the glass, that the guest leaves. Would this do just as well?" Martha, too, was on the small side, but hardly wrenlike. Nor was she, like Dickinson, often ill. Nor could she, in her chosen profession, be the recluse that the poet became in the early 1860s.

It is significant that the bulk of the poems Graham used for *Letter to the World* date from 1861 and 1862, when Dickinson was in her early thirties. She had had a playful childhood with her younger brother and sister and their companions; she made other friends during her school days at the Amherst Academy. However, death was always a presence in the lives of the community: women died in childbirth, children died from infections that had no known cure, and in April 1861 the Civil War began, bringing with it news of injuries and deaths of young men, some of them from Amherst. Higginson served briefly in the volunteer army, and Dickinson was much relieved to note that he emerged with only a minor wound. One of her dearest friends, Benjamin Newton, who had tutored her for a while, perished from tuberculosis after a debilitating decline. The "much-loved young director" of the Amherst Academy died as well.

At its New York premiere, the pruned and revised *Letter to the World* was peopled by the One Who Dances and the One Who Speaks (Graham and Erdman), Lover (Hawkins), March (Cunningham), Ancestress (Jane Dudley), Fairy Queen (Nelle Fisher), Young Girl (Sophie Maslow), and the Two Children (Nina Fonaroff and Marjorie Mazia), plus six additional men and women. Arch Lauterer designed a structure more elaborate than what he had managed at Bennington and more in line with what Graham had wished that the set piece might be—something like a "summer house, to make it dreamlike." In the end, the setting announced itself as a garden, with an ambiguous threshold upstage left—part tall metal garden gates, part Venetian shutter, and part open doorway. Opposite this was a white garden bench that could be tipped on its side or turned into a rocking chair and was portable enough to be lifted overhead to form a temporary shelter. Hunter Johnson's music for piano and percussion allowed for pauses, in which Erdman spoke, and shifted its mood to suit the social and emotional climates.

Letter to the World was the first dance in which Graham tried to portray in a group work the inner landscape of her protagonist, the first time her heroine relived events or sensations in memory. It is telling that in the original Bennington program she characterized the One Who Speaks and the characters billed as Two Children as "Characters in the Real World" and everyone else as "Characters in the World of Imagination." Interviewed years later, Erdman said that the whole dance took place in Emily's mind within the virtual moment it would have taken Graham to travel from the "house" to the bench where she sits when Erdman delivers the final line of the piece.

In the first section, titled "Because I See New Englandly," after Dickinson's poem, she and Erdman, wearing similar long gowns in different colors, stride about the stage on separate right-angling paths, as if to acquaint us with their parallel existence. After this prelude Graham is alone for a happy, scampery solo, with small leaps in a circle and skittering hops. (Martha Graham skipping? A shock, perhaps for some devotees.)

Now and then her gestures remind us that the whole of *Letter to the World* is taking place in the open air, with breezes to feel, skies to gaze upon, and flowers at her feet. The firmness with which she makes a deliberate gesture of placing her hands behind her back indicates a girl brought up to be a lady. When Erdman returns, it's with the line "I'm nobody! Who are you? / Are you nobody, too? / Then there's a pair of us." The two women bow to each other and hold hands as they dance—sisters who can whisper together.

Various characters pass through *Letter to the World* the way the bees and birds pass through the Dickinsons' garden. The poet attended parties when she was a young girl, and four couples make their several appearances festive ones. For them, the choreographer created imaginative versions of the reels and circle dances that young New Englanders of a certain class would have known. Their dancing is unlike anything Graham had made before, or would make again. These young people are here to have fun, and their steps are jaunty and swift-footed, the men taking good care of their partners. Among the party-goers is Cunningham, the jauntiest of all, who takes a few seconds in the group's first entry to leave his partner and try a few nimble, tricky steps for his own pleasure.

The two children linked to the "real world" periodically race through the action; at other times they enter it. In one of the scenes she has summoned up, the ensemble of eight marches as if down the aisle of a church, with the halting step befitting such a procession. Johnson's music evokes a familiar hymn: "Are You Washed in the Blood of the Lamb?" "Looking at death is dying" is Erdman's last word for now. And suddenly the men lift Graham overhead as if on a bier (the necessary manipulation is concealed by their veiled, kneeling female partners, so it's a shock when she appears high in the air, lying on her back, hands folded). The pallbearers ceremoniously bear her a short distance and lay her on the floor. In the hurly-burly that follows, the two little girls are lifted by the men and laid out side by side. Twin deaths? But after a pause, they sit up, exchange looks, and run happily offstage together. They've only been reenacting the tales they were told.

When Erdman recites the line "I'm saying every day / 'If I should be a Queen, tomorrow'— / I'd do it this way," the two girls, who've been sitting at her feet and listening to the stories she "tells" (as they do several times), gladly join the suddenly appearing Fairy Queen, who holds up a small maypole while they dance with its two ribbons. They're onstage again to assist the Young Girl (the adolescent Emily surely) being teased by an interested young friend (Cunningham) in a brief, impudently flirtatious scene. She expresses her elation by jumping over and over, opening her legs in the air like wings, before he pulls her offstage.

The Lover and the Ancestress vie for control of Emily's spirit. Even though Hawkins's character is identified in the program as "Lover," he could also at various points in the dance suggest Dickinson's father, or a friend of her brother's, or one of the men Emily considered her mentors, and a man she loved (or imagined loving). Despite his many straight-up-and-down jumps, the opening solo, as he performs it, doesn't convey elation, only strength and decisiveness.

A heavy beat in Johnson's score and the line "It's coming—the postponeless creature" cause the two Emilys to rush together and clutch each other. "It gains the Block and now it gains the door" (the two little girls rush across the stage) / "And carries one—out of it—to God." The Ancestress makes her first appearance from within slightly parted curtains at the back of the stage, instantly ominous, although that aforementioned theater program note describes her as "beautiful" as well. Jane Dudley, on whom the role was built, was at least eight inches taller than Graham. Dressed in black, and wearing a white ruffled bonnet, she evoked an implacable *Whistler's Mother*, but also, perhaps, Graham's own great-grandmother, severe in a family photograph, wearing a dark, long-sleeved dress and the headgear that every married woman was expected to don. (This relative, recalled Graham, had supervised her eldest great-granddaughter, Martha, remorselessly in the weighty business of ironing a handkerchief until it gleamed white and wrinkle-free.)

In *Letter to the World*, however, the seemingly gigantic woman represents more than a severe relative. She is death's harbinger, or alluring death itself, as well as signifying stultifying religious morality. To the ominous sound of a wood block, she comes up behind Graham, gestures fiercely, and clamps her arms around the smaller woman, encaging her. She then backs her over to the bench, sits, pulls her onto her lap, and rocks her stiffly (both a terrifying image of love frozen into a convention and the suggestion that this domineering creature may indeed bear Emily off to heaven). She's given to pointing a finger high, as a reminder of the rewards for virtue, or to climbing onto the bench—a black cloud hanging over the garden. From that elevated position, she, briefly, seems to have snared one of the partying youths (Cunningham).

One of the duets between Graham and Hawkins also suggests that, as well as feeling deeply the deaths, or potential deaths, of others she knew, Emily Dickinson had considered her own. After the somber ensemble has laid Graham on the floor and exited, the Lover comes to her. The idea of a duet between a living human and a dead one has become a cliché since *Letter to the World*, but it's uncannily moving as performed by Graham—even when seen in a silent black-and-white record film. This Emily isn't truly dead; she is only numbed and incapacitated by grief. Collapsed across Hawkins's bent knee, she suddenly, leadenly, rolls lower and is caught by him just in time. If, perhaps, he represents her love of life, his task is to revive her. He pulls her firmly to her feet, holds her up. You see a flicker of life. But he releases his grip too soon, and she falls backward. This happens several times. He twists her from side to side, lifts her, and swings her around almost roughly, and gradually her strength returns. The music gallops furiously as the Ancestress runs, bent over, her arms curved behind her, and the other women rush about in the same way (the critic Marcia B. Siegel likened them to harpies or furies).

The section ends with Erdman backing Dudley off the stage: "In the name of the bee / And of the butterfly / And of the breeze, / Amen!"

Suddenly the "garden" is a sunny place again, and Emily is a young girl. But it is Erdman's Emily who frisks about delivering lines from one of Dickinson's most charming poems: "Inebriate of air am I, / And debauchee of dew, / Reeling through endless summer days, / From inns of molten blue." Graham's Emily returns, delighted with herself—the "little tippler" of the poem. She shrugs her shoulders several times, as if the very gesture emancipates her from duties and she can do whatever she likes today. The long, full skirt of her remarkable magenta costume is open at the front, and under it, she's wearing black taffeta trousers, which she clearly enjoys showing as she swishes her skirt about. Her dance alludes here and there to a sailor's hornpipe: hopping, holding one bent leg up behind her, she lifts one hand to shield her eyes from an imagined sun. She makes her feet fly in precise little steps and clicks her heels together in the air. Her arms briefly reel in an imaginary rope. These images, however, are not presented as vignettes, but are embedded in the flow of the dance.

Cunningham rushes onto the stage, takes a look at this playful young woman, leaves, and reenters with a buoyant series of jumps. He's not too early after all! Erdman has welcomed him: "Dear March, come in!" And as he continues his ebullient dancing: "How glad I am! / I hoped for you before." The month of March ushers in the spring, and spring Cunningham does. But he's also a lad with whom the girl poetess greatly enjoys playing. She sits rocking and fanning herself with her hand while he dances, and when he comes to straddle the tipped bench, they seem to be conversing.

The two little girls run into the above scene and take a turn rocking, and in the end all four performers fall back and kick their legs in the air. It takes the Ancestress, stalking in and righting the bench with which they've been playing, to remind them of propriety.

The second half of *Letter to the World* turns dark again. The two Emilys enter, their heads covered with veils (wedding veils perhaps), and Graham, now costumed more soberly, removes her veil, regards it, and places it carefully on the bench, then picks it up again and runs with it. Her dancing expresses trepidation. She arches back under the weight of the veil, gazes to one side and the other. She throws herself repeatedly into big tipped-over turns on one leg that cause her full skirt to bell out into circle after circle. When the men enter, two of them flank her and wait quietly. Graham turns her head to look at each of them. Perhaps they are off to war and she is saying goodbye (Martha the performer was always brilliant at conveying her state of mind while doing very little).

The duet with Hawkins that follows is enigmatic. He bends tenderly over her as she sits, head bowed, on the bench. She "listens" to his dancing rather than keeping her eyes on him, but he alludes to her often as he jumps, paces, spins. You imagine him telling her something important. When he draws her to her feet, however, they are not joyful in their dancing. Once, he lunges, reaching toward some distant goal, and she rests quietly for a few seconds on the calf of his back leg. At another moment he places his hands on either side of her face as she wilts, and when she falls—seems to faint, even—across his widespread, bent legs, he leans over her, moving his hands along her body, inches above it, as if tracing her into memory (or perhaps it's that she can no longer remember or fully envision the feel of those hands). Holding their arms straight in front of them, his fencing hers, the two walk together, he behind her, while Erdman recites the poem that begins "I'm wife; I've finished that, / That other state." (Since no secret marriage had been discovered between Dickinson and any of her male friends, that is perhaps a dreamed-of one.)

In the end, the Ancestress-as-Death enters and with a knifelike gesture cleaves them apart, eventually forcing the Lover to retreat upstage and pass between the partly open back curtains, where he falls. Here Erdman recites some of Dickinson's most anguished lines. "There is a pain so utter / It swallows being up." And while Graham dances as if she were being ripped apart—convulsing, hitting her hands against the bench—Erdman raises Dickinson's outraged cry to heaven:

> Of course I prayed—
> And did God care?
> He cared as much as on the air
> A bird had stamped her foot
> And cried, "Give me!"

Erdman begins walking across the stage, sometimes backward, and exiting; each time she reenters from a different wing, reciting a few more lines as she goes. In the middle of this final section, Graham confronts the lurking Ancestress and, palm to palm, wrestles her into bending backward toward the ground and crawling away. Around this victory swirl images seen earlier in the dance. Graham, reentering in a simple white gown, reprises some of her previous movements, gathering her memories. In the end, she is alone. Erdman has crossed the stage for the last time, saying, "This is my letter to the world," and Graham follows her diagonal path from the portal to the bench, sits, and folds her hands in her lap. She will not be anyone's wife, nor burdened with a sense of sin. She will be the master of a universe of words.

In this extraordinary work, Graham experimented with mingling past and present, the real and the imagined, and Dickinson and herself as dedicated artists. Parsing the aspects of Dickinson's life that were pressed out onto the page through the poems, Martha created *Letter to the World* not as a simple narrative (although the defeat of all that the Ancestress represents gives the work dramatic momentum), but as a montage of images. The critic Stark Young wrote, "The reading of the poetry was imaginatively contrived, as if it were music calling out the movement's soul." To choreograph the dance, Graham had, in a sense, to become a poet herself. And, considering the dances she went on to create, its title has the glint of a manifesto.

~12~

MAKING PLAYS DANCE

I N 1941, Graham's image and her words reached a population larger than those who had seen her and her company in a theater or those students who had quailed before her uncompromising eye. Barbara Morgan's *Martha Graham: Sixteen Dances in Photographs*, which was published that year, included not only images but a chronology of Graham's choreography, put together by Louis Horst, and a list of all the dancers who had worked with her over the years. Morgan had started photographing Graham and her works after seeing a performance in 1935. Having grown up on a California peach ranch and begun her career as a painter, she had switched to photography when motherhood made that more feasible (her husband, Lloyd Morgan, was a photojournalist). Over the years, she indulged her fascination with dance by taking remarkable photos of modern dancers in action: Doris Humphrey, Valerie Bettis, Pearl Primus, José Limón . . . But Graham inspired her more than the others (the image of Martha in *Letter to the World*, plunging forward, her long skirt foaming up like a wave behind the leg lifted high behind her, has become iconic). Morgan shot photos of Merce Cunningham sitting on the floor, twisting himself into Graham exercises; she shot Graham alone in what looked like sunlight, naked or garbed in a makeshift practice dress. Years later, Graham celebrated the woman who had become her friend by commenting in the book's 1980 republication: "It is rare that even an inspired photographer possesses the demonic eye which can capture the instant of dance and transform it into timeless gesture. In Barbara Morgan I found that person." When Erick Hawkins was seeking funding, support, and performance opportunities for the Martha Graham Dance Company, he sent a copy of the book to Serge Koussevitzky to implement his request.

Graham appeared in a different guise in an anthology edited by Frederick Rand Rogers, *Dance: A Basic Educational Technique*. Her essay, "A Modern Dancer's Primer for Action," included not just a survey of her teaching methods and the attitude that a would-be dancer should have toward technique, the body, and dance itself; her introduction has the force of a mission statement, announcing her own approach to her work.

She began with a terse history, explaining the emergence of a new movement language more suited to contemporary life than ballet. "A break from a certain rigidity, a certain glibness, a certain accent on overprivilege was needed. There was need of an intensification, a simplification. For a time, this need manifested itself in an extreme of movement asceticism."

Then, she announced, came "a swing back from that extreme. All facilities of the body are again being used fearlessly, but during that time of asceticism, so-called, much glibness was dropped, much of the purely decorative cast aside."

For her, the "swing back" also involved an approach to narrative and theatricality. During the late 1930s and early 1940s she went to the theater fairly regularly (when she could afford a ticket)—not just to view what ballet companies were offering and what Doris Humphrey, Charles Weidman, or Hanya Holm were up to, but to see plays. In December 1942 she saw a revival of Chekhov's *Three Sisters*, in which her friend Katharine Cornell played Masha. Her letter to Cornell exemplifies how intently and with what insight she watched events onstage. Of the production's Natasha, she wrote, "Ruth Gordon was the viper that the part calls for, the deadly female thing that can eat the heart out of anything or anybody and emerge fresh and fed. It is a loathsome part because it is so attractive in the beginning. She plays with a dancer's use of space, even a slight gesture seems to have sufficient tension behind it to allow it to hang suspended in a kind of lovely evil design." The following week she attended Thornton Wilder's *The Skin of Our Teeth* with its author. A few days later, she accompanied composer Lehman Engel to see Alfred Lunt and Lynn Fontanne in *The Pirate*, a play written for the celebrated pair by S. N. Behrman.

The above may not be a typical week for her, but she had been combining the spoken word and movement since 1938 and educating herself as to how drama might develop through the rhythmic interplay between them. Teaching at the Neighborhood Playhouse, she had observed how actors prepared for a role and how a knowledge of movement could enhance a performance. Marian Seldes, who studied with her at the Playhouse, recalled that the actor Richard Boone said he had based his walk as Paladin in television's *Have Gun Will Travel* on Martha's classroom demonstration of how a cat moved.

Graham's choreographic project in 1941 was *Punch and the Judy*, a witty, satirical dance-play that employed snippets of a text drawn from the prologues for puppet plays written by Edward Gordon Craig under the pseudonym of Tom Fool. Erick Hawkins played Punch, Graham played The Judy. The capital *T* affixed to the article in the name suggests that she was distancing herself from her character, or refusing to pin herself down as just one of several equal contenders in the "squabble and scuffle" that characterized the battling family of traditional Punch and Judy puppet shows. Nina Fonaroff appeared as their Child. Jean Erdman, Jane Dudley, and Ethel Butler played the Three Fates and spoke (mostly Erdman's job) the text. Two of the three men Graham had acquired for *Letter to the World*—David Campbell and David Zellmer—were joined by Sasha Liebich (later known as Mark Ryder). Identified as "Heroes," they were costumed, respectively, as a Soldier, a Scout, and a Pony Express rider—appetizing figures whom The Judy "auditioned" as a replacement for her philandering husband. Merce Cunningham was given the role of Pegasus—not exactly the winged horse of legend, but an alluring figure representing free-flying imagination. In his review of the New York performance, John Martin suggested that the theme of the piece was "how to be happy though married."

Janet Soares, in her biography of Louis Horst, writes that Graham's faithful music director "may have hoped for a score by Aaron Copland" to accompany the new work, but in the end, the music was written by Robert McBride (Hawkins's idea). A handy solution, since the choreography was to be shown at Bennington in August, and McBride was on the arts faculty there—as, of course, was Arch Lauterer.

Lauterer's scenery for *Punch and the Judy* employed a bed that was set horizontally on a platform and framed by a wall at its foot and an entranceway at its head. Most remarkable—at least as seen in a silent 1940s film—is the wall at the foot of the bed. Its outer side appears to have slight indentations into which Graham fits perfectly; when facing it, she seems to drop a kiss into it, perhaps to prepare her for the next event.

The Fates congregate on and around a chair, a footstool, and a small table holding a large globe. It's established right away that these women are busybodies. Wearing headpieces and long, full-skirted gowns, they periodically dash away from their home base to rush around, pointing here and there, circling the stage, and, on occasion, tiptoeing back to where they came from. They whisper among themselves, and one of them pulls away a dark cloth to reveal the globe to be a crystal ball, above which she waves her arms, as if attempting an abracadabra.

With the exception of the Fates, all the characters seem to be part human, part puppet, with Graham herself only occasionally artificial. She contemplates Hawkins, slumbering on his back with his feet pointing up, shrugs her shoulders, and does a little dance of hesitation to and away from her spouse. Awakening, Hawkins kicks his legs into the air, as straight as if an unseen puppeteer has pulled them up on strings attached to his toes. He's full of himself—swaggering across the stage, jumping up behind the chair to kiss the head of the seated

Fate, and patting another (they might as well be his aunts). After launching into a little solo consisting of big hops and tricky in-and-out twists of one leg, he looks toward the audience and encouragingly mimes applause.

As in any Punch-and-Judy show, the conjugal relationship is defined in a very few minutes. Hawkins kisses Graham's hand, pulls her around a bit, and pushes her away. She retreats to the bed, hand to brow. He walks away "thinking," beckons her, and when she comes, kisses her, then slaps her. After which, they strike a family pose, she kneeling on one knee, he standing, a hand on her shoulder.

As their offspring, Fonaroff is less a puppet than a doll; straight-legged and slightly turned in, she holds her dress; takes awkward, jittery little steps; and hops herself into turns (her introductory solo is a high point of the dance). However, her entrance brings more domestic complications. When she runs around her parents and stamps her foot in a mechanical tantrum, Graham soothes her and Hawkins spanks her, which causes Graham to cover her own eyes in dismay. The Judy then whacks her mate, and the Child, spanked again, gets trundled off by Hawkins as if she were a wheelbarrow.

Graham is cheered up when Cunningham as Pegasus pops up from behind the set, kissing her cheek, greeting the Fates. She hangs on to him, and they pulse together as if he's taking her on a ride through the sky. Then, with a wave, he disappears again, and another optimistic vision of family life is attempted. Graham sits in the chair, reading a book; Hawkins lounges on the stool, his legs stretched out; Fonaroff rests on the floor, leaning against the chair. But the Fates pace around plotting, and in comes a temptation for Punch: Pretty Polly, another sometime character in old Punch-and-Judy shows, appears (played by Pearl Lack—later Lang). Up bounds Punch. She's so innocent, so lovely! (He mimes the ballet gesture for "beautiful," circling his face with one hand and kissing his fingers to let us know what he thinks of her.) He plants a reassuring kiss on his wife's head before sneaking away with this doll-like charmer in his arms.

Of course, Graham/The Judy has a fit, and the three ladies comfort her. She bats a wad of black fabric back and forth between her hands as if contemplating who knows what, then solemnly dons black gloves and whisks her skirt around to signal that she's putting this marriage to rest and contemplating a new partner. Indeed, with a little help from the Fates, her gesture ushers in the three Heroes, and she summons each in turn to show her his stuff. They appear identical except for their outfits, and they define their job descriptions in the most obvious terms. Liebich obliges with marching steps and big jumps. Pressed against Zellmer's back, Graham reaches around to shield his eyes with her hand. He drops down to cock an ear to the floor, and the two of them peer in various directions (while the three Fates sit on the floor, their skirts over their heads). He's sent away with a handshake. When Graham whips her skirt a third time, Campbell ties a bandanna over his mouth and mimes aiming two pistols while the alarmed women gallop in place. Graham sends all three men away,

However, after the Fates have rustled around, figuring out their next strategy, the Heroes reenter through a little arbor they have carried onto the stage. Hawkins rises from his nap and shakes hands with them, agreeing on a deal. Graham is blindfolded while the men compete, avoiding her attempts to catch one of them. In the end, the stereotypical three more or less deliver her to Hawkins. Horrified, she collapses. In the end, this Judy gives Punch a good swat, and the Fates deliver a final line: "Shall we begin again?"

Anyone seeing this somewhat dark comedy decades after it premiered might wonder what Hawkins thought when his lover created this tale of a botched, for-better-or-for-worse marriage, with infidelity contemplated as revenge for a mate's faithlessness. Also, Graham choreographed a fine part for him and cast herself as one who would stand by him despite any straying on his part or misgivings on hers.

The critics approved. Walter Terry of the *Herald Tribune* found *Punch and the Judy* "hilarious." Margaret Lloyd of *The Christian Science Monitor* called it "a polished little sinfonia domestica, a gem of observation and comment." Edwin Denby, writing for *Modern Music*, praised McBride's score but was sufficiently perplexed by the dance to devote his monthly column to it twice. Although he called *Punch and the Judy* "the one American choreography of first class quality that I have seen this season," he grappled with his impression that the characters, except for Punch and The Judy, had "only unreal puppet foils" to react to. "They themselves, part puppet, part human, never can act toward the others humanely."

I don't entirely agree with this most thoughtful of dance critics (there are several subtle, very "human" images of behavior, including one in which The Judy and the Child walk companionably toward the chair, hand in hand and chatting silently). However, Denby discerned that Graham was continuing to develop her role as the observer in her dance dramas, as well as playing a character in them. Except for the Fates, she is the only one of the characters in *Punch and the Judy*—as she was in *Every Soul Is a Circus*—who shows indecision and plots strategies. The stylizations in the new work suggest that the other characters are being manipulated not just by the Fates, but by unseen puppeteers, who may in turn stand for the machinations going on in Martha-as-Judy's mind.

Graham and Hawkins had been together for three years at this point, and their relationship affected the life of the company and occasionally tested her authority. Gertrude Shurr and Anna Sokolow had left, unable to endure Hawkins's presumption. What right had this upstart to order them around? Nevertheless, Hawkins figured in Graham's plans for the studio at 66 Fifth Avenue. Writing to him from California, she wonders whether he will want to teach a ballet class there in the spring. Three afternoons? Maybe two mornings as well, when she is teaching classes at the Neighborhood Playhouse? She encourages his desire to choreograph.

She also battened on his strength. According to Jane Dudley, "Once the scenery and props came into the studio, he saw to it that they got packed for performances and tours. He was like a janitor, and he was a good one, and, as there began to be added men, he got all the men in the company to serve as stagehands (they were permitted to in those carefree days), and they could knock the set down and put it into crates and then set it up on arrival."

Martha Graham, age two
(Library of Congress, Music Division)

(Clockwise from
bottom left) Martha
Graham with her
younger sister
Mary and their
nurse, Elizabeth
"Lizzie" Prendergast,
seated in front of
a photographer's
background
(Library of Congress,
Music Division)

A postcard showing the Cumnock School of Expression in Los Angeles (Published by Benham Indian Trading Company)

Artistic nude image of Martha Graham (standing) and her trio of dancers: (seated, from left) Thelma Biracree, Evelyn Sabin, and either Betty Macdonald or Susanne Vacanti (who took over Macdonald's roles) (Library of Congress, Music Division. Courtesy of Martha Graham Resources)

(From left) Thelma Biracree, Betty Macdonald, and Evelyn Sabin in Martha Graham's *Danse Languide* (Photograph by Soichi Sunami. Courtesy of the Soichi Sunami Estate and Martha Graham Resources)

Martha Graham and Ted Shawn flirting in a Spanish dance (Shawn's duet, *Malagueña*) in 1921 (Photograph by Albert Witzel. Jerome Robbins Dance Division, the New York Public Library)

Martha Graham as a Japanese maiden in one of Denishawn's solos (ca. 1919–23)

Ruth St. Denis (standing, right), admired by Ted Shawn (seated, far right) and members of their company, including Martha Graham (seated, second from left)
(Danvis Collection / Alamy Stock Photo)

Robert Gorham and Martha
Graham costumed and posing
for *Xochitl*, billed as an "Aztec"
ballet (1920)
(Photograph by Fred Hartsook.
Jerome Robbins Dance Division,
the New York Public Library.
Courtesy of Martha Graham
Resources)

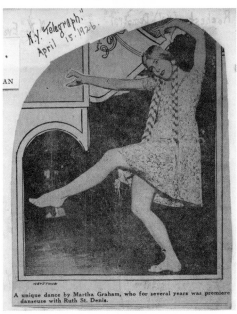

Martha Graham in *Maid with the Flaxen Hair*
(New York: *The Morning Telegraph*, April 15, 1926. Library of Congress,
Music Division. Courtesy of Martha Graham Resources)

The Marionette Show, by Martha Graham, for her trio: (from left) Thelma Biracree, Evelyn Sabin, and Betty Macdonald (November 18, 1926)
(Courtesy of Martha Graham Resources)

Betty May and Martha Graham as "Mammy" (ca. 1926). Graham may not have considered the racial implications of this role at a time when white singers occasionally used blackface makeup.
(Courtesy of Martha Graham Resources)

The Greenwich Village Theatre, where the Greenwich Village Follies were held (1923–24), on the Manhattan corner where Christopher Street, Seventh Avenue, and West Fourth Street come together

Martha Graham as the heroine/victim in Léonide Massine's version of *Le Sacre du Printemps*, danced by members of Graham's company, among others. The women attending her may be Gertrude Shurr and Eleanor King. (Courtesy of Martha Graham Resources)

Martha Graham
and Rich Currier
in a pseudo-
Spanish dance
onstage at
Mariarden, where
Ted Shawn and
Graham did some
summer teaching
(Bettmann / Getty
Images. Courtesy of
Martha Graham
Resources)

Martha Graham in her ballet *Ekstasis*
(Photograph by Soichi Sunami.
Courtesy of the Soichi Sunami Estate and
Martha Graham Resources)

Martha Graham demonstrates
her high kick to the identically
garbed members of her company,
seated on the lawn at Bennington
College. In 1941, they, plus
twenty-four apprentices,
danced in an early version
of Graham's *Panorama*.
(Photograph by Hans Knopf. © Jacob's
Pillow Dance Festival. Courtesy of
Martha Graham Resources)

An early cast in Martha Graham's *Primitive Mysteries* (1931). Standing at the back are (from left) Sophie Maslow, Jane Dudley, Helen Priest Rogers (substituting for a dancer unable to be there), and Freda Flier Maddow. Those identifiable kneeling at right are Nina Fonaroff and Ethel Butler.
(Photograph by Barbara Morgan. Courtesy of the Barbara and Willard Morgan photographs and papers, Library Special Collections, Charles E. Young Research Library, UCLA, and Martha Graham Resources)

(From left) Jane Dudley, Sophie Maslow, and Freda Flier Maddow on the fall 2006 cover of *Ballet Review*, announcing a later conversation between Maddow and Francis Mason within its covers

(Photograph by Barbara Morgan. Courtesy of the Barbara and Willard Morgan photographs and papers, Library Special Collections, Charles E. Young Research Library, UCLA, and Martha Graham Resources)

Martha Graham in Léonide Massine's *Rite of Spring*, 1930
(Lebrecht Music Arts / Bridgeman Images. Courtesy of Martha Graham Resources)

Miguel Covarrubias's illustration for the December 1934 issue of *Vanity Fair*, referring to the "Impossible Interview" within: "Sally Rand vs. Martha Graham"
(Miguel Covarrubias, *Vanity Fair* © Condé Nast)

Iconic 1940 image of Martha Graham in *Letter to the World*
(Photograph by Barbara Morgan. Courtesy of the Barbara and Willard Morgan photographs
and papers, Library Special Collections, Charles E. Young Research Library, UCLA,
and Martha Graham Resources)

Martha Graham, Erick Hawkins, and Yuriko in Graham's *Cave of the Heart* (Photograph by Philippe Halsman. © Philippe Halsman Estate 2023. Courtesy of Martha Graham Resources)

Martha Graham, as Mary, Queen of Scots, in her ballet *Episodes I*, faces her executioner (Kenneth Petersen). (Photograph by Martha Swope. © New York Public Library. Courtesy of Martha Graham Resources)

Martha Graham rehearses a 1986 revival of her 1929 dance *Heretic*,
set to variations on the music of an old Breton song.
(Photograph by Martha Swope. © New York Public Library. Courtesy of Martha Graham Resources)

Martha Graham ascending the stairway at the Metropolitan Opera House, 1980
(Photograph by Martha Swope. © New York Public Library)

Martha Graham in the garden behind her New York studio, surrounded by choreographers of her own generation and two later ones. (Clockwise from lower left) Twyla Tharp, Merce Cunningham, Erick Hawkins, Paul Taylor, Yvonne Rainer, Don Redlich, José Limón

(Jack Mitchell / Getty Images)

In September 1941, another letter that Martha wrote to Erick during her usual California visit is full of requests and suggestions. The topic of money comes up frequently in their correspondence. The studio floor needs a light coat of wax, but he must be tactful in requesting it, because she owes the landlord money. The lights will have to be turned back on at the apartment; she is behind in paying the electric bill but doesn't know how much it is; perhaps when she gets home she can borrow from Jean Erdman or from the Neighborhood Playhouse. They can pay Lincoln Kirstein for the lessons Erick is continuing to take at the School of American Ballet as soon as her check from Bennington arrives. He may need to borrow some money until it does come, because she has none at present. She reminds him that there's no virtue in poverty.

Hawkins had his own problems—artistic and personal—and he often confided them to his older sister. Back in the late 1920s, when he was still a student at Harvard, Fern had advised "Fred" (later he chopped off the first part of his given name, Frederick) that he "must learn to limber up. No matter what you think about anything or anyone. You can be a better mixer." (She also told him that he smiled too little.) He wrote her worriedly from Harvard about his homoerotic urges and possible experiences (she wrote back that she almost fainted when she read his letter, but rallied enough to provide counsel that focused on abstinence).

It's not surprising that more than a decade later he would be frustrated that an intimate relationship with Martha Graham entailed downplaying what in the 1940s could be considered a masculine prerogative, although Fern counseled him that competing with a genius was futile. Certainly he had a strong influence on Graham. On more than one occasion he was able to calm her when no one else dared. In turn, Graham—who had met with his sister and his father en route to the West Coast—went out of her way to placate and encourage him. In one letter attesting to her love for him, as well as the many ways in which she depends on him, she refers to his "locked heart," going on to say, "But there are deep ways of my woman's soul where you have lead [*sic*] me and I have gone into jungles with you where I have never been before." She wants to help him with his insecurities, "but sometimes I am so clumsy with you and I know you feel that I have a stone in my heart." She does not, she writes, want him to make sacrifices for her. (Indeed, she agreed at least twice to go on camping trips with him out West—this was when he learned that she couldn't swim and found lakes threatening.)

Speaking of Graham years later, Ben Belitt attested to her ability to be, in one minute, the domineering artist out to get what she wanted and, in the next, a wit and a charmer.

> She was lustrous, a commanding presence, one of a kind. She radiated charisma and power, even though at the table she was the most—well—deceptively accessible and flirtatious Irish colleen. If she wanted to make you this gift of her accessibility and her intimacy, to scramble you eggs . . . at 1:00 in the morning and reach for the pith of your brain, she did so with utmost gentleness or a benevolent mockery that made my whole identity squint . . . And it was this kind of laughing provocation that finally loosened me to regard her as a very great colleague with whom I could talk myself into stillness.

To her students, of course, she was both inspiring and a terror. One young man who studied with her later said, "The other teachers [at her studio] are great but they do not shoot electricity out of their eyes . . . nor can you see energy flow out of them . . . She never tells you anything with just her mouth. No! She tells you with every fiber of her body. The voice just happens to be part of her body." No one in her classes got away with just executing the movements; they had to deliver them as if each bore the moment's most important message.

She demanded much of her company members, but approached them differently. At this stage of her career she rarely demonstrated passages of movement that she expected dancers such as Hawkins or Cunningham to copy; more often, she provided an image or two and sent them off to work on their own—after which she would view, enhance, discard, and alter what they had come up with, and perhaps be spurred to embark in a new direction. Cunningham confirmed

what many who worked with her acknowledged: "She liked contention in the company. She needed it in her life. It was the way she could
work . . . It was always as though she needed something to push
against in order to continue."

On December 5, 1941, the Martha Graham Dance Company left to
perform in the southern states and also made its second appearance
outside the United States. On Sunday, December 7, the dancers were
on the train from Rome, Georgia, to Miami, preparing to embark for
an engagement in Cuba, when they learned that Japanese airplanes
had bombed Pearl Harbor. While in Miami, waiting for permission to
proceed, they heard President Roosevelt broadcast his intention to request Congress to declare war. The performances in Havana, Cuba,
on December 9 and 10, needless to say, were not the best that the
dancers had given. Jean Erdman had been born in Hawaii and spent
her early school years there; David Campbell too had roots in the islands. Cunningham had been unable to appear with the company;
scheduled to take the U.S. Army physical examination, he had gone
back to Washington. Welland Lathrop, who had studied with Graham at the Neighborhood Playhouse, took over Cunningham's roles
in *El Penitente*, *Letter to the World*, and *Punch and the Judy*, while Liebich substituted for him in *Every Soul Is a Circus*.

With a spring tour in the offing, the company returned to the
United States, a country gradually adjusting to war. Although Cunningham was eventually declared 1A, he was not inducted (he may, in
the end, have admitted to homosexual experiences). According to Agnes de Mille, Hawkins's poor eyesight rendered him unfit for service.
Eventually Liebich and Zellmer would be called up, and Campbell
would leave dance to head the drama department of the King-Smith
Studio School in Washington, D.C. Graham's company was, of course,
not the only dance organization to be depleted: gradually Lincoln
Kirstein, José Limón, and numerous others departed civilian life, as
did Belitt and Merle Armitage.

Civilian life involved restructuring. In January 1942 Congress's new Emergency Price Control Act enabled the Office of Price Administration to ration food and other commodities, as well as to set price limits. By spring, one needed food stamps to purchase sugar. Gasoline rationing began in November. By March of the following year, ration books were issued with variously colored stamps for meat, cheese, butter and other fats, canned fish, canned milk, and other items. The days of victory gardens, recycling, and blackout curtains on coastal areas lay ahead.

In a climate of patriotic fervor, Graham prepared a new work called *Land Be Bright* and premiered it at the Chicago Civic Opera House in March; it was relegated to the dustbin after two performances. The cast list gives you an idea of what it may have been like. Hawkins played "Chingachgook, the friend of Leather Stocking"; Cunningham took on the role of "Yankee, an orator," which suggests that he spoke some text; Graham was billed as "Betsy Ross, flag-maker." The eight company women were labeled "A chorus of Americans."

With Hawkins's assistance, Graham taught the usual June Course at her studio—an experience that unfailingly irritated her; she found too few students who flared into beauty and commitment among the merely eager and dutiful. In July, she and her company repaired to Bennington and a reduced summer session—the last of its kind. The college maintained a two-hundred-acre farm, and students were encouraged to labor on it. Doris Humphrey wrote to a former company member that Bennington "has reorganized its summer session to include science, agriculture, and so forth, and has re-organized the dance center almost out of existence."

Nonetheless, Humphrey and Weidman sent representatives to teach, as did Holm. Hawkins taught two levels of ballet. Horst coaxed and bullied students through his usual Pre-Classic Forms and Modern Forms classes. For the second year, American country dancing was offered, and Martha Hill had learned how to call the square dances that took place on certain evenings. New courses were given, subsumed under the heading of Government, Economics, and Science (among these were several gatherings titled Forum on War and the Future, at one of which Graham made an opening statement, and a course called Fundamentals of Food Production).

Although there was no festival, the Graham group resurrected *American Document*, and various members of her company presented their own work. In an August 1 concert, for instance, Cunningham and Erdman performed solos and three collaborative duets: *Seeds of Brightness*, to music by Norman Lloyd; *Ad Lib*, to music by Bennington's Gregory Tucker; and *Credo in Us*, to music by a close friend Cunningham had made while at the Cornish School in Seattle: John Cage. Fonaroff offered two solos. A week later, Maslow and Dudley presented their own dances and teamed up with the Humphrey-Weidman dancer William Bales to premiere pieces for what became a working trio. Woody Guthrie accompanied Maslow's *Two Dust Bowl Ballads*, and Burl Ives sang the songs that accompanied her *Folksay*, which incorporated spoken text from Carl Sandburg's book-length poem *The People, Yes* (Campbell, Liebich, and Zellmer were still available to fill out her cast).

Graham was working on a solo, the first she had made for herself since 1939. *Salem Shore* could be considered relevant to the home-front atmosphere. When the dance premiered in New York on the day after Christmas, a program note portrayed it as "A ballad of a woman's longing for her lover's return from the sea." Martha's sister (now Georgia Sargeant) read portions of Elinor Wylie's seventeen-verse poem, "The Puritan's Ballad," which imagined a dialogue between a mariner and his daydreaming sweetheart:

> My love came up from Barnegat,
> The sea was in his eyes;
> He trod as softly as a cat
> And told me terrible lies.

Unfortunately, the backstage microphone did not work properly for the first part of the dance, and the words that "Geordie" was reciting could barely be heard. Graham soon dropped the text from subsequent performances.

Paul Nordoff composed the score for piano, woodwinds, horn, and bass fiddle, and Horst directed it. Lauterer provided decor and props consisting of things that might be found on a beach. Margaret Lloyd of *The Christian Science Monitor* explained:

> A coil of rope or seadrift, indefinably emanating the idea of a crown of thorns, a black lace parasol with soft pink lining, a weathered fragment of shipwreckage, the widow's walk of an old Salem house, participate in the stress of emotional event. A pale cyclorama bordered with what might be mounds of sand implies the vast stretch of sea beyond.

A photograph of Graham bears out George Beiswanger's more explicit description of the first prop: "a twisted circle of sea-drift"; she looks through it as if it were a window opening on the ocean. The critics who wrote about *Salem Shore* used such words as "tender," "poignant," and "delicate." Denby thought Graham looked "wonderfully young."

Those words could not have been applied to the other work Graham was struggling with at the time. *Deaths and Entrances* had nothing to do with love of country or men in peril. Herself one of three sisters, Graham set out to create images of a more challenged—and exceedingly gifted—trio of siblings: Charlotte, Emily, and Anne Brontë.

There were reasons, aside from a family structure similar to hers, that made the Brontës appeal to Graham—for one, the fierceness with which the young sisters approached their artistic ambitions. In 1837, twenty-one-year-old Charlotte, the eldest, wrote to England's poet laureate Robert Southey about her urge to write poetry. His reply? "Literature cannot be the business of a woman's life: & it ought not to be." Fortunately, these daughters of a widowed curate in a small Yorkshire village—only one of whom lived past the age of thirty—were not easily dissuaded; in childhood, with their brother, Branwell, they created imaginary kingdoms and grew up writing poetry and stories around the dining room table. The sisters had the temerity to send a

London publisher a book of poems purportedly written by three young men: Currer, Ellis, and Acton Bell. Only two or three copies were bought, and their authors became a great deal better known with their novels, especially *Jane Eyre* (Charlotte), which sold extremely well; *Wuthering Heights* (Emily); and *The Tenant of Wildfell Hall* (Anne).

In *Deaths and Entrances*, its title gleaned from a poem by Dylan Thomas, the choreographer chose for herself the role of Emily, although the sisters were not named in the program. Emily Brontë had little in common with Emily Dickinson, the poet protagonist of Graham's *Letter to the World*, even though, of the three sisters, she was the one most comfortable with solitude and walking alone on the moor (the other two managed intermittent careers as governesses). In a letter to David Zellmer, to whom she felt particularly close (and who was at that point training to be a pilot in the air force), Graham remarks that the work she is struggling with has some similarities to *Letter*, but will be "so much more elemental, wild. In some ways it is more abstract. It has as its essence the aloneness one feels in a beloved country—the ecstatic happiness that such aloneness brings with none of the sadness or nostalgia of loneliness." This time, she thinks, she will not use words. Her working title was "Doom Eager," drawn from an Icelandic saga; it means, she writes, "that one lives to the limit the search for one's destiny." The decor was to be by Lauterer and the score by Hunter Johnson, her collaborators on *Letter to the World*.

Choreographing the dance may have been more onerous than usual. In the absence of fall tour dates for the Graham company in 1943, Cunningham and Pearl Lang were working in a new musical, *One Touch of Venus*, choreographed by Graham's friend Agnes de Mille and due to open on Broadway in October. They were available to Graham only on Sunday nights. After the leading male dancer in *One Touch of Venus* was fired during Boston tryouts, Merce Cunningham was called in to replace him. According to the scholar David Vaughan, Cunningham, who had to carry Mary Martin across the stage, "said the situation was unkempt." Fortunately for Graham, he soon quit. In addition, Hawkins was understudying both Curly and Jud Fry in the dream ballet that ends Act I of *Oklahoma!* (this other major musical in which de Mille was involved had opened on March 31). His stint involved his being in the theater on matinee days.

In between the first workshop presentation of *Deaths and Entrances* at Bennington in July 1943 and its second a week later, Martha reports to Zellmer that she is both relieved and let down after finishing and presenting the "strange" new work: "I feel the two days after such a thing as though I had been beaten. My nerves seem to sit out in public." Once recovered, and alerted to how the work might be bettered, she set about revising it in preparation for its Broadway premiere the day after Christmas (you can guess how she and her dancers spent the holiday). Hawkins had secured $2,000 for set and costumes from a wealthy philanthropist in Santa Barbara, and an additional $200 to have the music orchestrated came from a woman who had been taking classes at Graham's studio and whose name gave away her pedigree: Bethsabée de Rothschild. Her first contribution eventually led to twenty years of support.

The Martha Graham Dance Company had not performed in a Broadway theater since 1941, although it had been seen at those bastions of modern dance, the 92nd Street YMHA and the Central High School of Needle Trades. On December 26, the Forty-Sixth Street Theatre was filled with admirers, and people had to be turned away. However, the company's press representative, Isadora Bennett, was able to announce at the second intermission that the theater would be available for another Sunday performance three weeks later, at which *Salem Shore* and *Punch and the Judy* would again bookend *Deaths and Entrances*, the dance that had just startled public and critics alike. Edwin Denby began his review, "It isn't often I've seen the lobby in the intermission so animated in its discussion of a ballet as it was after Martha Graham's new 'Deaths and Entrances.'" John Martin of the *Times* praised the work as "an extraordinary experience in the dance theatre," but also mentioned the "general elusiveness of the work as a whole." Some writers—and undoubtedly some viewers—were more mystified than delighted. Graham reported to Zellmer that "the public seems baffled but moved in some way they do not understand."

She may have anticipated bafflement, because the program note for the new group work is unusually lengthy. It reads in part:

> The action takes place in a room and the halls of an ancient house. It concerns three sisters "doom eager," as the three Brontë sisters were "doom eager," to fulfill their destiny.
>
> It concerns the restless pacing of the heart on some winter evening. There are remembrances of childhood, certain dramatizations of well-known objects, dreams of romance, hatreds born of longings and madness. It is "imagination kindled at antique fires" . . .
>
> This is essentially a legend of poetic experience, rather than a story of incidents. In the secret life of the heart there are invisible actors and "Deaths and Entrances" with no barriers of period or time. Rather, there is a suspension of time and subsequent intensification of experience at the sight of some simple remembered object; a shell, a glass goblet, a vase.

Deaths and Entrances is indeed mysterious. The structure of the novel *Wuthering Heights* may have been a catalyst that further freed Graham from any traditional development of plot. In the novel, the tale of the ill-fated love of Catherine Earnshaw and Heathcliff (the orphan brought by her father into the household of Wuthering Heights) and the violence that resulted from it in the next generation is introduced from the perspective of "Mr. Lockwood," a newcomer to the village of Haworth. He has leased Thrushcross Grange, now owned by Heathcliff, but been forced by stormy weather to spend the night at Wuthering Heights (the domicile of Heathcliff, who had returned from abroad wealthy and vengeful). When the narrator is able to return to his rented house, the strange events he witnessed at Wuthering Heights cause him to question his resident housekeeper, Nelly Dean. So the story then emerges through *her* voice, with Lockwood prompting or querying her at intervals. It is left to him, returning to the place years later, to discover the ending. In other words, Brontë distanced and objectified her tale; the double perspective enabled a flexible approach to the passage of time; passing years could be condensed into a few sentences and crucial actions could be described in detail—an approach that may have affected not just *Deaths and Entrances* but also the narrative structures that Graham would continue to develop in the ensuing years.

Although the novel is suffused with the bleak beauty of the Yorkshire moors, that openness does not inform the dance (although their windswept quality often does). Denby, writing later, compared *Letter to the World* and other Graham dances in which "the real open air . . . is suggested" to ones such as *Deaths and Entrances* that "happen in a room of some kind, and in these pieces, when Miss Graham suggests in her gesture a great space about her, it is, so to speak, the intellectual horizon of the character she depicts."

In a silent film record made in the 1940s, Graham leaves the stage only once during the dance. And it's evident from the beginning that the character she represents is sifting through her memories, perhaps on the brink of a decision, as in *Letter to the World*, and that other characters appear onstage as if summoned by her. Often, when her recollections come to life, she is frozen, unseeing; sometimes others freeze, waiting for her to will them into action.

Among these are not only the women with whom she is listed in the program as "the three sisters," but also those billed as "three remembered children," who evoke the sisters' younger selves.* The heroine's memories are triggered by the small objects that these little girls occasionally bring in and set down and may later move or carry away. As a spectator, you may not fathom the particular significance of these; that's also true of a handkerchief and what look like armloads of black net. Lauterer's three set pieces are both practical and mysterious; they serve as tables, chairs, perhaps portions of a balustrade, yet are not easily identifiable as such; they're solid in themselves but fragments in relation to the whole "room" in which the events take place.

I used the word "heroine" because whatever anguish and possible

---

* In the 1943 cast, Jane Dudley, Graham, and Sophie Maslow played the adult sisters and Ethel Butler, Nina Fonaroff, and Pearl Lang were their remembered childhood selves.

madness Graham's character endures, in the end, when the three sisters, wearing long silk gowns, are grouped around a chess game, as they were when the dance began, it is she who triumphantly lifts a piece and makes the winning move—or changes the game. Like Emily Dickinson—and like Martha Graham—the heroine of *Deaths and Entrances* ends by choosing her destiny.

At several moments during the dance, Graham's gestures and focus reach toward stage right, beyond the place she is in—the kind of place that she later called an "arena of the mind." After the December 26 performance, she wrote:

> The company dances well, very well. They looked most lovely. Edythe did her best dresses for it and the men's clothes were tailored under Erick's eye and are wonderful. I have never seen such handsome men. The three of us, Jane, Sophie and I wore dresses with tiny trains but wide skirts reminiscent of the bustle period. The movements at times looked like mad birds moving. Jane wore cinnamon, Sophie gray and I wore black with green slippers and leaves in my hair.

In *Deaths and Entrances*, Graham limns the portrait of a woman encaged in dilemmas—in her life as in her work. "There are so many little deaths," she wrote, "those moments of doubt, loneliness, fear, anything . . . Just any moment when one ceases to be for a short time. Then there is an entrance again into the real world of energy that is the course of life, that is the immortality." As a choreographer-dancer, she had become expert at conveying conflicting desires with her actions and gestures—twisting this way and that; pacing, one elbow jutting in front of her to bring a hand to her forehead or near her cheek; tipping—plunging—forward, one bent leg lifted behind her; running hunched over, spinning.

Hawkins, identified in the program as the "Dark Beloved," and Cunningham, as the "Poetic Beloved," ratchet up her tension. While it might be tempting to identify the former as a lover (Emily Brontë had none) or the latter as the sisters' dissolute gifted brother, you can more easily see them as conflicting aspects of Graham/Brontë as an artist and/or as glimmering ideas about the characters dreamed up by the author of *Wuthering Heights*. It's telling that, interviewed decades later, the Graham dancer Bertram Ross—who rehearsed Hawkins's role with her for a revival of *Deaths and Entrances* (but never performed it)—explained that "she wanted a much darker Heathcliff, a ruthless charmer."

Hawkins enters the stage walking backward, Cunningham, seconds later, walking forward. They look at each other and at Graham. She doesn't turn to gaze at them, but their appearance incites remarkable dancing from her, which continues after they exit in opposite directions. Contractions cease to be a classroom exercise and become convulsions. In one startling move, she sits, her knees bent to the side, falls backward, then swings one leg like a lever to turn herself until she's sitting again, her legs briefly spreading in the process. She repeats this three times, as if perfecting a sentence about despair.

Graham makes it clear that the objects relate to her thoughts and to her memories. Trying out a few jaunty jig steps, kicking up her legs behind her, and running upstage in perky, tottering little steps (a bit like a child at play), she comes near the right-angled structure that looks something like a bookcase, and she suddenly halts. Turning her head, she sees the blue glass goblet that Fonaroff has hurried in and set down; she touches it lightly. That act brings on all three remembered "children" in their short dresses to burst into a bit of playful dancing. Arms around one another, they race along a diagonal path, form a brief circle, break away, and run out of sight. Only then does Graham take her hand off the goblet.

Throughout *Deaths and Entrances*, characters may appear onstage, perform certain actions, and then hasten away. The sisters, their childhood selves, the two men who haunt her thoughts, and two additional men (Robert Horan and John Butler) occasionally rush across the stage—fleeting recollections that fail to develop. You imagine the protagonist's family relations, both real and fictitious. The "remembered children" who play childish games, ducking under one another's clasped hands, don't always dance in unison—evoking for an instant those gifted little Brontë girls who wrote poems in hand-sewn notebooks no bigger than half an adult hand. In one scene, the three adult sisters take turns making "statements" in movement; they may connect briefly by joining hands or forming tableaux, but they are also contentious. In their various appearances throughout the dance, the adult trio and the younger one repeat steps or poses that you can identify as shared information, learned young. But each of the mature women also has her own way of dancing.

Graham's relationship to the character Hawkins embodies is a demeaning one. His movements are primarily abrupt, his jumps forceful. In their first encounter she comes trustingly close to him and hands him the goblet; he gravely returns it to its place. He behaves in this duet as if giving orders: "Go there!" "Take my hand!" One of his initial moves is to face her and, holding her hands, press her down to her knees; he then sinks down to kneel beside her, twisting their arms into a cage as he does so. He also picks her up, facing him, her legs apart, and tips her backward until the top of her head almost touches the floor, then lifts her up again and holds her stretched out sideways as he turns with her. When he finally puts her down, she collapses, still grasping—and pulling against—one of his hands, which he then yanks away.

Her meetings with Cunningham are briefer and gentler. He moves in a larger, calmer, airier way than Hawkins and more in keeping with her (once, for instance, he balances on one leg, tipped forward, his other leg lifted horizontally behind him, and she, kneeling beside him, duplicates that position as best she can before they both drop to the floor on their faces). In *Deaths and Entrances*, Cunningham and Hawkins repeat the male duality Graham devised back in 1939: Ringmaster and Acrobat in *Every Soul Is a Circus*, the Lover and "March" in *Letter to the World*, Punch and Pegasus in *Punch and the Judy*.

Some of the images in *Deaths and Entrances* are clear in their intentions; others are enigmatic. When Cunningham and Hawkins wrestle, Graham stands at the back, not seeing them, *thinking* them. On the other hand, an occasional movement of hers can convey a number of emotional states or decisions: she picks up her skirt on either side and walks along, her arms glued to her sides, but the outward flick of her wrists makes the fabric repeatedly spread out, then drop again; although the action is almost mechanical, it can make you think of a bird whose wings can be spread only so far.

Later in *Deaths and Entrances*, a party takes shape. While Cunningham stays immobile and unwatching, the sisters, Hawkins, and the two shadowy men perform a spirited dance of sorts, the couples holding both clasped hands out to the side; when they tip, their arms form rings, which, interlacing as they move, evoke the punitive early duet of Graham and Hawkins.

A few simple moments near the end convey Martha-Emily's feelings about the Dark Beloved and the Poetic Beloved who've been wrangling over her or with her. The three of them walk slowly, close together, side by side, Graham between Hawkins and Cunningham. Hawkins's arm is around her, and she and Cunningham hold hands. A pause occurs—a moment of doubt perhaps—and Cunningham twice circles Graham, jumping straight up and down repeatedly as he does so. The three resume their close connection, but in the end, Graham lets Cunningham's hand slip out of hers, and although he, pressing close behind her, puts his cheek against hers, she returns, not happily, to Hawkins.

In her final solo, Graham looks as if she's coming apart. She hovers over the chess game, rapidly picking up its only two pieces, putting them down again, backing away, moving in again, looking from left to right, making sharp little putting-down gestures when there's nothing in her hand. What is she planning? What should she dare? Her two sisters enter and position themselves over the chess game, as they were when *Deaths and Entrances* began, but while they make their initial moves—now one, now the other—she picks up the goblet and, shielding it in her hand, takes her place around the game. Just as the other two are preparing to make their next moves, she makes a sweeping gesture and plants the goblet on the "board." They recoil. She stands, turns away from them, and hails what must be her future. The curtain falls. We are not to know for sure what the goblet signifies, nor, for that matter, what the shell and the vases and the (mourning?) veils stand for. As often happened with Graham, once stirred by what she read, felt, and remembered, she worked intuitively, sensing what was "right" and what wasn't.

In one of her poems, Emily Brontë wrote,

Sleep brings no strength to me,
No power renewed to brave:
I only sail a wilder sea,
A darker wave.

Graham too had sailed a wilder sea. In the letter she wrote to Zellmer after the premiere of *Deaths and Entrances*, she confessed, "I do not think I [would] understand it if I were asked to chart it completely. It just came that way. I think the dancing is some of the most articulate and significant I have done but the idea is another thing. Perhaps the two do not need to go together or perhaps the material assumes a meaning of its own fashioning."

Evidently she was correct. When the program was repeated three weeks later, John Martin averred that "certainly no drama in our time has contained such psychological revelation, such a span of action, such statement of emotion in anything like such economy of form."

—13—

SPRINGTIME IN APPALACHIA AND A DARKER JOURNEY

O N FEBRUARY 17, 1941, Graham sent a long, handwritten letter to Aaron Copland proposing a collaboration. "At last, I
have my courage up," she began the missive, thereby initiat-
ing a process that was to expand over three years of correspondence
among six people. Finally, on October 30 and 31, 1944, three Graham
works, *Imagined Wing*, *Mirror Before Me* (later renamed *Hérodiade*),
and *Appalachian Spring*—their scores commissioned by the Library of
Congress—premiered at the library's Coolidge Auditorium in Washington, D.C. It's a testament to Graham's ability to juggle several projects at once that during those three years, while choreographing four
dances, presenting three New York seasons, touring, and teaching, she
also gestated two additional and remarkable works—one of which was
to be a landmark in both her career and Copland's and another that
set her on a new course.

The growing pains of what became *Appalachian Spring* reveal much
about Graham's choreographic development. A year and a half passed
before she sent Copland a scenario that fleshed out and modified what
she had described in that 1941 letter. The projected work, titled
Daughter of Colchis, had been inspired by Euripides's *Medea*, but she
made it clear to the composer that she was not planning a danced recreation of that tragedy. What she had in mind was almost, she wrote,

like the "revenge plays" of Japanese Noh theater. She mentioned having read somewhere that *Medea* "might be any wife's letter to her husband."

She had envisioned the projected work taking place in a New England house during the period in which Poe or Hawthorne set their tales, although in her typed manuscript she alluded to the structures of Greek drama and some of its costuming. (You might wonder whether she had seen or read Eugene O'Neill's 1931 *Mourning Becomes Electra*, which transported another play by Euripides to the American South during the Civil War era.) Perhaps influenced by the fact that the present war was gradually depriving her of male dancers, she limited the roles to the Passerby (a neighbor woman who would function as a kind of Greek chorus), the Woman, Her Fury, the Man, and His Muse ("tall, calm, heroic"). Graham told Copland that she'd like him to use a wordless human voice (belonging to the Fury) as one of the instruments.

The most potent conflict was not to take place between the Man and the Woman, but (interesting to consider in terms of Graham's later works) between the Woman and Her Fury, "herself." The piece she described was essentially a series of duets: Woman/Man; Man/Man (plus Passerby); Woman/Fury; Man/Fury; Woman/Man; Muse/Fury. Vivid ideas pop up in her description, some of them reminders of how much she learned during her Denishawn days about the ways in which costuming can abet not only narrative but mood changes. At times, the Woman is to wear a heavy nineteenth-century cloak; the Fury whirls her out of it, revealing her brilliantly dressed as "the beautiful, sinister barbarian." In their duet, the Fury, seated, functions like the conductor of an orchestra, directing the Woman, who behaves as if hypnotized and is spun off the stage, "leaving the Fury wrapped in her cloak and in her place." Near the end, Graham imagines the four main characters performing a "perverted square dance with the Fury as the caller." A final "tragically tender" solo for the Woman merges with a duet for her and the Man, and they end as they began, seated in two chairs, side by side, while the Passerby indicates to the audience that the piece is over. And according to Graham's minutely projected timings, this portrait of a relationship (perhaps resonating against hers with Hawkins) adds up to just twenty minutes.

Copland turned down the *Daughter of Colchis* script, although, re-membering Graham's use of his music for *Dithyrambic* and admiring her and her work, he did not close the doors on an eventual collabora-tion, instead suggesting something less dark, more akin to Thornton Wilder's 1938 play *Our Town*.

The following year offered a prestigious opportunity for Graham to set a dance to a commissioned score by Copland. During the sum-mer of 1942, Graham's company performed in Washington, D.C., in a series of outdoor concerts sponsored by the Coolidge Foundation. It was there that she met the season's benefactor, Elizabeth Sprague Coolidge, an accomplished pianist and, more important, a generous and knowledgeable patron of music. In advance of Graham's D.C. appearances, Hawkins had sent Mrs. Coolidge a copy of Barbara Morgan's *Martha Graham: Sixteen Dances in Photographs*, along with the hope that her foundation might commission two composers to write scores for Graham. Those he suggested were Copland and Paul Hindemith.

As the back-and-forth communications proliferated, those two were, in the end, the principal ones receiving the grants. Along the way, the Brazilian composer Heitor Villa-Lobos had also been considered along with Copland for the three-dance project. Graham had hoped to have a score from the latter, whose music, she wrote to Coolidge, "is so different from anything we have in this country, so rich in a re-gional sense." However, it was decided that the problems of long-distance communication made Villa-Lobos an impractical choice.

Copland provisionally accepted the invitation, with its promise of a $500 fee, in August 1942. Hindemith's name briefly reentered the list but dropped out again when Graham, unfamiliar with his music, instead proposed Carlos Chávez, whose work she knew and whom she had met in Mexico in 1932. Coolidge acted on that request. Graham wrote Copland, "I think I am the most fortunate dancer anywhere to have you and Chavez. I cannot believe it as yet." (However, not quite ready to abandon *Daughter of Colchis*, she also asked Copland if he would mind if she sent that script to Chávez.)* After many nerve-racking months, Chávez, busy in Mexico City, had yet to produce a feasible score, and Hindemith, who worked quickly, stepped up to receive the other $500 commission.

Coolidge originally considered presenting the dances in Pittsfield, Massachusetts, to honor the twenty-fifth anniversary of the Berkshire Music Festival, which she had founded. Harold Spivacke, chief of the Library of Congress Music Division, advised her against it: not with such prestigious composers and an admired choreographer with whom she was now on a semi-first-name basis ("I love having you call me Martha"). Why not present the new works in September 1943 in the Coolidge Auditorium, the building she had funded in the mid 1920s? It had been designed for music concerts, but with a width of thirty-one feet and a depth of nineteen feet, it might well house small-scale dance.

That was agreed upon, but further delays ensued. On September 18, 1942, the day before Copland met with Graham in New York to discuss their collaboration, he learned that he had passed the army's physical exam, although, because of his poor eyesight, he would not be sent into combat and could combine what the Army Specialist Corps might ask of him (lectures at army bases turned out to be one of them) with his own artistic practice. In March 1943, however, he wrote to Spivacke that he hadn't heard from Graham since December, at which time she had promised to send a script soon. It was May before he received it.

Her letter accompanying the provisionally titled "House of Victory" began contritely: "I approach you with fear and trembling on two counts; one is the lateness of this; the other is—will you like it at all and will it [be] something you can work with."

Copland found that he could work with it, and he began doing so while in Hollywood, employed from February to September writing and recording a considerable amount of music for Samuel Goldwyn's politically charged film *The North Star* (script by Lillian Hellman,

---

* Graham eventually made use of Chávez's score, *La Hija de Cólquide*, for her *Dark Meadow* (1946).

lyrics by Ira Gershwin, and a roster of Hollywood stars depicting Ukrainian peasants and the Nazis who occupied and brutalized their village). The film's message was clear: the villagers turned partisans were risking their lives for "a free world for all men."

Graham's scenario, also influenced by the ongoing war, promoted an image of American values in the nation's historic past. As Coolidge had suggested, she made her desires about the music known to the composer: she would need at most half an hour of music for an ensemble of ten or twelve instruments; she hoped to have it from him in June 1943.

In late July, Graham wrote to Spivacke, quoting from a letter Copland wrote her: he has sketched out the music up to a certain point but has been bogged down in delays to do with the movie. And, by the way, can he, Spivacke, asks Martha, prod Chávez to produce something? Whether angered or despairing about the progress, Graham's letters to Copland remain calm and gracious. In the one accompanying "House of Victory," she tells him that hearing his *Lincoln Portrait* (which had premiered a year earlier), she had realized all over again "how fortunate I am to be able to work with you. It is so utterly beautiful. That slow center part takes my heart. It is so just what it is, American, without any of the folk tricks."

Along the way, another unanticipated change of plans took her aback. She had counted on Arch Lauterer to design the set and had sent him a letter about what she might require. His reply shocked her. Not only were the Bennington students keeping him busy, but he hadn't felt that theirs had been a true collaboration nor that he had been given sufficient credit for his part in her success (her acknowledgment of his "artistic collaboration" in the program for her informal Bennington showing of *Deaths and Entrances* in July 1943 failed to mollify him). Graham fired off a response that included these words: "If you say that you cannot realize your dreams, your potentialities with me I am grieved but I see how that is. If you say it will not work or that it is money, then you are not fighting, Arch, and I could kill you for that." She ended the letter with "I send this with love always, Martha."

The "House of Victory" script predicted the kind of set that her old friend and two-time collaborator Isamu Noguchi would eventually design. She had seen a sculpture housed in New York's Museum of Modern Art: *The Palace at 4 a.m.* (1932) by Alberto Giacometti and been taken by its skeletal structure of slender sticks. In her script she wrote, "The scene is the inside and outside of a house . . . There will be no heavy construction; only the frame of a doorway, a platform of the porch, a Shaker rocking chair with a bone-like simplicity of line, and an old fashioned rope swing." This setting would be populated by The Mother, who would sit in the chair throughout the piece and speak lines drawn from the Bible, as well as directing everyday remarks to the Daughter (Graham's role), who is "what one thinks of as the Pioneer Woman"; the Citizen—"the kind of man that becomes the abolitionist, the John Brown"; the Fugitive—"really the slave figure of the CIVIL WAR but should have a broader feeling as well. He will be seen in the half-light and shadows"; Younger Sister; Two Children; and Neighbors—the men "a little like the Mark Twain figures."

Reading the scenarios—three in all—that Graham sent to Copland, you can almost imagine them resulting in a work akin to her friend Agnes de Mille's *Rodeo*, which the Ballet Russe de Monte Carlo had premiered in October 1942 and for which Copland had written the score. Likely, too, she had seen Kirstein's short-lived Ballet Caravan perform the 1938 work *Billy the Kid*, also set to music by Copland.

Liking Graham's idea (with some reservations), Copland made a few marginal notes on the script and set to work. It's clear from their correspondence that his ensuing comments influenced the direction she was taking, just as his music eventually ignited new ideas in her mind. At the end of May 1943, up in Bennington (to do some teaching in the college's summer session as well as work on *Deaths and Entrances*), she was ready to send him a revised script, and some days later he received a third, along with the tentative timings for each of the work's sections and the atmosphere of what she had planned: a courtship duet, a wedding, a party, the children playing, patterns signifying work, and more—"a telescoped day." These would be followed by the Fugitive's desperate attempts to escape pursuit and a solo for the Citizen (and bridegroom to be) who is "angry, violent, possessed . . . fanatical, at times mad." She dropped her plan to present brief scenes from *Uncle Tom's Cabin* on a small stage within the stage—scenes that should "have the effect of the pictures that take place in one's mind upon hearing that name." To Copland, she wrote:

> You may object to some of the things, such as the use of the Indian Girl. But please read it through and tell me if you think we can do it or if it defeats the end. I have thought of the use that Hart Crane made of her and also the "American Grain" of William Carlos Williams. I have as you will see taken out the Uncle Tom's Cabin episode altogether. I think you were right that it was dragged in by the hair of the head and I did not seem to be able to fix it so I started on a different aspect.

An "Indian Girl"? If he doesn't approve, she could, with a little reconfiguring, remove her too. However, "she is always with us . . . in the names of our cities, rivers, states, and in the play of all of us as children. She is the symbolic figure of the land, the Eve of our Genesis."

Whatever Copland's initial reservations, he sets to work with her latest script. She is relieved, assuring him that what she has planned "will come alive with your music in a new way. I am so anxious to deal in movement rather than in words." In late October, Copland comes to Graham's Fifth Avenue studio and plays on the piano what he has written so far. She finds it beautiful.

In the end, the "Indian Girl" is removed. So is the swing. Graham had wondered whether the composer would object to her plan to use the sporadic recitations of biblical text. He did. The text disappeared. (Copland later said that from the beginning he'd had misgivings about both the text and the Civil War allusions, "but only when Martha asked my opinion did I say so.")

A letter Martha wrote to Copland two weeks before the New York premiere of *Appalachian Spring* in 1945 shows that their collaborative exchanges continued even after the two Library of Congress performances. "I have reworked it," she told him, "particularly the points you spoke about. The variations, principally the last one of Erick's, the solo, certain points of my solo and May O'Donnell's. Hope it is better! I've also worked on the costumes."

By August 1943, Graham has received nothing from Chávez, and Spivacke writes to Coolidge, advising further postponement. Spivacke tells the understandably annoyed Coolidge that it would be unwise to cancel the commissions—better to accept the works, pay for them, and tell the composers to get the music to Graham by December 1943, but (a wise idea) not to inform them when the music will be used. The revised dates are set for October 30 and 31, 1944, the first evening now fortuitously celebrating Coolidge's eightieth birthday and all she has accomplished in the musical world.

Possibly unknown to Graham, Copland and Chávez *had* been exchanging letters, Copland gently prodding Chávez; they plan to agree on the instrumentation of their scores. Finally, in November, Chávez sends four of eleven proposed sections in the form of negative photostats; he hopes to send more in December. Graham has the music transcribed for piano, but tells Spivacke it is "in strict musical terms without stage awareness." Maybe she can work in counterpoint to its numerous short sections, but . . .

In January 1944 Graham gets a wire from Coolidge; she and Spivacke have decided to commission another score to replace Chávez's on the program. Hindemith is finally approached. However, the scenario based on elements of Shakespeare's *King Lear* that Graham has offered doesn't suit him; he prefers something more abstract. She meets with Hindemith in March and tells him he can forget her script.

Writing to David Zellmer in the middle of teaching the annual June Course in her Greenwich Village studio (the students "just as bad or worse than ever and more of them"), she describes the outcome of the meeting: "So what do you think he has decided on—a poem called 'Hérodiade' by Mallarmé. Do you know it? It is strange and beautiful and repellant in a way." She has heard some of the music, "very fine—deep and dark and utterly limpid and passionate in its tensions." During an afternoon she spends with Hindemith, his wife, Gertrud Hindemith—who is working on a master's degree in French philology at Yale, where her husband teaches—reads the poem aloud to Martha in its original French, hoping that her creative spirit may be stirred by rhythms and sonorities that English translations of the poem lack. And the Hindemiths make it clear to her that the composer was shaping his music around the orchestral equivalent of a female voice that corresponded to the rhythms of Mallarmé's dialogue between Hérodiade and a woman identified as "Nurse."

In April 1944 Coolidge commissions a third work to flesh out the program. Darius Milhaud, like Hindemith, had emigrated from Europe during the war and was teaching at Mills College. He would provide a piece of music under twenty minutes long. Martha Graham, wisely, refrained from sending him a scenario. Perhaps she had no time to dream one up. In an extremely bold step, she had secured Broadway's National Theatre for a week of performances by her company beginning on May 7, its ending marking the departure of three longtime company members: Sophie Maslow, Jane Dudley, and Ethel Butler (of whom Martha was particularly fond).

This was not just the usual season; it was an eight-performance retrospective featuring eleven dances ranging over the past thirteen years. Hawkins proved more than competent at getting the necessary money; it was he who asked Katharine Cornell if she would host a fundraising party at her apartment. She gladly complied; it raised $26,000. "Martha didn't know beans about figures," Hawkins recalled in a later interview. "Sometimes I had to go to the bank and put in a few dollars because she's overdrawn."

By August 5, up in Bennington and teaching in the college's summer session, Graham has received Hindemith's music as well as Milhaud's (which she has not yet heard). Aided by Horst and the pianist Helen Lanfer, she has been working with what Copland has sent, and she expects any day to receive the complete score and the two-piano version that he and Leo Smits have committed to a number of 78 rpm phonograph records in order to convey his preferred tempi. When it arrives, she writes to "Dear Aaron":

> It is so beautiful and so wonderfully made. I have become obsessed by it. But I have also been doing a little cursing too, as you probably did earlier, over that not-so-good script. But what you did from that has made me change in many places. Naturally that will not do any-thing to the music, it is simply that the music has made me change. It is so knit and of a completeness that it takes you in very strong hands and leads you into its own world. And there I am.

Copland is in Mexico, and she, both excited and fearful of not finishing the three dances in time, is nevertheless able to say, "When you see Chavez, give him my love."

And she sets to work, leaving it to Hawkins to correspond with Spivacke, employing his growing skills as a promoter and fundraiser to bring the event in Washington to fruition. Since the Coolidge Foundation is funding only the composers' fees, Noguchi's, and sala-ries for on-site rehearsals, it was up to him to find money for produc-tion expenses, transportation, and more. Graham telephoned Henry Allen Moe at the Guggenheim Foundation requesting another fel-lowship to cover her cost of living during preparations, and the foun-dation awarded her $200 a month for six months, beginning in August 1943.

Copland's music indeed made her change. The gradual transfor-mation of what had been a dramatic group piece punctuated by spoken text into the fresh, spare, profoundly poetic *Appalachian Spring* is both instructive in terms of Graham's development and fascinating to con-template. The strong musical hands that Graham mentioned in her letter led her into territory that differed considerably from that de-picted in the three scripts with which Copland had been working. When he first saw the piece, even the title surprised him. She had gotten it from the section titled "Dance" in Hart Crane's book-length poem *The Bridge* (1930) and was unconcerned that "O Appalachian Spring" appeared in a verse hymning a gush of water—"a white veil" seen from a mountain ledge, and not the end of a Pennsylvania winter. In the long run, Copland was tickled when people complimented him on capturing the essence of life in long-ago Appalachia.

The title was not all that startled him. Music he had created for the fugitive slave now accompanied a new character called the Revivalist in his dark evocation of a Hell ready to swallow sinners. Talking to the critic and historian Marcia Siegel in 1975, Graham mentioned this character in relation to Jonathan Edwards and Cotton Mather, those eighteenth-century preachers who ruled their congregations by invoking the terrors that awaited the sinful and unrepentant. Hardly have the Bride (Graham) and the Husbandman (Hawkins) finished their exuberant but quite chaste wedding dance—a little hoedown for two—when the Revivalist places his hat on the upraised hands of his four sprightly female followers, the better to deliver a warning to the couple about the lurking peril of sensuality. He repeatedly wrenches his body into a vertical pillar, scrabbles on the floor under the weight of a judgmental sky, flickers his hands to suggest rising flames, and ends by pointing his finger at the pair (by now crouched and praying on the steps of their new home). All that remains of the section that Graham had originally designated as "Fear in the Night—Negro" is the feverishness and the impression of lurking danger.

Yet Graham's own disavowal of the strict Presbyterianism of her youth also figures in *Appalachian Spring*. Near the end of the single day that the dance depicts, the other people, facing upstage, kneel to pray, but—even as she respects their devoutness—instead of joining them, she frisks among them and away from them, clasping her hands in prayer, yet avowing her spiritual freedom and kneeling to salute the earth.

Copland composed the score for thirteen instruments (double string quartet, piano, double bass, flute, clarinet, and bassoon). Complex in its construction, its open fourths and fifths nevertheless convey a sense of open space, and its melodies have what the composer's penciled notes characterize as "the folk feeling—without folk themes." The initial three notes of a chord that climb singingly and three more that follow reinforce the skeletal spareness of Noguchi's set: the frame of a doorway, a portion of an exterior wooden wall with a bench attached to it, slender poles linking this part of the structure to a platform bearing a pencil-slim rocking chair. A portion of a rail fence sits at the front of the stage to one side. This is a territory with few settlers. In Nathan Kroll's 1958 film of the piece, as in more recent performances, the Husbandman (played by Stuart Hodes) pauses as he enters the stage, running one hand over the boards of the single wall as if to assure himself of its sturdiness, and the Bride (Graham), following him, casts her eyes briefly up at the slender lintel, acknowledging an invisible doorway as she passes under it. This dwelling, then, is both solid and fragile, like the marriage taking place there. To celebrate that event, the cast members process solemnly onstage to Copland's quietly expansive prelude and take their places.

Graham used Noguchi's set more formally and symbolically than she did the suggestions of architecture and furniture that Lauterer had designed for *Letter to the World* and *Deaths and Entrances*. The shallow Coolidge Auditorium stage influenced her choreographic structure; the cast became less populous than the one originally planned. The stage, designed for music concerts, had only one exit and no wings. So no performer exits until the end of the dance. Instead, Noguchi's construction provides home bases for them. When not involved in the action, they wait, motionless, their eyes and thoughts on something else. Only the Revivalist stands on the low, slanted object (perhaps representing a stylized stump). Only the Bride or the Pioneering Woman sits in the rocking chair, and for the former, doing so seems to mark an achievement, an acceptance of this house and this marriage. The bench exactly fits the Revivalist's quartet of followers in their identical dresses and sunbonnets. The fence belongs to the Husbandman; from it, he can survey his land. When the Bride stands briefly at it, gazing into the distance, his arms, braced on the top rail, corral her there. Once, for a very few seconds, the Followers rest their elbows on it and gaze into the distance, as if to remind us that they too inhabit this vast landscape. (In the 1944 version, the Pioneering Woman stands at it even more briefly just before she leaves the stage.) But at times they also expand the virtual space; several times, the

Bride and the Husbandman exchange waves, as if he is traveling much farther away than just across the stage.

It is this use of space on Graham's part that inspired Edwin Denby's memorable words about *Appalachian Spring*: "The separateness of the still figures, one from another, which their poses emphasize, suggests that people who live in these hills are accustomed to spending much of their time alone. Their outlines don't blend like those of townsmen."

A section of lively music, designed by Copland for a wedding celebration that would have included two children, shaped Graham's vision of the Revivalist and his Followers. She may have purged from the dance the youngsters she had formerly envisioned, but not their innocence or their playfulness. In their opening dance, the women who accompany the Revivalist leap and skip and scuttle about in a squat, shaking the skirts they hold up as if they're shooing chickens. They clap their hands in time with the music or to punctuate its pauses; having dropped to the floor, they hit that rhythmically too. In a later sequence the Revivalist joins them in a celebratory dance. When he's not prophesying doom, he too can skip and hop; he knows the steps that might occur at a hoedown and offers some jaunty moves, such as smacking his lifted ankle with one hand. When the Followers walk bouncily in a circle, he, traveling in the opposite direction in a grand right and left, claps each one's hand in passing. The question-and-answer format that crops up in the music suits this leader and his devotees as well as it might have supported a children's game.

In his review of *Appalachian Spring*'s New York premiere, Denby, a poet as well as a dance critic, likened these women to "small wild animals that were not frightened away by people." However, the musical ejaculations that crop up in Copland's score induce not just jumps for joy or pauses left for hands to clap or strike the floor, but ecstatic amens. While in the throes of creation, Graham described the dance she had just finished choreographing for the four as "a kind of athletic prayer from a virgin body as revealed by a non-virgin heart." The women seem to worship the Revivalist as much as they do the God about whom he preaches. They fawn on him. When he falls back in ecstasy, they cheerfully support him back to his place, semi-recumbent though he is and walking in a squat—as if he were theirs to care for as well as, quite literally, to lean on. When he momentarily collapses onto the floor, they hover over him, rolling him into one pair's solicitous, adoring embrace and then the other way, into the arms of the other two. Years later, coaching Bertram Ross in the role, Graham told him that—as with the several mystics she was reading about at the time—for such revivalists, it was often "99% sex and 1% religion."

When questioned about his use of folk motifs in his score, Copland said, not entirely jokingly, that doing so didn't require royalty payments. His score included variations on a buoyant borrowed tune. In 1940, Edward Deming Andrews had published *The Gift to Be Simple: Songs, Dances and Rituals of the American Shakers*, the third of six books he wrote about the practices of these celibate religious communities that flourished in mid-nineteenth-century America and considered dancing a form of prayer. At the time, few people were familiar with the now widely known song "Simple Gifts," written in 1848 by Joseph Brackett, Jr., an elder in the Maine community of Sabbathday Lake. It was meant to be danced to:

> When true simplicity is gained,
> To bow and to bend we shan't be asham'd,
> To turn, turn will be our delight,
> Till by turning, turning we come 'round right.

Copland's use of the melody enabled not only devotional gestures from Graham's devout Christian group members but also their almost childlike delight in religion.

Only Graham and Hawkins danced to the musical passage that presented the song's tune recognizably for the first time—linking elbows to swing around, he slapping his thigh in rhythm, she switching her skirt from side to side—and the Husbandman's solo moments express not just his elation on the occasion; they allude to the space he intends to domesticate, the plow horse he will drive. He slides one foot expansively sideways, far ahead of the other, measuring his turf as he progresses along it.

Copland threaded his variations on the Shaker tune through *Appalachian Spring*—altering its instrumentation, shifting its elements, fragmenting it, sliding it underneath other passages, and reprising it with a weightiness that turns it almost hymnlike. Its melody returns with jubilant clarity just before the end of the dance. You can also, if you like, and despite the beauty of the score, hear moments when a cadence you might expect doesn't occur and liken this to the uncertainty that lurked in pioneer life and in a new marriage.

The second solo Graham created for herself occurs just before the calm, affirmative ending; it is set to music composed for what her script labeled "Moment of Crisis," and Copland's copy of it sums it up as "hysterical." The difference between the solo as audiences saw it in the 1940s and as it appears in Nathan Kroll's 1958 film, directed by Peter Glushanok (and in performances thereafter) is striking; changes to suit the camera account for only a few of the discrepancies. When Graham performed the role of a young bride for the first time, she was fifty years old and at the peak of her powers. In 1958, she was in her sixties and—although a remarkable performer—less reckless in her dancing than she had been a decade earlier. By then, she had substituted a trimly fitted pink silk gown with many ruffles for the full-skirted dark dress she wears in the sequences preserved in a partial early film. In that film clip, she rushes around the stage, twisting this way and that, many times flinging out a leg to whip herself back and forth in half turns, spinning, several times rolling up and down the steps leading into the house. In a few calmer seconds she kneels and makes a gesture that suggests roughly rocking a cradle (rather than rocking a baby in her arms as the Bride does in later versions), then reaching toward her motionless, unseeing husband (as does her later pink-gowned self). That done, she collects herself and retreats into her new house, gives the chair a whirl, and sits back in it kicking one leg, as if all her doubts have been laid to rest and the Bride has truly become a wife.

The most striking difference between the version of *Appalachian Spring* seen by audiences in the 1940s and the one performed by the

Graham company in later decades lies in the character of the Pioneering Woman. The role was created on May O'Donnell, who had just returned to the company as a guest artist after an absence of almost six years, during which time she had formed a short-lived company in San Francisco with another ex-Graham dancer, Gertrude Shurr, and then teamed up with José Limón in a program of solos and duets. A strong woman in her late thirties, she not only contributed to the choreography; she shaped Graham's vision of the role that in the earlier scenarios was that of a speaking "Mother" to Graham's "Daughter." Bonneted and plainly clad, O'Donnell seems, in the incomplete film, to relate more to the husband than to his chosen wife—checking him out and buoying him up for his new relationship to her daughter.

She is also more down-to-earth both in her movements and her manner of performing than Matt Turney, who played the Pioneering Woman in the 1958 film. Comparing them makes you realize yet again how open Graham was to change, but also how much of her earlier thinking and research might cling to a finished work's substratum, giving the piece a richness you can sense without fully understanding it.

Whereas Turney (like subsequent performers) makes big, expansive steps that lift her slightly off the ground, throwing one leg out to the side and opening her arms wide, O'Donnell, for the most part, keeps her body narrower, her rhythms tougher. Where Turney gently touches Hodes's lifted bent elbow, sidling around him as he stands motionless, O'Donnell reaches for Hawkins's hand, and when he gives it to her, the two of them, side by side, jump repeatedly. When he stands at his fence, she comes near him and twice bends far backward, one arm stretched behind her, as if expecting a revelation or a blessing. She does this again in another place onstage, but this time she slowly rotates in that extreme position while Hawkins orbits her, traveling sideways on his knees, and ends by bending low to embrace her ankles. When she sits on the steps briefly, he tilts forward, as if to whisper in her ear or kiss her cheek. Nothing like this occurs in the version of *Appalachian Spring* that we see today.

Turney—tall, slender, and delicately, exotically beautiful—joined

Graham's company in 1951; she and Mary Hinkson, both of whom had been studying in the University of Wisconsin's pioneering dance department, arrived together—among the first African American dancers to appear in a largely white modern dance company. Anyone knowing Graham's original plans for *Appalachian Spring* might guess that in Turney, Graham saw—and resurrected—traces of the American Indian girl she had wanted in the cast, as well as a hint of the originally planned speaking Mother, who was to have spent most of the dance sitting in the rocker with a light on her face. This Pioneering Woman wears no bonnet. Christian though she clearly is, it is also telling that when the four Followers freeze in a rapt position, eyes looking heavenward, she passes behind each and shivers her spread fingers behind each one's head, as if to say, "You too are holy." When the Husbandman kneels, asking her blessing, she opens his clasped hands with an expansive gesture of her own.

In praising the dance, critic John Martin called Copland's *Appalachian Spring* music "the fullest, loveliest and most deeply poetical of all his theatre scores." The news that the composer had received a Pulitzer Prize for it appeared on the front page of *The New York Times* on the same day, Tuesday, May 8, 1945, that the paper's headline announced "THE WAR IN EUROPE IS ENDED!" Amid national rejoicing, the Music Critics Circle of New York also gave the music its award for best "dramatic composition" of the year, and Copland was already at work scoring and editing the music into a suite for full orchestra. Graham wrote to the composer, "I am so very happy over your acclaim. It is certainly your year, Aaron. If I could sing I would sing." She ended her letter "With deep gratitude for working with me and letting me dance your piece, Martha."

In Washington, D.C., the program that ended with *Appalachian Spring* began with *Imagined Wing*. Along the tortuous route leading to this engagement, Graham had, as mentioned, been rereading Shakespeare's *King Lear*, envisioning a role for herself as his faithful youngest daughter Cordelia (six years later, she was to tackle it as a vehicle for Hawkins, titled *Eye of Anguish*). Perhaps delving into that tragic play led her to include Shakespeare in her plan for what the music's composer, Darius Milhaud, had titled *Jeux de Printemps*. In a letter to Copland, Milhaud had described his contribution to the Library of Congress program as "clear, gay, and springlike"—an antidote to his own prevailing sorrow over the war and all the losses involved. He had composed it for eight instruments: flute, clarinet, bassoon, trumpet, and string quartet. The musicologist Annegret Fauser identifies specific pieces by other French or European composers that Milhaud fleetingly echoed or hinted at in the six sections of *Jeux de Printemps*—ones by Gabriel Fauré, Erik Satie, Luigi Boccherini, and two of his own earlier works, plus a nod to Copland.

According to Marjorie Mazia, one of the six dancers cast in the work, Graham didn't much care for Milhaud's music and, with the performances in Washington only a week away, directed them to create solos, duets, and trios relating to Shakespeare, after which she would arrange order and transitions. Pearl Lang decided to channel the Dark Lady of the Sonnets. Nina Fonaroff was praised for her solo identified as "The Lady Distracted in her Dream."

Mazia's recollections stirred her interviewer, Ted Dalbotten, to interpret the title Graham chose for the last-minute *Imagined Wing* as somewhat ironic. In Shakespeare's *Henry V*, the character of Chorus introduces the siege of Harfleur in Act III with these words: "Thus with imagined wing our swift scene flies / In motion of no less celerity / Than that of thought."

The dance indeed wafted onto the stage, borne on the necessity for speed. Noguchi's contribution was aided by that of Jean Rosenthal, a gifted newcomer to dance lighting who was to illuminate fifty-three Graham dances before her death in 1969. A "solid canvas square changing color accents as the dancers saw fit" shifted the action to a forest, a marketplace, or a palace hall. In her role as the Prompter, the dancer Angela Kennedy delivered, in John Martin's words, "bits of amusing stage directions, in the manner of Shakespearean plays," and Yuriko, as Chorus, hurried around, opening and closing panels included in the set, thus enabling the fantasies dreamed up by the valiant creative participants (Hawkins, Cunningham, and O'Donnell rounded out the cast).

It's not surprising that the critic Robert Sabin found *Imagined Wing* "rather slight and improvisational in its effect" (although he applied "ingenious" to some of its episodes). Or that Martin labeled it "not notably successful." There's no way of knowing for sure how the several hundred music lovers, who had been sent special invitations to this last event in a four-day festival of music and dance, felt about the cobbled-together opening work; a celebratory atmosphere may have prevailed. Since Coolidge's eightieth birthday fell on the night of the first performance, the librarian of Congress and playwright-poet Archibald MacLeish presented her, in one of the intermissions, with a "specially printed volume" containing President Franklin Roosevelt's expression of gratitude for all she had accomplished in presenting the tenth edition of the festival, in establishing the foundation that bore her name, and in donating the auditorium to the nation's capital. Milhaud's piece was dedicated to her.

If some people, including Graham herself, dismissed *Imagined Wing*, the middle piece on the program, *Mirror Before Me*, thrilled many and daunted others. Martin found it "as dramatic as if there were gunplay and counterplot, though its movement is, in effect, slow and consciously controlled." Choreographing this duet for May O'Donnell and herself had not been easy for Graham. She found Hindemith's music beautiful but unnerving. While she grappled with it up in Bennington during the 1944 summer months (coping as well with her now-widowed mother as a visitor), she could be helped by Horst, who would conduct the chamber ensemble at the Library of Congress, and the rehearsal pianist Helen Lanfer, who would be part of that ensemble. Most important, Graham could seek additional help from her Bennington faculty colleague, the poet and translator Ben Belitt, since Hindemith had indicated which sections of the poem "Hérodiade" guided each of the eleven sections of the music that he termed a "recitation orchestrale."

Like other late nineteenth-century poets identified as Symbolists, Mallarmé eschewed naturalism and embraced visions, feelings, and sensations—twisting and spinning language and rhythms as he did so. His work has attracted scholars of every ilk bent on deconstructing his glistening jungles of words. It had a fevered effect on at least one reviewer of a translation into English: "A Mallarmé poem is typically a soufflé of synaesthetic delights, served up to all five senses with the icy skill of a Paris head waiter, crying out for orchestration by Debussy and illustrations by Manet. It will tend to strike a mystical note, as though spoken by the priest of a non-existent religion addressing an equally non-existent god."

Graham's original title, *Mirror Before Me*, was apt. Mallarmé's Hérodiade, having commanded the Nurse to hold that object up to her, addresses it with "O mirror! And continues:

Chill water, frozen in your frame by ennui,
How often and during what hours, saddened
By dreams and searching my memories,
Like leaves in the deep hole beneath your ice,
I appeared in you as a faraway shadow.
But, horror! On some evenings, in your hardened fountain,
I have recognized the nakedness of my scattered dreams.

The biblical story had spread far beyond its source into secular literature, drama, opera, and the visual arts. In it, Herodias, affronted by the imprisoned John the Baptist's denunciation of her for marrying her previous husband's brother, persuades her daughter to dance seductively before her stepfather, Herod Antipas, and, when promised a reward, to demand the saint's head on a platter. Some spectators, critics, and scholars familiar with that scenario have striven to connect the heroine of *Mirror Before Me* (retitled *Hérodiade*, like the music, in 1945 at Hindemith's request) with either Herodias or her daughter Salome or both. Mallarmé, who began writing the poem at the age of twenty-two and returned to it over the ensuing five years, appeared unconcerned about his evident fusion and alternation of the two, aware perhaps that certain ancient Greek versions of the gospels, as well as Gustave Flaubert's short story "Hérodias," call both mother and daughter by that name.

Mallarmé's "Scene" (Part 2 of the poem) takes the form of a dialogue between Hérodiade and the Nurse, with Part 1 a soliloquy by the latter. The poet was not telling a story, but prying open and nursing into bloom the visions and memories of his protagonist. Past, present, and future interweave. At the beginning of his dialogue, the aged Nurse, seeing Hérodiade, her mistress, return after a long absence, asks if this can be a ghost.

Graham imbibed the poem and knew its roots in the New Testament books of Matthew and Mark, but chose her own perspective. To her confidante Zellmer she wrote, "I am staging it as a performer, an actress or a dancer. The scene is a dressing room that is not a representational room but is recognizable. She is preparing her role. In that sense it might be anyone preparing for her Destiny. The excursions into the deep past, the soliloquy with self, the looking into the mirror of self, the withdrawal from [the] touch of the world on the spirit . . . I will not quote the poem. It is too obscure and the audience as a whole would never get past the Salome idea and the word virginity."

Graham's duet takes place in what the program describes as "an antechamber"—a liminal space that separates present reality from an unknown future. In a later speech to Juilliard students, she related the heroine's ordeal to the difficult moment in which an author confronts a first blank page or a choreographer enters the studio to begin work on a new dance. Mallarmé, she thought "must have meant himself in this and his struggle to perform the role as he visioned it." A couple of decades later, coaching two members of Israel's Batsheva Dance Company who were alternating in the leading part of the heroine, she linked the crucial dilemma to what she knew of their own lives: to one she talked about the tension of maintaining a career while raising a family; to the other, she emphasized the decisive moment in which she might lose her virginity.

Noguchi's three set pieces representing a clothes rack, a chair, and a mirror were all made of flat, interlocking white panels similar to those that interested him in his current sculpture. The clothes rack is the least complex as a symbol; over its X-shaped structure hangs the black cloth in which the heroine will eventually drape herself. For Graham, the chair was "the chair of memories that Plato speaks about," and Noguchi referred to the mirror as "an x-ray vision of herself . . . more of a reflection than she would really like to see, almost." She herself saw it as "a skeleton. The ribs are there. The bird that lies in the heart is there." And, more trenchantly, "When a woman looks into a mirror . . . and if she's approaching the time when she's no longer young, she sees her skeleton, she sees her bones." Graham at fifty was aware of menopause and all that it can signify. She was not concerned with the image of Mallarmé's heroine coiffed and bejeweled for a rite of passage. Too, for an artist like Graham, chastity in every sense of the word easily became a metaphor for the creative solitude in which to pare away what she deemed extraneous.

She had become familiar with the writings of Carl Jung, perhaps through Erich Fromm, who taught at Bennington, or through Joseph Campbell, who, since 1938, had been married to the Graham dancer Jean Erdman (originally one of his students at Sarah Lawrence College). Among Graham's readings were also books on myth and literature by authors who had been influenced by Jung or ventured down similar paths, such as Maud Bodkin's *Archetypal Patterns of Poetry: Psychological Studies of Imagination* and Jessie Weston's *From Ritual to Romance*. In *Hérodiade*, she traveled into the territory set forth by the Jungian psychologist Frances Wickes (whose client and friend she later became). Wickes's book *The Inner World of Choice* describes the "moment of choice," at which time "the ego must decide to step across the threshold into the perils of the unknown that lead to greater self-knowledge or to retreat into the safety of the known."

As seen in an archival film, Graham and O'Donnell enter from behind a slightly trapezoidal panel at the back of the stage (possibly the same one used in Coolidge Auditorium for *Imagined Wing*). If the performers in *Appalachian Spring* often direct their gaze beyond the confines of the stage toward an unknown wilderness, the opposite is true of *Hérodiade*; they rarely travel outside—or look past—the space defined by the three set pieces. Graham, in her grave entrance, turns to stage left to acknowledge the rack and then takes one step back, as if she has confronted an invisible wall. When she resumes her forward walk, she again rocks one step backward when she nears the front of the stage. She also acknowledges the chair, and she is standing before the mirror in profile to the audience—one arm bent above her head, the other stretched behind her—when O'Donnell enters, also solemn and ceremonious. They bow to each other. The women are identified in the program not as Mallarmé's Hérodiade and her Nurse, but as a Woman and Her Attendant.

Several times during the dance Graham approaches the mirror in various ways—for instance, kicking one leg forward, then the other back, or twisting her upper body as she strides toward and away from the object so that she flattens herself into a two-dimensional image like those in an archaic vase painting. Some of her movements, many of them springing into the air in agitated jumps, seem unique to this dance. Once, she stands, her elbows akimbo at chest level, and twists from side to side; you can almost imagine her formally shaking herself out of a garment. At another moment, crouched down on her knees, she travels a short distance by again and again wrapping one bent leg tightly around the one that, for the moment, bears her weight (anyone trying to do that may understand how such a move could symbolically lock in the virginity to which the text keeps referring).

Graham's movements suggest narrowness and restriction. O'Donnell seems to inhabit a larger space. She often sinks into a deep, obsequious bow; her feet are wide apart, her knees bent, and she spreads her curved arms as she bends over. Although she sometimes appears to expostulate and in her solos throws one leg high to the side, her posture is usually expressive of her lower stature. Once, she backs rapidly away from Graham like a scuttling spider, her legs still spraddled and her body leaning forward.

The accommodating gestures of this "attendant" mask both her distress at what the other woman is planning and her own urge to dissuade such an action. As in the poem, however, she is not to touch her mistress, who is steeling herself for what she is to endure alone (when, in Mallarmé's poem, the ancient Nurse asks Hérodiade for whom she is saving her purity, the answer is "for me"). Yet one of the first things O'Donnell does is to bend down and seem either to put a shoe on each of Graham's feet or to remove one (the gesture is smooth and vague, with Graham lifting one knee and then the other to accommodate it). Later, when Graham is balanced on the chair, O'Donnell repeatedly pats the air close to the sole of her one raised foot. When the heroine falls to the floor and remains motionless (which she does several times), her attendant's solicitous gestures hover above her. Once, Graham "interrupts" O'Donnell with an unmistakable "No! Stop!" gesture. At another moment you can almost believe that she has slapped the other woman, so sudden is her movement and so swiftly does O'Donnell retreat to the back of the space, one hand pressed to her cheek. Yet toward the end of this fateful duet, Graham places her hands on O'Donnell's shoulders, walks her backward, and sits her down on the chair, where she remains, back erect, not watching Graham's next resolute utterance. After that is over, when she rushes to her mistress and kneels, bent over, at her feet, Graham very gently helps her up; she is needed for one final act.

Although O'Donnell eloquently plays the role of a devoted servant to this woman who is insulating herself against sensuality and against vulnerability, she also at one point stands behind the mirror on which Graham is focusing, which means that Graham the performer sees the other woman instead of an imagined reflection. O'Donnell thought that her character assumed this position vis-à-vis Graham in order to "block her from looking through it into a future or a past." Others have envisioned the character as an alter ego, who both discourages the heroine and prepares her for her enigmatic ordeal.

Graham used costume expressively for this duet. In the archival film, she wears a remarkable one—a long, dark, translucent gown, beneath which can be glimpsed something white. The ingeniously cut dress has a pleated insert at the back, which fans out when she holds her skirt out with one hand. She can also wrap it partly around herself, as if girding for an ordeal by narrowing her silhouette. As the intensity of the dance calms down and she has summoned O'Donnell's help, she stands erect and still while the other woman slowly paces around her several times. The spectators can't easily divine that O'Donnell, without ever pausing, is also unfastening whatever holds Graham's dress together. So it's a surprise that when she stands in front of Herodias and takes hold of the garment, it slips off into her hands, leaving her mistress in a plain white gown.*

But there is more to be done. Behind Graham, who is standing, arms wide apart, ready to receive what may befall her, O'Donnell puts the discarded dress on the clothes rack, removing the black piece of fabric hanging there and carefully placing it on the chair. After running in a circle with tiny, rapid steps, like a moth circling a light, Graham, in a movement so smooth you cannot see how she accomplishes it, lifts that wide black strip, turns, and is suddenly almost encased—holding the resulting sheath out sideways from herself by means of one straight arm and the opposite bent one. If you know that the third part of the poems grouped as *Hérodiade* after Mallarmé's death deals with John the Baptist's experience of his own beheading, you can relate it to the image of Graham's pale face isolated by the blackness of that panel. O'Donnell leaves with the other garment. Graham lifts an arm to enwrap herself further before following her servant. Perhaps she travels into darkness, perhaps into beckoning light.

Graham's work of the preceding five years reached a climax in 1944. Although she was clearly the star, the conscience, and the contemplator of *Appalachian Spring*, she endowed the Husbandman, the Preacher, and the Pioneering Woman with individual characteristics and almost equal agency; the dance's ending can almost be predicted at its outset. She didn't make another "American" work until 1975, *The Scarlet Letter*.

* The Library of Congress program makes special mention of Graham's undergarment, "courtesy of Mr. J. R. Prince." It was made of a flexible form of Vinylite, a polymer trademarked by the Union Carbide Corporation. Those who understood the term might well feel that it rendered the heroine of *Hérodiade* both invincible and armored against disaster.

Hérodiade, on the other hand, situated her at a moment of crisis when, caught between memory and foreboding, she had to make a decision whose outcome her character couldn't for certain predict. That issue drove many of her ensuing works—dances in which she identified herself with heroines of Greek myth and bold women of Christianity: Medea, Ariadne, Clytemnestra, Alcestis, Phaedra, Hecuba, the Witch of Endor, Judith, Heloise . . . Donning these roles, she became the one who both remembered her past and reenacted those memories, the one who dreamed up everyone else onstage and envisioned what might—what *would*—come to pass.

AN ERRAND THROUGH THE MEADOW, THE MAZE,
AND THE HEART'S CAVE

THE YEAR 1945 WAS AN UNUSUAL ONE for Graham. For the
first time, she premiered no new dances. It was also a year of
tensions, both personal and professional. Erick Hawkins was
chafing at the fact that the group's programs and advertisements did
not list him more prominently. He worked hard for and with Graham,
but never felt himself in full control of anything. And why could Martha not follow the "Martha Graham and Company" in programs and
flyers with a line saying "with Erick Hawkins"?

Certainly she loved him and depended on him. In 1943 she had
sent a note to him from her mother's house in Santa Barbara. All it
said was "I loved you to call me your 'sweet wife.'" A letter she wrote
to him on her arrival at Bennington that summer attests to the mundane aspects of their conjugal relationship. "If you ever feel inspired, I
do wish you would see whether you could buy me a pair of non-
rationed play shoes. The only trouble is that I have to have some kind
of a heel. I wear 5 medium width or 5B, But do not do it if it is too
much bother or embarrassment." Two years later, however, she still
seemed uninterested in legalizing their love affair.

There's a hint of desperation in Hawkins's diary entries. He wants
to marry her and, if not her, then someone else: "I want to write

Mr. and Mrs. and to walk down the street & back into a house and show everyone this is where we sleep together." In 1945 he moved into his studio on East Seventeenth Street for almost a year. One indication of how much Graham depended on him and wanted to repair their relationship is that, according to him, she went out a couple of times to Long Island, where he was teaching classes at Adelphi College, and took a room at a nearby hotel.

During that busy spring, however, she also found time to write of her feelings and ideas to another man: Craig Barton, a friend of Agnes de Mille's husband, Walter Prude, who was connected with Bethsabée de Rothschild's foundation, and currently serving in Pakistan as a lieutenant in the U.S. Army's 380th Air Service Group. Barton sent Graham the gift of a sari as well as a money order so that she might purchase three copies of a new translation of the Bhagavad Gita, one for him, one for her, and one for B. J. Vaswani, the sadhu with whom he had become friends. "Dear Honey," he wrote. "I love you very much. Not in any possessive or jealous way. It is not dependent upon anything except that you have existed and do exist and are so, as a miracle is." In her answer, she reminds him of a past summer evening the two of them spent at the apartment of de Mille and Prude. Dinner over, the four were still drinking wine—Craig with his shoes off, Martha lying on the floor because it was cooler there. "There was no especial urgency about anything," Graham remembered. "Everyone seemed to exist in his own orbit and we slowly revolved and at times we touched . . . you, Agnes, Walter, and I." It is unclear how that relationship dovetailed with the one she needed and within which she struggled. (Later, Barton was to work for Prude, serve as Graham's personal representative, and form an enduring personal relationship with LeRoy Leatherman, who was also employed by Graham to manage her school and perform other services.)

The Martha Graham Dance Company began a weeklong season at the National Theatre on May 14, 1945. The ambitious programs included the New York premieres of *Appalachian Spring* and *Hérodiade*, along with *Letter to the World*, *Deaths and Entrances*, *Every Soul Is a Circus*, and Graham's solo *Salem Shore*. Jane Dudley and Jean Erdman had returned as guest artists, and Hawkins and Cunningham presented solos of their own devising—perhaps out of generosity on Graham's part, but perhaps also attributable to the necessity of filling the bills and keeping those two invaluable dancer-choreographers contented. Hawkins had been thinking for some time about *John Brown*, a solo for himself that involved a modest set by Noguchi, music by Charles Mills, and an "interlocutor" played by Will Hare. ("Too much talk and not enough action" was the feeling of Robert Sabin, reviewing it in Louis Horst's monthly magazine *Dance Observer*.)

Cunningham's solo pleased Sabin more. Merce had, the previous spring, found time to assemble a dance and music program of six short solos and compositions by John Cage, his adventurous former colleague in Seattle, whose contributions were described by the composer and music critic Elliott Carter as "a maze of shivery strange and delicate noises." The performance, which Graham attended, took place at Doris Humphrey and Charles Weidman's small Studio Theatre on West Sixteenth Street; for a later appearance in the Hunter College auditorium, Cunningham made more dances. Sabin's words about his witty solo *Mysterious Adventure* capture the quality that was to characterize Cunningham's onstage image for much of his career—one very different from the characters he portrayed in Graham's works: this "delicate study in eroticism brings us a primitive creature, who is strangely alert and who examines the 'object,' designed by David Hare, with all the intensity of a wild animal sniffing at a trap."

After the week of performances, Graham may well have been extra tired when she greeted the students who descended on her studio to take the annual June Course which ran from May 21 through June 16. And, of course, there had been regular spring classes at the studio; she taught an advanced class in the late afternoon and a beginner's one in the evening (sometimes spelled by a company member). Hawkins taught a men's class two nights a week; Horst taught either his well-known Modern Forms or Pre-Classic Forms, classes that linked dance with music or the visual arts. Graham was also still listed on the faculty of the Neighborhood Playhouse.

The day after the June Course concluded, she took off for Bennington for a month, accompanied by Marjorie Mazia, Nina Fonaroff, Yuriko, May O'Donnell, and "possibly Erick," as she wrote to the recently demobbed David Zellmer, adding, "Merce says he cannot go but he will come for the performances [at the college] on the 23rd and 24th." She has spoken to Martha Hill about Zellmer, and she added that he could go there as a member of the company—"because until you elect to do something else that is what you will always be."

Zellmer elected to remain a dancer for the time being. Sasha Liebich had also finished his military duties and, now billed as Mark Ryder, rejoined the company. The male contingent was augmented by Douglas Kennedy, one of several men Graham had, over the war years, recruited from the Neighborhood Playhouse but had not kept long.

A letter written by Graham to Harold Spivacke at the Library of Congress on September 13, 1945, is a good indication of how hard she drove herself:

I was glad to have some freedom from schedule and I did not know how tired I was emotionally until I stopped working. Then I simply felt that I was falling to pieces. It was that cursed teaching which I had to begin at 9 o'clock the morning after I closed my week of teaching here. I held together all right while I had to and then when I had no need to keep hitting, it struck and I knew I had gone a little too far. I hope it will be a lesson to me. I have not pushed too far as yet. This was a tremendous year, the most exciting and wonderful as far as the rest of the work and the public was concerned of my life so far. And sometimes success will make one ill when adversity can be sustained. But I am really well now. Not really that I was sick but I was very strung up and highly pitched in tension.

Only nine performances on the northeast coast had preceded the Broadway weeks, three of them in New York City spaces that had regularly presented modern dance: the Brooklyn Academy of Music, the Central High School of Needle Trades (now the High School of

Fashion Industries), and the 92nd Street YMHA. However, Graham was expecting a much fuller performing schedule for her company the following year. Sol Hurok had taken an interest in her—perhaps on advice from Barton, who had begun working in the impresario's agency in 1945. Hurok would also be presenting the company in New York in January 1946, with the two-week season advertised as "Hits from the Graham Repertory" (not the usual language associated with modern dance). That was to be followed in March by a strenuous, monthlong United States tour that Hurok was arranging. (There was talk of European tour too, but it didn't materialize.)

Since the tour had to be scheduled and publicized well in advance, audiences did not see Graham's *Dark Meadow*; it was put on the back burner. Cunningham, wishing to work intensively on his own choreography, agreed to stay on, but only for the tour, and therefore had not been cast in this most recent work. After that excursion, Mark Ryder or John Butler would take over his roles.

Cunningham had begun to venture beyond his solo concerts in collaboration with John Cage. In May 1947 at the Ziegfeld Theatre, Balanchine and Kirstein's Ballet Society (soon to be rechristened the New York City Ballet) premiered Cunningham's *The Seasons*, set to Cage's music, with costumes and decor by Noguchi. Merce danced in it himself, along with some of Balanchine's favorites: Gisella Caccialanza, Tanaquil Le Clercq, and Beatrice Tompkins.

Hawkins had gotten his wish to be acknowledged more generously in the company two months before this, when Hurok again presented the Graham company in New York. Graham's name in large type on the program's first page was followed by a pyramid in smaller letters with Hawkins's name as its peak and May O'Donnell and Pearl Lang's names a line below (Lang was performing Graham's role in *El Penitente*).

Some time before this, he had sought counseling; a woman psychiatrist had been recommended by the major Jungian psychologist Erich Fromm, a member of the Bennington faculty from 1941 to 1950. (The woman may be "Dr. Foster," or a person referred to in the correspondence between Graham and Hawkins as "Dr. Bone.") By the summer of 1945, Hawkins had not only read Frances Wickes's *The Inner World of Childhood*, but was deep into her *The Inner World of Man*. Three years later, he became Wickes's patient.

Graham shared Hawkins's interest in Jung's theories about archetypes, and almost a decade later, during a difficult period in her life, she too consulted Wickes and continued to confide in her when Wickes moved west. To the woman she addressed as "Dear Lady," she wrote, "When I think of the wonder that Jung released to the world and how he has revealed so much of what man is to man himself I am deeply thankful I lived at a time when it was in the world as idea." By then, her choreography had come to be shaped by her forays into Jungian thought. Her "inner landscape" was material to be probed.

In this, she was not alone. During the 1930s and 1940s, artists in other fields were also interested in Jung and Freud. In his early Abstract Expressionist period, the painter Mark Rothko, delving into myth and its roots in the unconscious mind, gave his art such titles as *Antigone*, *The Sacrifice of Iphigenia*, *Oedipus*, and *Altar of Orpheus*. He wrote,

> If our titles [by "our" meaning his fellow artists] recall the known myths of antiquity, we have used them again because they are the eternal symbols upon which we must fall back to express basic psychological ideas. They are the symbols of man's primitive fears and motivations, no matter in what land or what time, changing only in details, never in substance.

Graham, while conceiving *Dark Meadow*, was not only pondering archetypes and the anima as defined by Jung; she was still dipping into Maud Bodkin's work as well Jessie Weston's. To these were added John Alexander Stewart's *The Myths of Plato* (1905) and Francis Cornford's *From Religion to Philosophy: A Study in the Origins of Western Speculation* (1912), and more. She took copious notes on many of these.

Her linking of mythical images and Jungian psychological archetypes is most obvious in *Dark Meadow*—a dance unique in her repertory and one that amounted to a personal fertility rite that assured new beginnings. A passage from Cornford's book had given her a title for it; he quoted a fragment by the Greek philosopher Empedocles: "The Soul is conceived as falling from the region of light into the 'roofed-in cave,' the 'dark meadow of Ate.'" In this meadow, the Greek goddess promoted "delusion, infatuation, blind folly, rash action and reckless impulse." Cast out of Olympus, Ate lured men (and gods) to ruin. Graham's "dark meadow" is the individual's own unconscious, which he or she must confront in order to be born again, enlightened.

Would spectators confronted by this dance have been as baffled as they were fascinated? Even the critics were to find themselves in a different sort of dark meadow, in which mystification grappled with the undeniable power and beauty of the piece. The *Times* reviewer John Martin summed *Dark Meadow* as "a curious work, indeed, which at first pretty thoroughly defies comprehension." Eight years later, on tour and reading Alan Watts's *Myth and Ritual in Christianity*, Graham wrote that she was "at last beginning to understand *Dark Meadow* a little and to know where it came from."

She divided the work into four sections: "Remembrance of the Ancestral Footsteps," "Terror of Loss," "Ceaselessness of Love," and "Recurring Ecstasy of the Flowering Branch." Hawkins was identified in the program as He Who Summons and Graham as the Seeker—her identification of herself (drawn from her readings) as "One who seeks and finds by means of love." The men and women became "They who dance together." As She of the Ground, May O'Donnell functioned as a priestess or guide—as enigmatic a figure as the Pioneering Woman in *Appalachian Spring* or the Nurse in *Hérodiade*. In developing her scenario, Graham may have drawn one of four female archetypes from Bodkin's chapter on "The Image of Woman": the sibyl who knows the future and follows her own path toward that inevitability. O'Donnell's appellation, like the term "ancestral footsteps," was also taken from Graham's literary exploration.

Isamu Noguchi made for her a dry garden of smooth, gray phallic symbols: a tall form at one side of the stage opposite a slanted object resembling a tongue; a smaller, darker pyramidal sculpture behind the tall one; and, at the center of the back, an irregular pillar, the tallest creation of all. Don McDonagh, in his biography of Graham, memorably likened the set to a "biomorphic Stonehenge." In the summer of 1945, she set to work, having finally received from Harold Spivacke the music that Carlos Chávez had failed to deliver in time for the 1944 Library of Congress performance. Her task—not an easy one—may have shaped the resulting music-dance relationship. Wrote Elliott Carter, "The music is continuously danced *against* rather than *with*, and this greatly heightens the subjective tension."

Some of the most powerful dancing in *Dark Meadow* occurs during the passages for the six women and four men who celebrate what seems to be a fertility ritual. The circle, a familiar ceremonial pattern, becomes a well-traveled one. The women—wearing narrow skirts boldly patterned in black, white, and brown and tops that bare their midriffs—are Amazons, slapping their hips with cupped hands as they spring from side to side, hitting their feet against the resonant ground, lunging, skimming along in low skips and preparatory runs. Yet at a certain point each of the four men lifts a woman and, holding her bundled up in front of him like an offering, carries her away—the woman's arms reaching forward.

The movements that Graham devised for these celebrants, if performed by only one couple, might look explicitly sexual; with four pairs moving in unison, they become sacramental—formal and beautiful—the dancers' limbs interlocking with angular clarity. The men lift their partners onto one shoulder as if they're plunder to be carried away, but they also sit and, swaying slightly, anchor the standing women who lean away from them, aslant like ships' figureheads, then fall back to sit on their partners' bent knees. Although, in the longest passage, near the end of *Dark Meadow*, the powerful women are lifted, their arms and legs wrapped around the crouching men; set down the next moment, they kneel and, bent forward, support the males who arch backward over them.

Other elements contribute to the spring ritual over which O'Donnell presides—announcing changes and cleaning up afterward. She wears a remarkable costume, a narrow, knitted earth-colored sheath. Even though she may repeatedly step out on the same leg, raising the other behind her as she travels across the stage, the garment permits no great distance between those limbs. She resembles the Etruscan statuettes that Graham may have noticed in New York City's Metropolitan Museum, females whose gowns have no drapes or folds, but cover their bodies as smooth, unbroken surfaces.

O'Donnell's recurring appearances and those of the men and women bind together another tale—that of the Seeker and He Who Summons. It is Graham's story—her character's feelings and responses—that dominates. What she is seeking in this place is the sensual love that the men and women depict, as well as a balance in power between her and the figure played by Hawkins. The principal subject of *Dark Meadow*, however, is the fluctuations in the mind of Graham herself—that is in the artist as seeker. The landscape of the stage alters—or rather, how we think of it alters—in response not just to seasonal changes, but to those churning in her mind.

In an early silent film of *Dark Meadow*, Graham, clad in a long, one-sleeved gown, often rushes about the space, contemplating or leaning on the objects but also gazing beyond the boundaries of the stage, as if looking for answers in a strange land. Her dancing, as had become increasingly the case in her works, often expresses the tension between possible alternatives. Shall I go this way or that way? Thrust myself forward or shudder away? Throw myself into fury or control my emotions? One impulse yields to its opposite as, twisting and turning, she dedicates herself to ordeal. After one of O'Donnell's passages across the space, Graham rises from her seat on the tonguelike sculpture and throws herself into big tilted turns on one leg, the other leg high, her body seesawing down. These moves—familiar in several of her dances beginning in 1943—also seem an apt expression of confusion and a fierce attempt to unravel it.

Noguchi's set pieces are not the only symbolic objects onstage. One of these is carried in by O'Donnell and set atop one of the pillars. Graham pulls away the length of dark fabric that covers it to reveal a cruciform shape with down-pointing tips at the ends of its horizontal bar. Hawkins stations himself behind the structure, only partly visible; O'Donnell kneels behind the "tongue" and falls forward over it, her arms stretched ahead of her. Both dancers remain there while Graham begins a voyage along the fabric.

The black cloth becomes both the actual path along which she must travel and a metaphor for ordeal, a journey into darkness. After she lays the fabric out on a diagonal, she can crawl and roll over it, then gather it into a bundle and start over. A third time, holding up the edges of it that lie behind her, she walks along it, twisting until she is enwrapped; finally, suddenly (you can't be sure how she manages this), she's seated cross-legged on the floor near the motionless O'Donnell, the black fabric over her head like a shawl, bringing to mind women in the pueblos she had visited with Horst and with Hawkins.

The references to fertility accrue. Each of the three men plants an object on a stick in the "tongue"—once stood on end to show a white side, now turned and laid down again. One of these objects resembles a flail, another what might be a white bird, the third a small black ball at the end of a chain. O'Donnell, wearing a long, full green cloak, enters and turns the stage-left pillar to reveal its pale side. Then, sheathing it from behind with her cloak, she slowly squats, sliding the fabric down it. After this unmistakably sexual allusion, she spins offstage, the cloak flying out in her wake. Later, she brings on a small bowl of red fabric and holds it out to Graham, who touches the material, then puts it back into the bowl (the menstrual cycle figured in some rituals she may have read about, but the cloth might also have represented a child who was not to be). After the powerful sextet, O'Donnell sticks an eight-branched "plant" into the top of the structure down which she had slid her cloak and shivers her fingers, as if encouraging its growth.

If the dance's meetings between Graham and Hawkins were extrapolated from their context and presented in sequence, you might see a progression. His first solo, addressed to her, is remarkable. He skids backward on one leg, as if an errant wind were forcing him on a curving path. He travels forward across the space in small jumps. He cants himself backward and sideways, one leg held up in front of him, then runs forward, then repeats the two maneuvers. Bent over and spinning, he circles the stage. Throughout this "announcement," he keeps his eyes mostly on the ground, marking his paths.

When you look back on an earlier duet between Graham and Hawkins, you can view him as introducing her to movements similar to those occurring in the sextet. Prying her away from the now-white object against which she's leaning, he bends his knees to seat her on his thighs, then sets her on the floor and falls on top of her. Kneeling behind her, he holds her as she tries to walk along, lifts her and bundles her over his shoulder, then sets her down again. When she travels forward on her knees, he's behind her, his hands on her shoulders, guiding her. There's no joy in this, and after they've walked together on tiptoe toward the upended "tongue," he pushes her against it and backs away to his hiding place behind the central pillar. The "lesson" over, O'Donnell gathers up the red fabric and exits, tossing it up in the air as she goes—as if it were now no more than a plaything.

In their final coming together, Hawkins and Graham approach each other from opposite sides of the stage. They seem to have reached an agreement that has sexual overtones. He picks her up and turns with her in a way that is both like and unlike those in which the three men have lifted the three women. She lies supine, and he kneels over her, one leg lifted behind him. But they also travel side by side on their knees, as Graham did in *Hérodiade*, wrapping one leg tightly around the other in order to travel forward. Finally, for a brief but telling moment, they sit together on the floor, and she leans tiredly against him.

In the end, she has fallen into step behind O'Donnell, who leads her to the tall central pillar and leaves her there. She lies down briefly before it, less worshipping it than yielding to its power. When she rises, she's alone onstage, advancing toward the audience, and behind her, a branch of red buds rises from it. Whatever awaited her in this meadow has been probed and laid to rest, and a new beginning, a vernal equinox of the soul, is implied.

Even though Graham began in 1946 to ally her onstage persona with specific females of Greek myth and literature, she was at first skittish about naming them as such. When *Cave of the Heart* premiered as *Serpent Heart* during Columbia University's second annual Festival of Contemporary American Music, Graham identified herself as "One Like Medea" and Hawkins as "One Like Jason." When the tightened and revised piece was performed at the Ziegfeld Theatre in 1947, she had become the even more ambiguous Sorceress and he the Adventurer (although the program note alluded to Medea and her lover). In *Errand into the Maze* (1947), she didn't mention the mythic Theseus or his helper, Ariadne, and her antagonist was not the Minotaur at its center, but a "Creature of Fear." As the program notes, the labyrinth where he dwelt was "the maze of the heart." Only for spectators of *Night Journey*, later that same year, did she identify Hawkins as Oedipus and herself as Jocasta, a tragic figure who had committed incest and whose anguish was also, however obliquely, rooted in Graham's own relationship with a much younger man.

All three of these works continued the collaboration between Graham and Noguchi, which had begun in 1935 when he created the fence for her *Frontier* and the platform for her solo in *Chronicle*, resurrected with *Appalachian Spring* in 1944. A shift had occurred. What Noguchi had designed for this last piece represented a home, spare and stylized though it was. In *Hérodiade*, his flat white shapes, interlocking to create the three-dimensional ones, represented a chair, a mirror, and a clothes rack. Although they looked nothing like the familiar objects bearing those names, and even though Graham used them as if they were articles in her dressing room, they were charged with symbolic import.

Beginning in 1946, her dances seldom unfurled along a timeline in a specific place, and Noguchi's sculptures became the furnishings of a woman's mind. She and he worked together in a process enriching for both of them—she telling him her ideas, he responding, she subtly commenting, he coming back with changes. Years later, he wrote:

We breathe in, we breathe out, inward turning, alone, or outgoing, working with others, for an experience that is cumulative through collaboration. Theater is the latter kind. My interest is the stage where it is possible to realize in a hypothetical way those projections of the imagination into environmental space which are denied us in actuality . . . There is joy in seeing sculpture come to life on the stage in its own world of timeless time. Then the air becomes charged with meaning and emotion, and form plays its integral part in the re-enactment of a ritual. Theater is a ceremonial; the performance is a rite. Sculpture in daily life should or could be like this. In the mean-time, the theater gives me its poetic, exalted equivalent.

With his contributions, Graham began to render time and space flexible, as had the Cubist visual artists who preceded her. Pablo Picasso's 1932 *Girl Before a Mirror*, for example, doesn't show the girl pressed against her exact mirror image, but against her older self, or a self corroded by her thoughts. In Graham's refashioning of myths, events that happened in two different locations or in different years might appear simultaneously onstage, a few feet apart. As in the Noh plays she had read—alone or on the Pacific coast with Ramiel McGehee—time became elastic. A long voyage might occur in seconds, a thought expanded into minutes. The device of having some performers pause, frozen into stillness, while others expanded actual time during private recollection or the weighing of a decision, may have originated in *Appalachian Spring* owing to the single exit/entrance on the Library of Congress stage, but it became increasingly resonant as memory—a structural ingredient in Noh plays—an ingredient in the dance structures Graham created.

Cave of the Heart, set to a score by Samuel Barber, is sparsely populated: only four dancers weave through its plot. The stage is both an arena for action and a playing ground of the mind. The set is, in fact, akin to the designs Noguchi made for city parks. He diminished to small platforms the islands along the Aegean shores at which Jason and Medea stopped on their voyage from Colchis to his home in Iolcus. Set in a line, they became stepping-stones for the vainglorious hero to stride on, implying that Jason leaves his footprint wherever his ship has landed. At times, Hawkins's legs bridge two of these "islands," which lead toward a dark structure representing a biological heart—as magnified as the stepping stones are miniaturized. The other element is barely identifiable as a thick snake, into which is stuck a structure of straight golden wires that tremble slightly when jostled. You might at first imagine it to be a fiery tree under which Graham can lurk. It may also prod one who is familiar with the tale of Jason and Medea to link that object with Medea's identity as a granddaughter of the sun.

The subject of the dance is a possessive love so consuming that it leaves devastation in its wake. In critic Robert Horan's words, Barber's score for twelve instruments provides a fine scaffolding for the tragedy: "Brilliant, bitter and full of amazing energy," it alternates, "like the swing of a pendulum, between relaxed lyrical flow and tense angularity." Graham, clad in a long black dress with slim lines snaking around on it, wears her long hair in a ponytail—high on her head and skewed to one side. Jason has betrayed Medea by acquiring another mate, the Princess Glauce, in order to cement an advantageous alliance with her father, Creon, the king of Corinth. In the tale as Graham reconstructs it, the little princess played by Yuriko might as well be an adoring pet; she often perches on Hawkins's shoulder, twines around him, leans into his embrace.

The first image of the three protagonists shows them as a single object, one standing behind the other. At first hidden, then crawling forward between the others' legs, the princess is born into a new and tragic life. Graham mingled Jason's fascination with his young love with images that suggest a ship—Yuriko standing on Hawkins's thighs, canted forward like a vessel's prow as he strides forward, while Graham walks backward in front of them, leading them on. The fourth character, the Chorus (a role created by O'Donnell), periodically comments or intervenes. Her gestures and rushing about imply impending crises, implore mercy; briefly, intent on avoiding the inevitable tragedy, she tussles with Medea. Photos of the dance around the time of its premiere show O'Donnell also wearing a dark gown with a serpentine design traced on it. But by the time Graham had reworked the piece for her Broadway season (when a small orchestra replaced the piano accompaniment of the Columbia University performances), the Chorus's costume had changed to the one she wears in recent performances: a remarkable brown-and-red-striped skirt and a matching top with sleeves as wide as its length.

At times the movement presents Jason as two-dimensional—a handsome figure from a Greek vase painting. But that's rarely true of Medea, torn between passion and fury. She lurks beneath the golden structure, at one with the "snake" that supports it. The cord that ornaments her dress also evokes a snake. And in the terrifying solo that climaxes *Cave of the Heart*, she draws from her bosom a red cord representing the serpent of jealousy that gnaws at her heart. Contracting her rib cage as if vomiting rage, dragging herself along the floor, bracing herself on her hands while she whips her head and that long hank of hair in circles, she has turned herself into an instrument of vengeance. As she sidles along on her knees, she devours the little red snake (actually crumpling it into one hand) even as she's pulling it from the breast of her gown. It becomes a plaything to be lifted overhead in triumph. She holds it out, away from herself, taking a hard look at it before dropping it in a pile and falling onto it like an animal ready to devour its prey. Horan described this demented solo as "frightened flashes of unpredictable movement, a kind of crippled hunted lurching of the body from one stage area to another."

The Princess, dancing to suddenly sweet music, is very pretty—and so young and vulnerable. When Jason steps out in a lunge, she sees it as an invitation to treat his back leg as a ramp and walk up it to sit on his shoulder. However, Medea's rage is not simple jealousy. It was she and her guile and her magic that had enabled Jason's seizing of the Golden Fleece, she who did away with all that hindered his mission, she who killed for him. True to the tale, Graham, all ceremonious politeness, graciously presses a poisoned crown on her rival's head and watches while the girl writhes, trying unsuccessfully to tear it off before running offstage. There are no offspring for Medea to sacrifice in *Cave of the Heart* as there are in Sophocles's drama. It is the dead princess whom she drags onto the stage, wrapped in a long length of purple fabric. When she displays to Jason his young love's body, he falls on it and, rolling, is engulfed with her. Graham's Medea nuzzles the bodies as if relishing the smell of death, then walks into the golden wires of what the audience suddenly sees as a vestment. Plucking it from its stand, she whirls around in it as if aflame. But as the curtain falls, it's stuck into the central "heart," and she is suspended within it, swinging her legs, flying home to her grandfather Helios, the sun.

The duet *Errand into the Maze* did not feature Hawkins as Graham's partner and adversary. He may have been busy with his own *Stephen Acrobat*, and, according to Agnes de Mille, he was also on call as an understudy to both the hero Curly and the villain Jud Fry in the ballet de Mille had created for the 1943 musical *Oklahoma!* Graham cast Mark Ryder in the part of the creature at the heart of the maze, and in the initial version of the dance, he was all but unrecognizable in the horned mask that Noguchi provided, a creature that looms up in nightmares.

Graham's title came from the opening lines of a poem, "Dance Piece," by her Bennington colleague Ben Belitt:

> The errand into the maze,
> Emblem, the heel's blow upon space,
> Speak of the need and order the dancer's will.
> But the dance is still.

The maze is represented by a length of white tape or rope that lies in erratic curves along the floor, a path the heroine must traverse to reach her destination. Initially alone onstage, she attempts to control what can only be terror, her body contracting repeatedly as if she's both shuddering and gathering strength for her mission by breathing strenuously. Graham and the composer Gian Carlo Menotti (new to her) must have worked closely together; his struggling melody and harsh chords underline, for instance, the emphatic way she whips her head sharply around, throws it back, and wrenches it resolutely into place again several times.

The path leads to an irregular V-shaped portal that could be interpreted as a vulva. The dancer raises her knees high as she steps on tiptoe along the white tape's every curve, the music sounding like a light march. She approaches the threshold and steps across it. Yet the entire space of the stage is her territory; it can represent either the area outside her destination or the inner place of reckoning; it grows and shrinks in relation to her feelings. A Graham movement learned by every student in her classes involves standing on one leg and, over and over, circling the other slightly bent leg forward and then oppositely to the back to create a figure eight. Performed with the dramatic intent that Graham brought to it in *Errand into the Maze*, it suggests someone preparing for violence, whipping herself on. When the trumpet in the score calls a warning, she rapidly gathers the white path inside the V and lashes it hastily back and forth around the sides of the structure, committing herself to her challenge despite her dread.

Conjured up by her imaginings, the partially masked Creature of Fear appears several times. It was a brilliant idea on Graham's part to have the dancer performing the role keep his arms hooked over a three-foot pole athwart his shoulders; rounded at the ends, it looks like a giant bone. He is both monstrous and effectively hampered by this yoke. Athletic nevertheless, he leaps in a circle around her, angled forward, his legs lifting behind him. Although he's implacable, he shows no malice (he is, after all, his victim's creation). When she falls and begins rolling across the floor, he walks heavily back and forth over her, smacking each foot against the floor; you fear that he might step on her. Crouching over her, he strikes one end of the pole against the floor. Even as constricted as he is, he can grab her hands and swing her in circles before she makes a dismissive gesture, and he moves slowly out of sight, turning on his knees. He can walk bent over, with her lying on his back, taking small, precise steps as if he were hooved. In one of their encounters he presses her back across his thighs, trapping her against himself with one elbow; both of them have their hands free as he revolves, as if they've suddenly and briefly merged into a single being.

Menotti's music provides her with high, sweet notes, to which she dances, raising one arm and kicking one leg high as if sensing victory, but a low, pulsing rhythm tells us she's not done with him yet. Leaning backward, her knees bent, she advances along a diagonal, beating her fists against her thighs. Suddenly he looms over her, jumping straight up, as if on a pogo stick, as he travels sideways behind her. This is the moment when she must win or lose. Grasping the pole, she stands on his thighs and, not without setbacks, forces him to fall gradually backward to the floor and slowly release the pole, until he twists to lie sprawled, facedown, inert.

Now victorious—and seeming to wonder at that—Graham unwraps the cord, steps onto the portal's threshold, and gazes into what must be her future, slowly and sensuously circling that one lifted leg in its figure-eight pattern. She strokes the smooth sides of the V before passing through it and opening her arms to the freedom of a new day.

In August 1946 Graham sent a letter to composer William Schuman, including tentative scripts for two dances, one of which she hoped to premiere in 1947. She could not, she explained, be too definite about how she would relate her choreography to a scenario written earlier, but she assured him that, in relation to one of her choices, "There is no telling of a story. It is the enactment of an emotional experience." Her source was "Tam Lin," a ballad published in the late nineteenth century by Francis James Child in his *The English and Scottish Popular Ballads*. Martha typed out the entire poem, some of which she wished to have performed onstage by a folk singer. Schuman may well have found the proposal daunting, beginning with the first verse:

> O I forbid you, maidens a',
> That wear gowd on your hair,
> To come or gae by Carterhaugh,
> For young Tam Lin is there.

The eponymous hero of the ballad is in thrall to a fairy queen and guards her domain in the woods of Carterhaugh. His task is to demand any passing maiden to pay him with her jewels or, if she has none, with her virginity. The story is complicated, and Graham did not intend to deal with it. She read and wrote primarily to stimulate her creativity, and her slant on the story was more personal: "The legend concerns those forces that may separate any two people at any given instant from the state of hearts union and the endeavor of two people to dispell [sic] these powers." The fairy queen at times represents both the "figure of love" and that of death.

Schuman must have replied very tactfully, expressing his preferences for the slightly shorter, less worked-out scenario that Graham thought of as "Jocasta's Dance." She wrote back that she was glad he'd made that choice; it's the piece she said, "I would like best to dance. I think because I can hear your power and rich dark tragic sense musically. Of course it is all in my imagination. But I think I can feel on my skin what you will write." She knew how to make a potential collaborator feel like a valued one.

Eventually Graham considered *Night Journey* as the third part of a trilogy, following *Cave of the Heart* and *Errand into the Maze* (although she didn't necessarily intend these three works to be performed together). In the first, the heroine revenges herself on a faithless lover; in the second, she conquers the demon of her own fears; in the third, she becomes the victim of an incestuous mating. In 1947 Graham turned fifty-three and Hawkins thirty-eight. She loved him fiercely and, according to de Mille, tried in various ways to further his career, to give him what he wanted. But the age difference may have preyed on her, and in *Night Journey*, she turned that fact into art.

Her Jocasta was not a powerful heroine in charge of her destiny— no Emily Brontë, no Emily Dickinson, no Medea. How was she to know that her consort Oedipus was fulfilling a prophecy he was straining to evade: that he would kill his father and marry his mother. After he successfully answered the riddles put to him by the Sphinx, who menaced those trying to enter Thebes, causing the creature to commit suicide, he was made the city's king; protocol demanded that he marry the widowed queen. The influence of Noh plays is more obvious in *Night Journey* than in any of Graham's previous works. In those Japanese dramas dating from the fourteenth century, the principal actor, the *shite*, recollects and reenters a crucial event in his life in order to understand it and perhaps find peace. In the words of the Asian theater scholar Faubion Bowers, that event "is poetically recalled and discussed by the characters and chorus, and their movements become dreamlike glosses to the idea carried by the words." *Night Journey* begins with Jocasta alone, holding a rope overhead. It ends with her twisting it around her neck and sliding to the floor. Tiresias, the blind seer, swirls in to pluck the rope from her hands with his stick, ordering her not to die without reexamining her life.

Graham took her title from Maud Bodkin's chapter on the myth of rebirth, which describes a pattern that the author called, after Jung, the "Night Journey myth." The seven women who embody the Chorus of Greek drama are the "Daughters of Night," an appellation of the Moirai, or Fates, that Graham found in Francis Cornford's *From Religion to Philosophy*.

Her first solo is a dramatization of her anguish; her every rush about the stage, her every flung-up leg, her outstretched arms, and her every twist seem both evasive and desperate. Finally, she retires to her bed—a slanting, comfortless structure that hints at the connected forms of a man and a woman. Lying there, she remembers Oedipus. He enters as the hero who saved the city, escorted by seven women who bear laurel branches that symbolize his victory, and they dance in his honor. Noguchi created a path of four stones for him to stride along, as he did for *Cave of the Heart*, but these four, leading to the "bed," are larger and marked with runic signs. He steps onto the bed, pulls Jocasta to her feet, sets her on his shoulder, and deposits her on a small stool while he makes himself known to her.

In Sophocles's drama, Jocasta had assumed the son she bore to King Laius to be dead; as an infant he had been left to expire on a hillside in order to thwart the very prophecy that is now coming true.

Graham's duet for Oedipus and Jocasta is the heart of the dance and takes up most of its length. Its subtext is "How could I not have realized that he was my son?"

No record film of the original *Night Journey* has been discovered. Graham and Hawkins separated in 1950, and it was with some trepidation that she decided in 1961 to reinvestigate the dance. The men in her company were now all much younger than she. Perhaps revisiting a subject that didn't flinch from that would be prudent in more ways than one. She settled on Bertram Ross, who had joined the company in 1949, to play Oedipus. The two of them would rehearse in secret, and if she felt the piece wasn't working, the experiment would be terminated. She handed Ross a complex piece of brown material that would serve as a cloak and told him to go into the studio and try things with it. Whereas Hawkins had performed a solo that, according to Ross, involved a lot of spinning around the stage, the new solo was in part a debate with the fabric. Knowing Oedipus's story, including the fact that he had, before his encounter with the Sphinx, killed her husband, Laius, at a crossroads, Ross stepped in and out of openings in the enigmatic, crisscrossed elements of it, wrapped and unwrapped himself in it. An effort to get it out of the way resulted in his thrusting his arm over and over again through the fabric, wrapping it around the arm as he did so. The result had phallic import, but could also allude to Oedipus, said to have been born with a clubbed, or swollen, foot.

Ross's action with his own foot is similar to what Hawkins and Graham had devised. Standing on the stool behind her, he slowly lifts one leg and brings it over her shoulder. In the film, Graham watches that foot as it passes over her; she is, Ross thought, questioning whether she might have recognized it. When he does it again, however gently (and Hawkins apparently had been rougher), he touches the heel of his foot to her rib cage, and her body contracts in response.

The duet as it stands reveals the arrogant conqueror falling in love. Onstage, Jocasta is clad in a pale garment that could have been a nightgown were it not for her enormous, eye-shaped brooch. She is vulnerable in a way that Graham in Nathan Kroll's admirable film of *Night Journey* is not; the black gown with flying-wing panels that she wears in the film was apparently one of several possible designs for her role as Clytemnestra.

The interplay between remembering and entering the memory is brilliantly choreographed. Graham, looking extremely small and vulnerable, is escorted by Ross, partly wrapped in his cloak, to their bedchamber. Moving one of the branches from side to side as she gazes at him, she has already revealed her willingness to flirt. Yet when they reach their destination and he keeps reaching around her to touch her breasts or her groin, she seems to be trying to escape, to be raising a hand to call for help.

From moment to moment, Graham's choreography shifts fluidly between showing the two as lovers and revealing them as mother and son. He lifts her, but when he sets her down, a new picture develops: he lies athwart her bent legs while she bends over him, rocking him. Seconds later, with his help, she steps onto his thighs, yet after they gently kiss, he tips her backward until her head barely grazes the floor, as if she were his to do with as he likes. Then, when he tilts her upright again, he sinks lower, until she is cradling his head against her breast. In this mating burdened with fugitive recollections, he falls on her where she lies on the floor; they kiss again, then roll apart.

The melodies in Schuman's score are often quiet, mournful, with chords underneath that mutter of impending danger. The music's patterns, wrote Walter Terry, "give Graham exactly what her dance style needs most—abrupt, harsh rhythms, staccato phrases that are brief and insistent, long-held steely notes against which she seems to lean and swell." It turns strident after Tiresias (Ryder in the original cast, Paul Taylor in the film) has entered to proclaim the mating incestuous, using his staff as a pogo stick; its impact on the floor adds its own ominous sound.

The women of the chorus lunge onto the stage, their hands before their eyes. The composer gives them rasping, almost percussive sounds as, standing on one leg, they contract their bodies violently in time to his repeated chord. Gradually they sink to the floor, still shuddering. Behind them, the couple moves onto the bed, where the rope Jocasta had held when the dance began becomes not only a snare but a symbol of the umbilical cord that once bound the two together. Now they tangle themselves in it. They are standing, leaning away from each other yet roped together, when Tiresias climbs onto the bed behind them and touches the taut rope with his staff. The rope slackens; they fall.

Graham provides a final vivid illustration of the fatal birth that impelled the tragedy. Oedipus has climbed onto the "bed," the women cluster at its foot, and he plunges forward—hands raised near his mouth, as if to suggest that he's howling—into their arms and onto the floor. The denouement comes quickly. Jocasta retreats to her bed, Oedipus plucks the brooch from her gown and places it over his eyes. Blinded thus, he gropes his way out of her memory. Awakening, she picks up the rope, passes it around her neck, and slowly slides to the floor.*

Ben Belitt, interviewed years later, likened *Night Journey* to his poem "School of the Soldier," about his war experiences. "It was the violence, the whole ambiance of the 1940s that attracted us both, I suppose, and brought us each to dwell on the 'nocturnal': night journeys, night marches, unknowns, blood pieties . . . Here was a perfect fable for the times, concerned with tremendous acts of supererogation— patricide, incest, the wasting of whole kingdoms, the fall of philosopher kings and their relation to violence."

In the coming years, Graham would continue to draw roles for herself from history and legend. But these works of the 1940s seem to have been not only inspired by the times and by her readings, but forged from her own most powerful terrors and desires. Audiences received them as great, daunting, perhaps mystifying works of art; for her they were also lessons in endurance, confrontation, and survival.

* Graham may have tired during the filming of *Night Journey*; in it her final fall to the floor happens swiftly.

—15—

ANGELS AT PLAY AND TWO CHRISTIAN HEROINES

PRECARIOUS FINANCES were Graham's lot for years. She occasionally had to borrow money from friends, even from company members. Hawkins was adroit at securing funds for theater rentals and production costs. The dancers sewed their own costumes on material bought cut-rate from the fabric stores on Orchard Street (they also ironed them before performances). Between 1948 and 1950, however, the group's increased exposure had the potential to make Martha's life a little easier.

Late in 1947 her name became familiar to many who hitherto hadn't known beans about modern dance and hadn't cared much about finding out more. Craig Barton, now acting as Graham's manager and personal representative, persuaded Ralph Edwards, host of the popular radio show *Truth or Consequences*, and the show's producers to feature Martha Graham as the mysterious celebrity. Each week, several selected contestants were telephoned during the show on the basis of their mailed-in completion of the following sentence: "We should all support the March of Dimes because . . ."* As the weeks passed, the prizes (refrigerator, washing machine, automobile, and

---

* Those who competed were obligated to include a donation to the organization that Franklin Roosevelt had established in 1938 as the National Foundation for Infantile Paralysis.

more) accumulated until a lucky person guessed the given star's identity. Graham (Miss Hush) followed the boxing champ Gene Tunney (Mr. Hush) and the movie icon Clara Bow (Mrs. Hush) onto the show.

The stint involved her delivering, twice per airing, a riddle with clues to her identity and a nod to the coming holiday:

> Second for Santa Claus, first for me.
> Thirteen for wreath, seven for tree.
> Bring me an auto, a book, and a ball,
> And I'll say Merry Christmas in spring, not in fall.

Truth or Consequence's ratings rose during the weeks that Graham appeared, and on December 6 the contest set a one-day record for mail: 119,000 pieces. The March of Dimes received more than $800,000 in listeners' donations. After three weeks, Ruth Subbie identified Miss Hush correctly and won $21,500 worth of prizes. It's not clear whether a fee might have come Miss Hush's way, but she said that she had been glad to contribute to a good cause.

Those who worked with Graham or followed her career guessed the speaker's identity pretty quickly, and she soon found that celebrity came at a price. Don McDonagh, in his biography of Graham, cited a United Press writer who cornered her near her studio and began pestering her with his guesses: "Miss Graham's complexion began to take on the purplish black hues of her ballet costume. She said 'Arrggh' quite clearly, thought a moment, and added, 'Arrggh.'"

She became known to a perhaps more elite public after Angelica Gibbs's lengthy profile in the December 27 issue of *The New Yorker*. Although the piece was intelligent, well researched, and, for the most part, respectful, Gibbs acknowledged that Graham could confuse spectators (and interviewers). "It may dismay a literal person to be told by Miss Graham that a particular dance can most easily be understood by people who know what winter means, but her collaborators—poets, dancers, composers, stage designers, and so on—profess to be entirely at home with such circumlocutions."

The summer of 1948 brought more changes. Martha Hill re-created the Bennington School of Dance at Connecticut College in New London, where most of the dorms were set around a great expanse of lawn, and a fine theater, Palmer Auditorium, had just been completed. Louis Horst, Arch Lauterer, and Ruth and Norman Lloyd taught the summer session, extending the atmosphere of community that had developed among them over the Bennington years. Hawkins worked on his new solo, *The Strangler*. José Limón, formerly a member of the Humphrey-Weidman Company, was also in residence; Doris Humphrey, plagued by an arthritic hip, had ceased performing in 1944 and was functioning as the artistic director of the company Limón had just founded. There, too, was a trio: former Graham dancers Sophie Maslow and Jane Dudley plus William Bales from Humphrey-Weidman.

Graham asked company members to teach classes in her technique; she was busy working on a new dance in which neither she nor Hawkins appeared. Beautiful and long-lived, it began as *Wilderness Stair* (after a poem by Ben Belitt) but was soon renamed *Diversion of Angels*—an evocative image also created by the poet. Lines that he wrote for her after watching a rehearsal became a program note:

> It is the place of the Rock and Ladder, the raven, the blessing, the tempter, the rose. It is the wish of the single-hearted, the undivided; play after the spirit's labor; games, flights, fancies, configurations of the lover's intention; the believed Possibility, at once strenuous and tender; humors of innocence, garlands, evangels, Joy on the wilderness stair; diversion of angels.

In September, getting some rest and visiting her mother in Santa Barbara, Graham told an interviewer that, for her, the place Belitt hymned resonated with the open spaces and big skies of the country around Santa Fe. The territory of love, however, was clearly on her mind. Flanked by a jubilant quartet of women and one extra man, each of the dance's three principal couples presents one aspect of a triad: exuberant, youthful love; passion; and mature companionship. The main women are differentiated by costume color: in the original cast, Helen McGehee wore yellow, Pearl Lang red, and Natanya Neumann blue (not long after the premiere, the women who played this last role appeared in white). Originally, the dresses were of different lengths, with a short dress for McGehee and a long one for Neumann, emphasizing the voyage from adolescence. The men are clad identically; unless you look closely, they're almost interchangeable. Three of them may have been new to some audience members; Stuart Hodes and Bertram Ross had been demobbed from the army (the G.I. Bill fortunately covered their dance classes). Dale Sehnert may have done military duty as well. Their presence recharged Graham's choreography.

Watching live performances of *Diversion of Angels* and one on film, in addition to passages from it that figure in Nathan Kroll's 1957 film, *A Dancer's World*, you can revel in the openness of much of the movement. Over and over, arms winging, the dancers lift one leg high to the side and lean away from it; they may tilt this image from side to side or take it into the air. The Woman in Red endows that canted pose with more earthly passion; stepping out onto one leg, she balances there and, with her other leg still held high, contracts her body, as if shuddering in sensuous delight. She repeats this step several times as she crosses the stage.

Another image is not so unequivocally open. The dancer stands on one leg, but pulls the other leg, turned in and bent, strongly across her body; leaning ecstatically back, arms raised, she twists her upper torso against the force of that lifted leg. The Woman in White initiates and repeats that step, but the cadre of secondary women know it too.

Norman Dello Joio's music underscores the moods of the choreography closely. It turns rapid, dense, and playful when the Woman in Yellow cavorts with her partner, leaping into his arms and onto his shoulder. Their love is a game. But when a sweet melody swells, the tempo slows and the performers become pensive.

In a sense, the Woman in White resembles the heroine Graham portrayed in other dances, in that she seems to be recalling the earlier phases of love in her life—flirtatious adolescent play and sensual rapture. She and her partner are alone onstage when the dance begins, he holding one of his hands, fingers spread, behind her head like the rays of a halo. These two, unlike the other pairs, are together at the end of the dance, when the Woman in Red races across the stage and disappears. In the final moment, the man uses both hands to make them more closely resemble a real crown. When he presses it emphatically down on his partner's head, she sinks under its virtual weight.

This couple's duet reveals even more ambiguities. Consider this. The man lies on his back, and supported by his lifted arms, the woman kneels on his bent knees to hover over him. When she rises, he rolls onto his belly, raising his flexed feet behind him and arching his upper body off the floor, his hands locked behind his head. She steps carefully onto his thighs and sits on the stool created by his feet, gazing around her. This image (surely arduous for him to maintain) implies that he's a boat on which she may consider taking a journey. But she steps off to gaze at something in the distance, and the dance goes on.

If you were to analyze the movements in *Diversion of Angels*, this most athletic of her previous dances, you might find the vocabulary small. Yet you don't feel this while watching the dance. Exuberance sends the dancers into leaps and jumps and runs that skim over the space. Angels at play indeed, albeit often in small choirs. The stage fills and empties like a shimmering current. Various dancers pause—sometimes frozen in intricate poses together—while the action goes on around them. Once, the paths of the Woman in Red and the Woman in White intersect, and the latter waits, balanced on one leg, gazing elsewhere while the other "speaks," circling her closely in a series of falls. A circle is one of the predominant patterns, with the four men and/or women periodically surrounding a couple or one of the female soloists. Once, the men encircle the Woman in White, bounding from side to side and leaping around her as she balances on one leg, the other drawn across her body in that equivocal gesture, her curved arms lifted high. And cartwheels are a recurring maneuver. They are not just executed as a burst of energy that spins the world; the men lift their partners spread-eagled and rotate them like wheels as they carry them offstage. Pearl Lang, who understood this dance to be a turning point in Graham's movement style, remembered Martha telling her dancers,

"I'd like this to look like a Chagall. Figures are in the air and upside down and sideways. You are not standing on the floor."

As usual, Graham made changes in *Diversion of Angels* after its August 13 premiere at Palmer Auditorium. One of these was to dispense with Noguchi's contribution: a stretched backdrop of gray fabric, which workers backstage poked at to suggest the hills and valleys of a changeable landscape. For the piece's summer premiere, Louis Horst had assembled an orchestra of Juilliard students to play Dello Joio's score. At the dress rehearsal, the young musicians didn't meet Horst's exacting standards. He hounded them so mercilessly and for so long that eventually Graham and Hawkins intervened. Horst walked out and later presented his resignation as musical director of the Martha Graham Dance Company. He conducted the performances and had a quiet conversation with Graham later, but his unhappiness and his resentment of Hawkins had been simmering for quite a while.

The severance with her longtime partner pained Graham immensely. Horst's career went on without her, however, and his influence expanded. *Dance Observer*, the publication he had created, continued to serve the dance world. As long as he was able, he played the piano for whatever choreographer needed him. Many dancers who had taken his composition classes at Neighborhood Playhouse or Graham's studio or Bennington (or, starting in 1951, at the newly founded dance department at the Juilliard School) had gone on to form their own companies: O'Donnell, Maslow, Dudley, Lang, Sokolow, Nina Fonaroff (who had also become Horst's companion), Anna Halprin, and many more in the next generation. He also never lacked for the company of smart, attentive young women dancers who enjoyed dining with him.

Nor was the schism between Louis and Martha permanent. By 1954 their friendship had burgeoned again. When he received the Capezio Award in 1955, she was there; when she received hers in 1960, he was there. Graham was solicitous of his health, and years later, near the end of his life, convinced him to move into an apartment near hers so that she could periodically check on him.

Hawkins had long wished to wed Graham, even though their disagreements had caused them to live separately during parts of 1946 and 1947. On September 7, 1948, the two of them married in the First Presbyterian Church of Santa Fe, with their friend Cady Wells as one witness and the church organist as the other. On the certificate, Graham put down a birth date that sheared years off her age. Hawkins was thirty-nine; she admitted to being forty-six. That figure is somewhat less surprising than the truth: the bride was fifty-four years old. (Years later, Hawkins said that he never considered Graham's age a factor and neither knew nor cared how old she was.) According to one source, he, now legally sanctioned, moved back into her apartment at 257 West Eleventh Street, between Seventh and Eighth avenues—a healthy crosstown walk from the studio at Fifth Avenue and Twelfth Street. But he kept his own studio at 6 East Seventeenth Street. The bride began to receive congratulatory messages addressing her as Mrs. Erick Hawkins. In at least one letter to him, she tried out her new name: "Martha Hawkins."

This may have been one of the summers when the two of them briefly camped out in the New Mexican desert, an anomalous experience for Graham, who was unaccustomed to cooking over a campfire. Many years later she told an interviewer, "I was terrified, because sleeping in sleeping bags on the ground is not my area. But I did it, nonetheless. And I got so I could cook very well over stones and bake potatoes and everything. I must say it was not my way, but I wanted Erick to do it, he loved it so, and so we did it. But I was always afraid I was going to wake with a snake on my stomach, because they have a way of doing this, you know." In retrospect, you can view the ending of *Diversion of Angels* as foreshadowing what was to come in the Graham-Hawkins marriage. Whatever her experiences in love and hopes for its future had fueled this resolutely beautiful work, she seems to have also been pondering her role as a wife whose husband, to put it bluntly, could be considered one of her employees, as well as an ingredient in her vision. Over the next year, members of her company noticed that despite an occasional loud-voiced fight between the two of them, Graham also seemed at times to be attempting to inhabit (or playact) a wifely role, making herself appear small and devoted beside Hawkins.

By this time, he had created ten dances of his own, most of them solos and most involving spoken text. Now she presented one of these on her company's programs. *The Strangler*, to music by Bohuslav Martinů, was Hawkins's approach to the Oedipus drama; he chose as its subject the hero's meeting with the oracular Sphinx, thus predating the tragedy that drove Graham's *Night Journey*. It premiered at Connecticut College, with Hawkins as the hero, the actress Anne Meacham as the Sphinx, and the actor Joseph Wiseman (later Pearl Lang's husband) as the Chorus. It was reported that Wiseman, exiting the stage after the curtain descended, remarked in passing, "All's well that ends." The critics offered praise but not much enthusiasm.

Despite the good publicity and renown that the company had received, and despite Hawkins's success in raising money, funding had not kept up with artistic stature. The Martha Graham Dance Company had its usual Broadway season in February 1948, but a 1949 season in New York turned out not to be feasible, and Graham didn't present a new work until January 1950. Instead, with Charles Green as a manager and Eugene Lester as the company's new music director, the company undertook a sixteen-week tour of the United States. On the Hurok tours, the company had had its own Pullman car; traveling between one-night stands by bus made this tour more arduous in every way. Some critics and audiences were enthusiastic; others expressed bafflement; still others, inevitably, disliked what they saw.

A surprising new group dance by Graham premiered on this 1950 tour, one in which she did not appear. Hawkins played its leading role: Shakespeare's King Lear. Hawkins later said that it was he who had persuaded her to tackle the play. She certainly thought about it for a long time. Almost five years earlier she had written to David Zellmer that she was working on a script that "will have little to do with the actual play Lear as we know it, any more than Deaths and Entrances is the Brontes or Letter is Dickinson really." Neither did the three daughters of Lear have anything in common with the three Brontë sisters, nor with the three daughters of Dr. George Graham. The virtuous Cordelia

(Lang) was countered by her sisters, the greedy and unloving Regan (Yuriko) and Goneril (Judith Janus, who appeared in the Graham company only during 1949–1950). Stuart Hodes played the villainous Edmund, Bertram Ross was Edgar disguised as Poor Tom, and Robert Cohan and Marie-Louise Louchheim appeared as Chorus. Vincent Persichetti composed a score for the nineteen-minute work.

Graham extracted her title, *Eye of Anguish*, from the play. Cordelia has asked the Doctor whether her father will recover from his madness, and he replies, prescribing draughts that will promote sleep:

> There is means, madam:
> Our foster-nurse of nature is repose,
> The which he lacks; that to provoke in him,
> Are many simples operative, whose power
> Will close the eye of anguish.

In making the piece (subtitled *The Purgatorial History of King Lear*), Graham was unable, it seems, to transfer to Hawkins's role the depth and complexity that she built into in her own parts. As sensitive as she was to the individual qualities of her dancers and as devoted as she was to Hawkins despite their differences and their quarrels, she apparently couldn't choreograph for him as if she *were*, in some way, him—that is, keeping him as the focal point around which the work spun.

Surely conceived as her gift to him—although he created much of his own movement material—the piece was praised and criticized equally. John Martin found it "a kind of frantic fantasia on themes from 'King Lear,' violent in movement and mood, attempting to give both the external story development and the inner madness of Lear at the same time. In this it does not altogether succeed," despite the fact that "some of the individual phrases of movement are exciting and occasional lashes of action theatrically telling." More than one New York reviewer remarked on the fine theatrical device of having Lear and his daughters at one moment wrapped in a "tremendous red cloth." (Doris Hering of *Dance Magazine* said that *all* the performers were so enmeshed.) In the end, Martin was still balanced on a mental tightrope:

Hawkins, who wore a headdress that appears in a photograph to look like a mane of dried grass, "fairly knocks himself out as Lear, but not to any great effect . . . and the performance is a fine one even if the work itself is no great shakes." Horst, with his own axe to grind, called the work "The Angst of Eyewash."

The year 1949 must have been an especially difficult one for Graham, in part because of her sister Mary's slow death from cancer. Martha saw her briefly in mid-July and wrote to "Darling—my husband" that Mary was extremely thin, "terrifyingly beautiful—and very ill." Coping with pain and refusing food, she passed away in her sleep days after Martha's visit.

The events of that year also stirred Graham to affirm herself as a soloist. She had not made a solo for herself since *Salem Shore* in 1943. In January 1950, now in her midfifties, she premiered two very dissimilar ones: *Judith* and *Gospel of Eve*. The first of these had been commissioned for the Louisville Orchestra; one of its most prominent backers, Louise Kain, had suggested a collaboration between the orchestra and the choreographer. Given the choice of a composer to work with, Graham selected *Night Journey*'s William Schuman and sent him a tentative script, along with biblical quotes that inspired her.

The heroine of an Apocryphal Gospel was a fitting role for her in that it juxtaposed enterprise, courage, and strength to wiles deemed feminine: Judith, a virtuous widow, almost single-handedly saved her besieged city, Bethulia, from an army sent by the power-crazed Assyrian king Nebuchadnezzar. Accomplishing the task by garbing herself seductively and promising secret information, she entered the tent of Holofernes, the general camped outside the city with his troops, got him drunk enough to pass out, and beheaded him with his own sword. On the base of Donatello's statue of Judith and Holofernes that stands in Florence's Palazzo Vecchio are the words "Kingdoms fall through luxuries, cities rise through virtues; behold the neck of pride severed by the hand of humility."

Schuman's *Judith* was conceived as a concerto in five movements in which the dancer would function as a solo instrument and for which the orchestra would be onstage, partly concealed by a scrim. The first movement, a nearly five-minute adagio, represented in its dark tones the plight of the starving Israelites who were near surrender. In the second movement, Judith, in a familiar Graham structural device, recollects her heroic act and garbs herself for her ordeal. The music's third movement (tranquillo) suggests her prayers for strength. After she has garbed herself and disappeared into the tent, the presto movement, with its ominous timpani and agitated strings, invokes the beheading. She reappears in triumph, perhaps during the three-minute andante meant by the composer to represent Judith's homeward journey bearing the head of Holofernes. Graham described her action that occurred during a moment of silence near the end of the work: "Slowly, slowly I pulled down the curtain until Judith stood there alone and in her hands she had two branches of white flowers and the dance ended by her crossing the stage with those flowers."

The original set for the Louisville premiere on January 4, 1950, was created by William Sherman and Charles Hyman (Hyman married the Graham dancer Ethel Winter later that year). For the piece's Carnegie Hall debut that year, Noguchi redesigned it. His vision of Holofernes's domain was a portal akin to the bony one in *Errand into the Maze*. Two crossed supports end in arrowheads or spear points; a third one looks more like a penis. The horizontal rail joining them has the stylized head of a snarling beast, and a length of deep purple fabric hangs over it. Another large set piece resembled a lyre; according to Martin Friedman, it also served as a loom. Graham changed costumes at least once during the piece.

Gospel of Eve, which premiered later in January during the company's season at the Forty-Sixth Street Theatre, recaptured the far lighter tone of her popular *Every Soul Is a Circus*. Its flippant title refers, of course, to the literary forerunner of all women who tempt their husbands to do whatever they require. While *Judith* presented Graham as a virtuous woman who didn't hesitate to seduce and murder a man who threatened the life of her city and its inhabitants, *Gospel of Eve* showed her as a frivolous lady who whiles away her time trying to decide which hat would be most beguiling. The piece involved many of these moments, as well as a number of heart-shaped mirrors. The theatrical designer Oliver Smith provided a setting (mostly chairs), Miles White was credited with costumes, Paul Nordhoff wrote a score, and the wonderfully gifted Jean Rosenthal, who'd been lighting Graham's dances since 1943, provided the atmosphere.

Judith garnered accolades. Not so *Gospel of Eve*. John Martin found it "little more than an extended gag," praising Graham's comedic skill and tactfully—as was his wont—hoping that the dance would improve after a little tightening. Walter Terry of the *New York Herald Tribune* wrote a more illuminating review, noting that the piece was

> in the area of gesture, rather than large scale movement where the choreographer has worked major miracles of hilarity and dramatic point. These gestures—the useless flutter of a hand, a shrug, a grimace of exasperation, a prissy manipulation of stage props—all contribute to the characterization of a woman whose whole life appears to be dedicated to self-embellishment, self-admiration and the arrangement of surrounds to enhance that self.

However, Terry perceptively noticed in *Gospel of Eve* the sadness that can underlie comedy, writing of the passage in which Graham's character "discards the empty mannerisms of a foolish female and permits us to see the real anguish, the poignant loneliness of a woman whose attempts to build beauty end with the veneer."

Graham, now twenty to thirty years older than her dancers, didn't enjoy touring, although she was stoic about it. She was evidently nervous about an opportunity that loomed. Bethsabée de Rothschild had pledged $10,000 to support possible appearances of the company in Europe that summer, and negotiations to make that feasible had begun.

Performances were scheduled in Paris and London in the coming year. Then, a rarity: Graham injured herself. Accounts of how this happened vary. Ethel Winter thought that an accident occurred during New York rehearsals *before* the trip to Paris and that Graham re-injured her knee once abroad. Stuart Hodes remembered rehearsing a passage in *Every Soul Is a Circus* during which she clung to one of his arms and, as he hoisted it, repeatedly leaped and landed on an already problematic leg. Bertram Ross had the impression that Hawkins had set her down hard from a lift. Graham herself said that one knee "went" during a deep plié in that dance at the first Paris performance. She hated the alternative forced on her: a second program of pieces in which she did not appear. It included *Eye of Anguish*. Rage though she might, the company had to cancel its London appearances.

In London, Hawkins borrowed a bit of money from some members of the company and went off to Stratford to see Laurence Olivier and Vivien Leigh perform Shakespeare's *Titus Andronicus*. He'd deserted Martha, most of them thought. However, a letter that Martha wrote to Erick on July 27 from the Mission Inn in Santa Barbara, where she was recuperating, offers a different perspective: "I am more grateful to you than I can ever say for the consideration and care you gave me in Paris and London. You made things so much easier at a hard time. I only wished I could have so behaved that you might know how much I mean that. I made a mess of things again and it is done. I realize that I am ill and I have to find a way out of this 'primeval forest of evasions.'"

She spent the next months recovering from the torn cartilage. She had decided against an operation and kept her leg strong by swinging it while wearing a heavy iron boot. De Rothschild succored her during much of that difficult time; supporting Martha had become a major project for her, from which she derived great pleasure.

The disaster in Europe delayed acceptance of Graham's work there by several years; it also wrecked her wavering marriage and damaged the professional relationship that went with it. Inevitably, it reshaped her choreography. Two extraordinary letters document the falling-out between her and her husband-partner. On August 27, 1950, from his New York studio, Hawkins sent Graham a single-spaced, typewritten letter, twenty-seven pages long; it had taken him several days to compose it. Graham's September 3 answer, written in Santa Barbara, covered eleven single-spaced typewritten pages.

Although Erick's letter acknowledges Martha as a genius and his superior in art, he wrote that he wanted equality in their partnership; being, in effect, prince consort to a queen chafed at his own ambitions as a choreographer. It would be a mistake, however, for anyone reading the letter to sum up his feelings too simplistically. He had contributed a great deal to helping her expand her career, and he makes that clear. Yet he feels that she has not always been happy with what he did, especially when he seemed to be pushing her toward more touring. And he is not happy that the newspaper critics rarely praise him as a dancer and or as a choreographer. Too, Graham's technique is hard on his body, especially since he hadn't started to study dance until he turned twenty-one and graduated from Harvard.

His letter also reveals his bitterness about a more personal issue. Graham was still perhaps reacting to that inevitable time of change in any woman's life. She had become jealous of any attention she saw Hawkins paying to another woman, no matter how innocently. In Europe, on one of the occasions that triggered their breakup, she had berated him in front of other people, convinced that he had been unfaithful to her with the embarrassed young company dancer who was also present. He wrote in his long, long letter that he got on well with both her and Jean Erdman and enjoyed their company, but had been careful not to get too close to either of them for fear of angering her.

If Erick's letter enraged her or reduced her to floods of tears, Martha didn't admit to either, only writing back that his words had "brought a certain agony." Nor does she remind him of the ways in which she has fostered his ambitions as a dancer and choreographer. She does confess, however, to resenting his youth, at a time when she was facing the slow onset of age. "The only way I knew to work was changelessness through myself"—seeing herself as "a kind of goddess," with unchanging youth "the fetish of my power . . . I was curious in that I preached life and talked of life and yet in some inner way I refused to recognize the laws of life." She now understands, she says, the Chinese view "toward age and life as evolution," while she had made herself "a martyr to time." She writes that she "may have been too full of self-love to love you as you deserved or needed, but I loved you as far as I knew how. Now I see it was not a very wonderful love for you to have." Later in the letter she tells him, "I shall always be able to say that you were the most wonderful experience of my life. Not because of what we have done together but because of the inner vision you have had and the greatness of your thinking and feeling."

She laboriously types out for him five paragraphs from *Reason and Emotion* by John Macmurray, a book she'd read on the train to California, acquainting Hawkins with the author's belief that relationships with others are more important than considering everything from the individual's viewpoint. "I know of no clearer way," she writes, "to explain to you that at last I am awake." And after talking about plans for the school, at which she hopes he will continue to teach, and praising his performance of Lear in Paris, she ends her letter, "And above all else in the world I would have you release your powers whatever is necessary to bring that about. I could wish it would be with me but if it cannot be then I still want it." After signing the missive, she continued writing in longhand, the letters getting smaller and more cramped as they approached the bottom of the page.

In September of that year (1950), intent on moving forward in her life and career, Graham sought the help of the lay analyst Frances G. Wickes, whose works she admired and whom Hawkins had seen briefly two years earlier. This relationship turned into an extraordinary one, though over the next few years they were able to meet only occasionally, as Wickes had moved out west. In one letter, written to her in 1951 from New London, Graham says, "I am not a very satisfactory patient," but what "patient" wrote letters to her therapist like those that Graham sent? She, of course, destroyed the responses that she received, but Wickes saved those addressed to "Dear Mrs. Wickes" or "Darling," which might end with, for example, "Your hand is on my life. Love, Martha."

To Wickes, Graham recounts her anguish over the breakup with Hawkins and her slow reacquaintance with happiness; to Wickes she confesses her own guilt over her unwise behavior; to Wickes she describes her works in progress, the things she has seen, and the people she has met—always including her concern for Wickes's well-being (serious eye trouble and back trouble). She can be said to have bared her soul.

In one letter, begun on July 16, 1951, she notes that the next day would be the anniversary of the "London fiasco" and what she refers to in a later letter as "That Night." But she had left New York for her usual summer job in New London, and two days earlier, driven there by de Rothschild, she had gone immediately to the beach. She had taught her first class to a group of about sixty, and she despairs of the students:

> All I can do in these five days is to make them a little more aware through shock and an attempt at building and progression. But then again it will be a painful experience if they get it at all and perhaps it is better and kinder to let them sleep as they are now . . . to employ what I call the "rocking chair" method of dancing . . . comfortable, rhythmic, monotonous, safe . . . Perhaps they should never leave the chair to stir those depths of the shadowy pool near which they rock their lives away.

She goes on to link that perceived apathy with the solo relating to Joan of Arc that she is working on, commissioned again by the Louisville Symphony Orchestra and scheduled to be performed in December 1951:

> I think I never want [the students] to be on fire if it is so painful for them as it is for me. I wonder how long one can stay on fire. It is a curious fire. Perhaps it is good for Joan. I wonder. At least I think I know what it does mean to burn slowly from within . . . to feel possessed by flame as to be infinitely hot and about to disintegrate into an ash at any instant. It may be very beautiful to watch. People speak of my radiance, that I look as though I had found a new life . . . Perhaps it is the final glow and not a beginning.

The "Joan" she writes of, of course, did indeed burn into ash, and Martha transformed the "final glow" into a beginning.

Norman Dello Joio, whose music accompanied *Diversion of Angels*, provided the score for Graham's solo. He had been struck by stories of Joan, the female warrior, when he was a twelve-year-old church organist. In 1950 he had composed *The Triumph of St. Joan*, a three-act opera, for his students at Sarah Lawrence College. In 1951 he wrote an instrumental version, and in 1955 he revised and shortened the opera, retitling it *The Trial at Rouen*. It was his 1951 work that accompanied Graham's *Triumph of St. Joan*.

In an article for *The New York Times* in 1956, Dello Joio wrote that he had been drawn to the story of Joan in part because it recounted "the ageless conflict between excessive imagination and those who hold to the status quo." (One can't help wondering if the hearings of 1953–54, conducted by Senator Joseph McCarthy with the aim of flushing out supposed communists, influenced the composer's third version.) The conflict between creative vision and long-established beliefs about art were certainly familiar to Graham.

Like the performances of her *Judith* in Louisville, *The Triumph of St. Joan*—with scenery by the architect and theater designer Frederick Kiesler and lighting by Jean Rosenthal—balanced the passages of dancing with ones for the musicians alone. As in her 1955 *Seraphic Dialogue*, Graham's expansion of *The Triumph of St. Joan* into a group work, the heroine was shown in three differently costumed aspects of her life: the Maid who receives the heavenly vision, the Warrior who rides into battle to save France from the English, and the Martyr. One minor point: Graham, whose legs hadn't been seen by audiences since her Denishawn days and the sometimes filmy garments they required, wore tights when she wielded her huge wooden sword—not to fight the invisible enemy as much as to contemplate doing so.

Graham had turned fifty-nine in 1953. That fact; the loss of her partner; her knee injury, healed though it was; and the success of *Diversion of Angels* conspired to influence her creative choices. She appeared in only one of the four dances she choreographed between 1952 and 1958: *Canticle for Innocent Comedians*, *Voyage*, *Ardent Song*, and *Seraphic Dialogue*.

Canticle premiered in April 1952 at the Juilliard School, then up in Morningside Heights. The noted music school's Dance Division, acquired the previous year, was established by William Schuman and directed by Martha Hill, so it was inevitable that Graham technique would be taught there, either by Graham or her dancers.

Graham again took her title from a poem by Ben Belitt: "A Canticle for Innocent Comedians," but a program note for the dance hints that the "comedians"—meaning players, not clowns—stood for the five elements that Saint Francis of Assisi christened in "The Canticle of the Sun," which he had begun to compose in 1224. In it he praised God's "creatures" as Brother Sun, Sister Moon, and her stars, Brother Wind, Sister Water, Brother Fire, Sister Earth, and Sister Death. Graham honored those gender distinctions in her casting and listed each—preceded by "for" to indicate that in the cosmic universe, dancers were only stand-ins.*

The movable set pieces that shaped the choreography and provided an environment were ones that Kiesler had created for a music performance at Juilliard, where he was in charge of scenic design. These "mobiloids," as he called them, could form bridges, doorways, steps, and resting places. Blue on the inside, blond wood on the outside, they could be turned, angled, or tilted. Various of the six or seven women dancers, stepping in rhythm, wheeled them smoothly into place or offstage, sometimes with other performers sitting or standing on them. *Canticle for Innocent Comedians* began with almost all these set pieces, mostly waist-high, clustered at the center rear of the stage, where they created a compressed stadium around and within which dancers walked, as if winding up the dance to come. You could imagine them as reorganizing the cosmos to acknowledge the pull of tides and the coinciding of orbits. Graham, increasingly delighted with her dancers, created an anthology of small pieces—mostly solos and duets.

---

* For Sun: Bertram Ross; For Earth: Mary Hinkson; For Wind: Robert Cohan with Matt Turney; For Water: Helen McGehee; For Fire: Stuart Hodes with Linda Margolies, Mary Hinkson, Patricia Birsh; For Stars: Helen McGehee and Robert Cohan; For Death: Pearl Lang with Bertram Ross. Miriam Cole and Dorothy Krooks are also listed in the original cast.

Bertram Ross, as the Sun, appeared between these on his passage through the day. In his opening solo he suspends himself and turns smoothly upside down within a narrow, freestanding curved panel. Reviewing a 1987 revival, Anna Kisselgoff wrote of the Sun hanging upside down in his dark little "sky" when he encounters the Moon: "The effect is astoundingly right: the sun as tender fool." Here is my description of the characters as they appeared in that revival:

> Earth is a serene woman who carries flowering branches and strikes deep, wide poses. Wind leaps, whirls, tumbles, and is gone. Water, a pretty mermaid, thrashes on a "bridge" in a foot-trapping gown. Fire is a trickster who vaults over walls and teases the chorus of women. Stars perform a rapid, bright duet. Death comes as a fascinating Spanish dancer, veiled in black, and the Sun becomes her doomed and hypnotized partner.

Thomas Ribbink's score was one of the weakest among Graham's collaborations. The Moon danced her solo passages in silence, a wise decision Graham made after watching the movements that Yuriko created after the two had discussed ideas about the orbit and rhythms of the moon. For many, this dancer's solo and her duet with Ross were the high points of the work. The two were wheeled onstage in a structure representing conjoined windows. Yuriko recalls it being made out of two-by-fours—three sections the same size and the fourth larger. A narrow ledge spanned the base of all four windows.

The Moon moves slowly and expansively, opening her arms and lifting her chest as she turns in her own curving paths. Eventually the Sun follows her, copying her moves, or answers her, each time accompanied by a sudden rush of music. Lying atop the windows, she reaches a hand down to him. No fancy lifts; Sun and Moon are partners, forever paired, touching only every ten years, when her shadow eclipses him.

Graham had been pondering *Voyage* for almost three years before it premiered in 1953. References to it in her letters to Frances Wickes, as well as in her archived notes and the edited version of these published as *The Notebooks of Martha Graham*, show it swimming around in her mind along with passages from books she has read. The roots of *Voyage* tangled briefly with a work that she, about to leave New York for California in July 1951, imagined being titled "Point of the Wolves" or "Promontory of the Wolves," in reference to California's Point Lobos cleaving the Pacific Ocean. The wolves were "the hungry ones who tear at the heart with that cruel hunger that only wolves have." By August, in Santa Fe with de Rothschild, with Craig Barton and LeRoy Leatherman there for a week as houseguests, Graham was fighting dark moods and thinking further about the piece. As she told Wickes, she had flung out her arms and thought she might instead title the piece "I Salute My Love," and she wrote elsewhere that love was her life. That moment called up many lists: "Twilight, Moon-rise, Moon-full, Moon-set, Deep Dark, Dawn" is one of them; fallout from *Canticle for Innocent Comedians* would be reignited in *Ardent Song*.

Graham, like *Voyage* itself, was evolving. In the margin of her notes she scribbled a quote from Robert Payne's *The Wanton Nymph: A Study of Pride*: "a grief which turns into a triumph, a solemn vow to endure & die dancing." She confided to Wickes that she thought it necessary "to transmute a sentimental experience into something constructive and perhaps creative" and hoped this might be done "without embarrassment of unnecessary revealment." The wolves have slunk away. And drawn to the phases of the moon, she begins to envision "I Salute My Love." It might have the flavor of Moorish Spain and begin with a muezzin calling the faithful to prayer. She's thinking of a bullfight and the "querencia," the spot to which the embattled animal keeps returning. As is frequently the case, she thinks in triads, whether she's jotting down the phases of the moon or "Love, Death, Life." Soon she is envisioning a balcony at night or a courtyard or "some cool remote room of a tropical house"; "a meal is finished, except for wine." Three men philosophize, the woman is silent.

Graham's scenario went through many phases. Gradually, the other characters she has thought about—including a Keeper of the Gate, three matadors, three dancers, and more—slip away. The querencia becomes "the arena of the woman's being." In her, each of the three men can see "the image of woman he holds in his heart." Graham's images of the dance become increasingly vivid and specific. For instance, "Image—woman seated—man kneeling between her wide knees—Her feet clasp about him & he falls backward—down steps as she rises." Above this, on a slant, she writes "Voyage. Bob?" Meaning Robert Cohan. And above "man & woman with crossed daggers," she writes "Voyage. Stuart"—meaning Stuart Hodes.

Some of the visions Graham conjures up became part of what became *Voyage*: "As he draws hair pin out of her hair each man kisses her—rips part of her dress from—exits blinded with the piece he carries—." The flowers she mentions appear, made, by Noguchi, of wood. A green cape is considered. The scene is to be an uncharted inland sea, over which the men must travel into their own natures. Noguchi's set consisted of a stylized boat and a frail, freestanding sculptural portal. For a time, Graham labels Cohan as the Poet, Hodes as the Warrior (Conqueror), and Bertram Ross as the Clown (lover). The passage of the night and the emergence into dawn endure as life-affirming themes: death and rebirth.

Graham began to work with the three men at night in her studio. At her request, William Schuman was orchestrating a piano piece of his that created an atmosphere of unspecific drama. Decades later, the three men remembered loving the intimacy and intensity of the experience— the discussions, the improvisations. At *Voyage*'s premiere, Graham wore a Hattie Carnegie gown of black and brown silk; her colleagues were dressed in evening clothes of polished cotton. According to Hodes, "Bert Ross's [suit] was blue for truth, Bob Cohan's green for freshness and adolescence, and my tux was red for passion." Yet when Graham perched atop the arch, the men, jumping as they circled her, began stripping off their jackets. Taking turns exiting and returning minus shirts, shoes, and socks, with their trousers rolled up, they eventually launched themselves into primitive behavior—described by one observer as "a kind of war dance about her." In Ross's recollection, they "picked her off" her arch and "zoomed her all over the stage and put her on top of Hodes. She was like a bird of prey that knocked him down."

Apparently the men initially "conversed," their mouths moving, but no sound emerging. As civilized behavior went the way of the costumes, Hodes and Cohan slipped under Graham's cape while she was dancing, only their heads sticking out, and then swung her around by the fabric. As mentioned above, the three men had also taken her hair down, each drawing out one pin. Over the course of the dance, Graham had a duet with each suitor—the one with Ross the gentlest—yet formed no lasting alliances with any of them. By the end, they had all returned to the party, fully dressed and well-behaved. The cocktail engagement turned savage rite had buttoned itself up again before the four left the stage.

Unlike the three cardboard suitors in the lighthearted *Every Soul Is a Circus*, these men suggested aspects of a single man's personality as Graham's character assessed it—his youthful zest, his ruthlessness, his sweetness—and the lust that lay beneath these. Unusually for Graham, the male personas not only lured her but also invaded and dominated her.

Her process, through all the intellectually and emotionally fevered images in her notes and through the many rehearsals, seems to have been—at least partly—instinctive. In June 1953, a month after *Voyage*'s premiere, she wrote to Wickes, wishing that the analyst who advised her so wisely had seen it: "I know you could tell me exactly what I am creeping about and trying to evade . . . I have a fair suspicion what it may be."

In hindsight, one can imagine what that suspicion was. If her desire had been to investigate her relationship with Hawkins as a way of moving forward in her life, *Voyage* may have served her well (although it didn't succeed onstage with the public or most of the critics). Yet she wasn't done with it. In 1955 she renamed it *Theater for a Voyage*, thereby transforming the protagonists into performers one step removed from the characters they embodied and transcending her own grief.

The lunar images that had preoccupied her for several years shaped *Ardent Song*, set to a score by Alan Hovhaness. By now, audiences, especially those in New York City who had been following Graham's career, were familiar with the dancers' traits that the choreography made shine. Yuriko, small and valiant, was to embody Moonrise; swift, sharp Helen McGehee to portray Moonset; strong, glamorous Pearl Lang, Dawn. Radiant Mary Hinkson with her beautifully arched feet, plus Matt Turney of the long limbs and serene air and Linda Margolies, represented Moon High. Stuart Hodes emanated strength and masterliness; Robert Cohan could be slippery; Bertram Ross was both noble and vulnerable; David Wood was smaller and bolder.

Graham was preparing *Ardent Song* for the company's debut at the Saville Theatre in London on March 18, 1954. It didn't escape her that this would be her chance to redeem herself to British dance lovers after the canceled 1952 performances. The piece had had a difficult birth, and Graham, forced to ready ten works for the two-week London season, hadn't finished it by the time the company sailed for England on the *Queen Elizabeth*. It was to premiere during the second week and had been conceived to last more than three-quarters of an hour. At almost the last minute, Graham attempted to cancel its appearance but was forcefully dissuaded to do so by Gertrude Macy, who was producing the season.

In order to fill a gap in the work, when four couples were circling Yuriko, Cohan—in Hodes's recollection—"would do a move, the second couple would repeat it, then the third, then the fourth. Then he'd think up another move. Twelve moves, ten seconds each." Graham rallied and provided more material. Hinkson, Margolies, and Turney improvised a rapid trio and eventually, collaborating with pianist Helen Lanfer, nailed it down. *Ardent Song* was an "enormous success" in London, according to Graham, and she thought she knew why: "It has some lovely things in it," she wrote to Wickes, "but it also has some very fine theatrical wooing ways. These will be pruned before New York."

Fortunately, the small audiences and the critics' baffled, disapproving words during the first week were outweighed in the second week by a rousing review by Richard Buckle in the *Sunday Observer*. "Now," he wrote, "I conjure every idle habit-formed creature, in need of a third eye to see new beauty that he should visit the Saville Theatre and watch Martha Graham. She is one of the great creators of our time." Graham wrote a long letter to Horst, marveling that "a ballet fan turned the tide for me."

However rickety the construction of *Ardent Song* had been, the work contributed to that change in the tide.

By March 28, Martha could write to Wickes that "The weeks in London went by with me seeing nothing of London except the inside of my own heart." In that letter, she told Wickes of the grueling schedule: Every day she left the hotel before 9:00 a.m. and returned close to midnight.

Her spirits must have been lifted further by the company's reception by audiences in Holland, Sweden, Denmark, Belgium, France, Switzerland, and Austria. She wrote Horst that one man had ridden his motorbike more than two hundred miles between Hanover and Amsterdam to see a performance, and another had made a similar trip from the polar circle to Stockholm. Only in Florence—where Graham and her company shared the stage for four of its six programs with an opera company during the city's Maggio Musicale week—were audiences irritated, confused, and loud about expressing those feelings. France awarded her a medal from the City of Paris, the first time a dancer had been so honored. The U.S. State Department talked about a tour to the Far and Middle East the following year. Willy-nilly, Graham had become a cultural ambassador.

In preparation, Graham expanded her solo, *The Triumph of St. Joan*, into *Seraphic Dialogue*, a work for small ensemble; it premiered in May 1955 in another season of American modern dance at the ANTA Theatre in New York, during which eleven companies participated.

Her earlier solo had not used all of Dello Joio's score, and she had been offstage changing her costume while the Juilliard Orchestra played its other sections. Now her choreography used all the music.

Seraphic Dialogue linked the passages for the three performers portraying Joan as Maid, Warrior, and Martyr with interludes for the Joan who recollects those three incarnations at the moment of her ascension into heaven. Noguchi created one of his most beautiful sets. The pyramid of slender brass rods allude to the metal framing of the stained glass shapes that glow in church windows. Within the stage-right structure hangs a long sword made of the same brass, and the stage-left one incorporates a cross about two feet square (you don't recognize these until they are detached). Three brass circles, one above the other, are suspended within the structure like vertical halos.

Seraphic Dialogue marked Graham's clearest and most potent use of memory as a structuring device. Wearing long, plain, differently colored cloaks, Joan's three avatars enter in a measured procession and seat themselves side by side on what looks somewhat like a golden-wired sawhorse. Standing before Saint Michael on his high central seat between and above his helpmeets, Saint Catherine and Saint Margaret, the Joan who has conjured up these former selves is moved by Saint Michael's fluttering hands to recall the stages of her life.* She often splits her legs apart, slides to the floor, and lays her cheek against its surface, or bends slowly, hinging at the knees. When she jumps repeatedly—perhaps recalling battle—her legs are slightly apart and bent behind her. Her focus is on the stage-right structure, which will also come to represent the stake at which she is to be burned.

In the video version of *Seraphic Dialogue*, Patricia Birch embodies the maiden Joan with admirable subtlety. After Saint Margaret and Saint Catherine have removed her blue cloak, her raptness and swooning devotion bespeak her innocence as she gazes at the sword and stake that suggest to her only her mission, not her fate. But when she accepts her destiny, the country-girl kerchief she has tied under her chin is transformed into a flag for her to wave as, feet planted wide apart and knees bent, she pulses in place as if riding into battle.

Saint Michael descends from his "window" in order to rouse Joan's fighting spirit. Graham designed a remarkable costume for him, its green top and purple bottom bisected horizontally and vertically by slim white lines of fabric, forming two conjoined squares that descend from his wrists to his ankles. When he spreads his legs slightly apart,

---

* Cast at the premiere: Linda Margolies (Joan), Patricia Birsh (Joan the maid), Mary Hinkson (Joan as warrior), Matt Turney (Joan as martyr), Bertram Ross (Saint Michael), Lillian Biersteker (Saint Catherine), and Ellen van der Hoeven (Saint Margaret).

he looks like a flat rectangle, although he is anything but two-dimensional in his role. He conveys to Joan the warrior what may happen to her in battle—pressing her down with the sword that he has taken from its place, lightly pricking her with it, and, after she has staunchly accepted it from him, lifting her as she embraces it. He trudges along holding her horizontally, binding her and her sword together and guiding her toward the English invaders against which she must lead the French army. When, wounded in battle, she collapses, he holds her limp form against him and keeps moving, the sword held aloft. That this small girl should lead an army!

The third "Joan" clutches the cross to her breast as she dances. The shuddering contractions of her rib cage seem to help pull it to her—her shield, her faith. And, in the end, she collapses against what has become the stake.

Joan's other selves remain motionless and expressionless until they are summoned to dance. Throughout, the unrobing and re-robing of each of them is executed with the utmost formality by the two saints who assist Michael in these tasks and add their own fragments of ecstatic dancing.

In the end, the Joan-who-remembers reappears in a plain, slim-fitting golden gown. Noguchi's gates—the gates of Heaven—open, so that, helped by the two lesser saints, she can ascend backward up the two steps toward Saint Michael, who waits to receive her. The two close the structure's shining gates and resume their places. He, with fatherly gentleness, places his hands around the new saint's head, crowning her.

Whatever may have compelled Graham to revisit Joan of Arc, she created a work in which a brave young woman struggles to become a hero, battles the odds, pays the cost, and is glorified. Graham didn't premiere another piece until 1958.

─16─

TRAVELING INTO ASIA AND ONWARD WITHOUT ERICK

A SNAPSHOT TAKEN IN LATE OCTOBER 1955 shows members of the Martha Graham Dance Company waving and smiling beside a Japan Airlines plane. Wearing light overcoats and (most of them) hats, they have embarked on a new job, that of being cultural ambassadors. The Korean War having ended two years earlier, the Soviet Union and the United States were competing for influence in the Far East, where countries, many in the process of decolonization, wavered over the possibility of communism.

The U.S. State Department hoped to capture the hearts and minds of citizens halfway around the globe. President Dwight Eisenhower spoke of "the broader considerations that might follow what you would call the 'falling domino' principle. You have a row of dominoes set up, you knock over the first one, and what will happen to the last one is the certainty that it will go over very quickly." Catch the first before it topples, he implied.

In an April 1954 news conference, the American National Theater and Academy (ANTA), authorized by the State Department, convened advisory panels to select groups to send abroad. As dances such as Graham's were perceived as "serious" American art rather than simply entertainment, it's not surprising that her company was chosen for export to Asia, given the names of the panelists: Doris Humphrey;

Martha Hill; Lincoln Kirstein; Bethsabée de Rothschild; Walter Terry; Ballet Theater's founder-director Lucia Chase; *Newsweek*'s music and dance critic Emily Coleman; Hyman Faine, executive secretary of the American Guild of Musical Artists; and, later, Agnes de Mille.

Graham herself is not shown in that first snapshot at the airport. She had arrived in Tokyo a few days earlier in order to acclimate and reinvigorate herself for her company's appearances in Japan and the strenuous ensuing tour. The publicity had been persuasive. Beginning with the group's first performance in Tokyo, her dances were viewed by audiences far larger than any experienced in the United States. A strike in Seoul, Korea, prevented the planned November performances there, but between the middle of that month and the first week of February 1956, Graham's dances were viewed in Manila; Bangkok; Kuala Lumpur; Jakarta; Rangoon; Dacca (now Dhaka); Calcutta (now Kolkata); Madras (now Chennai); Colombo, Ceylon (now Sri Lanka); Bombay (now Mumbai); New Delhi; Karachi; and Abadan. And after the stint in Iran, the company went to Israel for performances organized by de Rothschild.

The dancers were welcomed at airports and train stations and toasted at parties. In India, Graham met Jawaharlal Nehru; in Iran, the shah, Reza Pahlavi, invited the company to a banquet. De Rothschild, who was traveling with the company, arranged a visit to Agra to view the Taj Mahal on one of the performers' rare free days. They also bought souvenirs and had a considerable amount of fun.

Graham, writing to Frances Wickes from Ceylon, marvels at the company's "unbelievable success." In Rangoon, it was reported that four thousand people had attended the performances taking place in a field adjoining the golden Shwedagon Pagoda. Food was cooked and served surrounding a huge teakwood stage with walls of straw matting. Buddhist student monks in saffron robes sat in front of the box office until they were admitted free of charge. How many monks? Eight hundred in all, it was guessed. On opening night the ambassador presented Graham to the audience, and the prime minister made a speech and draped around Martha's neck a rope of jasmine and red roses held together with silver thread. In Jakarta, an editorial in a left-wing, anti-American newspaper proved so admiring that Washington, D.C., sent it by wireless around the world.

Jakarta had been "hot, hot, hot" and mosquito-ridden, according to a report sent home by LeRoy Leatherman, while the weather in Rangoon was blessedly cool. During this period of renascence for Indian classical dance, which had been repressed under British rule, major dancers came to greet Graham, speak with her, perform for her. Uday Shankar—noted for his fusion of Indian dance forms with Western theatrical techniques—was at the airport to welcome and embrace her (she remembered him from his American tour in the 1930s). In Bombay, the great Balasaraswati gave a private performance for the visiting dancers; while there, they also saw Shanta Rao dance in the Mohiniyattam tradition. In Chennai, they were invited by the Bharata Natyam dancer and educator Rukmini Devi to visit Kalakshetra, the music and dance academy she had founded.

Audiences may have been puzzled or startled by Graham's compositions, but they were impressed, often adulatory. And she was now prepared to introduce her ideas about dance while guiding the company members in public lecture-demonstrations that included her movement technique as well as excerpts from her own influential repertory.

The dancers adjusted to the occasional unusual stage, such as one with a splintery dance floor, one with a steep rake, or one open to the sky. Dressing rooms and toilets were often makeshift. They coped with injuries and unfamiliar food and dealt with unexpected situations. "Lee" Leatherman had to have his appendix out in Colombo. Craig Barton, advance man for the company, became snowbound in Iran. Two of the women dancers had a catfight backstage, and in New Delhi, one of them, who'd been worrying everyone, had what may have been a nervous breakdown (Martha calmed her, and her parents came and took her home). At a party given by people from the American Embassy, Stuart Hodes slipped as he was dashing into the swimming pool and ended up with a dislocated big toe. Donald McKayle hurt his back. At Christmas, six of the dancers were too ill to perform.

Paul Taylor (called "Pablo" by Graham), new to the company,

offered in his autobiography, *Private Domain*, a story that reveals how the grandeur Martha projected in public could be countered by the more relaxed persona she revealed when the occasion warranted it. Bumping along in a tour bus to visit the Elephanta Caves of Bombay with the company, she requests a rest stop and disappears into the ferns beneath a palm tree. A family of gibbons scolds her for invading their territory but apparently doesn't watch her closely. Back in the bus, she tells her friend Bethsabée that the monkeys' "concepts of modesty are terribly old-fashioned" (did they perhaps cover their babies' eyes?).

Throughout the tour, de Rothschild—although a baroness, a member of the great French banking family, and one who, as a member of the Free French forces, had participated in the landing for the Normandy invasion—was identified as the company's "wardrobe mistress," supervising the laundering and packing of costumes (finding that her ironing sometimes scorched the costumes, the dancers took to arriving early at the theaters to do it themselves). On the other hand, in Kuala Lumpur, this modest and shy benefactor of Graham and her company bought—and had sent to New York for Graham's living room—an antique Chinese bed on which Martha might occasionally lounge for a photographer.

When she returned home and was recovering from the monthslong endeavor, Graham could ponder her future onstage and the growing individuality and creative instincts of her company members. She was also acquiring new performers. One result of the tour was that several young dancers who attended the performances in Japan eventually migrated to New York. Three of them—Akiko Kanda, Takako Asakawa, and Yuriko Kimura—joined the Martha Graham Dance Company, while Kazuko Hirabayashi became a choreographer and a prominent teacher.

The ideas that Graham had been formulating for her next work—her longest to date—may have been sparked in part by a work that Erick Hawkins premiered in 1957. His *Here and Now with Watchers* was unusually lengthy, lasting for seventy-five minutes, and it was the only offering on his program. The spare, poetic array of eight duets and alternating solos for himself and Nancy Lang was set to a score by a young composer he later married. In view of the audience, Lucia Dlugoszewski performed her music for "timbre piano," a piano whose strings she hit and stroked with a variety of objects.

The following year, Graham went him one better. Her dance would unfold over two hours, with two intermissions. It would be neither spare nor plotless, however, and its poeticism was of a meatier sort than that of Hawkins's. She had been delving into the *Oresteia*, Aeschylus's fifth-century BCE Greek trilogy: *Agamemnon*, *The Libation Bearers*, and *The Eumenides*. The role she chose for herself was that of Clytemnestra, queen of Mycenae and wife to its king, Agamemnon, and she structured her eponymous composition around that character's vision of the tragic events that had engulfed her, some of which were of her own conniving.

The crisis that incited the nine-year Trojan War differed considerably from the previous Graham-Hawkins marital crisis. Clytemnestra's sister Helen—queen of Sparta and the wife of Agamemnon's brother, Menelaus—had been kidnapped by the Trojan prince Paris. Agamemnon's mission was to cross the Aegean Sea, conquer Troy, and bring Helen back to Greece. Clytemnestra slew him on his homecoming. Her reason? Before setting sail for Troy, he had deceived her into thinking that he had arranged a marriage for their eldest daughter, Iphigenia, but had instead sacrificed her, believing that Artemis, a goddess he had offended, would thus be propitiated and provide the long-awaited wind that would allow his fleet to embark from the port of Aulis and start a war.

Another family crisis loomed. When Agamemnon finally arrived home victorious after a voyage lasting more than ten years, he also brought with him the war prize who had been warming his bed: the Trojan prophetess Cassandra. And during her husband's long absence, Clytemnestra had fueled her rage at the loss of her daughter by taking a lover herself: the handsome Aegisthus.

A betrayed wife, a grieving mother, an adulteress, and a queen strong enough to commit murder whatever the cost . . . you can see what attracted Graham to the role and to this tremendously ambitious undertaking. Perhaps one can relate her choice of subject matter to the demons that simmered beneath the polite, even cordial relations that endured between herself and Hawkins.

She cast the principal characters sagely. Small, innocent-appearing Yuriko played Ismene, the younger of Oedipus's two daughters, and tall, enigmatic Matt Turney was Cassandra. Sharply pretty Ethel Winter assumed the role of the abducted Helen of Troy. Bertram Ross doubled as Agamemnon and his son Orestes. The lean, long-legged newcomer Gene McDonald played four roles: Hades, Paris, the Watchman, and the Ghost of Agamemnon. Helen McGehee's clarity and assertiveness molded her Electra, and Paul Taylor easily conveyed the louche sensuality of Aegisthus. For the first time, Graham acknowledged her own physical limitations by casting Ellen Siegel as the young Clytemnestra. Nine other dancers filled out the tapestry of events.

In preparing *Clytemnestra*, Graham passed on to her cast a list of reading material: *The King Must Die* by Mary Renault and some provocative nonfiction tomes: Joseph Campbell's *The Hero with a Thousand Faces*, Robert Graves's *The White Goddess*, C. W. Ceram's *Gods, Graves, and Scholars*, and two books by Jane Ellen Harrison: *Prolegomena to the Study of Greek Religion* and *Ancient Art and Ritual*. She may also have revisited the collection of red-figured and black-figured Greek vases in the Metropolitan Museum—drawing from them processional images flattened into two dimensions and endlessly circling.

In *Clytemnestra*, she undertook her most complex voyage to date into the realm of memory. Clytemnestra, following the Messenger of Death (David Wood) toward the Underworld, is compelled to recall her deeds and re-create her visions—just as in Aeschylus's tragedies, she reappears as a ghost among the living. In the work's four parts, Graham was almost never offstage; the actions swirled around her while she reposed on Noguchi's white throne or slept near Clytemnestra's lover Aegisthus on the low platforms that served as a bed, dreaming events into onstage life. Memories not only invaded her but goaded her into action.

One of the Prologue's set pieces consists of a tall, flat white structure with an irregular vertical crack dividing it in two. Entering the stage one by one, each of the protagonists pauses behind it, staring through that narrow fissure. Cassandra lunges out from behind one side of it, then from the other, staring forward—alone able to perceive the destiny it shields. Halim El-Dabh's score included chanted and spoken words by two singers who, from either side of the proscenium arch, identify the tragedy's characters when they appeared onstage.

Another of Noguchi's creations resembled a prison of slim ribbons at the center rear of the stage; descending from above, it could also be opened by members of the cast. The first time it rises again it reveals Clytemnestra, and as she advances, the down-thrusting of her hands on each chord of the music indicates her refusal to recall her past; it takes the commanding figure of Hades, holding up two branches, to force her to do so. She crawls, implores; he backs her away. Finally she sits on the throne and watches four women being grasped by four men. As if in a frieze, side by side, the pairs simultaneously perform different brief, cruel struggles, but all these duets end with the women on the floor. It's as if this condensation of the war between Trojans and Achaean Greeks leads Clytemnestra to dig deeper; when she staggers and falls, Hades straddles her, jumping over her as she rolls to evade him.

And now, as her memories intensify, she begins to understand— and envision—how her anger and grief began. A man enters bearing a huge white X of crossed spears and places it on the floor; two others drag in Iphigenia and lay her across it, tip it upright, and carry her away. Later, Clytemnestra will be forced to confront again the kidnapping and immolation of her daughter. Nor is it the last time that a man will rush away with a woman in his arms or on his shoulders.

The dancers are all costumed in one color scheme: black, or black and white, with, for the women, occasional patterned panels in antique shades created by dancer McGehee. Six furiously powerful women represent the Furies, sometime circling as if around a ritual fire (or a painted vase). Pairs of the dancers are escorted, one couple at a time, along opposite diagonals by two men carrying the crossed lances: Helen and Paris, Orestes and Electra, Cassandra and Iphigenia. Later there will be duets, also solos—frantic and pleading for Iphigenia, knowing and sorrowful for Cassandra.

A dance for the Watchman of the House of Atreus opens Act I, anchoring the plot in Mycenae. He laboriously pushes across the stage a large, flat, tear-shaped object that lies on the floor, seemingly impaled on the long stick that is its handle—a symbol perhaps of unavoidable disaster. One of this act's most potent scenes begins with Aegisthus caressing Clytemnestra, even as he keeps bending her over the seat of the throne and pressing the large knife that sits beside it into her hands. He finally induces her to seize it and, hypnotized by it, dance her way into revenge. Another memorable sequence is the entry of the victorious Agamemnon, borne in on two crossed spears and holding a lance erect. He is welcomed home by Clytemnestra, who's being adoringly feminine, while he is also eyeing Cassandra, who stands immobile. Agamemnon slings one cloak to his wife and another that wraps around his captive mistress's legs, thus introducing the two women and marking them both as his property.

In staging the slaying of Agamemnon and Cassandra, Graham brought into play her uncanny skill at stripping dramatic action to its essence. Two women enter, each bearing a long, curved stick; stretched between these these and spread on the floor is a purple and crimson length of fabric, along which Clytemnestra escorts Agamemnon to his bath. When he has mounted the small platform at the back of the stage, the women lift the curtain's arching rods and stand them together in front of him, touching at the top (it can't be accidental that, so placed, the cleft fabric resembles a giant vulva). Each time the women swing open its portal briefly, Clytemnestra makes a single stab at Agamemnon, and after Cassandra has run wildly in anticipation of her own destiny, she too becomes a victim in the murder scene that is finally revealed in full. Other cast members carry the scene of carnage away.

With similar brevity, Graham conveyed Aegisthus's flight and death, Orestes's matricide, and his appearance, in the Epilogue, to be judged by Athena and Apollo on their respective platforms. The Furies who've pursued him await the verdict. But Graham rarely lets the audience forget that all this is being relived in her heroine's memory as she prepares for her voyage to the Underworld. Before the final vision of her alone onstage, she participates in a small formal dance anchored to its center—a dance in which she, Orestes, Electra, and the ghost of Agamemnon (who walks stiffly, shod in the platformed *kothurnoi* of ancient Greece's tragic actors) meet and separate, circle, and briefly expostulate. This last gathering suggests that these four are enmeshed in their destiny and could repeat it over and over, like those figures depicted on ancient vases whose first experiences merge with their endings only to return to their beginnings.

On the third night of the company's season in New York's Adelphi Theatre, the company premiered a very different dance—this one for four denizens of the Garden of Eden—even though, at times, *Embattled Garden* suggests outtakes from *Clytemnestra*. This time the protagonists were identified in the program as Eve, Adam, Lilith, and the Stranger, played respectively by Yuriko, Ross, Turney, and Glen Tetley. A program note identifies the Stranger as "the biblical snake, the tempter" of the Book of Genesis. At times, he watches the action upside down, hanging from Noguchi's "tree," which resembles a gigantic long-handled comb set on end. He is allied with Lilith (Adam's first wife, according to the Talmud) from the moment the curtain rises to show her sitting beneath the tree, cooling herself with a small red fan. Many years later, Graham told a dancer that the four were like "neighbors who share a backyard fence and occasionally cocktails." You can imagine a bit of mate swapping as well.

Much of the dance takes place on two conjoined platforms, each of which has a large hole at its center. Painted in red, orange, dark green, and black geometrical shapes, they might well evoke a gaudy 1950s conversation pit, although the tall, slender rattan poles that pierce the platforms hint at the reeds that surround a pond and can be pushed aside when needed. The scorching score by the Spanish composer Carlos Surinach brings out the Latin heat in the work's shifting liaisons, and the women's gowns—one yellow, one red—have vertical ruffles at the back that allude obliquely to flamenco dancers' trains.

At times, Lilith and the Stranger seem to monitor the actions of Adam and Eve—watching, assisting, reassuring them. At one point Lilith bends Eve backward over the Stranger and ties her hair into a ponytail, as if girding her for battle (or independence). At another she carries Eve back to the platform from which she came. When the dance ends, Eve is again sitting at Adam's feet, and he is—strangely—stroking her long black hair upward along his body. The party's over.

In January 1959, Lincoln Kirstein jotted down the following words in his diary:

> With Martha Graham, discussing possibility of a collaborative work half by her, half by Balanchine, in which part of her company could dance in ours and vice versa. Spoke of key characters of feminine distinction so far unattempted, she having already drawn from ancient Greece, the Bible, Joan of Arc. I proposed Alice in Wonderland, which seems to me the essence of Martha's spirit; she thought I meant the Red Queen or Ugly Duchess. But she consented to consider Elizabeth or Mary, Queen of Scots.

Alice in Wonderland? One can only imagine Graham's response to that initial proposal. However, she not only considered the project; she chose Mary to impersonate and began to work on a possible structure.

Kirstein had been both fascinated and confused by Graham's early work during the days when Frances Hawkins managed both his Ballet Caravan and Graham's company. Writing about Graham back in 1937, he confessed that she had "repelled me so strongly that I was continually drawn back to see her almost to exorcise myself of curiosity, or to lay the ghost of all the irritating questions which raised themselves when I watched her."

He changed his mind a year later when he saw and lavishly praised her *American Document*, and it must be remembered that he had suggested that Hawkins, while a member of Ballet Caravan (and someone he had known from their Harvard days), take some classes at the Graham studio, inadvertently setting Martha's romance with Erick on its course.

The friendship between her and Kirstein was occasionally thorny, but he found her "personal intensity . . . exhilarating." Balanchine had met her and seen her dance (he found her not only intriguing but also appetizing) and was interested in collaborating with her. The music for the proposed two-part dance consisted of orchestral pieces by Anton Webern, who had died in 1945, having stepped outside his house in Allied-occupied Vienna before curfew in order to smoke a cigar without disturbing his sleeping grandchildren and been mistakenly shot by an American soldier. In the end, Balanchine chose four of his pieces, Graham two.

Graham selected Webern's first published composition—his 1908 *Passacaglia for Orchestra*, opus 1—and his 1909–10 *Six Pieces for Orchestra*, op. 6, which he revised in 1928. Balanchine said that this composer's orchestral music "fills the air like molecules; it is written for atmosphere. The first time I heard it, I knew it could be danced to."

Graham heard something more dramatic—the formality of the passacaglia structure, the stress and struggles of atonality. As might have been expected, she chose to relive the ill-fated drama of Mary as she mounted the scaffold to be beheaded by order of Elizabeth I, her rival for the throne of England. The casts that the two choreographers selected affirmed their intent to collaborate, even though they choreographed their sections of the ballet separately, and primarily for their own companies. Grahamite Paul Taylor felt as if dancers were being "traded around like hockey players." Chosen by Kirstein (who called him "Geek"), he was the only Graham dancer in *Episodes II*. He walked into the spotlit center of an empty stage and stayed there, goaded by Balanchine into what seemed to him at the time like arbitrary physical entanglements. He toiled endlessly to make them flow together. When he queried Balanchine about the solo's subject, the choreographer offered, "Is like fly in glass of milk, yes?" Grateful, Taylor took that image as a direction and convoluted extraordinarily with it.

The Balanchine dancers handed over to Graham were Sallie Wilson, who played Queen Elizabeth; corps members William Carter and Paul Nickel, who served as "heralds"; and Kenneth Peterson as Mary's executioner. Graham did her usual in-depth research, but didn't spend much time distinguishing among her own company dancers, who played Mary's second husband (Gene McDonald); Rizzio, her private secretary (Richard Kuch); and Chastelard, a poet attached to her court (Dan Wagoner)—all of whom had either been murdered or executed. Bertram Ross portrayed Mary Stuart's third husband, the conniving Bothwell, and Helen McGehee, Ethel Winter, Linda Hodes, and Akiko Kanda undertook the Scottish queen's ladies-in-waiting, all of whom were named Mary.

Balanchine's *Episodes II* was plotless and had no set, while Graham's *Episodes I* was memorable for its theatrical ingenuity. A high black platform with a box on it could be turned to show Elizabeth enthroned or become the scaffold on which Mary was beheaded. Graham as Mary is first seen in a stiff black gown. When she unfastens it and steps out of it as a young woman clad in white to meet Ross's Bothwell, it remains standing by itself, the discarded carapace of royalty. After her ladies-in-waiting have dressed her in a red gown, she and Sallie Wilson reconceive Mary's long pursuit to take the throne of England from Elizabeth. Standing on small mounds on opposite sides of the stage, they play a genteel game of tennis. The balls, attached by cords to the slender racquets, fly out but always return to the sender, never entering the opponent's terrain. In the end, as Graham kneels to meet Mary's death, the halberd becomes an axe, and a beam of red light pours like blood over her cast-off armorial gown.

John Martin of *The New York Times* felt that "Somehow ghosts of Miss Graham's inventions hover over [Balanchine's] episodes, and in his final section, to the Ricercata in six voices from Bach's 'Musical Offering,' he returns us with a lovely affirmation to a reconciliation with normality. And only then does the essential unity of the work as a whole dawn on us." Those who attended performances of the work may have sensed such a unity, but as Martin notes, Balanchine's plotless *Episodes II* had more in common with his *Agon* or *Ivesiana* than with the fierce drama of *Episodes I*.

Graham, possibly to counter the New York City Ballet's stressful but prestigious commission, had been thinking about a more lighthearted new dance that focused on her own creative process—not to exalt it but to reveal herself bedeviled by it. *Acrobats of God* premiered a year later. She took her title from the *Athletatae Dei* of early Christianity—men who, like Saint Augustine, labored against the "impure" urges that beset them—and affixed it to the dancers who struggled with their bodies in other ways. Noguchi bowed to her recent collaboration with the ballet barre and those who toiled at it daily, constructing a high, narrow, slightly curving version of that classroom staple perched on seven slender supporting legs. Performing atop it required unusual precision and steady nerves. The small orchestra was augmented by three mandolin players who sat onstage, grave and motionless, until called on to add some sweetness to Carlos Surinach's score.

In creating her onstage persona for the work, Graham satirized herself—or rather, an aspect of herself: the one who dithers over choices, postpones decisions, and encourages dancers. As in her 1939 *Every Soul Is a Circus*, her adversary and helper is a ringmaster with a long, flexible whip (a role created for David Wood). Consider him her alter ego (or a reincarnation of Louis Horst)—the one who admonishes her to get on with it and stop the nonsense.

In playing herself as choreographer at bay, Graham made subtle use of her dramatic skills and comedic timing. Her choreography for herself disguised her infirmities by making them part of her character. Since her arthritic toes barely bend now, she travels the stage in flurries of pattering little steps as she dithers over what to do next. Many times she bows to the man with the whip, and he to her—both bending from the hips with exaggerated deference and an extended "after you" hand. Often, however, she remains seated on a stool, her head—at first, and again near the end of the dance—behind an empty, suspended frame, while the celestial acrobats (five men and five women) attempt to bring life to what she is envisioning.

Occasionally the performers use Noguchi's set piece as a barre; so, briefly, does Graham. But far more imaginative and whimsical use is made of it. Four women, helped to stand atop it, do deep pliés, while the men imitate the move from below—first standing, then upside down, their feet mirroring those of the women. In a different sort of ingenious maneuver, four of the men link arms and, with three women seated on those links, cross the stage stepping sideways. As if that weren't tricky enough, the men kick high every other step, and when they're not kicking, the women are beating their own feet together. It's as if you're seeing an elaborate music box being wheeled across the stage.

A dancer, or several of them, will occasionally leap across the stage and be gone, while Graham watches them anxiously. One small joke for those familiar with her work: the man with the whip lashes it into a snaking path on the floor, and one of the women steps boldly along it for a few seconds, placing her foot on one or another side of its curlicues. Watching her, Graham makes strongly rejecting gestures (no, she will *not* copy something she'd dreamed up for *Errand into the Maze*).

The lifts she devised with the help of the dancers are both perverse and lovely: women—their backs draped over a male shoulder, their legs spread, or belly down with airplaning arms—are picked up and carried away. Once, one of them perches on her partner's slanted-forward spine, and he carefully, awkwardly walks along so as not to dislodge her. At another time a man leaves his partner in a headstand, flashing her legs around while he does a few exercises at the barre; then he returns to pick her up and tote her away. There are clever little contrasting duets. And Graham, playing her role, is hard on her minions: one of the men endures a brief spate of semi push-ups while she gestures him to keep going.

It's difficult to tell whether the choreography forced into being has gotten slightly out of control or has resolved itself into whatever she (Graham the character) hoped she had in mind.

Whatever the result, she and her whip-wielding partner are at peace, standing in front of the barre, when the characters finally reenter one by one to take their places facing their leaders upstage and, when all have arrived, to bow to their creators.

One might well believe Graham's mind to be working on the subject of rebirth in the late 1950s. In 1959, she turned sixty-five, when most U.S. citizens retire and begin to reap their Social Security benefits. She had a sizable company of lithe and powerful young men and women and did not need to perform in every dance she made. Too, in 1954, although she and Hawkins had divorced after a long separation, the loss of that relationship may have continued to affect her choices.

The role she chose for herself in a work that premiered along with *Acrobats of God* during the company's Broadway season was that of Alcestis, one of the most perplexing heroines of Greek drama and, saliently, one who was resuscitated from the world of the dead perhaps reinvigorated by her ordeal. Euripides depicted her as heroic in that she is willing to give her life for her husband, Admetus, who has been granted eternal life by Apollo, *if* he can find someone willing to expire in his stead. However, she is dead or on the brink of death or not yet fully returned to life for most of Euripides's play.

Graham pruned from it a number of the work's characters, choosing to depict only Alcestis, Admetus, Hercules, and Thanatos, the god of death, along with a chorus consisting of eight women in pink gowns and five athletic men. Noguchi provided her with two massive set pieces: an L and a wheel. These look as if they've been carved out of stone, but are easily tipped over by members of the cast and set into new positions as the dance progresses. A smaller slanted slab of wood serves as a ramp or an uncomfortable place to lounge.

Vivian Fine wrote her original score based on a scenario devised by Graham, later expanding it for full orchestra. People educated, as

Martha had been, during the late nineteenth century or the early twentieth knew their Greek myths, and these influenced her approach to *Alcestis*. In addition, she may have encountered reproductions of an 1869 painting by Frederic Lord Leighton, *Hercules Wrestling with Death for the Body of Alcestis*, in one corner of which a naked Hercules grapples with the black-draped and winged Thanatos, while Alcestis lies pale and dead nearby. Robert Browning's long 1871 poem "Balaustion's Adventure" offers vivid images of the duel as planned by Hercules to revive the heroine:

> I will go lie in wait for Death, black-stoled
> King of the corpses! I shall find him, sure,
> Drinking, beside the tomb, o' the sacrifice:
> And if I lie in ambuscade, and leap
> Out of my lair, and seize—encircle him
> Till one hand join the other round about—
> There lives not who shall pull him out from me
> Rib-mauled, before he let the woman go!

Graham knew Euripides's play well: Admetus plays gracious host to the unexpected Hercules, who is on his way to his eighth labor (getting rid of the four man-eating horses of Diomedes). Yes, there has been a death in the household, but Admetus indicates that the one being mourned is a lowly member of the household. Hercules is fairly drunk and full of food before he learns the truth and rouses himself to battle Thanatos and revive Alcestis.

According to Fine, Graham also drew ideas from Theodore Morrison's book-length poem *The Dream of Alcestis* (1950). His Alcestis, dying, dreams of treading in circles in a "stony valley, among sand and thorns." In the poem, Death appears as a masked, godlike figure, but Alcestis, emboldened by a vision of Persephone doomed to spend half of every year in the Underworld, is not passive, calling Death a "liar and ravisher." She is fighting with him when Hercules enters to save her. Death yields. Alcestis sees again the toiling, hooded figure she has recognized as her dying self, and as they merge, running and leaping, those watching over the queen at her bedside "looked at each other / And marveling said, 'Her brow is cool. She sleeps.'"

The poem's structure as a healing dream and its shape-shifting Alcestis surely stimulated Graham, as doubtless did the Admetus depicted by Morrison: one who refused to believe in the gods and their meddling in human affairs. The dance Graham envisioned also had to deal with some of the play's implications—such as Admetus's gradual transformation from being willing to let his wife die in his stead and his recognition that without her his life will be empty. And Alcestis herself, powerless though she was to influence events alone, would have to be prominent in the work—as if, even in her semicomatose state, she was present and aware.

Fine's music for *Alcestis* provides a key to the dance's structure. Its four parts are titled "Alcestis and Thanatos," "The Reveling Hercules," "Battle Between Hercules and Thanatos, Dance of Triumph," and "The Rescue of Alcestis." Graham didn't follow this plan to the letter. She wrote in her notebooks, "A 20th century treatment of Alcestis can logically present a group of 3 characters, a variation of the eternal triangle, here composed of husband, wife & rescuer, a 3-dimensional group as complicated in its combination of realism & lyricism as an Alexandrian marble, a Laocoön or a Niobe." And she envisioned her character not only in dialogue with Thanatos, but—as in Morrison's poem—present at the climactic struggle in which Hercules conquers the hungry god of death and brings Alcestis back to life: "Trio—fight between Herakles & Thanatos with the eloquent, almost inanimate, certainly passive—Alcestis." Bringing those three adjectives together would seem a task one might indeed label "herculean."

Graham cast the three characters wisely. Gene McDonald, pale, tall, slim, and long-legged, took on Admetus. Bertram Ross embodied the malicious Thanatos, and Paul Taylor's soft-edged muscularity suited him to the role of Hercules. Photographs taken of the first production reveal such penultimate moments as McDonald reaching graciously out to Graham, who is still covered in a translucent salmon-pink veil; men tilting the L-shaped set piece into a new position; Taylor leaping in the background, the wheel set on its rim and balanced there by some of the women. Another image shows what follows. The six women of the chorus stand at the back of the stage. Four men, wearing trunks with pink fabric tubing around them, dance vigorously around the disk, which is now lying flat. Thanatos raises high the black veil of death with which Alcestis had earlier lain down. One more man (David Wood) lies half under the wooden ramp, as if bracing it with his feet for those about to descend it. Atop Noguchi's L stand Admetus and Alcestis, touching hands delicately and formally, she looking forward from where she stands, holding up a small branch, serene—almost passive—and full of wonder. And ahead of them, vaulting off the end of the ramp and onto the stage floor, is Hercules, knees bent, body curling forward as he triumphantly flourishes the pink veil that had, seconds earlier, hidden Alcestis from her repentant husband.

If you consider, however warily, the relationship between Graham's own life and the roles she assumed onstage, you may see in *Alcestis* the larger story of a woman who is willing to sacrifice herself for her self-centered (but reformed) husband's sake and, in the end, empowered, is reborn into her marriage (if only onstage) but, more important, regains her life.

17

TO COMBAT THE ONSLAUGHT OF AGING

MARTHA GRAHAM was exceptionally photogenic, whether posing or being captured in motion by the high shutter speed of a camera held by Barbara Morgan (whom she continued to count among her friends). Studying images of her, you can imagine how she wished herself to be seen.

In 1948 Irving Penn took one of his famous black-and-white "corner portraits" of her when she was about fifty-four years old. She stands in the meeting place between two high white walls joined at an angle. Her long, dark, short-sleeved, off-the-shoulder satin gown is plain, except for what appear to be three big flowers of the same material lined up along its neckline. Her hands are behind her back, her elbows touching the walls. She rests her weight slightly on her right hip. Her eyes are half closed, but her gaze is steadily forward. She is not smiling. She looks completely contained and very enigmatic.

Twenty years later she posed for Jack Mitchell, seated on the terrace of her East Sixty-Third Street studio. She wears a blue-and-white checkered suit. Her hair is pulled up into a fashionable 1960s pompadour; her lips are enlarged in the style she admitted to having stolen from Joan Crawford. She is in her mid-seventies and looks both glamorous and careworn.

She is not alone, but artfully enshrined among the choreographers whose works, along with hers, are to be shown in a 1969 season at New York's Billy Rose Theatre. Framing her on assorted perches and looking relaxed sit her onetime husband and leading man, Erick Hawkins; two of her important former dancers, Merce Cunningham and Paul Taylor; and the younger choreographer Don Redlich. José Limón sits at her left and slightly lower than she is. But between Taylor and Redlich stands a very intense Yvonne Rainer, and at Graham's right, on a level with Limón and, like him, slightly in front of her, sits Twyla Tharp, her mouth momentarily downturned. These last two—the youngest in this multigenerational gathering—admired Graham, had studied with her however briefly, and had gone on to be as radical as she once had been.

The years spanned by these two images were ones in which Graham was redefining herself on the stage; there, as in the rehearsal studio, she took joy in feeling challenged. Readers may recall that decades earlier, her father the doctor had concluded that his eldest daughter was akin to a horse that ran "better on a muddy track." The doctor who first attended her in 1967 said, "With Martha, if there wasn't stress around the corner, she would go looking for it and create stress for herself. She functioned better that way." Although throughout her life she could be charming, brilliant, and stoic, yielding to fits of temper was a purgative for her; a dancer she'd fired in a rage should know better than to quit.

Not until *Alcestis* in 1960 did the dances in which she herself appeared reflect her need to come to terms with aging. That inescapable fact does not mean she expected less of herself. The company's 1961 season in New York consisted of eight dances, two of them premieres; she appeared in four: *Acrobats of God*, *Alcestis*, *Night Journey*, and the new *Visionary Recital*. Twenty-four additional dancers were listed in the program.

Graham billed *One More Gaudy Night*, a new work in which she did not appear, as a fantasy that "might be considered as a possible prologue to a tragedy." The play in question was Shakespeare's *Antony and Cleopatra*, its title drawn from the former's "Let's have one other gaudy night" (Act III, Scene XIII). The "sad captains" he summoned to drink with the pair were also onstage; "Gaudy" (played by Linda Hodes) became a character as well. Ethel Winter as Cleopatra and Paul Taylor as Antony feasted with six revelers, a musician, and the two captains. A god and a goddess showed up. According to John Martin, Halim El-Dabh's music with its "Eastern drums" at times contributed an Egyptian atmosphere more attuned to the State Fair Midway than to antiquity. Members of the cast positioned parts of Jean Rosenthal's set to suit. A comedy then. And not, apparently, a major Graham work.

Rebirth was a theme she was drawn to explore over and over, and the program note for *Alcestis* avoided alluding to Euripides's tragedy. Instead it announced that "the myth becomes a festival of the seasons— the death of Winter, the triumphant return of Spring." The note accompanying *Visionary Recital* was more opaque. It begins, "Along the corridors of memory walk images of love, hate, desire, despair, calculated cruelty and shame" and continues, "This is a visionary recital of 'events whose scene and action are set in the world of the Imaginable'— which is the heart of man." The moral is that a hero may be "blinded by his own strength and reborn through his vision." To music by Robert Starer, three aspects of Samson and three of Delilah meet and move together and apart. Graham portrayed the biblical heroine as the Awakener, Matt Turney played the Betrayer, and Akiko Kanda was the Seducer. Bertram Ross partnered Graham as the Dedicated (which indeed he was), while the labels for Paul Taylor and Dan Wagoner respectively were the Destroyer and the Tempter. Graham choreographed dances for the three heroes and duets with each heroine.

Rouben Ter-Arutunian's set, a forest of rope curtains shimmering in Rosenthal's lighting, created the "corridors of memory," where the Delilahs waited. Graham's persona controlled the other two aspects of herself and the partner whose strength she destroyed. Both music and set had been commissioned by "Mrs. Frances G. Wickes"—not only Graham's former Jungian psychologist but also a devoted friend who preserved every letter Martha had written to her.

When the piece was presented the following year, it had been retitled *Samson Agonistes*, and Graham no longer performed in it.

In the 1960s, her method of putting together a dance work did not involve demonstrating steps. You can read numerous accounts of rehearsals that boil down to this: Martha gathers her dancers, shows them pictures, recommends reading, and tells them stories—perhaps a partial scenario. She may then send various individuals or duos away to work by themselves on a particular passage; when she sees the result, she becomes the master editor—deleting this, repeating that, suggesting an alternative, or coming up with a wholly new idea. Or she may set a studio full of dancers to work on images from information she has proffered. One result of this is that the dancers look at home in the movement—like themselves, or rather like the selves she wishes them to be at the moment.

They drew, of course, on her movement vocabulary, which had become less uncompromisingly fierce than it was during the 1930s and 1940s. At some point she began to call her dances "ballets." Ballet's sleekness—its pointed feet and turned-out legs—was borrowed and adapted. Members of the company during those years have also said that what she'd seen and felt during the tour of Asia fed into her classroom technique and influenced her style. Nonetheless, in classes and performances, dancers perfected her lexicon of movements, ones that reveal stress and emotions three-dimensionally—one part of the body pulling and twisting against another, the spine caving in and the dancer then recovering to press forward. Direct attack had evolved into indirect complexity.

In her handwritten notes, whether planning or recollecting, she gave names to steps she often used. Some of the terms dated back to her days as a Denishawn dancer: "Bali position," "Bali attitude," "Bali turn," "Javanese foot movement." These aren't authentic, of course; they're been altered to fit her needs. A "Javanese step" involved walking forward while thrusting one arm, then the other, strongly out to one side or the other, the fingers curled, the arms so straight they almost bent the other way. She borrowed from herself too: a "Cave turn" (revolving in a tipped-over arabesque) was invented for *Cave of the Heart*.

Her teaching was often physical. Bertram Ross hadn't been long out of the army when he took his second class at the Graham studio. As he recalled, this was a day in 1947 on which she had decided to weed out those she felt were insufficiently talented or dedicated. During this fraught procedure she looked at Ross and said, "Not you, darling, you just got here." As Ross remembered it,

> Moments later, when I was sitting in second, my back round, she placed her hands under my armpits and put her legs against my back and picked me up.
>
> "I can't breathe," I said.
>
> "You will, darling."
>
> She took me in front of the mirror, pulled my hair, and aligned me. I did not believe I had an attractive body, but she said, "There, that's how you should be and that's the way you will be. See how beautiful it is?"

It's no surprise that in 1962 the Graham school had to fight a suit brought by a former student who claimed that a too-vigorous physical correction had seriously damaged her back. With support from the Batsheva de Rothschild Foundation for Arts and Sciences, the injured student was paid a $28,000 settlement, and teachers at the Martha Graham studios were warned to refrain from pushing and pulling students into the desired positions. As a result, a teacher might stand behind a malfunctioning student, laboring to put a correction into words and fairly itching to lay hands on him or her.

Graham often refused to be designated in print as a "choreographer." Perhaps this avoidance had a generous component, hinting as it did at the dancers' creative involvement, but it also identified her primarily as a dancer, which is how she thought of herself. In an interview published in *The Washington Post* in May 1984, she made a revealing statement about her dread of misusing the body: "As a dancer, you take that body and you train it, almost like a little animal—you discipline it, care for it, feed it, and you adore it. It's a symbol of your life—it is your life."

Before she reluctantly retired as a performer in 1970, that animal, despite the care it received, was resisting discipline. It was not only her toe joints that had stiffened; her hands were bent at the knuckles into claws—almost a travesty of the gesture she expected all her students to assume in class whenever they contracted their bodies in a cosmic gasp. None of these infirmities, however, had prevented her from being mesmerizing onstage.

If her 1962 *Phaedra* was more noteworthy than the previous year's *One More Gaudy Night* and *Visionary Recital*, that could have been because she played the title role, and the entire plot was seen through the eyes and memory of this Cretan princess. Akin to her *Night Journey*, in which Jocasta mates with Oedipus without realizing that he is her son, the myth of Phaedra tells of a woman who, egged on by the goddess Aphrodite, lusts after her stepson, Hippolytus. Having made a vow of chastity to the goddess Artemis, he spurns Phaedra's advances; she, humiliated and enraged, tells her husband, Theseus, that the young hero raped her. The story, which does not end well, has been retold in countless plays. Graham drew what she needed from them and also probably from Mary Renault's historical novel *The King Must Die* (1958).

In his memoir, *Private Domain*, Paul Taylor, who played Theseus, paints a devastatingly witty if affectionate picture of initial rehearsals for *Phaedra*: long, late nights during which the dancers sit on the studio floor while Graham, who has clearly had a few drinks, tells them several times the backstory of how Pasiphaë, the mother of Phaedra, became the half sister of the Minotaur; and shows them pictures of Cretan bull leapers. Martha occasionally staggers (his word) to the studio's small kitchen, where a refrigerator door slams, a glass falls to the floor and shatters, and a dog named Roderick yelps.

Yet as a powerful artist, she seemed unstoppable. Noguchi designed a set that both reflected and influenced Phaedra's view of the conflict. Artemis (Helen McGehee) can retreat to a tower downstage right, while on the opposite side of the space stands the "home," where Aphrodite (Ethel Winter) hangs from, or stands on, pegs inserted into a large structure that resembles paired shells (or ears, or a highly stylized vagina). She is given to spreading her legs wide apart. The besotted Phaedra first glimpses Hippolytus in partial views. He (Ross) stands behind a three-story structure of small doors. Each door that she opens reveals a different portion of his anatomy. The moral derived from the tale seems to be that our transgressions are not our fault; the quarreling gods who wish to control us are leading us astray. Did Aphrodite introduce Hippolytus to Phaedra as "your new stepson"? No, she revealed him as the anonymous and faceless possessor of strong muscles and a bulging crotch.

It may have been in part the sight of those tightly fitted trunks that appalled two members of the United States House of Representatives who had attended a performance in Cologne during the Martha Graham Dance Company's 1962 State Department–sponsored tour of Europe and the Near East. To the surprise of the art world, Graham and her supporters had to deal with the charge of obscenity that Representatives Peter Frelinghuysen of New Jersey and Edna Kelley of New York introduced in Congress. Why, these two wanted to know, should a work such as *Phaedra* be given government support?

They could also object to the sex-instigating Aphrodite, or the lascivious flashback of a duet in which Graham and Ross enacted the tale of rape that Phaedra was "describing" to her husband. Another twist in time: the seductive Pasiphaë (Linda Hodes), holding a horn in each hand, was carried in by four male dancers, half hidden by the yards of translucent black fabric that, as the men manipulated it, swirled around her like the unreliable dream of a rutting bull.

Graham and her dancers were performing in London when the two congresspeople testified before a House Subcommittee on Foreign Affairs. Their attempt to have the dance censored failed, and the publicity it stirred up added a bit of zest during the company's London performances and helped earn the company a warm welcome when it returned to New York.

Graham's mother had died in April 1958, and Martha no longer took the train west. No longer would she spend time at El Mirasol to recuperate from her busy New York schedule. Not one to brood over the past, she asked to be sent the letters she had written to her mother over the years. She then destroyed them. Her influence was expanding; she had become a world traveler, and for the first time, her technique had begun to be taught abroad and her works performed by other companies.

Baroness Bethsabée de Rothschild had decided to form a dance company in Israel and in 1964 named Graham its artistic adviser. Martha, who felt greatly indebted to Bethsabée, was present at auditions for the Batsheva Dance Company and returned to Israel several times in the succeeding two years to supervise rehearsals of her *Cave of the Heart, Diversion of Angels, Errand into the Maze, Dark Meadow, Embattled Garden, The Learning Process* (which featured excerpts from *Clytemnestra*), and later *Hérodiade*. Graham often fitted costumes on the dancers herself and stayed in an apartment that de Rothschild created for her within her own home.

The relationship began to disintegrate in 1967, when de Rothschild founded the Bat-Dor Dance Company, to be headed by Jeannette Ordman, a ballet dancer from South Africa who was a gifted teacher and had, it is said, "captured the heart of the Baroness." De Rothschild had thought to combine the two companies, but that didn't happen, and in a few years, amid a tangle of plans and responsibilities plus a redefining of artistic directions, she withdrew her support of Batsheva, and Graham rescinded Batsheva's rights to perform her works.

Graham also became artistic adviser for the school that Robin Howard, intoxicated by Martha's work, founded in London in 1966, which three years later became the Place, housing the London Contemporary Dance School and the London Contemporary Dance Theatre. Howard, also for a time the executive director of the Graham

Foundation, sent staff members of his school to New York to learn how Graham's school operated. Robert Cohan moved to London to head the new school and was eventually joined by two former Graham dancers, Jane Dudley and Nina Fonaroff—the first as director of Graham studies, the second as head of choreography.

That Graham managed all this, as well as choreographing a dozen more dances for her own company between 1962 and 1968 and appearing in five of them, attests to her endurance. It was the impression of one of the doctors she consulted in the 1960s that she had never been to a doctor for ailments, with the exception of a visit in the early 1930s when she had a cyst removed. She still, however, resorted to vitamin B shots when performances loomed. She outlived her Denishawn rival, Doris Humphrey, who passed away late in 1958 and was memorialized in the summer of 1969 at Connecticut College during the American Dance Festival. She coped with the loss of Louis Horst in January 1964, but she had no hand in the initial stages of reconstructing *Primitive Mysteries* as a tribute to him in the summer of that year, since she had been in Israel. She arrived home, raging, to make last-minute adjustments. It was said that during the performance, she was not among the audience, but sat in a backstage dressing room with her memories, clutching Robin Howard's hand.

She must have done considerable thinking about what she could do—should do—onstage. In some of the dances she made during the 1960s she resorted to the structure that had served her well before: casting herself as a heroine remembering her past. As in *Clytemnestra*, she made use of surrogates. In 1962, when she expanded her solo *Judith* into *Legend of Judith*, a work for nine dancers, Linda Hodes played the Young Judith. The 1968 *A Time of Snow* opened with a young girl laying flowers on the tombs of the medieval lovers Heloise and Abelard, and Noemi Lapzeson was cast as the Young Heloise, the intellectually gifted niece of Canon Fulbert who had been tutored, beloved, and impregnated by the scholar-theologian-composer Peter Abelard. Graham wore a wimple to play Heloise as the abbess she eventually became, and she brought her earlier self to life when she, now remote from desires of the flesh, recalled her affair with Abelard (Bertram

Ross). In this unhappy history of twelfth-century Paris, four men (called "scholars" in the program), sent by Fulbert (Robert Cohan)—in Graham's plan not only furious, but somewhat attracted to his niece himself—castrated Abelard, who retired to a monastery. He and Heloise wrote letters to each other for the rest of their lives. Graham's preliminary notes for the work involve dividing the stage between the two of them.

However, in an earlier, more complex venture into Christian territory, *The Witch of Endor* (1965), Graham dispensed with surrogates entirely. The role she gave herself doesn't even have a name in her principal source: 1 Samuel 28:7. In this most complex and contradictory book of the Bible, King Saul, in disguise, seeks the advice of "a woman that hath a familiar spirit," even though he has banished sorcerers and necromancers from the kingdom of Israel. Whether by the witch's powers or by fakery, the "familiar spirit" that Saul hopes will help him as hordes of Philistines mass against the Israelites appears as the ghost of Samuel, and his news isn't good: Saul and three of his sons will perish in the coming battle.

Ming Cho Lee provided Graham with thrones—one for Saul (Ross) and one for the David who slew Goliath (Cohan). There was also a structure from which a ramp could descend, as well as a wall that could rise or descend. "Spikes" protruded from the wings as part of the scenery. Graham's notes give a hint to the complexity of the scenario she developed, focusing on the relationship between Saul and David (David kept changing sides, all the while protecting Saul from those who would kill him). Her cast included two women attendants, three guards for each of the battling heroes, and David Wood as "the voice of evil in Saul." There were solos, conflicts.

With the help of her colleagues Graham came up with some startling dramatic devices, one of them for tall Gus Solomons, Jr., who played the ghost of Samuel. In wishing to provide the "enormous gesture" she required, he recalled "wearing heavy boots, which were bolted to a stool, which was bolted to the stage floor. So, I was a figure over 10 feet tall, and I could lean precipitously out into space, like a skier on a downhill run. I waited behind a pierced 'drawbridge' upstage left for my cue, and when the panel descended, I was revealed for my solo."

The Witch of Endor has been portrayed in slew of paintings; sometimes she's a hag, sometimes a madwoman, sometimes a Pre-Raphaelite beauty. This gave Graham considerable leeway. Her "prophecy" must have come—in part at least—as a reenactment. Jottings in her Notebooks refer to a "red leg" that she reveals at times, as well as preliminary ideas, many of which involve fabric (the spacing is hers):

> Cover Saul with veil
> (sits on edge of throne)
> on low tone
> goes around throne wrapping
> Saul in veil   silence
> high kick? 3 high kicks (low tone) st. L.
> 2 X twitches to St.L. (foot out & in) Torn between?
> (Saul following wrapped in veil—crawling)
> 2 X twitches to center
> Witch moves St. L.
>
> Saul rolls to throne with veil—rises on it . . .

Some of her images are more violent:

> "The Evil spirit was upon him"
> pushes Saul
> rides Saul
> stands on Saul.

Unlike the woman in the Bible, Graham's witch was not a gentle soul who restores Saul's strength after their session by cooking a fatted calf and other treats for him. When Ross as Saul falls on his knees before her, she "throws him away & he spins." This witch, say her notes, "beats Saul with her Cape" and "thrusts him away."

Why did she choose such a character for herself? The Witch of Endor can't control fate; she can only reveal what it has in store. Yet, as choreographer and the work's leading lady, she can bring to life the predicted events and the surrounding scenario by entering them, remembering them, perhaps trying to influence them. Ironically, in performing the finished piece, Martha, now seventy-one and having vision problems, had to rely on one or another member of the cast to guide her to the spot onstage where she needed to be.

Clive Barnes, now the *New York Times* dance critic, called *The Witch of Endor* "a dance of great psychological complexity, whose strands are not always as neatly, or more important, as clearly placed as they might have been."

Between *The Witch of Endor* and *A Time of Snow*, Graham launched a larger-scale piece and returned to ancient Greece, compressing the events of the Trojan War into *Cortege of Eagles* (1967). In *Clytemnestra*, she had already told some of the story through the lens of the title character; now she cast herself as Hecuba, wife to Priam, King of Troy, and the mother of Hector, adding three more ill-fated offspring and a grandson. For inspiration, she delved into Homer's *Iliad* and several of Euripides's plays: *Hecuba*, *The Trojan Women*, and *Andromache*. Writing of the work's revival in 1985, Anna Kisselgoff of *The New York Times* aptly called it "a movie of the mind. Its filmlike texture is a function of Miss Graham's astute playing with theatrical time structures. Even if you do not know the names of the Greek and Trojan figures (they are listed in the program), the emotions and acts they depict are always identifiable." In fact, the piece had already been reenvisioned for television as part of *Three by Martha Graham* (1969).

Watching *Cortege of Eagles* in this televised version (directed by John Houseman and introduced by him in a voice-over), you notice Graham's reliance on stillness. Throughout the piece, twos or threes of the characters freeze into tableaux while others of them fight or mate. Occasionally three men leap across the stage as if bound for the battlefield; occasionally five dancers billed as Captive Women of Troy appear in various identical outfits. Every character is a Trojan, with the exception of the kidnapped Helen (Matt Turney), Achilles (Bertram Ross), and the Thracian king Polymnestor (also Ross). Charon (William Louther in the film) takes no sides. In charge of ferrying souls to Hades, he is a busy creature, masked and slithering around seductively and jutting out his hips as if his job turns him on, or as if he's a carnivorous animal preparing to pounce.

Graham's choosing to play Hecuba meant that almost throughout *Cortege of Eagles* she is helpless, a mother unable to save her children, even when one of them reaches out to her or kneels at her feet and clings to her. Only when it's too late for Hecuba to rescue anyone does she turn into an aggressor. Polymnestor, the enemy who killed her son Polydorus, arrives and bows elaborately to her, mocking respect. She gives him the gold bracelets that her now dead husband Priam had put on her wrists, and she takes the small dagger that he offers her. If Polymnestor had turned his back, assuming that Hecuba would commit suicide, he was wrong; she pulls his head back and blinds him with the weapon. Then she leads him by the hand to feel the face of the dead Polydorus (Robert Powell). Finally, she sits cradling the dagger as if it were a cherished baby. The dead arise to parade past her, leaving her as she began: alone.

Here is one among the many striking images that Graham, a wizard with fabric, devised. At one point, the captured women arrive, hooded in black and staying close together as they walk. You only realize after a while that these veils are not individual, but part of a single long piece of black material that they lift off themselves to lay over the fallen Astyanax (Lar Roberson).

Cortege of Eagles was set to music by Eugene Lester, with lighting by Jean Rosenthal. Graham, however, didn't use Isamu Noguchi's scenery and props exactly as he had intended. He had made huge shields, but Martha "converted them to towers, to parts of the palace . . . [and] pushed them together at one point so they'd look like the gates of Troy. Isamu kept saying, 'What happened to my shields? My shields!' And Martha said, 'Isamu, get off my stage. They're not shields, they're part of the palace.'" Concealed behind these movable structures, corpses could be pushed offstage. It is with Noguchi's large, highly stylized, two-dimensional weapons that Achilles and Hector (Robert Cohan) battle with vicious formality before the winner, Achilles, drags his enemy's body away.

The audience sees only glimpses of the love between Hector and his wife, Andromache (Mary Hinkson); she pushes his corpse awkwardly along the floor, their limbs tangling as she rolls with him. Polyxena (Helen McGehee) works her way into the foreground—quick-footed, repeatedly jumping, and trying to avoid her destiny: Achilles grabs her to be sacrificed to the gods in order to secure calm weather for the victorious Greeks' voyage.

In her 1991 book *Blood Memory*, Graham wrote, "The last time I danced was in *Cortege of Eagles*. I was seventy-six years old . . . I did not plan to stop dancing that night. It was a painful decision I knew I had to make." Interestingly, the last role that she created for herself was, like her character in *The Witch of Endor*, nameless, known only by the mythic soubriquet that gave the work its title: *The Lady of the House of Sleep*. However prominent Graham was in this 1968 work and however central her character, her physical strength was not what it had been.

The title had come from Joseph Campbell's *The Hero with a Thousand Faces*. He mentions the Lady of the House of Sleep as a character who appears in fairy tales and myths:

> She is the paragon of all paragons of beauty, the reply to all desire, the bliss-bestowing goal of every hero's earthly and unearthly quest. She is mother, sister, mistress, bride. Whatever in the world has lured, whatever has seemed to promise joy, has been premonitory of her existence—in the deep of sleep, if not in the cities and forests of the world.

For much of the action, Graham wore an immense gown that, if she so wished, could easily have concealed two additional dancers on their knees. Parts of it could be manipulated by her attendant (Dudley Williams), who at one point swings the cloak around and above her, making her appear momentarily winged. The hero who seeks her (Ross) arrived with a more sinuous—hence equivocal—alter ego (Cohan), whom he must combat. But he must also struggle against the coils of plastic rope in which the Lady, with the help of four henchmen, seeks to entangle him (four women are also part of the cast).

Robert Starer's score (his fourth for Graham) created a brooding atmosphere, as did Jean Rosenthal's lighting and Ming Cho Lee's set: a cluster of silvery "trees" and three increasingly small rectangular metal platforms layered atop one another to form a pyramid. One photo shows Ross, wrapped in a great length of fabric, poised atop this structure behind Graham, who stands below him grasping the supine Cohan's upraised feet; together the three create a human version of Lee's pyramid. In reviewing the piece, Marcia B. Siegel remarked that the stage was so full of scenery that the dancers' paths were inevitably short, and diagonal passages impossible.

The original program note alluded to Campbell's works and identified Ross as the hero. When Graham reworked *The Lady of the House of Sleep* the following year, he became "a man, perhaps a hero," and what he attained, thought Anna Kisselgoff, had become not self-realization, but possibly death as represented by Graham.

However one interpreted the work, what Graham had intended was murky. And Barnes, although praising the work's theatrical images in his May 1968 review, felt that "Miss Graham restricts herself to little more than a demonstration of her presence."

Her onstage presence was to become even less evident. She created two fine lyrical works for her company to accompany the dramas: *Dancing Ground* in 1967, paired with *Cortege of Eagles*, and *Plain of Prayer*, which premiered in May 1968 along with *A Time of Snow* and *The Lady of the House of Sleep*. She made only one new piece in 1969: *The Archaic Hours* for eighteen dancers. Not until 1973 did she choreograph again or undertake new roles. The journey on which she embarked at the age of seventy-nine was not a fictionalized one, but a gradual—and painful—reconstruction of herself.

18

CHOREOGRAPHY AS MEAT AND DRINK

IN A TWO-PAGE SPREAD in *Vogue* advertising Blackglama furs, with the firm's usual inspired heading, "What Becomes a Legend Most?," Martha Graham, Rudolf Nureyev, and Margot Fonteyn are depicted swathed in sable. Nureyev wears a fur turban that has a tail. Fonteyn's coat has been pulled back to bare her shoulders. Graham is garbed in a garment with wide metallic bands at the neck and around the cuffs of its capacious sleeves. Nureyev, the apex of this glamorous triangle, clasps a hand of both women in one of his. Martha is now eighty-two, but her face and neck no longer reveal a single wrinkle. She gazes slightly upward, and you can imagine her delivering a blessing on the other two as well as affirming a momentous pact. These two ballet stars appeared in her company's 1975 season. The trio got to keep the coats, valued, it is said, at about $6,000 each.

At a fundraising gala the previous year, Graham had presented the two dancers in *Lucifer*, a piece in which Nureyev played the deeply conflicted fallen angel of the Bible and Fonteyn performed the angelic role that Graham had designed for the company member Janet Eilber. *Lucifer* became part of the Martha Graham Dance Company's unusually long season: thirty-two performances at Broadway's Mark Hellinger Theatre. It announced a period that would stretch over almost two decades—years during which famous dancers, stage and film actors, visual artists, and fashion designers materialized to support Martha and (some of them) to make guest appearances in her works.

Because she felt more alive when performing—or preparing to do so—than at almost any other time, her artistic transition was a difficult one. She was, wrote Joan Acocella in *The New Yorker* years later, "a complete stage animal." When her dancers were performing, she sat in the theater's downstage-right wing watching them. Jim McWilliams, the Graham company's stage manager between 1985 and 1995, told an interviewer that the stagehands at New York's City Center called her "The Babe." She wouldn't leave the building until they had struck the show, and, remorseful that they couldn't always get out to eat prior to showtime, she paid for a kitchen in the scene dock.

More than once, her friends Ben Garber and William Kennedy took her on vacation with them to St. Martin. Was she grateful to these two—partners in life and in Kennedy's design firm? Yes, but she missed the city's action, even though, when her long-ago dancer Bonnie Bird visited her at Garber and Kennedy's four-thousand-square-foot house in the Westchester enclave of Cross River, she seemed in no hurry to get back to choreography. It may have been that Graham— a great actress in life as in work—intended to give that impression. Agnes de Mille may have been right when she described her old friend in those years as looking like "a little Oriental deity, a little goddess, an empress, like a miniature Japanese doll. She was tiny and costly, rare and superb. And very remote. How unlike the plain girl we used to know, with the thunder in her head!"

That thunder, however, stilled temporarily between April 1969 and May 1973. During those years, Graham choreographed no new dances. Instead, she redesigned herself with the help of friends, some of whom were doctors. The plan hinged in part on getting her to stop drinking. The lighting designer Jean Rosenthal, who had worked closely with her, told Garber that she thought Graham's alcohol addiction "began as a whip. Martha got a sense of power and could physically do things when she'd had just a few drinks. It started that way. Her physical feats were going, and so the drink helped her, and then more drinks. And then it became quite a problem."

The dancer Armgard von Bardeleben, a six-foot-two Graham student who became a company member in 1973, visited Graham and her sister Georgia while they were vacationing on Fire Island. Martha, she was told, needed company. The experience was enlightening:

> Geordie met me at the ferry, and at their house we had drinks right away. By the time I'd finished my glass, their bottles were drained. Each of them had a bottle. Martha wanted to nap, so we helped her into bed. This was at about noon. I went for a swim. When I returned, Martha was on the deck and she scolded me for swimming. No lifeguards were on the beach and she was afraid there might be sharks. I was amazed that she was completely sober and together again after two hours.
>
> Fortunately, the bottles contained white wine rather than hard liquor.

Ben Garber, who had studied dance at the Graham studio before turning to design, had been monitoring Martha's need for alcohol. As a houseguest in his and Kennedy's mansion, she foraged for the small bottles of wine she had managed to procure and hide in the cachepots the two men collected. They understood her strategy. The wine was part of their determination to wean her off harder stuff. In the end, the attempt was unsuccessful. When the two men moved to Huntington Palisades in Southern California, they continued to look out for her. In the 1970s, when she was possibly feeling suicidal, she had a bad fall in the shower of her New York apartment. It was perhaps that event that galvanized her into taking Garber up on his offer to finance her plastic surgery by an expert in Los Angeles.

The doctor who gave her a physical examination prior to the operation was amazed that a woman of her age, bruised on her face and all the way down her spine, had not only avoided serious fractures but had managed the flight from the East Coast. The facelift, paid for by Garber, was eventually followed by two more in New York. In 1982 Graham's physician talked her out of a fourth procedure, telling her, "If you get another, your face is going to look like a Viking ship."

She also startled the New York doctor, who'd provided her facial cosmetic surgeries gratis. She didn't want a general anesthetic; possibly, given only a local one, she, in his words, "just put[s] herself out of it." He had never, he said, had a patient like that. When convalescing from the procedure in California, she had refused to stay in the hospital for the recommended time. "Get me the hell out of here!" she told her saviors. She was obeyed.

She recovered from the alcoholism, relapsed, was hospitalized, and recovered again. But only temporarily.

On returning from her company's national tour in the 1960s, she drank herself into a stupor on the afternoon before its final date in Brooklyn. Garber knew her well. Discovering her asleep, balled up in blankets, he awakened her, noted that she had lost control of her bladder, stripped off her clothing, got her into the shower and held her there, made coffee and saw that she drank it, got her dressed, and delivered her to the theater. Reader, she danced *Legend of Judith* that night. It has also been recorded that for at least one performance that season, a bucket was placed in each of the stage's four wings, into which she could exit in case she needed to throw up. Nearsighted, she had also, while exiting during a performance of *The Witch of Endor*, banged into the striking array of fake spears, their blades sticking from the wings partly onto the stage.

If she became fretful during her recovery, no one recorded that. Dr. Allen Mead, her physician between 1967 and her death, in 1991, said that when he visited her, there was no subject on which she couldn't talk. She had a mind, he said, "like a snapping turtle." Not only intellectually accomplished, she seems also to have retained the charm that her turn-of-the-twentieth-century upbringing had instilled in her. With Mead—by his own account a "sports nut"—she conversed knowledgeably about golf and asked to be updated on pros like Sam Snead (in turn, she recommended books on Greek art and mythology to him). They had, recalled Mead, "a lot of fun together."

Between 1973 and her last unfinished work in 1991, in addition to weathering performances in New York and on tours, Graham choreographed or revised twenty-seven dances. For most of this time she was revered, guided, protected, and dominated by a man who may have come into her life as early as 1967. According to Garber, Ron Protas was a young fellow with a camera who showed up backstage at one of the Graham company performances, wanting to take photographs. Or: "He would call our house in Cross River and say, 'Oh, I'm in Katonah. Can I come by?' And before I could even say 'It wouldn't be convenient at this moment,' he would be there."

Understanding that Graham was more fulfilled by her creative process than by anything else in her life, Protas encouraged her to keep making works. He was also, however, instrumental in separating her from people who had been of immense importance to her choreography and her dancers. In July 1972, according to Agnes de Mille, Martha accused LeRoy Leatherman, who'd managed her company for fifteen years, of mishandling funds. He departed. Harold Taylor, a member of her board of directors, quit the board in 1973, accusing her of wishing only sycophants to advise her. Later that year, her longtime manager Gertrude Macy was confronted for supposed mishandling of money, and the accompanist Ralph Gilbert was reprimanded for trying to control the way the classes were being taught. Both quit.

These were not the only departures. Trying to keep her image vital to company members and students at the school while she was recovering, Bertram Ross and Mary Hinkson put together studio showings in which Graham's choreography was danced to taped music, minus costumes, with tables and chairs standing in for scenery. One program in May 1972, for instance, consisted of the sarabande from *Dark Meadow*, a chorus section from *Clytemnestra*, *Errand into the Maze* (performed by Diane Gray and Lar Roberson), *Embattled Garden* (performed by Gray, Judith Hogan, Jeff Phillips, and Peter Sparling), and Stuart Hodes's *Hieros*, a weaving together of Graham's classroom technique accompanied by a recording of Sandy Bull playing his guitar.

In 1973, although Graham had featured Ross in two new works and Hinkson appeared in another, she accused the two of attempting to "steal" her company. Deeply disturbed, Ross—who had not only inherited Erick Hawkins's roles but had played Graham's heroes and/ or lovers in many more recent works—quit. Hinkson held on until attacked by both Protas and Graham over contract negotiations. Bethsabée de Rothschild had a more distanced view of their departures: "I think she needed to break with Bertram Ross and Mary Hinkson, not because Ron Protas prejudiced her against them but because she needed to break with her past. Change was vital to her renewal."

One must also wonder what role paranoia may have played in Graham's slicing away of her past. When Ethel Winter, not only a one-time leading dancer in her company but a favorite of hers, was asked whether she thought that the amount of alcohol Martha had consumed affected her relationships, she unhesitatingly replied yes.

When Graham began to create again, the two pieces that premiered at the Alvin Theatre in May 1973 featured male protagonists, as if—retired as a performer and with a number of gifted and highly individual men on hand—she wanted to test her ability to build works around someone unlike herself. Although in both pieces a woman guides the hero's steps, she offers him no clear fulfillment. Still, the title and some of the text for her *Mendicants of Evening*—drawn from Robert Fitzgerald's translation of Saint-John Perse's poem "Chronique" and recited onstage by the actress Marian Seldes—might well have expressed how Martha wished to think of herself:

> Great age, you lied: a road of glowing ember, not of ash . . . With face alight and spirit high, to what extreme are we still running? Time

measured by the year is no measure of our days. We hold no traffic
with the least nor with the worst. Divine turbulence be ours to its last
eddy . . .

Seldes, wearing a long, floating dress, was billed as the Witness.
Ross played the Poet, and Matt Turney appeared as the Guide. Those
billed as the Mendicants of Evening (a term within Perse's poem) performed duets. One could imagine the joyful, fiercely physical encounters between Phyllis Gutelius and Tim Wengerd, Yuriko Kimura and
Lar Roberson, Diane Gray and Ross Parkes, Takako Asakawa and
David Hatch Walker as representing Graham's gradual and nostalgic
leave-taking of youth.

The atmosphere was that of dusk, with a distant chiming in David G. Walker's electronic score. Hanging panels by Wojciech Fangor,
both monolithic and insubstantial, created hidden doorways. The
costumes contributed to the "divine turbulence": Turney and Ross
wore immense cloaks that trailed behind them or swirled into the air,
and Ross, buffeted by imagined winds, fought his entanglements in
different fabrics and the limbs of others. Three additional women (Janet
Eilber, Peggy Lyman, and Traci Musgrove) swelled the cast. The
younger dancers occasionally leaned against these taller, more experienced ones or were briefly held by them. In the end, one of the
cloaks was bequeathed to a member of that next generation, and Ross,
stripped of his draperies, advanced toward what could be imagined as
a creative rebirth into a world not created by Martha Graham.

A year later, the dance was renamed *Chronique*, and Graham embarked on the inevitable part of her process. As usual, after a work of
hers had premiered, she could see its faults more clearly and get to
work fixing the problem. Sympathetic reviewers often remarked that a
newly premiered Graham dance needed a few tweaks from her to become more itself.

She was in familiar Grecian territory with *Myth of a Voyage*, which
premiered in 1973, the day after *Mendicants of Evening* made its initial
appearance at the Alvin. The title of Alan Hovhaness's accompanying
music, *Dream of a Myth* (his third score for Graham), acknowledged

the piece's retrospective slant. The dreamed-of voyage in question was the homecoming of Odysseus (played by Ross Parkes) as the dreamer. Ming Cho Lee's maze of hanging ropes became the ship's rigging, Penelope's loom, and an entangling web. The hero relived being enchanted in turn by Circe (Yuriko Kimura), Calypso (Phyllis Gutelius), and Nausicca (Mary Hinkson), as well as encountering his favorite, the Goddess of Change (Takako Asåkawa). Guided by the Gray-Eyed One (Matt Turney), he wended his way homeward through those who played sailors, sirens, suitors, and their girlfriends. Colorless papier-mâché animals' heads were used as hand puppets.

The hero relived . . . In the medieval Japanese Noh plays that had begun to interest Graham early in her career, the protagonist looks into the past in order to reawaken and examine his or her feelings and decisions. The device produces a narrative form far more contemporary than a simple procedure of recounting events from beginning to end. Its flexibility is akin to that of film, with its flashbacks and flashforwards, montages, and dissolves that, stirred together, enrich the plot. That perspective enabled Graham to be the key figure in her own narratives (if not the most active)—the one through whose mind the past is constantly being envisioned, queried, and reshaped.

In May 1977, *The New York Times* published a substantial profile and interview of Graham by its dance critic Anna Kisselgoff: "Martha Graham—Still Charting 'The Graph of the Heart.'" In it, Graham speaks of not wanting to work with big groups: "I want the intensification, rather than the spread. I'm more interested now in working with individuals than in making great stage spectacles."

She did not yet know that the company's performance in London the previous July would be the last one Robert Powell, a dancer she cherished, would give, nor could she have guessed that he was to commit suicide in the coming October. She also could not have foreseen that over the years between the late 1980s and 2001, the AIDS epidemic would plow its way through the dance world. Seven men—valued performers who had contributed much to her work—would eventually succumb to the disease: Charles Brown, Mario Delamo, Kevin Keenan, Jean-Louis Morin, Lar Roberson, Philip Salvatori, and Tim Wengerd.

Dancers who interested her were stimulated by her focus on them. As the Graham company member Christine Dakin put it, "Martha lived for her work. She lived by working. She lived by working with the dancers. That was it." Her new ways of choreographing empowered them, and the chance for the women to take over her roles in earlier pieces put them in touch with the ideas that had compelled her.

Interviews that Francis Mason elicited from them about working in her later dances convey much about the studio atmosphere.

Janet Eilber: "When she started making a new ballet, Martha would bring in books and photos and quotations. We always accused her of stalling, but she was only trying to fill us with the motivation and the idea of where she was going to be choreographing from. She completely understood the 'shadowing' of the Puritan ancestors and how the past influences one's actions . . . She would tell us of her family, of her grandfather who was supposed to be a farmer but was really a poet. She was aware of the footsteps from the past and her ancestral blood. 'Within you is a drop of blood from every woman who has ever existed before,' she would tell us. 'So, yes, you have the ability to be Medea; you have the ability to be Jocasta—there's a piece of her in you.'"

Peggy Lyman: "For about two seasons she had trouble choreographing in her new method of having to stay seated and talking us through new steps instead of demonstrating everything herself by moving with us. Working with her was draining, because nothing we could do was ever enough. Never trusting her first instinct, she would invent wonderful stuff but throw it away . . . She always wanted to find a means to say the same thing in a more powerful or more direct way. And when she hit her stride, we learned that if we didn't get out there and improvise for her, we weren't going to earn a part in the new piece. She might say, 'Peggy, this is your music,' and I'd go into the studio with the music and play around. I knew who my character was and I knew whom I would be interacting with. So I'd bring some improvised material to Martha and she would edit it. She'd say, 'No, do two of those,' or 'Do it in the other direction.' Or, more often, just 'No, take it out—it doesn't work.' That's how I learned to choreograph, and it was very exciting to be working with her this way."

Peter Sparling: "We were reviving *Plain of Prayer*. Since there was no film of it, some of the choreography had to be recast . . . We'd listen to the music, she'd describe what it was she saw, I'd improvise, she'd ask that I set something that she could work with, and then leave the room. She'd return later, we'd look at what I'd made and deconstruct it. Those were the greatest lessons in dance composition that I have ever had, watching Martha take movement and reorganize it, re-pattern it, and put it into sentences and phrases that made some kind of sense to her."

Peter London (working on *Night Chant* with her in 1988): "Martha would give me imagery, saying 'Okay. Do . . .' and name a movement from her vocabulary. She would say, 'It's a wide open space and he's flying through the air. Do that, using a pitch turn.' A pitch turn is a grand battement while your torso cascades in a spiral around your standing leg. After I did that, she'd take it further: 'Come up in a sharp contraction and feel some sort of aggressive feeling, too, an attack or a sacrifice. You are prepared to make some sort of sacrifice.' That's the way we worked. I would use my mind plus her imagery and vocabulary to try to create a movement."

Terese Capucilli: "If there wasn't a storm, Martha made one. But it wasn't the kind of storm that can stifle people. If you're constantly being hammered and pushed, there's a kind of storm where you can't see the other side because you can't even stand up. But Martha knew how to create a storm where the energy pushed you through it, or wound you into it, or wrapped it around you, forced you to become entangled with it, to find your way out of it. It's like in *Errand into the Maze*, that same finding your way out of the labyrinth. She was able to let each person find for themselves what it is that they're trying to do, or what it is that they need."

Over the last decades of Graham's career, the modern dance world changed. The 1968 photograph described at the beginning of the previous chapter shows her nestled among prominent choreographers of the generation after hers, but also those of the subsequent one. The fact that two women who had studied with her only briefly—Yvonne Rainer (born in 1934) and Twyla Tharp (born in 1941)—were to share the upcoming Broadway series put together by Charles Reinhart signified a change in how modern dance was presented.

Those who had banded together in 1962 to form Judson Dance Theater—prominent among them Rainer, Trisha Brown, David Gordon, and Steve Paxton—were intent on reinventing what a dance could be. In the antiestablishment years of the 1960s and early 1970s, they investigated the mundane and redesigned virtuosity as something other than physical feats. Choreographers who had taken Robert Dunn's pioneering composition course were giddy with making discoveries about space and time in relation to movement. They climbed buildings, walked on walls, and appeared in public parks. Since they didn't require proscenium stages (or have the funds to pay for them), they were able to give a particular work more performances than the usual single one that they could afford. And spaces such as Greenwich Village's Judson Church, or lofts such as the original Dance Theater Workshop on West Twentieth Street, also offered shared programs for smaller audiences when a choreographer hoped to premiere a single work.

In this context, many of Graham's new works may have seemed "old-fashioned" to some. In truth, few of her current ones could be listed among her greatest dances. It is worth noting that when her 1931 *Primitive Mysteries* was reconstructed in 1982 and appeared at the Brooklyn Academy of Music, audiences were astonished and thrilled by the power of the choreography and that of the women performing it. The same was true of the 1988 presentation of the "Steps in the Street" section of her 1936 *Chronicle*, with its endlessly jumping dancers.

In her 1977 interview with Anna Kisselgoff, Graham had hinted that her plans for the following year involved "a different form than what

I've used." Only one of the three new works she created in 1978 involved what might be considered a different form, even though that one, *The Owl and the Pussycat*, harked back to some of her earlier displays of comedic inventiveness. Lines from one of Edward Lear's *Nonsense Songs* were recited by Liza Minnelli on opening night (and thereafter by Janet Eilber), as she wandered around Ming Cho Lee's playground clad in a green lounge suit speculating on the unlikely mating. Yuriko Kimura's Pussycat had a curving couch to recline on, while the Owl (Wengerd) perched on his arch of a ladder. The Pig (Bert Terborgh) sold them the ring from his nose to use for the wedding, presided over by the Turkey (Sparling), while the narrator concluded the piece with Lear's lines:

> They dined on mince, and slices of quince,
> Which they ate with a runcible spoon;
> And hand in hand, on the edge of the sand,
> They danced by the light of the moon,
> The moon,
> The moon,
> They danced by the light of the moon.

In this charming showpiece, shards from earlier works cropped up. The Turkey in his frock coat, with its coat hem wired into a series of little points, seems to echo the minister of *Appalachian Spring* in denouncing the perils of damnation that await the unfaithful, and he gives the amorous couple little slaps on each cheek like the Christ figure in *El Penitente*.

Ecuatorial was set to a remarkable score: Edgard Varèse's thundering piece of the same name featuring two Ondes Martenots and a male voice. The artist Marisol created separate dwellings—a jagged golden platform for the Celebrant of the Sun (Mario Delamo) and a coiled structure that harbored the Celebrant of the Moon (Kimura). In their skimpy gold costumes and headdresses, the solar entities briefly invaded each other's territories and swirled a dark cloak to hide each other's light.

Two potent rivals also appeared in *Flute of Pan*, each with her own rock (by Leandro Locsin) from which to agonize or gloat. The subtitle, *Fragments of Songs from "The Iliad,"* suggested that the whole might be a collage of incidents culled from the Trojan Wars. To the sounds of a traditional Rumanian flute and organ chords, Lyman, clothed in green and sporting a gold wig, battled Eilber, who wore a silver outfit. Each acquired a partner (Wengerd and Sparling), both of whom, possibly on some quest or voyage, also struggled with Lucinda Mitchell. Linda Hodes, veiled in black, followed Eilber and seemed to be trying to take care of her. Helen? you wonder. Achilles? Later a chorus of six women, gowned and turbaned in purple, formed frieze-like patterns. The performers moved dreamily from pose to pose without the percussive force and emotional impetus expected from Graham.

Not all the critics admired the new pieces; to at least one, they seemed like "stylish schema of her masterpieces."

> The characters in them are figures standing for people—beautiful and passionate; she presents them unequivocally with their desires full-blown, their feet set on a course. They succeed or fail, but they don't change . . . The new dances, sumptuous and theatrical, engage your attention without feeding your heart.

Graham may have tired—if only temporarily—of revisiting and transforming Greek myths. According to Ben Belitt, her friend and former colleague at the American Dance Festival, she was after two things in her dances:

> She was seeking the "hot points" inside something which could then coalesce—the whole encompassing significance of "mazes" in relation to their "errands." That's what drew her so obsessively to mythology and metaphor. They gave incandescence and specificity to a complex combination which charged her, as you would charge the acids of a battery, and allowed her to unfold things "not known in advance," because I think the unforeseen was part of her secret. She worked blindly, as a poet might . . . She "divined" in order to know.

In 1974, the year before she created *Lucifer*, Martha had immersed herself in the Bible and American literature. Having choreographed *Jacob's Dream* for Israel's Batsheva Dance Company, she revised it a year later, changed the costumes for ones by Leandro Locsin, and called the revised dance *Point of Crossing*. That same year, she retold Nathaniel Hawthorne's *The Scarlet Letter*, and in 1977 she confined her creative gifts to choreographing a sensual duet for Elisa Monte and David Brown, whose title, *O Thou Desire Who Art About to Sing*, she drew from Saint-John Perse's *Winds*.

> Very great mendicant tree, its patrimony squandered, its countenance seared by love and violence whereon desire will sing again.

> "O thou, desire, who art about to sing . . ."

The heroic Judith had appealed to her for decades: an Israelite widow with a mission to destroy Holofernes, the Assyrian enemy king whose army waited at the gates of her city, ready to attack. Seducing him with her beauty, she puts him to sleep with drink, then beheads him. The original 1950 solo had more than affirmed Graham's recovery from her knee injury. Able to lift thirty-pound ankle weights, she had had no problem performing the twenty-four-minute work. Of that first Judith, Pearl Lang remarked, "Martha had to make that dance so she could cut off Erick's head."

After expanding her solo into a group work, *Legend of Judith*, in 1962, Graham reworked the subject completely in her 1980 *Judith* and passed the leading role to Lyman. A program note from a 1981 performance in Ann Arbor, Michigan, reveals her vision of her heroine, drawn from the deuterocanonical Book of Judith 16: 6–9:

> The Assyrian came from the mountains of the North . . .
> He threatened to set fire to my land.
> Judith . . . disarmed him by the beauty of her face.
> She put off her widow's weeds

to raise up the afflicted in Israel;
she anointed her face with perfume
and bound her head with a headband,
and put on a linen gown to beguile him.
Her sandal entranced his eye,
her beauty took his heart captive,
and the sword cut through his neck.

Graham went one better than the ancient heroine: her Judith danced for Holofernes (Bertram Ross) before demolishing him. She had told the composer, William Schuman, that she did not wish to make the biblical heroine "in any way inhuman or goddess-like." In the 1980 version she also fiddled with time, casting Linda Hodes as the Young Judith, Helen McGehee as the Teller of the Tale, Robert Powell as the Listener, and David Wood as the Tyrant (presumably Holofernes's commander Nebuchadnezzar).

The costumes for this final *Judith* were designed by the fashion designer Halston (born Roy Halston Frowick). Beginning with *Lucifer* in 1975—entranced by Graham and enjoying talking with her—he not only dressed more than eight of her dances but also garbed *her* and gifted her female dancers with discarded pieces from his shows. Anne O'Donnell, one of the nurses who cared for Graham during her final years, had only to telephone him and say that the black work gowns he'd created for Martha had become shiny with wear, and he would provide new ones, free of charge. (O'Donnell also noted that when Halston visited Graham, his hostess "acted like a young girl again.") Thanks to him and to the hairdresser and the makeup artist who accompanied Graham on the company's tours (as often did he), Martha developed a new personal style. Greeting those who visited her in her studio, she wore one of Halston's superbly designed pantsuits with covered buttons, her hair tied in a ponytail by a matching swatch of material. Onstage to take bows after the company's performances, she would be garbed in one of his shimmering caftans, often wearing her hair in two sculpted bunches that subtly evoked the Hopi maidens of the Southwest that she loved.

One might be surprised that, having carved out a major career with the support of very few (Louis Horst and Frances Steloff among others), she was content in her old age to be dependent on an array of helpers. Maybe her image of herself as a great lady reinforced and upheld that necessity, but she was under no illusions about aging. Her hairdresser, José Aznarez, remembered her greeting him with, "I'm so happy to see you because I feel like the grandmother of God today." When not working in the studio or greeting visitors such as Doris Duke, Madonna (a former student of hers), Liza Minnelli, Alice Tully, and Jacqueline Onassis (the latter working with Martha on her 1991 autobiography *Blood Memory*), she gladly accepted the ministrations of her nurse, Helen O'Brien, who, beginning in 1987, was on duty for twelve-hour days, and O'Donnell, who took care of her from seven at night to seven in the morning and also accompanied her on tours. If Graham had been working in the studio until 6:00 p.m.—and she wanted to be there every minute if that were possible—she'd have tea when she got home, nap, and awaken hungry for homemade soup, a lot of fruit, and conversation that wasn't about dance.

According to O'Brien, Graham was "immensely curious about everyday things. She enjoyed talking to ordinary people about their lifestyles, their feelings, their routines, what they did when they went home at night, their families." When they were in Tucson, Arizona—whether on tour with the company or to visit her sister—O'Brien might be called on to drive her patient out into the desert. O'Donnell's nightly duties also occasionally involved taking notes dictated by Graham, then stepping aside when Ron Protas arrived to collaborate on further notes. O'Donnell remembered that Martha thought nothing of phoning Protas as late as 2:00 a.m. to recount her latest idea. And she stayed up late after a performance, wanting to read the reviews when they came out. A five-minute nap was all she ever needed to refuel. "Inactivity drove her crazy," said O'Brien of Graham's days. "She wanted to be where the action was."

Quite a lot of "action" surrounded her *Frescoes*, whose official premiere took place in New York during the Graham company's 1980 season at the Metropolitan Opera. (The 7:00 p.m. gala performance was followed by a 10:00 p.m. haute cuisine dinner at Le Poulailler and midnight dancing at Régine's.) *Frescoes*, however, had first been seen two years earlier, celebrating the Metropolitan Museum of Art's installation of Egypt's Temple of Dendur. The structure—built, it is thought, during the last centuries to be labeled BCE—had regularly been flooded when the first and second dams near the city of Aswan caused the waters of the Nile to rise. The third Aswan Dam, constructed during the 1960s, had created Lake Nasser and would have submerged the temple forever. Because of the Metropolitan's initiative to salvage it, its gigantic portals were documented before being taken down, disassembled, and packed into 660 boxes. Three years later, in 1965, it arrived in New York via freighter, a gift to the United States by the Arab Republic of Egypt, and was reconstructed in the museum.

The temple's history, its original site, and its present one influenced Graham's choreographic choices. A precipice above the Nile had served as its rear wall, but when it finally opened in the Metropolitan Museum, it had become a freestanding building with a granite stage surrounding it and its immense gate. A channel of water reflected the structure; a slanted skylight towered above it. The principal deity originally worshipped in it was Isis. But her consort, Osiris, whose scattered body parts she traveled the world to reassemble, was also depicted in the sanctuary, the innermost of the temple's three chambers.

Walking down the long corridor leading to the Sackler Wing, where some of the museum's extensive Egyptian collection is displayed, Martha may have been struck by a small, light-complexioned statue of Isis, naked except for her jewelry and a gigantic, vaselike headdress perched above her golden curls; Halston costumed the *Frescoes* dancers in flesh-colored unitards that clung to and outlined their torsos and limbs. Graham divided the dance into four "Frescoes"—an allusion to the temple carvings whose colors had long since washed away. Christine Dakin and Charles Brown assumed the roles of Isis and Osiris in the first and fourth section. In the second section, Eilber played the youthful Cleopatra and Sparling her Antony. In the third, Lyman and Wengard portrayed the couple later in life, and in the last part they came together with Isis and Osiris. A chorus passed through between these scenes or waited in smaller groups (by 1981, Terese Capucilli and Jacqulyn Buglisi had been singled out in programs as Cleopatra's handmaidens, Iras and Charmian).

Graham's choice of these famous lovers avoided all the complications of rulership and warring nations that had attended the fraught historical relationship of Antony and Cleopatra. Their duets were performed to two arias from Samuel Barber's opera *Antony and Cleopatra*, which Martha may have heard on a 1968 LP recorded by Leontyne Price and the New Philharmonia Orchestra conducted by Thomas Schippers. The words that begin the arias are drawn from Shakespeare's play of that name: Cleopatra's speech that begins "Give me some music—music, moody food / of us that trade in love" and the final moments of the play in which she, committed to suicide, calls out to her maidservants, "Give me my robe, put on my crown. I have immortal longings in me." Graham's Isis and Osiris, however, danced to the sounds of howling winds, their two-dimensional poses alluding to the temple's long-lost frescoes and its themes: death and fertility, the renewal of love.

Later, when the piece was staged in a theater, the dancers portraying Antony and Cleopatra began by succeeding Osiris and Isis in posing momentarily, just like their predecessors, atop the set's faux-stone structures. Again, Graham used memory as a structuring principle. Men carried in the dead body of Antony, yet as the red robe that Cleopatra wore to mourn her lover flew upward into a canopy and the sail of a ship, the pair relived moments of their love affair beneath it, even as he sank back into death again and again. The seas over which the partners voyaged were invoked in other ways: Isis sat sideways on Osiris as he rode the imagined waves, buoyed up by three men. In the end, the red fabric, held back by Iras and Charmian, enwrapped Cleopatra as she leaned out to become the figurehead of the imagined ship bound for an eternity where Antony awaited her. Love defies death and persists beyond it.

Frescoes itself, however, had a fairly long, sturdy life. It could be adjusted. The same two principal dancers could perform all the duets; cuts could be made. When the company went to the Middle East on a tour sponsored by the State Department, audiences, remembered Lyman, loved *Frescoes*.

It was also seen during the last week of the Graham company's 1982 spring season on a special program in homage to Graham's old friend and collaborator, the composer Samuel Barber, who had died the previous year. In addition to it and *Cave of the Heart*, Graham returned yet again to the Greek dramas to prepare a third work, *Andromache's Lament*, set to a piece by Barber and sung from the orchestra pit by the soprano Julia Lovett. Barber had drawn the text of his music, titled *Andromache's Farewell*, from Euripides's play *The Trojan Women*. In it, the heroine was lamenting the death of her son Astyanax, who'd been thrown from the walls of Troy to ensure the Greeks' victory. Lyman's solo as Andromache was one of dread and mourning, clutching herself in agony, staring into the distance, falling to the floor. David Brown played her husband, Hector; eleven-year-old Tali Ben-David (the daughter of Linda Hodes) played Astyanax's corpse, and Donlin Foreman appeared as the Greek king Menelaus. Red-robed women and warriors swelled the scene.

Graham revisited her past in other fruitful ways. As Anna Kisselgoff wrote, "In search of herself, she has always revealed us to ourselves. The questing heroine—and occasional hero—is her central figure." The 1982 *Dances of the Golden Hall*, she noted, "looks ornate, it glitters with the gold of Halston's tiaras and tigerskin half-robes, it specifically recalls India's temple sculpture rather than an abstraction of that imagery." In an interview with Kisselgoff, Graham referred to the work as her "Denishawn piece," inspired also, she said, by Ashoke Chatterjee's 1979 book, whose title she had borrowed (the Indian dancer Shanta Rao, who illustrated its traditional Bharata Natyam poses, had sent the book to Graham as a gift).

In Martha's golden hall, Shiva Nataraja, the creator, preserver, and destroyer of the universe, performed his cosmic dance (although Graham's allusions to the god occur only very subtly in the movement). Yet in this dance it is a woman (Elisa Monte) who places her foot on the fallen David Brown. Perhaps her avatar is Kali, the fiercest of Shiva's consorts.

The year 1983 marked an important cultural event in the dance world: the seventieth anniversary of *Le Sacre du Printemps*, the ballet by Serge Diaghilev's Ballets Russes that had premiered in Paris in May 1913 with choreography by Vaslav Nijinsky, music by Igor Stravinsky, and costumes and decor by Nicholas Roerich. By the time this tale—of a virgin who dances herself to death to ensure the coming of spring—had reached its 2013 centennial, Pina Bausch, Maurice Béjart, Angelin Preljocaj, Molissa Fenley, Glen Tetley, Hans Van Manen, Yvonne Rainer, Paul Taylor, Mark Morris, and many others had created their own versions to Stravinsky's epochal score (written when the composer was still in his twenties). In 1987, the Joffrey Ballet would rekindle interest with its production of *Sacre*, enabled by painstaking, yearslong research by Millicent Hodson and Kenneth Archer into its original iteration and direction.

In 1983, Graham, perhaps spurred on by her 1930 participation in Leonide Massine's 1920 reconstruction of *The Rite of Spring*, decided to choreograph her own version. Several months after it premiered during her company's 1984 season at the New York State Theater, she turned ninety.

She told *The New York Times* that she had choreographed much of her *Rite* without consulting Stravinsky's score and then adapted her composition to his. Neither did her choreography acknowledge all the original work's subtitles—no "Ritual Action of the Ancestors," no "Augurs of Spring . . ." Also, her scenario made much of the chosen victim's relationship to the presiding tribal leader, the shaman (George White, Jr., in the original cast). It is he who advances unexpectedly behind a procession of three men—each of whom holds a wary and watchful woman arched upon his shoulders—and, without hesitating, selects the last woman as the one to be sacrificed. It is he who winds thick white ropes around her and later uncoils them, he who parades with her standing on his shoulders, he who finally offers up her dead body. His costume, seamed only along his arms, flourishes a white panel when he faces front and a black one when he turns his back on the proceedings.

The eight attending men, costumed by Halston, wear only black trunks, and the eight corresponding women are clad in skin-colored unitards that make them appear bare-breasted; their long white skirts, open in front, hang from black waistbands. Only in the beginning do these people reveal any individuality. Gazing skyward, the men stalk in various directions, their clasped hands pulling their straight arms down to their groins and their bodies into contractions. Only occasionally does one or another of them break briefly away into a leap of some kind. Whether airborne in a circle around the sacrificial virgin, charging toward and away from her, or posing symmetrically on either side of her (men alternating with women in tightly spaced lines of either six pairs or eight), the celebrants often wrench themselves from one position into another, suggesting an addiction to ceremony that's almost voracious and prefigures the inevitable extinction of a life.

Yet their synchrony and the unusual designs they make are as exact as those of the figures on a piece of ancient pottery. You cannot guess which woman is to perform the ritual until she is selected. Nor do her comrades exhibit sympathy when they undo her hair and alter her costume. Graham's vision of the solo in which the Chosen One is to dance herself to death is enigmatic. Shortly after she (either Terese Capucilli or Christine Dakin in the original cast) begins whirling, turning with one leg thrust high and her body slanted toward the floor, falling, jumping repeatedly, and thrashing her arms, the observers leave the stage, and she is alone—except for the shaman who waits on the stairs at the back. In the end, two of his male assistants stretch out an almost serpentine torrent of green fabric that stands for the spring to come, and the awkwardly inert body of the victim is lifted and displayed.

Only after being arrested by the power of the dancing and the music might one wonder how personal this rite may have been to Graham herself—a woman for whom choreography was the most powerful element in her life, and dancing until she died a possibility she may have craved.

In *Tangled Night* (1986), she dispensed with a heroine whose memory ignited the action and—with the help of Ming Cho Lee's constructed ship—brought a new perspective to the notion of a voyage. In it, a man (Foreman) searched for some unknown vision, perhaps an artistic revelation. Competing strenuously for his devotion were a wife (Jacqulyn Buglisi) and a sea goddess with snaky green hair (Dakin). Seven male dancers were costumed as seamen (also by Lee), and their six partners behaved more like furies than wives. In the end, the men bore Buglisi—their figurehead—away.

The accompanying music, the Norwegian composer Klaus Egge's Second Piano Concerto, was new to Graham, but the dance, commissioned by the Norwegian Foundation, had been initiated by the Danish-American Edward H. Michaelson, the vice chairman of her company's board of directors. Here again, a quote from Saint-John Perse subtitled the work: "The Sea, woven in us, to the last weaving of its tangled night, the Sea, in us weaving its great hours of light and its great trails of darkness."

Not only unfamiliar music but also new ideas fueled Graham during her final years. For what turned out to be her last completed work, she set her dancers frolicking on and around a structure she had discovered during the summer of 1990, when her company appeared at the Spoleto Festival in Charleston, South Carolina: the joggling board. Invented in nineteenth-century Scotland, it had soon spread to the United States, where, according to its publicity, "it became almost as commonplace as a swing set or hammock is today." You can, however, realize that a narrow, flexible plank, mounted at either end on a stanchion that ended in a rocker would not have the lazy swing of a hammock. To be on the safe side for what was to become her *Maple Leaf Rag*, Martha bought three such structures from the Old Charleston Joggling Board Company.

When the lighthearted piece premiered at New York's City Center on October 2, its creator was ninety-six years old and ready to revisit her past in another way. Not long after the curtain rose, the audience heard her taped voice imploring, "Oh, Louis, play me the 'Maple Leaf Rag'!" Decades earlier, Horst had played it to cheer her up; now Scott Joplin's piano piece, along with his "Bethena" and "Elite Syncopations," was recruited to mobilize twenty-four dancers and cheer up the audience when Chris Landriau played it on an onstage piano.

The suspended board could be used for reclining, leaping over, or standing on to practice pliés: three men did the last, while three women, lying on the floor beneath them, lifted their bent legs to create a mirror image. The board is flexible, but the choreography treats the stage floor itself as another kind of springboard. Two bold men flip into near handstands at either end. Five women caper on and off the stage (with or without their Calvin Klein skirts). Men leap their way to somewhere else. Prancing on and off the stage, couples, one by one, frisk through short duets, and all five pairs end up sitting embraced on the board.

There are a few sly jokes. In the original cast, Floyd Flynn shoves himself along under the structure until his head disappears briefly under Terese Capucilli's hanging-down skirt (she, seated on the board, seems both affronted and pleased). Their little onboard romance is full of eager sentiment and pretend huffs, but when it's time for them to move temporarily offstage, he hoists her and tilts her horizontally; her legs—bent into pincers—point the pair into the wings.

Intermittently, a woman (Maxine Sherman) in a long gray dress passes through to resounding repeated chords, holding the front of her skirt up into a full circle as she turns slowly along her path. Is she indeed a wandering moon? A ghost from Graham's history? In the end, Capucilli has her skirt maliciously whipped off by her departing boyfriend and, thus bereft, clutches herself, looking vulnerable and mildly appalled. Then the lights go out. At the time, I imagined Graham saying to herself, "If I can't have fun now that I'm ninety-six, when can I?" But she could also have been portraying her own dilemma: a temporarily blocked artist hunting strategies.

Having completed *Maple Leaf Rag*, Graham—or her company—returned to *Eyes of the Goddess*, a dance she had started, managing to create almost fifteen minutes of it, but laying it aside in order to make the Joplin piece. The decision may not have been hers alone; she had been commissioned to create a new work by the Spain '92 Foundation, a part of the Spanish government's Columbus Quincentary; it would be set to sections of *Symphonic Variations* by Carlos Surinach, a composer whose music had served Graham well in *Embattled Garden*, *Acrobats of God*, and *The Owl and the Pussycat*. Watching it, one could sense that Graham had been working against time, hurling things into a simmering pot, hoping to refine them later. She told Pascal Rioult that his role was to be that of "a street vendor in an old Spanish town . . . a common man selling his wares from a cart." The two-tiered cart designed by Marisol bore a tree hung with symbolic objects, some of which could be pulled off by a rushing horde of revelers. Trickster, prop man, death figure Lyndon Branaugh reached out a long crook to drag various of the five soloists to their destinies. He ensnared Camille Brown with a hoop. Mario Camacho wielded a cruciform sword to duel with him. Capucilli waved a big, floppy fan to taunt and deceive a suitor. A mirror was held up in which Joyce Herring might view herself. When the group assembled as if for a photographer, they held in their teeth small, almost featureless masks that Rioult collected afterward.

No one can be sure to what degree Graham would have revised her early labors on *Eyes of the Goddess* or what she might have decided to add to it. The title itself hints at a mystery. The dance was a jewel box, its shining objects awaiting the discerning eye that would eventually sift through them. Labeled "unfinished," the piece premiered on October 10, 1991. Martha, however, would not be in the audience. The previous April 1, a month or so short of her ninety-seventh birthday, she had died of pneumonia.

What had this artist experienced over her long, long creative career? Enough of life and thought to lead her deep into what mattered most to her: choreographing nearly two hundred works and dancing in most of them for forty-four years. Like a horse retired from jumping who cannot glimpse a hurdle many yards away without ignoring its rider's wishes and galloping toward it, Graham could never resist the alluring obstacle of an embryonic dance. How she raced toward it! How she leapt to bring it to life!

AFTERWORD

T HE MARTHA GRAHAM DANCE COMPANY survived the death of its founder. In addition to maintaining dances from Graham's repertory, the company commissioned new works from the following choreographers: Kyle Abraham, Alleyne Dance, Aszure Barton, Baye & Asa, Sidi Larbi Cherkaoui, Lucinda Childs, Marie Chouinard, Sir Robert Cohan, Michelle Dorrance, Maxine Doyle, Nacho Duato, Mats Ek, Andonis Foniadakis, Liz Gerring, Larry Keigwin, Michael Kliën, Pontus Lidberg, Lil Buck, Lar Lubovitch, Andrea Miller, Josie Moseley, Richard Move, Juliano Nunes, Bulareyaung Pagarlava, Annie-B Parson, Nicolas Paul, Yvonne Rainer, Annie Rigney, Pascal Rioult,* Jamar Roberts, Steve Rooks,* Troy Schumacher, Hofesh Shechter, Bobbi Jene Smith, Susan Stroman,* Pam Tanowitz, Sonya Tayeh, Micaela Taylor, Twyla Tharp,* Doug Varone, Luca Vegetti, Gwen Welliver, Robert Wilson,* and Yin Yue.

*Those who contributed dances before Janet Eilber became the Martha Graham Dance Company's artistic director.

~~~

NOTES

1. FROM COAL-FED ALLEGHENY TO SANTA BARBARA'S OCEAN

3 *"Mary was blond"*: Martha Graham in an interview, quoted by Agnes de Mille, *Martha: The Life and Work of Martha Graham* (New York: Random House, 1991), 20.

3 *"I'm Dr. Graham's daughter"*: Ernestine Stodelle, *Deep Song: The Dance Story of Martha Graham* (New York: Schirmer Books, 1984), 2.

4 *which the often-rebellious*: Martha Graham interview, Lucy Kroll Papers, box 240, folder 7, page 3 (transcribed from reel 1, side A), Library of Congress.

4 *"The city has always"*: Herbert W. Casson, *The Romance of Steel: The Story of a Thousand Millionaires* (New York: A. S. Barnes, 1907), 270.

5 *"in his sweet way"*: Martha Graham interview, December 6, 1971, Lucy Kroll Papers, box 240, folder 6, page 3 (transcribed from reel 10, side A), Library of Congress.

5 *"hellers"*: Ibid., 4.

5 *"We didn't go to school"*: Martha Graham interview, February 10, 1972, Lucy Kroll Papers.

5 *"little Fu-Manchu shoes"*: Ibid.

6 *"first attempt to make"*: Ibid., 3. Several varying accounts of the nursery fire have found their way into print. See Martha Graham, *Blood Memory: An Autobiography* (New York: Doubleday, 1991), 33, and Don McDonagh, *Martha Graham: A Biography* (New York: Popular Library, 1975), 9.

7 *"You're like a horse"*: De Mille, *Martha*, 21.

7 *"Mother said, 'I can't'"*: Martha Graham interview, February 10, 1972, Lucy Kroll Papers, box 240, folder 7, page 3 (transcribed from reel 10, side A), Library of Congress.

7 *"It's a butterfly!"*: Loïe Fuller, *Fifteen Years of a Dancer's Life: With Some Account of Her Distinguished Friends* (London: H. Jenkins Ltd., 1913), 31.

7 *"I had found my dance"*: Isadora Duncan, *The Art of the Dance*, ed. Sheldon Cheney (New York: Theatre Arts Books, 1969), 65.

7 *Ruth St. Denis wrote*: Ruth St. Denis, *An Unfinished Life: An Autobiography* (Brooklyn, NY: Dance Horizons, 1969), 51–53.

8 *"the old Diblee estate"*: Martha Graham, quoted in Stodelle, *Deep Song*, 7.

8 *"I remember running"*: Martha Graham interview, February 10, 1972, Lucy Kroll Papers, box 240, folder 7, page 4, Library of Congress.

8 *"no child can develop"*: W. Adolphe Roberts, "The Fervid Art of Martha Graham," *The Dance Magazine*, August 1928.

8 *may have experienced California*: See Marlin L. Heckman, *Santa Barbara in Vintage Postcards* (Charleston, SC: Arcadia Publishing, 2000).

9 *"Nothing ever erupted there"*: Anna Kisselgoff, "Martha Graham," *New York Times*, February 19, 1984.

9 The Greaser and the Weakling: Information can be found at imdb.com.

10 *the corsage of violets Dr. Graham had bought*: De Mille, *Martha*, 21.

12 *"one of the treasures"*: Martha Graham, quoted in Jack Anderson, "Martha Graham Returns to Her Roots," *New York Times*, June 25, 1986.

13 *"The interpreter of 'Privacy'"*: Anonymous review in *Olive and Gold*, yearbook of the senior class of Santa Barbara High School, vol. 7, no. 1, June 1913, Martha Graham, editor. Published by the senior class, www.e-yearbook.com/yearbooks /Santa_Barbara_High_School_Olive_and_Gold_Yearbook/1913/Page_8.html.

13 *"The purpose of a true"*: "The School of Oratory," University of Southern California Yearbook, 1904–1905, 73 (circular of information).

14 *Cumnock students studied*: Porter E. Sargent, *A Handbook of American Private Schools*, vol. 2, 5th ed. (Boston: Porter E. Sargent, 1918), 689.

2. DENISHAWN DAYS: LEARNING FROM MISS RUTH AND TED

16 *"I entered, burnoose flying"*: Ted Shawn with Gray Poole, *One Thousand and One Night Stands* (Garden City, NY: Doubleday, 1960), 34–35.

17 *"It is well enough"*: Redfern Mason, "Ruth St. Denis Back in Dance of Sea Nymph," *San Francisco Examiner*, October 13, 1915, Denishawn Collection. Scrapbooks: clippings, announcements, and programs, New York Public Library for the Performing Arts.

17 *"assisted by Ted Shawn"*: Christena L. Schlundt, *The Professional Appearances of Ruth St. Denis and Ted Shawn: A Chronology and an Index of Dances 1906–1932* (New York: New York Public Library, 1962), 19. This billing was used for St. Denis's southern tour in spring 1914, the cross-country tour of 1914–15, and the concert and vaudeville tour of 1915–16.

17 *performed at a benefit*: Suzanne Shelton, *Divine Dancer: A Biography of Ruth St. Denis* (New York: Doubleday, 1981), 122.

17 *the word "obey"*: Ibid., 123.

17 *"inspire like hell"*: Jane Dudley quoting Ruth St. Denis in Francis Mason, *Martha Graham Remembered* (unpublished), © 2009 Francis Mason, All Rights Reserved.

18 *a film of them*: Denishawn Dance Film, 1915(?)–1917 (streaming video file, 7 minutes, 15 seconds), Performing Arts Research Collections, Jerome Robbins Dance Division of the Performing Arts Library, *MGZHB 4–856, New

York Public Library. Also https://digitalcollections.nypl.org/items/d08ab170 -f875–0130-dc17–3c075448cc4b.

18 *"those morning hours"*: Martha Graham, "Ruth St. Denis—1878–1968," *New York Times*, August 4, 1968.

18 *As Suzanne Shelton noted*: Shelton, *Divine Dancer*, 128.

18 *"To follow her commandments"*: Bliss Carman, *The Making of Personality* (Boston: L. C. Page, 1908), 212, https://archive.org/stream/makingpersonali02carmgoog #page/n230/mode/2up.

19 *At Denishawn, a student could learn*: Paul Scolieri, *Ted Shawn: His Life, Writings, and Dances* (New York: Oxford University Press, 2019), 91–92.

19 *The program advertised*: Louis Horst Scrapbooks, vol. 1 (1915–1920), New York Public Library. Also Shelton, *Divine Dancer*, 136.

20 *Decades later*: This demonstration occurred in a morning class at the Martha Graham School in the late 1950s, in which Jowitt participated.

20 *Shawn choreographed dances for Lillian Gish*: De Mille, *Martha*, 49.

21 *Graham evidently performed*: Ibid., 56.

21 *"exceedingly shy"*: St. Denis, *An Unfinished Life*, 187.

21 *"She's hopeless"*: Tape 2, track 2, typed manuscript dated January 26, 1969, and headed "Shawn autobiographical," Performing Arts Research Collections, Jerome Robbins Dance Division of the Performing Arts Library, New York Public Library.

21 *"If one saw Martha"*: St. Denis, *An Unfinished Life*, 187.

21 *"The first time I"*: Louis Horst, letter to Janet Mansfield Soares, n.d., quoted in Janet Mansfield Soares, *Louis Horst: Musician in a Dancer's World* (Durham, NC: Duke University Press, 1992), 23.

21 *"a dance with a circular skirt"*: Martha Graham quoting Ted Shawn describing *Serenata Morisca*, Lucy Kroll Papers, box 240, reel 10 (transcript), February 10, 1972, Library of Congress.

22 *"The former Denishawn dancer"*: Jane Sherman, *The Drama of Denishawn Dance* (Middletown, CT: Wesleyan University Press 1979), 22–25.

22 *uncredited Japanese servant boy*: Graham, *Blood Memory*, 61.

23 *"[She] said she wasn't interested"*: Martha Graham interview, Lucy Kroll Papers, box 240, reel 10 (side A, folder 7, item 8), recorded February 10, 1972, Library of Congress.

23 *The brochure for the summer*: Louis Horst Scrapbooks, vol. 1, New York Public Library.

24 *Lizzie Prendergast came down*: Tape 2, track 3, item 2, typed manuscript, "Shawn autobiographical," January 22, 1969, New York Public Library.

24 *"the weakling exoticism"*: Oliver M. Sayler, ed., *Revolt in the Arts: A Survey of the Creation, Distribution and Appreciation of the Arts in America; With contributions from Thirty-Six Representative Authorities in the Several Arts* (New York: Brentano's, 1930).

24 *Humphrey later accorded Shawn*: Doris Humphrey to Jowitt in a 1959 conversation when the latter was a member of Juilliard Dance Theater, founded and directed by Humphrey.

24 *never "deeply fond" of Shawn*: Martha Graham, Lucy Kroll Papers, box 240, reel 9, side A, Library of Congress.

24 *"things he did about Miss Ruth"*: Ibid.
24 *"The artist in me"*: Martha Graham, letter to Ted Shawn, dated "Monday night." Since the last performance of the tour took place in Montclair, New Jersey, on Saturday, April 21, the Monday when Graham wrote the letter is assumed to be April 23. Found by the Jacob's Pillow director of preservation Norton Owen in a large box of Shawn memorabilia donated to the Pillow in early 1994.
25 *"I wish to go to this man"*: Tape 2, track 2, typed manuscript dated January 26, 1969, and headed "Shawn autobiographical," Performing Arts Library, New York Public Library, MGZMD-137. (Typed transcript of interview also available, "Shawn autobiographical.")
25 *"Miss Ruth was a goddess"*: Graham, *Blood Memory*, 70.
26 *The score for* Xochitl: Tape 2, track 2, typed manuscript dated January 28, 1969, 256–57, and headed "Shawn autobiographical."
26 *"anthropologically and archaeologically"*: Ibid., 257.
27 *"completely on the half toe"*: Baird Hastings, "The Denishawn Era," in *Chronicles of the American Dance: From the Shakers to Martha Graham*, ed. Paul Magriel (1948; New York: Da Capo Press, 1978), 233.
27 *"I love this dance-drama"*: *The Morning Press*, October 25, 1920, cited in Soares, *Louis Horst*. Also in Elizabeth Kendall, *Where She Danced* (New York: Alfred A. Knopf, 1979), 168.
28 *Also, as Jane Sherman*: Jane Sherman, *Soaring: The Diary of Letters of a Denishawn Dancer in the Far East, 1925–1926* (Middletown, CT: Wesleyan University Press, 1976), 5.
28 *"lithe and graceful"*: *The Morning Press*, March 30, 1917, cited in Kendall, *Where She Danced*, 162.
28 *"there wasn't time"*: *Doris Humphrey: An Artist First; An Autobiography*, edited and completed by Selma Jeanne Cohen (Heightstown, NJ: Princeton Book Company, 1995), 40.
28 *In both programs*: Christena L. Schlundt, "Into the Mystic with Miss Ruth," *Dance Perspectives* 46 (Summer 1971).
28 *"a light comedy number"*: Ted Shawn, quoted in Scolieri, *Ted Shawn*.
29 *Bowen had an even more strenuous*: Schlundt, "Into the Mystic with Miss Ruth."
30 *St. Denis, however, credited Duncan*: Shelton, *Divine Dancer*, 149.
30 *"Through all the program"*: Keene Abbott, "Ted Shawn Delights with Artistic Dances," *Omaha World-Herald*, October 25, 1921.
30 *"Miss Graham exhibits"*: *Pioneer Press* (St. Paul, Minnesota), October 3, 1921.
31 *"will stand out"*: "Austin Applauds Ted Shawn, Dancer," *Austin American*, November 8, 1921.
31 *Dates that failed to materialize*: In his *One Thousand and One Night Stands*, Shawn says that the company was booked into the Metropolitan Opera House, but that may have been a slip.
31 *may have been in early 1922*: Ibid., 102.
31 *St. Denis took over her role*: Schlundt, "Into the Mystic with Miss Ruth," 41.
32 *"wanted me to come over and kiss her"*: Louis Horst, interviewed by Jeanette Schlottmann Roosevelt in Mason, *Martha Graham Remembered*.
32 *to look at Tanagra figures*: Ibid.

32 *The tuppenny printed program*: Louis Horst Scrapbooks, Jerome Robbins Dance Division, New York Public Library.

33 *Philo nibbled*: In Graham's *Blood Memory*, 97–98, she mistakenly attributes this episode and the London tour to *Greenwich Village Follies* instead of to Denishawn. The *Follies* didn't have a London engagement.

33 *"Talking about colours"*: Fashion column, *Dancing Times* (London), July 1922.

3. DANCING ON BROADWAY, BECOMING A TEACHER

35 *The special curtain*: Gerald Bordman, *American Musical Theatre: A Chronicle*, 3rd ed. (New York: Oxford University Press, 2001), 320. Also *The Greenwich Village Follies* clipping file, New York Public Library for the Performing Arts at Lincoln Center.

36 *only eighty percent*: Burns Mantle, *The Best Plays of 1923–1924* (Boston: Small, Maynard & Company, 1924), 196, 320, 445.

36 *she was reportedly paid*: Martha Graham, interviewed by Don McDonagh, *Ballet Review* 2, no. 4 (1968), 26, cited in Stodelle, *Deep Song*, 44.

36 *"large, beautiful and generally underdressed"*: "The Greenwich Village Follies," *New York Times*, September 21, 1923.

36 *she was able to see*: Martha Graham, interviewed by Don McDonagh, *Ballet Review* 2, no. 4 (1968), 26.

36 *a glimpse of the Moscow Art Theatre*: Mantle, *The Best Plays of 1923–1924*, 356.

36 *Graham had a special*: New Winter Garden program, September 20, 1923, Performing Arts Research Collections—Theatre, MWEZ + n.c. 5606, New York Public Library.

36 *He did not receive*: Ibid.

37 *"The most amusing"*: Alexander Woollcott, "'Greenwich Village Follies' the Most Amusing of Series," *New York Herald*, September 22, 1923.

37 *"ballet ballad"*: John Murray Anderson and Hugh Abercrombie Anderson, *Out Without My Rubbers: The Memoirs of John Murray Anderson as Told to Hugh Abercrombie Anderson* (New York: Library Publishers, 1954). Also Jean Henry, torn clipping of a review in *Greenwich Village Follies* clipping files, New York Public Library, stating that "*Garden of Kama* continued the Ballet Ballad formula."

37 *Given that Shawn*: Ted Shawn interviewed by John Dougherty, "Reminiscences: From Childhood to the Dissolution of Denishawn," January 30, 1969, tape 2, track 3, MGZMD-137, Performing Arts Library, New York Public Library (typed transcript of interview also available, "Shawn autobiographical," 295).

38 *"And as her lord lingers"*: Promptbook for *Garden of Kama* (see *Greenwich Village Follies* file, 1923, New York Public Library).

38 *"Kashmiri Song"*: This last was recorded by Rudolf Valentino in 1923 and subsequently by singers as diverse as Richard Tauber and Deanna Durbin.

39 *"Just as the dawn"*: Promptbook.

39 *"Two Sailors"*: Program.

40 *"My mother says"*: Promptbook.

40 *"I danced in floating yellow chiffon"*: Graham, *Blood Memory*, 92.

40 *"MARTHA GRAHAM, Who Can Be"*: "'Village Follies' Wander Joyously on Jaunt away from Home," *Journal*, September 21, 1923. *Greenwich Village Follies* clippings (tattered and incomplete), New York Public Library.

40 *"a remarkably gifted pantomimic dancer"*: Fragmentary newspaper clipping reviewing the *Greenwich Village Follies*, New York Public Library.

40 *"weakest in its humor"*: "Greenwich Village Follies Come to Winter Garden: Fifth Edition of Annual Revue Is Filled with Clever Dancers and Pretty Girls—It Is Weakest in Its Humor," *The Sun*, September 21, 1923, New York Public Library.

40 *"the Kama episode"*: *New York Times*, from the *Greenwich Village Follies* file, New York Public Library.

40 *"no more pictorially beautiful"*: Fragment from *Journal of Commerce*, September 22, 1923, New York Public Library.

41 *ninety-two pastoral acres*: The number is debatable. Soares mentions forty acres in her *Louis Horst*, 37.

41 *According to Shawn, he left*: Ted Shawn interviewed by John Dougherty, "Reminiscences: From Childhood to the Dissolution of Denishawn."

41 *She's shown on the lawn*: With Rich Currier and as part of a larger group. *Class at the Denishawn School of Dancing, including Doris Humphrey, Charles Weidman, Martha Graham, Louise Brooks, Robert Graham*, 1923. Still photograph by Cutter Studio, viewable online at https://digitalcollections.nypl.org/items/510d47df-87e7-a3d9-e040-e00a18064a99.

42 *Shawn had to scold her*: Scolieri, *Ted Shawn*, 13–15, 16–17.

42 *"she began to teach"*: Ibid., 8.

42 *harvested poison ivy*: Ibid.

42 *He was appalled*: Ibid.

42 *There is some evidence*: Ibid.

42 *A program for the fifth edition's*: Poli's Theatre, April 19, 1925, in box of loose programs 12–392, New York Public Library.

43 *"I wasn't in sympathy"*: Horst in Mason, *Martha Graham Remembered*.

43 *fairer-haired Americans*: Graham, *Blood Memory*.

43 *"Martha and I had a little tiff"*: Louis Horst, letter to Jeanette Schlottmann Roosevelt, quoted in Soares, *Louis Horst*, 43.

43 *yank a telephone*: Graham, *Blood Memory*, 82.

43 *one of which*: De Mille, *Martha*, 197, 202.

44 *persuaded George Eastman*: Rouben Mamoulian in McDonagh, *Martha Graham*, 44.

45 *Enid Knapp, who had studied*: See Edith Knapp Botsford, "A Vision Shared," *University of Rochester Library Journal* 26, no. 3 (Spring 1971).

45 *As Don McDonagh pointed out*: McDonagh, *Martha Graham*, 44–45.

45 *liking, he said*: Carl W. Ackerman, *George Eastman* (Boston: Houghton Mifflin, 1930), 76.

46 *musicales in the Eastman mansion*: Harold Gleason, "Please Play My Funeral March," *University of Rochester Library Journal* 26, no. 3 (Spring 1971).

46 *"In this consummated whole"*: John Rothwell Slater, cited in Arthur Jay May, Introduction, "George Eastman and the University of Rochester: His Role, His Influence," *University of Rochester Library Journal* 26, no. 3 (Spring 1971).

46 *The Eastman Theatre would rival*: Vincent Lenti, "A History of the Eastman Theatre," *Rochester History* (ed. Ruth Rosenberg-Naparsteck) 49, no. 1 (Janu-

ary 1987). See also Vincent Lenti, "A History of the Eastman Theatre" at www.libraryweb.org/~rochhist/v49_1987/v49i1.pdf.

47 *"different from any face"*: Thelma Biracree, interviewed by Don McDonagh, August 15, 1972 (sound disc, part 2, disc 3), *MGZTL 4–2544, New York Public Library for the Performing Arts.

47 *long red kimono*: Graham, *Blood Memory*, 106.

47 *"lots of tension things"*: Thelma Biracree, interviewed by Don McDonagh, August 15, 1972 (sound disc, part 2, disc 3), *MGZTL 4–2544, New York Public Library for the Performing Arts.

47 *Charles Weidman thought*: McDonagh, *Martha Graham*, 54.

47 *Johansson had accompanied*: Charles Weidman in McDonagh, *Martha Graham*. Also in Soares, *Louis Horst*, 38.

47 *"Learning how to dance"*: Martha Graham, untitled essay in Virginia Stewart, *Modern Dance* (1935; New York: Dance Horizons, 1970), 55.

47 *Eastman was a stickler about timing*: McDonagh, *Martha Graham*, 44.

47 *One of these accompanied*: Joel Shapiro, "Martha Graham at the Eastman School," *Dance Magazine*, July 1974 (sidebar by John Mueller).

48 *"had an original thought"*: Thelma Biracree, interviewed by Don McDonagh, (sound disc, part 1), *MGZTL 4–2544, New York Public Library for the Performing Arts.

48 *"Rhythmic Drama to Music"*: Otto Luening, *The Odyssey of an American Composer: The Autobiography of Otto Luening* (New York: Charles Scribner's Sons, 1980), 271.

48 *And according to Luening*: Ibid.

48 *Graham's first appearance*: "Martha Graham Presents a Student Group in a Program of Dances Assisted by Louis Horst, Pianist at the Anderson-Milton School, August 2, 1927." Concert program, Martha Graham Collection, box 308, no. 13.

49 *To women between sixteen*: 1923 brochure for Anderson-Milton School, New York.

50 *when Barlach's work was exhibited*: Deborah Jowitt, "Dances with Sculpture," *Tate Magazine*, no. 8 (2006), 96–101.

50 *"a bit heavy"*: Louis Horst, quoted in Soares, *Louis Horst*, 47.

50 *"Who's Satie?"*: Ibid., 48.

50 *he slapped her*: Stodelle, *Deep Song*, 50.

50 *"always giving me a good shove"*: Martha Graham, Lucy Kroll Papers, box 240, folder 6, p. 5 (transcription of reel 1, side A), December 6, 1971, Library of Congress.

50 *"Oh Louie"*: Martha Graham, interviewed for Lucy Kroll Papers, ibid.

50 *"I was her whetstone"*: Horst in Mason, *Martha Graham Remembered*. Also Jeanette Schlottmann Roosevelt, *Conversations with Louis Horst*, transcript of audiotapes, ©1933–2012, Reading Room, Jacob's Pillow Dance Festival, Inc., Lee, Massachusetts. All rights reserved.

51 *to anchor a gift-wrap bow*: Matthew Tannenbaum, *My Years at the Gotham Book Mart with Frances Steloff, Proprietor* (New York: Worthy Shorts, 2009), 16.

51 *Martha accompanied Louis*: Horst in Mason, *Martha Graham Remembered*.

51 *"Her teeth stick out"*: Nina Fonaroff in ibid.

51 *"She began to develop"*: Jeanette Schlottmann Roosevelt, *Conversations with Louis Horst.*

51 *"was teaching some of the East Indian movements"*: Martha Hill in Mason, *Martha Graham Remembered.*

52 *"was all tension"*: Bette Davis, *The Lonely Life: An Autobiography* (New York: G. P. Putnam's Sons, 1962), 45.

4. EMBARKING ON A CHOREOGRAPHIC CAREER

53 *nineteen cents a yard*: Martha Graham interviewed by Don McDonagh, *Ballet Review* 2, no. 4 (1968), 24.

53 *Morris Green and A. L. Jones*: McDonagh, *Martha Graham*, 48.

53 *Frances Steloff borrowed*: Anna Kisselgoff, "Martha Graham Dies at 96; A Revolutionary in Dance," *New York Times*, April 2, 1991.

54 *"We would have paid her!"*: Thelma Biracree interviewed by Don McDonagh, August 15, 1972 (sound disc, part 2, disc 3), *MGZTL 4–2544, New York Public Library for the Performing Arts.

54 *In her* Blood Memory: Graham, *Blood Memory*, 110.

54 *dance staged by Shawn*: "A Unique Dance Theatre at Denishawn," *The Graphic*, August 20, 1917.

54 *A photo by Soichi Sunami*: *The Dance Magazine*, June 1927. The caption says the women "add the classic Greek touch to Roxy's ballet."

54 *The theories of François Delsarte*: See Wikipedia's very thorough presentation of Delsarte's system and contributions.

54 *painter Federico Beltrán Masses*: "Federico Beltrán Masses." See entry in Wikipedia.

55 *sporting a wig*: Photo captioned "A Unique Dance by Martha Graham . . ." *New York Telegraph*, April 15, 1926.

55 *"a lady in a sweeping blue gown"*: The singer was Mabel Zoeckler. Author unidentified (a fashion editor), *The Bookman*, June 1926, Martha Graham Scrapbooks, box 308, Martha Graham Collection, 1896–2003, Library of Congress.

55 *"Childish things"*: Martha Graham interviewed by McDonagh, *Ballet Review* 2, no. 4 (1968), 24.

55 *"indefinable but unmistakable"*: George Beiswanger, "Martha Graham: A Perspective," in Barbara Morgan, *Martha Graham: Sixteen Dances in Photographs*, 1941. Republished (New York: Morgan & Morgan, 1980).

55–56 *tickets costing $1.10*: Program for Graham's "Dance Recital" at New York's Forty-Eighth Street Theatre on April 18, 1926, viewable online as [Martha Graham, Forty-Eighth Street Theatre, April 18, 1926], Library of Congress.

56 *Horst later remembered*: Louis Horst interviewed by Jeanette Schlottmann Roosevelt, 1959–1960 (transcript), Library of the Performing Arts, New York Public Library.

56 *"an inner compulsion"*: Beiswanger, "Martha Graham: A Perspective," in Morgan, *Martha Graham: Sixteen Dances in Photographs*, 144.

56 *"strikingly poignant"*: *Rochester Democrat and Chronicle*, May 29, 1923, Martha Graham Collection, Scrapbooks, box 308, Library of Congress.

56 *"in no way really romantic"*: Deborah Jowitt, "A Conversation with Bessie Schönberg," *Ballet Review* 9, no. 1 (Spring 1981), 39.

57 *"presents a series of pictures"*: "The Blessed Damozel Comes Down from Rochester," *The Dance Magazine*, July 26, 1923.

57 *"mime and posture"*: R.M.K., *Musical America*, April 24, 1926.

57 *"plastic qualities"*: Ibid.

57 *"a symbolic piece"*: Ibid.

57 *In one photo of the trio*: *Marionette, No. 1*, still photograph. Martha Graham Collection Box 248/7, #57. Viewable online at https://www.loc.gov/item/ihas .200153381/.

58 *At a 1927 performance*: H. H., *Musical America*, March 5, 1927.

58 *"clad in a heavy gold kimono"*: *The Dance Magazine*, August 1926.

58 *"come to life"*: Fashion editor at *The Bookman*, June 1926.

58 *"her shawl was made"*: Karen Bell-Kanner, *Frontiers: The Life and Times of Bonnie Bird; American Modern Dancer and Educator* (London: Harwood Academic Publishers, 1998), 17.

58 *"tight skirt that flares"*: Robert Bell, "Echoes of the New York Stage," *Washington Post*, March 6, 1927.

59 *"like a white moth"*: Ibid.

59 *"something sad and scarfy?"*: Louis Horst interviewed by Jeanette Schlottmann Roosevelt re November 1928 concert at the Klaw Theatre (transcript), 65, *MGZMT 3–2273, New York Public Library.

59 *Graham tells her interviewer*: "The Leading Question—'Why Is a Fat Lady?' Martha Graham, Premier Danseuse, Gives the Answer," *New York Telegram*, April 19, 1926.

59 *full concert in the school's Kilbourn Hall*: Kilbourn Hall was an intimate theatrical space within the Eastman School of Music in Rochester, New York. The program for May 27, 1926, can be viewed at www.loc.gov/item/ihas .200153286.

60 *"There must be no sudden"*: Lydia Barton, "Pioneers and Pathfinders," *Stage and Screen*, February 1926.

60 Flute of Krishna: The resulting silent film (now with an introduction by Janet Eilber and added music) can be accessed via the George Eastman Museum. (The process made Krishna, traditionally blue, appear as green-skinned.)

62 *Graham was able to write*: Martha Graham, letter to Stewart Sabin, September 25, 1926.

62 *"She is exquisite"*: Ibid.

62 *"pretty little things"*: Quoted in McDonagh, *Martha Graham*, 55.

63 *Arthur Waley's translation*: The six volumes of Lady Murasaki's *The Tale of Genji* were published in English between in 1921 and 1933 (New York: Houghton Mifflin).

63 *close to 260 plays and musicals lit up Broadway*: Burns Mantle, *Best Plays of 1926–1927* (New York: Dodd Mead, 1928).

63 *An unusual number of major European dramas*: Ibid.

64 *she too was praised*: Ginnine Cocuzza, "Angna Enters: American Dance-Mime," *Drama Review* 24, no. 4 (MIT Press, 1980), 93–102.

64 *"To Ravel"*: *The Dance Magazine*, December 1927. The reviewer may have been referring to Graham's 1926 *Danse Rococo*.

66 *"certainly one of the finest"*: L. M., *New World*, October 17, 1927.

66 *"a helluva thing to play"*: Louis Horst, interviewed by Jeanette Schlottmann Roosevelt, 1959–1960, New York Public Library of the Performing Arts, *MGZMT 3–2261, 70.

66 *"To Honegger's mad music"*: *The Dance Magazine*, December 1927.

67 *Graham had confided*: Frances McClernan Kemp, "The Blessed Damozel of the Concert Stage," *The Dance Magazine*, March 1927.

67 *"But it will not be a sarabande"*: Ibid.

67 *"Out of emotion"*: Quoted in Merle Armitage, *Martha Graham: The Early Years* (New York: Da Capo Press, 1978), 97.

68 *"clad in sculptured folds"*: Stodelle, *Deep Song*, 49.

68 *"very cute"*: Louis Horst, interviewed by Jeanette Schlottmann Roosevelt, 1959–1960, 74.

68 *"they suggest modern reproductions"*: John Martin, *New York Times*, April 23, 1928, "Martha Graham at the Library of Congress" Collection, Scrapbooks 308, 1926–29 (8–11), #49, Library of Congress.

68 *Horst mentioned*: Louis Horst, interviewed by Jeanette Schlottmann Roosevelt, 1959–1960.

68 *"Bavarian wood carving"*: Nickolas Muray, *The Dance Magazine*, July 1924.

68 *A photo by Soichi Sunami*: Kemp, "The Blessed Damozel of the Concert Stage."

69 *"more than a dancer"*: H. H., *Musical America*, March 5, 1927 (a review of the February 27 concert at the Guild Theatre).

69 *"one of those artists"*: Bell, "Echoes of the New York Stage."

5. TAKING ON NEW YORK, MODERNISM, AND NIETZSCHE

70 *a substitute program of twenty solos*: Presented by the Cornell Dramatic Club, December 7, 1927.

71 *"He was fearless"*: Letter from Martha Graham, September 27, 1962, Adolph Bolm Collection, Library of the Performing Arts, Dance Division, New York Public Library. Quoted by Cyrus Parker-Jeanette in "Wandering Dancer," Library of Congress Information Bulletin, February 2005. Adolph Bolm materials donated to Music Division of the Library of Congress.

71 *"the Shawns, I'm ashamed to say"*: Doris Humphrey, letter to her mother, quoted in *Doris Humphrey: An Artist First*, 73.

71 *"so hard to keep her studio going"*: Doris Humphrey to her mother, June 7, 1927, ibid., 74.

72 *"the usual Graham emotional pyrotechnics"*: Doris Humphrey to her mother, August 27, 1927, ibid., 75.

72 *"an electric men's convention"*: Louis Horst, letter to Jeanette Schlottmann Roosevelt, cited in Soares, *Louis Horst*, 56.

72 *Horst, Tamiris, and Elsa Findlay*: Louis Horst, transcript of interview by Jeanette Schlottmann Roosevelt, Jacob's Pillow Archive.

73 *Graham sat and watched*: Soares, *Louis Horst*, 73.

73 *"as is being done"*: Barton, "Pioneers and Pathfinders."

73 *"said to be in the nature of"*: John Martin, "Graham Dance Recital: Artist More Eloquent When She Is Lyrical Than When Dramatic," *New York Times*, February 13, 1928.

74 *"a dignified way of earning a little money"*: Marcia B. Siegel, *Days on Earth— The Dance of Doris Humphrey* (Durham, NC: Duke University Press, 1993), 121. Also in Doris Humphrey's letters, folder C274.4 in the Doris Humphrey Collection, New York Public Library.

74 *"stage direction and dramatic composition"*: Program of the Manhattan Opera House, May 4, 1928.

74 *one of four Mourning Women*: Program for Neighborhood Playhouse performance directed by Alice and Irene Lewisohn in conjunction with the Cleveland Orchestra (Nikolai Sokoloff, conductor), Manhattan Opera House, May 4–6, 1928.

75 *"beautifully composed"*: Stark Young, "Orchestral Dramas," *New Republic*, May 23, 1928.

75 *"in the past [Louis]"*: Benjamin Zemach in Mason, *Martha Graham Remembered*.

76 *"strong, free, joyous, action"*: Program for Graham's solo concert at New York's Booth Theatre on January 20, 1929, www.loc.gov/item/ihas.200182484/. Taken from Friedrich Nietzsche, *On the Genealogy of Morality: A Polemic* (1887, translation).

76 *"long-sleeved, tightly fitted"*: Stodelle, *Deep Song*, 51.

76 *"she dared anyone to move her feet"*: Bessie Schönberg quoting Martha Hill in Jowitt, "A Conversation with Bessie Schönberg," *Ballet Review* 9, no. 1 (Spring 1981), 41.

76 and *"don't forget," she wrote*: Duncan, *The Art of the Dance*, 108.

76 *both had been intrigued by the essays*: St. Denis, *An Unfinished Life*, 97; Shawn with Poole, *One Thousand and One Night Stands*, 196.

76 *"I have been feeding"*: *Doris Humphrey: An Artist First*, 99.

77 *"I owe all that I am"*: Martha Graham, quoted in Roberts, "The Fervid Art of Martha Graham."

77 *introduced Graham to their ideas*: Soares, *Louis Horst*, 34.

77 *"the art of dancing stands at the source"*: Havelock Ellis, *The Dance of Life* (New York: Houghton Mifflin, 1923), 36.

77 *"the loftiest, the most moving"*: Ibid., 65. Note: The celebrated German Jewish Rahel Varnhagen (1771–1833) hosted salons for philosophers in Berlin.

77 *Music, he wrote, did not copy*: Harlow Gale, "Schopenhauer's Metaphysics of Music," *New Englander and Yale Review* 48, no. 218 (1888): 362–68.

77–78 *"come with all sorts of conventional notions"*: Martha Graham, quoted in Roberts, "The Fervid Art of Martha Graham," 13.

78 *"one who loveth leaps"*: "The Higher Man," in Friedrich Nietzsche, *Thus Spake Zarathustra*, translated by Thomas Common (New York: Boni and Liveright, 1921), part 4, chapter 63, section 18, 294.

78 *"I tell you, one must still"*: Ibid., "Zarathustra's Prologue," part 1, 32.

78 *"heavy feet and sultry hearts"*: Ibid., part 4, chapter 73, section 16, 329.

78 *"Lift up your hearts"*: Ibid., "The Higher Man," section 18, 294.

78 *"I have never danced a solo"*: "The Dance of the Greeks" in Duncan, *The Art of the Dance.*

79 *"Philosophical experience as set forth"*: Schlundt, "Into the Mystic with Miss Ruth," 27.

79 *"The Dance, Its Place in Life and Art"*: Martha Graham Scrapbooks, 1926–1929, box 308, Library of Congress.

79 *"she began to hold inner qualities to the light"*: Margaret Lloyd, *The Borzoi Book of Modern Dance* (New York: Alfred A. Knopf, 1949), 51.

80 *"retained the same thematic characteristics"*: John Martin, "Kreutzberg Superb in Dance Recital; Brilliant Audience Welcomes Him—Miss Graham's Unique Performance," *New York Times*, January 21, 1929.

80 *"Martha did a jump"*: Jane Dudley in Mason, *Martha Graham Remembered.*

80 *"Some of her latest and most interesting dances"*: *Theatre Arts Magazine*, March 1929, item #61 in Martha Graham Collection, 1926–1929, Library of Congress.

80 Its *"lyrical calm"*: John Martin, "Martha Graham's Recital," *New York Times*, March 4, 1929.

80 *"frighten away somnolescence"*: John Martin, "The Dance: One Artist; Martha Graham's Unique Gift and Steady Development—Current Programs," *New York Times*, March 19, 1929.

81 *"a masterpiece of Miss Graham's new style"*: Mary Watkins, *The Dance Magazine*, May 1929.

81 *She performed the piece on a small*: Stodelle, *Deep Song*, 58.

81 *Horst groused about the amount of practice*: Horst-Roosevelt transcript 1959–1960, envelope 2 of 4, p. 72, New York Public Library.

82 *Graham had written a letter*: Martha Graham to Evelyn Sabin from a westbound train, February 13, 1929 (obtained from Lionheart Autographs). A possible earlier letter hasn't been located.

82 *"sinister subdivisions"*: [Mary Watkins?], "Martha Graham Wins Acclaim in Dance Performance: Capacity Audience at Booth Theater Applauds Season's Final Appearance," *New York Herald Tribune*, April 14, 1929.

83 *"The feature of the evening"*: "Miss Graham Ends Season," *New York Telegram*, April 16, 1929.

83 *she represented "the central melody"*: Sigmund Spaeth, program notes for performance by Martha Graham and Group, presented by the Community Concert Organization of Watertown, New York, Library of Congress.

83 *"relentless march of destruction"*: [Mary Watkins?], "Martha Graham Wins Acclaim in Dance Performance."

83 *"puckish humor"*: "Miss Graham Ends Season."

83 *"Two girls on the left"*: Ibid.

84 *"laughing falls"*: Dorothy Bird gave these instructions to a Jowitt class on Graham in New York University's Department of Performance Studies during Bird's 1980 or 1986 visit.

84 *thanks to 1931 film footage of it*: New York Public Library for the Performing Arts, *MGZIC 9–1559, cassette 1.

85 "Alors, nous passerons les seuils": Anonymous poem, "Bretons Tetus," set to music by Charles de Sivry and included in Théodore Botrel, ed., *Chansons de "la Fleur-de-Lys"* (1793). Sheet music given to Jowitt by Martha Hill.

85 *"Never," wrote the dance educator Elizabeth Selden*: Elizabeth Selden, *The Dancer's Quest* (Berkeley: University of California Press, 1935), 93.

85 *heads are turned sharply*: Bessie Schönberg in Jowitt. "A Conversation with Bessie Schönberg," *Ballet Review* 9, no. 1 (Spring 1981), 31–63.

86 *Those positions, says Schönberg*: Ibid., 46.

87–88 *"this solitary dancer, not even a girl"*: Lincoln Kirstein in Armitage, *Martha Graham*, 26.

88 *and told her company members*: Schönberg quoting Hill in Jowitt, "A Conversation with Bessie Schönberg," *Ballet Review* 9, no. 1 (Spring 1981), 36.

88 *She could on occasion huddle*: De Mille, *Martha*, 185, quoting her own *Dance to the Piper* (New York: Atlantic Monthly Press/Little, Brown, 1952).

88 *"Her discipline had made her transcend her personality"*: Martha Graham to Evelyn Sabin, summer 1928.

88 *"virile" gestures*: Martha Graham, quoted in Roberts, "The Fervid Art of Martha Graham," 13.

89 *"Here, as the breath"*: William Sharp, "The White Peacock" (Part III of *Sospiri di Roma*), included in *A Victorian Anthology, 1837–1895*, ed. Edmund Clarence Stedman (1895).

89 *"The interpretation of Charles Griffes' Tone Poem"*: Kenneth Burke, *The Dial*, June 1929, Martha Graham Scrapbooks, #2, Library of Congress.

89 *one "cloud form"*: Program for Neighborhood Playhouse presentation, April 26 and 27, 1929.

89 *"the phantoms of his mind"*: Ibid.

89 *"unforgettably beautiful"*: Louis Horst, quoted in Soares, *Louis Horst*, 82.

89 *"Not until the music"*: Burke, *The Dial*, June 1929.

90 *at a "Garden Dinner"*: Martha Graham Scrapbooks, June 1929, box 309, #98, Library of Congress.

90 *In a* Dance Magazine *article*: Marks Levine, "Does Classical Dancing Pay? A Rebuttal," *The Dance Magazine*, July 1929.

90 *"We aren't country people," she told the interviewer*: Typed translation from German of an article in *Der Tag*, May 20, 1929, Martha Graham Scrapbooks, box 308, #92–94, Library of Congress.

6. FROM *RITE OF SPRING* TO A SEATTLE SCHOOL

91 *"Out of emotion comes form"*: Martha Graham (1927), in Herschel B. Chipp, *Theories of Modern Art: A Source Book by Artists and Critics*, 157, translated by Kenneth Lindsay from *"Über die Formfrage," Der Blau Reiter* (Munich: R. Piper, 1912), 74–100. Also "Seeking an American Art of the Dance," in Sayler, *Revolt in the Arts*, 122. Cited too by W. Adolphe Roberts in Armitage, *Martha Graham*, 97. Concept mentioned by Louis Sullivan in 1896, and expanded upon by Thomas E. Hibben in the January 5, 1928, edition of *The American Architect and Building News*, 250.

91 *"The form is the outer expression"*: Wassily Kandinsky, "On the Problem of Form," 1912, in Chipp, *Theories of Modern Art*, 157.

91 *"the spirit of the individual artist"*: Ibid.

92 *form is not only "determined by function"*: Thomas E. Hibben, cited in Sayler, *Revolt in the Arts*, 122.

92 *"the execution of this form"*: Ibid.

92 *"can only be in the personal vocabulary"*: Ibid.

92 *"decorative non-essentials"*: Henry-Russell Hitchcock and Philip Johnson, *The International Style: Architecture Since 1922* (1932; New York: W. W. Norton, 1966), 81. "Absence of Ornament" opens chapter 7, "A Third Principle: The Avoidance of Applied Decoration."

92 *"It would seem to me"*: Robert C. Stanley, quoted in Sheldon Cheney and Martha Candler Cheney, *Art and the Machine: An Account of Industrial Design in 20th-Century America* (New York: McGraw-Hill, 1936), 98.

92 *"The best inspiration for the architect"*: Dorothy Todd and Raymond Mortimer, *The New Interior Decoration: An Introduction to Its Principles, and International Survey of Its Methods* (New York: Charles Scribner's Sons, 1929), 20.

93 *"beginning to be manifest"*: Graham in Sayler, *Revolt in the Arts*, 254.

94 *This dance, said the woman*: Janet Eilber in Mason, *Martha Graham Remembered*.

95 *invitations went out*: The Dance Repertory Theatre began its weeklong season with a shared afternoon performance on Sunday, January 5, 1930, Scrapbooks, box 309, items #11–20, Martha Graham Collection, Library of Congress.

95 *"she is a snake"*: Doris Humphrey, quoted in Soares, *Louis Horst*, 84.

95 *José Limón recalled*: José Limón, *An Unfinished Memoir*, ed. Lynn Garafola (Middletown, CT: Wesleyan University Press, 2001), 52–53.

95 *"New Dance Theatre Scores a Success"*: *New York Times*, January 6, 1930.

96 *the* Times *reported*: "Dance Season Ends," *New York Times*, January 13, 1930, Scrapbooks, box 309, item #19, Martha Graham Collection, Library of Congress.

96 *"a beautiful choreographic poem"*: Richard Hammond, "Music and the Dance Theatre: Abstract Dance. Dance Repertory Theatre of Martha Graham, Tamiris, Doris Humphrey, Charles Weidman," *Modern Music* 7, no. 2 (February–March 1930), 20–23.

96 *she moved "with exquisite dignity"*: John Martin, "Martha Graham Gives Delightful Dance," *New York Times*, January 12, 1930, Scrapbooks, box 309, item #20, Martha Graham Collection, Library of Congress.

97 *she outshone the other three*: G.N.W., *New York Telegram*, January 12, 1930.

97 *"the robust, four square methods of Tamiris"*: Ibid.

97 *"The Pessimist waves the kerchief dolorously"*: Margaret Lloyd, "A Study in Angles—and Curves," *Christian Science Monitor*, July 30, 1932.

97 *"Martha was as simple"*: Jowitt, "A Conversation with Bessie Schönberg," *Ballet Review* 9, no. 1 (Spring 1981), 51.

98 *The* Columbus Enquirer-Sun *headlined*: "Dancers Thrill Audiences," *Columbus Enquirer-Sun*, January 16, 1930.

99 *"If her dance technique was in part non-understandable"*: "Dancers Present Modern Numbers," *Amsterdam Evening Recorder*, February 12, 1930.

99 *The program explained*: The Neighborhood Playhouse's fifteenth anniversary performances at the Mecca Temple, organized by Irene Lewisohn, Scrapbooks, box 309, 1929–1930, #30, Martha Graham Collection, Library of Congress.

100 *"a pyramid of stairs"*: Richard L. Stokes, "Music," *The Evening World*, February 21, 1930.

100 *Oscar Thompson of the* New York Post: Oscar Thompson, "Music: Symphonic

Made Visual in Alliance of Neighborhood Playhouse Mimes with Sokoloff's Orchestra," *New York Post*, February 21, 1930.

100 *"a brilliant satire on the fox-trot"*: Stokes, "Music."

100 *"a composite expression of the desires"*: *New Year's Eve in New York*, a symphonic poem in three sections by Werner Janssen. An element in the Neighborhood Playhouse performances.

101 *"little Martha throwing herself"*: Jowitt, "A Conversation with Bessie Schönberg," *Ballet Review* 9, no. 1 (Spring 1981), 51.

101 *Brooks Atkinson of the* Times: Martha Graham Scrapbooks, box 309, 1929–1930, #33, Library of Congress.

101 *Mary Watkins of the* Herald Tribune: Ibid., #34.

102 *exasperated them*: Tamara Karsavina, *Theatre Street: The Reminiscences of Tamara Karsavina* (London: Dance Books, 1981), 285.

102 *"tyranny of the bar"*: Igor Stravinsky, *The Observer*, July 3, 1921, interview quoted in Peter Hall, *Stravinsky: The Rite of Spring* (New York: Cambridge University Press, 2004), 110.

102 *The critic André Levinson*: Shelley C. Berg, *Le Sacre du Printemps: Seven Productions from Nijinsky to Martha Graham* (Ann Arbor, MI: UMI Research Press, 1988).

102 *"a spectacle of pagan Russia"*: Ibid., 67.

103 *According to Agnes de Mille*: De Mille, *Martha*, 156.

103 *Bessie Schönberg remembered*: Jowitt, "A Conversation with Bessie Schönberg," *Ballet Review* 9, no. 1 (Spring 1981), 54.

104 *sitting "in a corner, shawl over her head"*: Eleanor King, *Transformations: A Memoir; The Humphrey-Weidman Era* (Brooklyn, NY: Dance Horizons, 1978), 60.

104 *Martha "might have held back"*: Anna Sokolow, *"The Rite of Spring* at Seventy-Five," Dance Critics Association Conference, cosponsored by the Museum and Library of the Performing Arts, New York Public Library, November 5–7, 1987.

104 *"enough alike to be brother and sister"*: Graham quoting Massine, Lucy Kroll Papers, box 240, folder 7, p. 4, December 7, 1971. Transcript of interviews with Graham on tape #9, Library of Congress.

104 *Graham later said*: Graham, *Blood Memory*, 130. Also Soares, *Louis Horst*, 87.

104 *Massine suggested that Graham*: King, *Transformations*, 60.

105 *According to Richard Hammond*: Oliver Daniel, *"The Rite of Spring* in America: Graham—Stokowski—Massine," *Ballet Review* 10, no. 2 (1982).

105 *Graham herself later remarked*: Oliver Daniel, *Stokowski—Counterpoint of View* (New York: Dodd, Mead, 1982). Also Soares, *Louis Horst*, 87.

105 *"When I danced it in 1930"*: Stodelle, *Deep Song*, 71. Also Soares, *Louis Horst*, 87.

105 *"The Rite of Spring at Seventy-Five"*: Dance Critics Association Conference, cosponsored by the Museum and Library of the Performing Arts, New York Public Library, November 5–7, 1987. See Suzanne Levy, *Dance Research Journal* 19, no. 2 (Winter 1987–88), 52–54.

105 *silent film of a rehearsal*: A black-and-white record film of the dancers of the La Scala Ballet rehearsing Massine's *Sacre du Printemps* is housed in the Jerome Robbins Dance Division of the New York Public Library for the Performing Arts, Dorothy and Lewis B. Cullman Center.

105 *"In the 'Harbingers of Spring' section"*: Eleanor King, *"The Rite of Spring* at Seventy-Five," Dance Critics Association Conference.

106 *"Navaho-style things"*: Ibid. If Massine had taken Stokowski's advice and seen and been influenced by American Indian dances out west, that might indicate that his 1930 *Sacre* was not identical to his 1920 one. He had seen some tribal dances in Washington, D.C., when on tour with Les Ballets Russes in 1917.

106 *Rady recalled a sequence*: Lily Mehlman Rady, *"The Rite of Spring* at Seventy-Five," Dance Critics Association Conference.

106 *"My set, stamping along"*: King, *Transformations*, 65.

106 *Graham had been tactfully told by Stokowski*: Ibid., 60.

107 *Stokowski . . . often attended rehearsals*: Ibid., 61.

107 *perched on a sawhorse*: Ibid., 62.

107 *"the quadruple shock"*: Alex Ross, *The Rest Is Noise: Listening to the Twentieth Century* (New York: Farrar, Straus and Giroux, 2007), 81.

107 *"great crunching, snarling chords"*: Donal Henahen, "Philharmonic Incarnations of Spring," *New York Times*, March 23, 1984.

107 *"a delirious spin"*: Unnamed critic cited by Neil Baldwin in "Defining Modern Dance: Martha Graham and *The Rite of Spring* in America," a paper he delivered at Sacre Celebration, a conference at York College, Toronto, on April 20, 1913.

108 *Sokolova, as Nijinsky's doomed heroine*: Lydia Sokolova, *Dancing for Diaghilev: The Memoirs of Lydia Sokolova*, ed. Richard Buckle (London: John Murray, 1960), 165.

108 *"thought about trying to hear things"*: Marcia B. Siegel's notes, taken during a class conducted by Bonnie Bird for Jowitt's course "Isadora Duncan and Hellenism," in New York University's Department of Performance Studies in 1984 and 1990.

108 *the women on the 1987 panel all remembered*: Oliver Daniel on the timing of the "Danse Sacrale" in his essay *"The Rite of Spring* in America: Graham—Stokowski—Massine," *Ballet Review* 10, no. 2 (1982). Presented at the conference of the Society of Dance History Scholars. Listening to a relevant phonograph recording, he clocks Graham's final sacrificial dance as being four minutes and fifty-six seconds long.

108 *"She was in the air practically all the time"*: Bessie Schönberg, *"The Rite of Spring* at Seventy-Five," Dance Critics Association Conference.

109 *"Once again you fix your longing"*: Tom Beck, "The Literary Sources of 'Die Glückliche Hand,'" *Tempo*, no. 189 (1994), 17–23, www.jstor.org/stable /945150. See also cast members listed in box 309, #45 (Tuesday, April 22, 1930), Library of Congress.

109 *"Martha showed us"*: Bell-Kanner, *Frontiers*, 13.

109 *Dorothy Bird*: Dorothy Bird and Joyce Greenberg, *Bird's Eye View: Dancing with Martha Graham and on Broadway* (Pittsburgh: University of Pittsburgh Press, 1997). Bird gives space and resonance to her description of Graham's classes at Seattle's Cornish School, 32–36.

110 *"Here in this class"*: Martha Graham, quoted in Bell-Kanner, *Frontiers*, 13.

110 *"Miss Aunt Nellie"*: Ibid., 12.

111 *"Feel as if you have whiskers"*: Martha Graham, quoted in Bird and Greenberg, *Bird's Eye View*, 21.

111 *And how hard they worked*: Bonnie Bird taught a class at Senta Driver's studio for Jowitt's NYU students. And in 1981 Driver invited Bird to come to her studio and teach her company members the movements that figured in classes that Martha Graham taught in 1931–38.

111 *having the power to split a rock*: Bird and Greenberg, *Bird's Eye View*, 37.

112 *Jean Mercier, the director of*: Nellie Cornish in ibid., 19.

112 *"uniform and rhythmic grace"*: "Greek Drama Stalks Stage at Cornish," *Seattle Times*, July 30, 1930.

113 *Dorothy Bird mentions "Dance of Grief"*: Bird and Greenberg, *Bird's Eye View*, 48.

113 *"I haven't yet gotten over the thrill"*: Martha Graham to Evelyn Sabin from Santa Barbara, California, August 13, 1928, Evelyn Sabin Papers, (S) *MGZMD 414, Jerome Robbins Dance Division, New York Public Library.

113 *According to Horst's diary*: Soares, *Louis Horst*, 89.

7. PRIMITIVE MYSTERIES AND THE BIRTH OF MODERN DANCE

114 *"a sort of Ford plant for the reproduction of sculpture"*: Sayler, *Revolt in the Arts*, 167.

115 *Lillian Gish laments the invention*: Lillian Gish, "On Behalf of the Silent Film," in ibid., 225.

115 *"We are no longer preoccupied"*: Paul T. Frankl, *Form and Re-Form* (New York: Harper & Brothers, 1930), 3.

115 *"Fatuous in our adoration"*: Graham, "Seeking an American Art of the Dance," in Sayler, *Revolt in the Arts*, 250.

115 *"dance toward freedom"*: Martha Graham in Armitage, *Martha Graham*, 99.

116 *"I arrived when they were dancing"*: Martha Graham to Dorothy Elmhirst, September 7, 1931; Soares, *Louis Horst*, 100.

117 *show a striking correspondence*: In letters exchanged between Jowitt and Claude Stephenson (the folk arts coordinator and state folklorist at New Mexico Arts), Stephenson pointed out that of the thirteen to seventeen possible segments of a Matachines dance, these three are always a part of it. Given the many Matachines performances, he thinks it likely that Graham would have seen one, as well as have read and heard about the dance prior to beginning work on *Primitive Mysteries*. Louis Horst's journal (cited by Soares, *Louis Horst*, 105) reveals that he and Graham had seen a Matachines dance in Santa Fe, but that entry is dated September 1932, almost a year after *Primitive Mysteries* premiered.

117 *"It is a participation in a rite"*: Graham, quoted by Anna Kisselgoff, "Martha Graham Explores Primitive Mysteries," *New York Times*, January 31, 1999.

117 *"the metaphor was"*: Interview with Jean Nuchtern by Katy Matheson for the Dance Division of the Performing Arts Library, New York Public Library, audio file #1, transcript, *MGZMT 3–585, 27.

118 *"It is not a dance you go to"*: Marcia B. Siegel, *The Shapes of Change: Images of American Dance* (Boston: Houghton Mifflin, 1979), 50.

118 *"a few incisive strokes"*: Arlene Croce, *Writing in the Dark, Dancing in the New Yorker: An Arlene Croce Reader* (New York: Farrar, Straus and Giroux, 2003).

118 *as Siegel has pointed out*: Siegel, *Shapes of Change*, 58.

118 *The dancers entering from stage left*: Seen in a 1964 performance of *Primitive Mysteries* (1931) at Connecticut College. The revival was part of a memorial program that honored Louis Horst, who had died that January.

119 *a night-blooming cereus*: Kisselgoff, "Martha Graham Explores Primitive Mysteries."

119 *Dorothy Bird, a member of*: Bird and Greenberg, *Bird's Eye View*, 76.

119 *When Yuriko danced the leading role*: Yuriko Kikuchi, interviewed by Jowitt, January 20, 2015.

122 *Graham laid a broom handle*: Bird and Greenberg, *Bird's Eye View*, 74.

123 *spent the night in her dressing room*: McDonagh, *Martha Graham*, 80.

123 *sent helpers down to Orchard Street*: Don McDonagh, "A Chat with Martha Graham," *Ballet Review* 2, no. 4 (1968), 24.

123 *the input of . . . the early dancers*: Virginia Briton, Hortense Bunsick, Grace Cornell, Louise Creston, Dorothy Bird, Ailes Gilmour, Georgia Graham, Pauline Nelson, Mary Rivoire, Joan Woodruff, Lillian Ray, Ethel Rudy, Bessie Schönberg, Lillian Shapero, Gertrude Shurr, Anna Sokolow, Martha Todd, Ruth White. These are the members of Graham's company in 1931. Only twelve appeared in *Primitive Mysteries*.

123 *a tiny film clip*: Marcia Lerner Hofer confirmed (in "'Primitive Mysteries': A History, Analysis and Memoir," summer 1979) that the film showed Helen Priest Rogers, who didn't dance in that first production but had seen the original version.

123 *Barbara Morgan's remarkable 1940 photographs*: Morgan, *Martha Graham: Sixteen Dances in Photographs*.

123 *"could lift up a truck with no problem"*: See "Interview with Jean Nuchtern, 1979," New York Public Library Digital Collections, at https://digitalcollec tions.nypl.org/items/dfd5b790-c318-0133-8d14-60f81dd2b63c.

124 *Graham could inspire the dancers*: Hofer, "'Primitive Mysteries,'" 1. (Hofer danced in the piece's 1964 revival.)

124 *"to be noticed as an individual"*: Ibid., 16.

124 *a work of "major importance"*: John Martin, "Martha Graham Acclaimed in Dance: Her Group, Appearing in the Repertory Theatre, Seen as Equaling the Best," *New York Times*, February 3, 1931.

125 *"a grand girl but a bad dancer"*: Doris Humphrey to her mother, November 31, 1930, cited in King, *Transformations*, 114.

125 *"Not just tilting"*: Bird and Greenberg, *Bird's Eye View*, 81.

125 *"a suggestion of the Dionysiac rites"*: Martin, "Martha Graham Acclaimed in Dance."

126 *"both stark in their simplicity"*: Ibid.

126 *Graham joined de Mille*: De Mille, *Martha*, 121.

126 *Martha gripped the young woman's hand*: Bell-Kanner, *Frontiers*, 22.

127 *"overwhelmed by the gray Germanic wave"*: Robert Reiss, "Miss Graham Dance; Irish Players Score Against Philadelphia," *Philadelphia Record*, November 16, 1932.

127 *"Mary Wigman, through her greatness"*: Soares, *Louis Horst*, 90.

127 *"would almost seem impossible"*: Martin, "Martha Graham Acclaimed in Dance."

128 *Jane Dudley recalled struggling*: Jane Dudley, "The Early Life of an American Modern Dancer," *Dance Research: The Journal of the Society for Dance Research* 10, no. 1 (Spring 1992), 18.

129 *In a sample 1930s Graham class*: In November 1981 Senta Driver invited Bonnie Bird to come to her studio and teach the members of her company, Harry, movements taught by Martha Graham in her 1931–38 classes. Notes on the class courtesy of Marcia B. Siegel.

129 *a snake balancing*: Bessie Schönberg, interviewed in Marian Horosko, comp., *Martha Graham: The Evolution of Her Dance Theory and Training 1926–1991* (Gainesville: University Press of Florida, 2002), 25.

130 *"This angularity is only apparent"*: Frances Hawkins, quoted in Lloyd, "A Study in Angles—and Curves."

131 *a man in the audience began to question*: Mikhail Fokine, "The Old and the New in Dance at Odds," *Literary Digest*, May 19, 1931. His angry rebuttal of the episode published in the Russian magazine *Novoye Russkoye Slovo*, translated as "The Sad Art," appeared in the May 31 issue of *The Dance Magazine*. The brouhaha is also described in Soares, *Louis Horst*, 96–97, 112.

131 *"Ugly girl makes ugly movements"*: Mikhail Fokine quoted by Walter Terry, "Coq d'Or Created in 16 Days, Says Michel Fokine on Boston Visit," *Boston Herald*, November 4, 1937.

131 *Words he wrote*: Victor Dandré, *Anna Pavlova in Art & Life* (New York, Benjamin Blom Inc., 1972), 272.

133 *"when Miss Graham told me she intended"*: Aaron Copland, reminiscences assembled by Marta Elaine Robertson for Mason, *Martha Graham Remembered*.

133 *"a defiant howl of a piece"*: Howard Pollack, *Aaron Copland: The Life and Work of an Uncommon Man* (New York: Henry Holt, 1999), 152.

134 *Graham fell back and rose repeatedly*: Ibid., 154.

134 *"Orgiastic abandon"*: John Martin, quoted in Pollack, *Aaron Copland*.

134 *"we were all pink in those days"*: Horst in Mason, *Martha Graham Remembered*.

134 *"A primitive evocation of natural forces"*: Graham, program note, Library of Congress.

134 *"a Pierrot who wears his rue with a difference"*: John Martin, "Martha Graham, Dancer, Is Cheered," *New York Times*, December 7, 1931.

134 *"Miss Graham wrought a dance pattern"*: Russell Rhodes, "Graham Shows Grace, Rhythm," *New York Telegraph*, November 22, 1932, 33.

8. CREATING DANCES FOR PLAYS

136 *they glowed at the remembered luxury*: "Martha Graham's Early Technique and Dances: The 1930s, a Panel Discussion," in *Choreography and Dance* (ed. Alice Helpern), vol. 5, part 2 (1999). The entry details the Brooklyn Academy of Music's NEXT WAVE Festival presentation on October 1, 1994, of "Radical Graham: A One Day Symposium" at the New School for Social Research. Participants: former Graham company members Thelma Babitz, Dorothy

Bird, Jane Dudley, Freda Flier, Marie Marchowsky, and Sophie Maslow; Deborah Jowitt moderator.

137 *Lincoln Kirstein wrote admiringly*: Lincoln Kirstein, *Thirty Years: The New York City Ballet* (New York: Alfred A. Knopf, 1978), 68.

138 *Among those whom Laura Elliott had coached*: "Neighborhood Playhouse Studios shows off its student, afternoon program and evening programs," May 23 and 24, 1932. Louis Horst, Scrapbooks, 1915–1959, *MGZRS, Dance Division of the Performing Arts Library, New York Public Library.

138 *Horst developed the two courses*: The material was published in his *Pre-Classic Dance Forms* (1937) and *Modern Dance Forms* (1960).

139 *"to get European recognition"*: Martha Graham, application to the John Simon Guggenheim Memorial Foundation for a grant to perform in Europe, February 29, 1931, courtesy of the John Simon Guggenheim Memorial Foundation.

139 *"one of the greatest dancers"*: Leopold Stokowski to Henry Allen Moe, recommending a Guggenheim grant to Graham, ibid.

139 *"the only dancer in America"*: Henry Cowell to Henry Allen Moe, recommending a Guggenheim grant to Graham, ibid.

139–40 *a "creative art on a par with the drama, music and sculpture"*: Wallingford Riegger to Henry Allen Moe, recommending a Guggenheim grant to Graham, ibid.

140 *"one of the greatest creative artists of the day"*: Carlos Salzedo to Henry Allen Moe, recommending a Guggenheim grant to Graham, ibid.

140 *"I do not think our dancers"*: Edith J. R. Isaacs to Henry Allen Moe, recommending a Guggenheim grant to Graham, ibid.

140 *"To me the answer to the dancer"*: Graham to Henry Allen Moe, February 23, 1932, ibid.

140 *"the native dances of Mexico and Yucatan"*: Moe to Graham, February 26, 1932, ibid.

140 *In her "charming French," the great Spanish dancer*: "Martha Graham at Guild," *New Haven Register*, November 27, 1932.

141 *The land she called "dangerous" and "insatiable"*: Graham to Henry Allen Moe, August 6, 1932, courtesy of the John Simon Guggenheim Memorial Foundation.

142 *"To this tumultuous flood of Chavez's chaotic music"*: Bonnie Bird to her mother, in Bell-Kanner, *Frontiers*, 33.

142 *"a single musical line"*: John Martin, "Martha Graham in 3 New Dances," *New York Times*, November 21, 1932.

143 *"an exquisite thing"*: Bonnie Bird to her mother, in Bell-Kanner, *Frontiers*, 33.

144 *"vulgar plausibility"*: Stark Young, *Theatre Arts Monthly*, quoted in Katharine Cornell, *I Wanted to Be an Actress: The Autobiography of Katharine Cornell* (New York: Random House, 1939).

144 *"the disciplined fury"*: Brooks Atkinson, "The Play: Fleeing the Wimpole Street Ogre," *New York Times*, February 10, 1931.

145 *According to Agnes de Mille*: De Mille, *Martha*, 189.

146 *"Miss Cornell and Mr. McClintic gratefully acknowledge"*: Program for Cornell's December 1932 appearances at New York's Belasco Theatre in *The Rape of*

Lucrece, Thornton Wilder's translation of André Obey's *Le Viol de Lucrèce*, Martha Graham Scrapbook 310, #62, Library of Congress.

146 *"The high, white tones of her voice"*: "The Play: Katharine Cornell Presenting Thornton Wilder's Translation of Andre Obey's 'Lucrece,'" *New York Times*, December 21, 1932.

146 *"Stilted" was one of the words*: Stark Young, "Sorrow's Sharp Sustaining," December 20, 1932. Reprinted in Stark Young, *Immortal Shadows: A Book of Dramatic Criticism* (New York: Hill & Wang, 1948), 33–37.

146 *"I agreed with one of the critics"*: Cornell, *I Wanted to Be an Actress*, 118.

146 *Samuel "Roxy" Rothafel was opening*: *New York Times*, December 25, 1932. See also Martha Graham Scrapbooks 310, #42, Library of Congress.

147 *a preposterous surfeit*: Bonnie Bird in Bell-Kanner, *Frontiers*, 35.

147 *"The stage floor was still moving"*: Ibid., 35–36.

148 *"He especially loved Martha's dances"*: Ibid., 36.

148 *"She ran furiously, she leaped"*: John Martin, "The Dance: The First Experiment at Radio City," *New York Times*, January 8, 1933.

149 *"We diehards made a point"*: Martha Hill to Janet Mansfield Soares, cited in Soares, *Louis Horst*, 111.

149 *"It took exactly one week"*: "Roxy Slips," *New Haven Register*, January 15, 1933, Martha Graham Scrapbooks 310, #53, Library of Congress.

149 *speech that Hecuba delivered*: Marian Seldes, "A Chronology," in Mason, *Martha Graham Remembered*, 5.

149 *one student actor*: Graham, *Blood Memory*, 121.

150 *"roped into [it] against her will"*: Bonnie Bird, letter to her mother, quoted in Bell-Kanner, *Frontiers*, 39.

150 *Natalie Hays Hammond and Alice Laughlin*: Courtesy of Martha Graham Resources, 1931–33.

152 *"Martha hates directing plays"*: Bonnie Bird to her mother, cited in Bell-Kanner, *Frontiers*, 39.

152 *"possessed of a kind of loveliness"*: John Mason Brown, "Two on the Aisle," *New York Post*, February 6, 1933.

152 *"Sometimes they were motifs"*: Stark Young, "Moments of Miracle," *The New Republic*, March 1, 1933. See also his *Immortal Shadows*, 254.

153 *The dancers she supplied*: John Martin, "The Dance: With Drama," *New York Times*, June 18, 1933.

153 *In this tale, of a young woman*: Production details may be seen in Folder #114, Martha Graham Scrapbooks 309, Library of Congress.

154 *"moved into a new field"*: John Martin, "Martha Graham Ends Dance Series," *New York Times*, May 5, 1933.

154 *"first-rate artist" had gone astray*: Lucille Marsh, *Dance Culture*, January 1933.

155 *"a darling—old-fashioned"*: Bonnie Bird to her mother, quoted in Bell-Kanner, *Frontiers*, 41.

156 *"By every sign, she is the actress"*: Martin, "Martha Graham Ends Dance Series."

156 *"some soft white nun's veiling"*: Cornell, *I Wanted to Be an Actress*, 127.

156 *"an eager child, rushing toward love"*: Richard Lockridge, *New York Sun*, December 21, 1936.

156 *"moves gracefully and lightly"*: John Mason Brown, *New York Post*, December 21, 1936.

157 *"I went up to her"*: Graham, *Blood Memory*, 146.

157 *"Martha suddenly got the idea"*: Bonnie Bird, quoted in Bell-Kanner, *Frontiers*, 47.

9. SUMMERING IN BENNINGTON, FORGING *FRONTIER*

158 *grainy film clips*: In the summer of 1938 at Bennington College, Doris Isabelle Ewing filmed her colleagues and teachers in color. The copyrighted mp4 version is housed in Bennington's Crosset Library and can be viewed at https://crossettlibrary.dspacedirect.org/handle/11209/10136.

159 *"The Big Four" of modern dance*: Sali Ann Kriegsman, *Modern Dance in America: The Bennington Years* (Boston: G. K. Hall, 1981), 11.

159 *"Bennington was the first time"*: Norman Lloyd and his wife, Ruth; José Limón and his wife, Pauline; and Bessie Schönberg participated in a 1959 discussion held at Connecticut College, moderated by Jeanette Schlottmann Roosevelt and Martin Masters. See Elizabeth McPherson, ed., *The Bennington School of the Dance: A History in Writings and Interviews* (Jefferson, NC: McFarland, 2013), 312.

160 *"simplicity, directness, and relation"*: Robert D. Leigh, *Bennington College Bulletin*, *Bennington School of the Dance* 2, no. 1 (August 1933). Material in the Vermont college's Crossett Library. Also cited in Kriegsman, *Modern Dance in America*, 33, note 1.

160 *Graham in turn recommended Martha Hill*: Kriegsman, *Modern Dance in America*, 6.

160 *They were offered*: *Bennington College Bulletin* 2, no. 3 (February 1934), 5.

161 *"one step ahead"*: John Martin, quoted in Kriegsman, *Modern Dance in America*, 12.

161 *"The modern dance, in common"*: Robert Devore Leigh, quoted in *Bennington College Bulletin* 2, no. 3 (February 1934), 1, cited in Kriegsman, *Modern Dance in America*, 11.

162 *"The endless chains of pupils"*: T.B.W., "The Bennington School of the Dance: Another Successful Session Draws to a Close," *Brooklyn Eagle*, August 11, 1935.

162 *Graham's dancers often assisted*: Soares, *Louis Horst*, 115.

162 *she offered to lend a tweed coat*: Bell-Kanner, *Frontiers*, 50.

163 *"Tookie the Tin Chicken"*: Bird and Greenberg, *Bird's Eye View*, 100.

163 *"a sensational pot roast"*: Ibid., 61.

163 *"Italian style" green beans*: Ibid.

164 *"a fussy Rotarian type"*: Bonnie Bird, quoted in Bell-Kanner, *Frontiers*, 57.

164 *"Oh those first-year parties"*: Norman Lloyd, quoted in McPherson, *Bennington School of the Dance*, 231.

164 *Bessie Schönberg later reminded*: Ibid., 229.

164 *"At 12 o'clock"*: Ibid., 231.

165 *"To the American dancer I say"*: Martha Graham in Stewart, *Modern Dance*, 55.

165 *"An American dance is not a series"*: Ibid., 56.

165 *a hundred times*: Freda Flier Maddow in Francis Mason, "A Conversation with Freda Flier Maddow," *Ballet Review* (Fall 2006), 48.

165 *According to Bonnie Bird*: Bell-Kanner, *Frontiers*, 49.

166 *The work began with Graham*: Bird and Greenberg, *Bird's Eye View*, 97–98.

167 *"the essence of the ferocious"*: John Martin, "The Dance: Graham Again," *New York Times*, November 25, 1934.

167 *"grim gauntness"*: *Musical Digest*, December 1935.

168 *"cutting the stage space"*: Isamu Noguchi, *Essays and Conversations*, ed. Diane Apostolos-Cappadona and Bruce Altshuler (New York: Harry N. Abrams / The Isamu Noguchi Foundation, Inc. 1994), 51.

168 *five dancers braided*: Bonnie Bird, in Bell-Kanner, *Frontiers*, 70.

168 *a black-and-white film*: Martha Graham and Company, video recording, *MGZHB 6–2116, New York Public Library for the Performing Arts.

170 *"[Walt] Whitman's unrealized dream"*: Lincoln Kirstein, quoted in de Mille, *Martha*, 221.

170 *"Miss Graham steps"*: Leopold Stokowski, in Armitage, *Martha Graham*, 35.

170 *she wisely declined*: W. J. Henderson, *New York Sun*, November 1, 1935.

171 *Actors playing various types of citizens*: Archibald MacLeish, *Panic: A Play in Verse* (Boston: Houghton Mifflin, 1935).

171 *"the attempt to use the crowd"*: Ellen Perley Frank, "MacLeish Relives an Early Stage Work," *New York Times*, July 6, 1980. See also "A Note on the Verse" in *Panic: A Play in Verse*, x.

171 *"nervous, not muscular"*: "A Note on the Verse," in *Panic: A Play in Verse*, viii.

172 *"was mostly occupied by Martha Graham"*: John Houseman, *Run-Through: A Memoir* (New York: Simon and Schuster, 1972), 154.

172 *"arrangement of the crowd"*: Stark Young, cited in ibid., 155.

172 *"Although the poet"*: Unnamed "critic of the left," cited in ibid.

172 *"so full of dust"*: Jo Mielziner, quoted in ibid., 153, footnote.

173 *Martha Hill had decided*: Janet Mansfield Soares, *Martha Hill and the Making of American Dance* (Middletown, CT: Wesleyan University Press, 2009), 49.

173 *"part of the national consciousness"*: Martha Graham, program note for *Panorama*, in Kriegsman, *Modern Dance in America*, 131.

174 *he based his composition*: Norman Lloyd, quoted in ibid., 132.

174 *"so we rigged them up"*: Martha Graham, November 12, 1976, quoted in ibid., 134.

174 *"huge, jointed, scissor-like"*: Bonnie Bird, quoted in Bell-Kanner, *Frontiers*, 79–80.

175 *"Rarely has a dance ended so brilliantly"*: Henry Gilfond, *Dance Observer*, March 1935.

175 *Silent black-and-white footage*: *Panorama*: excerpts; [and] *American document*: excerpts [video recording], *MGZIA 4–3793, New York: Library and Museum of the Performing Arts.

176 *The "dignified" opening*: Edna Ocko, "Martha Graham's 'Panorama,'" *New Theatre*, no. 2 (September 1935), 27.

176 *John Martin was impressed*: *New York Times*, September 1, 1935, noted in Kriegsman, *Modern Dance in America*, 135.

177 *"the first full-length"*: Martha Graham, 1936–37 souvenir program note for Bennington performance, 1935, cited in Kriegsman, *Modern Dance in America*, 46.

177 *"an American Salzburg"*: T.B.W., *Brooklyn Eagle*, August 11, 1935.

177 *Jacques Barzun spoke*: Kriegsman, *Modern Dance in America*, 49.

178 *"I do not make social"*: Martha Graham, quoted in "Martha Graham Compels Her Audience to Interpret," *New Canaan Advertiser*, August 20, 1936 (paraphrased by the writer).

178 *"The figure like a giant bird"*: Stanley Burnshaw, "Five Dancers in Fourteen New Works," *New Masses*, December 10, 1935.

178 *"might be taken for"*: Edwin F. Melvin, "Martha Graham in an Evening of the Dance," *Boston Evening Transcript*, February 6, 1936.

178 *"magnificent struttings"*: *Boston Traveler*, February 6, 1936.

178 *"costumes deemed contemporary"*: "Chatter," *Santa Barbara Press*, September 22, 1935.

179 *"skillfully manipulated"*: Russell Rhodes, "Cheer Dance at Guild: Martha Graham Triumphs," *New York Telegraph*, November 12, 1935.

179 *"apricot"*: Pitts Sanborn, "Dance Group in Program at the Guild," *New York World Telegram*, November 11, 1935.

179 *twenty-five pounds*: Caption for full-page photo in box 313, #59, Martha Graham Scrapbooks, Library of Congress.

179 *"not specifically American"*: G. G., "Martha Graham Gives New Dance: 'Horizons,'" *New York Post*, February 24, 1936.

179 *"the dances do not interpret"*: Martha Graham, program for Guild Theatre, February 1936.

180 *a variation on* Frontier: J. M. [John Martin], "Martha Graham's Recital," *New York Times*, February 24, 1936.

180 *"new sentient warmth"*: H. G. [Henry Gilfond], *Dance Observer*, April 1936.

180 *the other did not*: *New York Herald Tribune*, February 24, 1936.

180 *"a monstrous corkscrew"*: G. G., "Martha Graham Gives New Dance."

181 *"prolonged applause"*: Stanley Bigelow, *Los Angeles Evening News*, April 11, 1936.

181 *"showered with blossoms"*: Eleanor Barnes, "Miss Graham Given Ovation," *Los Angeles Daily News*, April 8, 1936.

181 *"an Edith Wharton"*: Eugene Stinson, "Martha Graham, Modernist Dancer, Pleases in Recital Here," *Music Views* (Chicago), April 28[?], 1936.

181 *"one woman in the audience"*: Marion Park Louis, *Peninsula Herald* (Monterey), March 29[?], 1936.

181 *"You find her magnificent"*: Arnette Burgess, "Dance," *The Peninsulan*, May 1936.

181 *"I would find it"*: "Dancer Turns Down Bid to Nazi Festival," *Daily Worker*, March 16, 1936. Graham's refusal was also noted in the *New York Post* that day and a day later in the *Chicago Tribune*.

181 *"So many artists"*: Martha Graham, quoted in Victoria Phillips, "Cultural Diplomacy and Fighting the Atheist Totalitarian 'Other': Modern Dancer Martha Graham, the Military, and Radio Free Europe," June 16, 2016, www

.osaarchivum.org/files/fellowships/visegrad/reports/2016/PHILLIPS
-201601.pdf.

182 *"Martha was always very intense"*: Theodora Wiesner interviewed by Theresa
Bowers in McPherson, *Bennington School of the Dance*, 253. See also Theodora
Wiesner, letter to Theresa Bowers, quoted in Soares, *Martha Hill and the Making of American Modern Dance*, 70.

182 *"no more than open dress rehearsals"*: Kirstein, *Thirty Years*, 49. See also Lincoln
Kirstein, "Blast at Ballet," in *Three Pamphlets Collected* (Brooklyn, NY: Dance
Horizons, 1967), 41–42.

10. WORKING THROUGH WAR AND LOVE; ERICK ARRIVES

184 *December 1934 issue of* Vanity Fair *featured a drawing*: Gouache on paper for
Vanity Fair, private collection, http://bloximages.newyork1.vip.townnews
.com/santafenewmexican.com/content/tncms/assets/v3/editorial/1/f1
/1f185b40–44f3–11e4–8be8.

184 *In the end, Rand snipes*: Irving Drutman, "High Priestess of the Dance," an
appreciation of Martha Graham by Irving Drutman, *Cue*, September 26,
1936.

184 *the comedian Fanny Brice garbed herself*: www.artnet.com/artists/albert
-hirschfeld/fanny-brice-singing-modernistic-moe-d-APCHhF-UWZF
-P0QKRTMg2.

185 *Graham said she was a fan of Brice's*: Lucy Kroll Papers, box 240, folder 6, item
#3 (transcribed from reel 4, side A).

185 *"She is thin, plain, gaunt, unadorned"*: Harry Salpeter, "Martha Graham," *Mademoiselle*, February 1937.

185 *her refusal to take her company to Berlin*: *The New York Times* printed Graham's
letter of reply to the invitation from the Ministry of Culture of the Third
Reich to present her company at the 1936 Berlin Olympics. Quoted in Soares,
Louis Horst, 123; mentioned in "Dancer Turns Down Bid to Nazi Festival,"
Daily Worker, March 16, 1936.

185 *performed at the Sixth Plenum Celebration*: Martha Graham Scrapbooks,
box 311 (1935–36), #2, Library of Congress.

186 *Eleven days later she spoke on "Dance and the Theatre"*: Ibid., #3.

187 *"a red cascade"*: Ibid.

187 *John Martin found it so transformed*: John Martin, "Martha Graham and Her
Group Present Second Program of Season at Guild Theatre," *New York Times*,
February 28, 1936.

189 *A writer for* The New Masses *wonders*: "A Note on the Modern Dance," *New
Masses*, January 19, 1937.

189 *"the colors suggest blood and desolation"*: "Martha Graham and Group," *Dance
Observer*, January 1937.

190 *into a mourning veil*: Margaret Lloyd, *Christian Science Monitor*, January 5,
1937.

190 *"'Chronicle' does not attempt to show"*: Program, March 2, 1937. A clip of a reconstructed *Chronicle* may be viewed at danceinteractive.jacobspillow.org
/martha-graham-dance-company/chronicle/.

190 *"dryness" and "overformalism"*: John Martin, "Martha Graham in Dance Recital," *New York Times*, December 21, 1936.

190 *"passionate performance" made the difference*: John Martin, "Martha Graham and Her Group Present Second Program of Season at Guild Theatre," *New York Times*, December 28, 1936.

191 *"a lively work of art"*: John Martin, "Martha Graham Scores in Dances," *New York Times*, March 3, 1937.

191 *Eleanor Roosevelt, chatting with Graham*: "My Day," March 1, 1937. See https://erpapers.columbian.gwu.edu/my-day (look up by date).

191 *Martha had not wanted to dine*: Soares, *Louis Horst*, 131.

192 *Horst's favorite restaurant*: Carlus Dyer (ed. Francis Mason), "Carlus Dyer on Graham," *Ballet Review* (September 2017), 82, 83.

192 *"long, white, loose-fitting gown"*: Ibid., 84.

192 *Bessie Schönberg said*: Jowitt, "A Conversation with Bessie Schönberg," *Ballet Review* 9, no. 1 (Spring 1981).

193 *Graham wrote him that she had gone to Brentano's*: Dyer, "Carlus Dyer on Graham," 84.

193 *on the summer solstice*: Carlus Dyer in Mason, *Martha Graham Remembered*.

193 *the Spanish Civil War heroine Dolores Ibárruri*: See Imogen Morley, "Anatomy of a Speech: ¡No Passarán!—Dolores Ibárruri," https://imogenmorley.wordpress.com/2017/08/20/anatomy-of-a-speech-no-pasaran-dolores-ibarruri/.

194 *Graham and Horst had visited him*: Bird and Greenberg, *Bird's Eye View*, 254.

194 *Cowell had constructed an "elastic form"*: Norman Lloyd, "Sound Companion for Dance," part of "Henry Cowell, a Dancer's Musician," *Dance Scope* 2, no. 2 (Spring 1966), 11–12.

194 *John Martin praised Cowell's "deeply poignant music"*: John Martin, "The Dance: New England: Festival Notes—Martha Graham Premiere," *New York Times*, August 15, 1937.

194 *Immediate Tragedy was the "apogee of all her works"*: Limón, *An Unfinished Memoir*, 83.

194 *"Lest there may be something"*: Martin, "The Dance: New England: Festival Notes—Martha Graham Premiere."

195 *"wiry concentration, her awkward"*: Lincoln Kirstein in Armitage, *Martha Graham*, 24. See also Lincoln Kirstein Diaries, Journals, (S) *MGZMD 123–20 (May 26, 1933–January 24, 1934), folder 21, Dance Collection, New York Public Library.

195 *"keystone masterpiece"*: Ibid., 33.

195 *Martha wrote to Dyer*: From Graham at 66 Fifth Avenue to Dyer at 125 N. Catalina Avenue, Redondo Beach, August 9, 1937.

195 *Holm later wrote*: Hanya Holm, "Trend Grew Upon Me," *Magazine of Art* 31, no. 3 (March 1938), 137.

196 *The dramatic poem by Michael Gold*: "Strange Funeral in Braddock," www.ideals.illinois.edu/bitstream/handle/2142/30246/gold-stra.pdf?sequence=2.

196 *The text crucial to Blecher's work*: Ellen Graff, *Stepping Left: Dance and Politics in New York City, 1928–1942* (Durham, NC: Duke University Press, 1997), 61.

197 *"would spend the late afternoons alone"*: Dyer, "Carlus Dyer on Graham," 87.

197 *their friendship lasted much longer*: www.vintagememorabilia.com/index.cfm /page/martha-graham-autograph-love-letter-signed-carlos-dyer/.

197 *"who would bring me to re-birth"*: Martha Graham to Carlus Dyer, April 16, 1938 (Good Friday), quoted in Dyer, "Carlus Dyer on Graham," 87.

197 *"in the greatest tradition of Stravinsky"*: George Antheil in Armitage, *Martha Graham*, 76–77.

197 *"stunned and shaken"*: Armitage, *Martha Graham*, foreword.

198 *"A hint of Spanish feeling"*: Margaret Lloyd, *Christian Science Monitor*, November 3, 1938.

198 *"'Deep Song' is not meant to be"*: Program for Martha Graham and Company, March 10, 1939, Library of Congress (online).

199 *when Martha announced, "Erick and I come in here"*: Erick Hawkins, in Kriegsman, *Modern Dance in America*, 260.

200 *she told Marcia Minor*: Daily Worker, October 7, 1938.

200 *although he later said*: Kriegsman, *Modern Dance in America*, 193, 198.

200 *The* American Document *scenario*: "Dance Libretto, *American Document* by Martha Graham, with Four Scenes from the Dance," *Theatre Arts* 26, no. 9 (September 1942), 565–74.

200 "Say, who are you that mumbles in the dark?": Langston Hughes, "Let America Be America Again," www.poetryfoundation.org/poems/147907/let -america-be-america-again.

200 *"The people is the grand canyon"*: Carl Sandburg, *The People, Yes* (1936; New York: Harcourt Brace, 1990), 253–54.

204 *The few filmed fragments*: Selections from Panorama and American Document, Bennington School of the Dance (16mm, silent, approximately 15 minutes).

204 *Jean Erdman, who joined her company*: Jean Erdman, interviewed in Kriegsman, *Modern Dance in America*, 194.

205 *"an experiment of immeasurable significance"*: Joseph Arnold Kaye, *Dance* 5, no. 1 (October 1938), 11, quoted in Kriegsman, *Modern Dance in America*, 197.

205 *"The whole piece was so nobly framed"*: Lincoln Kirstein, "Martha Graham at Bennington," *The Nation* 147, no. 10 (September 3, 1938), 230–31.

206 *"as successful a combination"*: John Martin, *New York Times*, August 7, 1938, cited in Kriegsman, *Modern Dance in America*, 197.

206 *"the stripped clean, poetic words"*: Lloyd, *The Borzoi Book of Modern Dance*, 62.

206 *"bloodless, characterless, humorless"*: Walter Terry, *Boston Herald*, October 16, 1938.

206 *"the monotony of equal thrusts"*: Edwin Denby, "With the Dancers," *Modern Music* 16, no. 2 (January–February 1939), 130. Also in Martha Graham Collection, box 314, Library of Congress.

206 *"beauty and power"*: Kaye quoted in Kriegsman, *Modern Dance in America*, 11.

206 *"undoubtedly the most exciting"*: Merce Cunningham, letter to Bonnie Bird, in David Vaughan, *Merce Cunningham: Fifty Years* (New York: Aperture, 2005), 23–24.

11. ENTER THE MEN

208 *"I WANT TO TELL YOU"*: Telegram sent October 12, 1938, to Erick Hawkins (then on tour with Ballet Caravan), c/o Mrs. Stringer, Fisher Theatre De-

partment, Erick Hawkins Collection, box 55, folder 1 (ca. 1939–1990), Library of Congress.

208 *"with so little experience"*: John Martin, "Martha Graham Offers New Dance," *New York Times*, October 10, 1938.

208 *letter to Ted Shawn*: Discovered by Norton Owen, director of preservation at Jacob's Pillow, Lee, Massachusetts, in a box of Shawn memorabilia donated to the institution in 1994.

209 *the family's years in Missouri*: Fern McGrath to Erick Hawkins, July 28, [?], Erick Hawkins Collection, Library of Congress, box 54/5, folder 6.

210 *"unfit as yet"*: Lincoln Kirstein, Lincoln Kirstein Papers, (S) *MGZMD 97, December 10, 1934, New York Public Library for the Performing Arts, Dance Division.

210 *surprised Kirstein by naming Hawkins*: June 8, 1934, excerpted from Kirstein's handwritten diaries, 1932–35. I am grateful to Alastair Macaulay for sending me the relevant material.

210 *"kept up very well"*: Ibid., March 2, 1934.

210 *"sweet & very enthusiastic"*: Ibid., June 9, 1934.

210 *"hard-headed, thick"*: Ibid., November 27, 1934.

210 *"slightly uppity & fractious"*: Ibid., December 2, 1934.

210 *"an elaborate & funny imitation"*: Ibid., December 21, 1934.

210 *"was mad with love of life"*: Ibid.

210 *Erick wouldn't joke*: Ibid., January 13, 1935.

210 *Lynn Garafola has pointed out*: Lynn Garafola, "Lincoln Kirstein, Modern Dance and the Left: The Genesis of an American Ballet," *Dance Research* 23, no. 1 (April 2005), viewable at https://core.ac.uk/download/pdf/161441848.pdf.

211 *"Erick's failure"*: Lincoln Kirstein Papers, February 7, 1934.

211 *he noted in his diary*: Ibid., January 24, 1935.

212 *"Improving some"*: Ibid., March 2, 1935.

212 *Balanchine thought her talent*: Ibid., February 10, 1935.

212 *"effective" and . . . "also OK"*: Ibid.

212 *he "liked [Graham's] body"*: Ibid.

212 *"do something for us"*: Ibid.

212 *"but not using her group"*: Kirstein's suggestion to Frances Hawkins, March 12, 1935.

212 *Horst, according to Kirstein, hated what he saw*: Lincoln Kirstein Papers, March 5, 1935.

212 *Anna Sokolow—an emerging choreographer herself—did too*: Told to Kirstein by the actor Margot Loines. Ibid.

212 *"thinks the turns"*: Ibid.

213 *"The reason people grow old"*: Martha Graham to Erick Hawkins from California, undated four-page letter, Sunday afternoon, 1939, Erick Hawkins Collection, box 55, folder 1, item #3, Library of Congress.

213 *"sweet little girl from Brooklyn"*: Graham to Hawkins, ibid., item #7.

213 *"I dare not go into"*: Ibid., item #6, Friday (Graham has just arrived in Santa Barbara by train).

213 *"I wish I could make it so much better"*: Ibid., item #7, Monday (six-page letter).

214 *"make you feel free"*: Ibid., item #13, Monday night (five-page letter).

214 *"If you should feel that it is"*: Ibid., item #12, Monday (yellow lined paper, green ink), written from her studio.

215 *José "is marvelous in movement"*: Ibid., item #2, Sunday morning (1939), written from the Cliff House in San Francisco.

215 *Puccinelli "thinks you are"*: Ibid.

215 *She's "very happy about that"*: Ibid., item #14, Monday (Graham has just returned to New York).

215 *"the more I know you American bred men"*: Ibid. (continued Tuesday night), written in bed.

215 *Christensen "filled the stage"*: Ibid.

216 *"very beautiful and very moving"*: Ibid.

216 *"I spoke to you of the Ringmaster"*: Erick Hawkins Collection, box 55, folder 1, item #2, Library of Congress.

217 *"Every soul is a circus"*: Vachel Lindsay, *Every Soul Is a Circus* (New York: Macmillan, 1929), 3–14.

217 *"Lady, you don't know me very well"*: Merce Cunningham in Mason, *Martha Graham Remembered*.

217 *silent black-and-white record film*: Copies of record films of several Graham works (courtesy of Janet Eilber, artistic director of the Martha Graham Center of Contemporary Dance, and Oliver Tobin, director of Martha Graham Resources).

221 *"Miss Graham mimes"*: Claudia Cassidy, "Martha Graham Dances at the Civic," *Chicago Journal of Commerce*, March 11, 1940.

221 *"The circus she creates"*: David Diamond, *Modern Music*, December 1939.

222 *At least two writers*: Cecil Smith, "Martha Graham Adds Charm to Vigor in Dance," *Chicago Tribune*, March 11, 1940; "Nik" (Nathan I. Krevitsky), "Martha Graham and Group," *Chicago Dancer*, March 10, 1940.

223 *Graham reports how much she admired*: Martha Graham (interviewed), "Noted Dance Artist Approves of Shag and Hop of Jitterbugs," January 22, 1939, syndicated in seven newspapers.

223 New York Post *photographs her*: Ibid.

223 *At various times throughout the year, a photograph*: For information re Yale Puppeteers, see J. G., "Yale Puppeteers Open Their Season: It's a Small World Is Titled Their New Vehicle," *New York Times*, November 7, 1938.

225 *An early program note*: In "Martha Graham in Concert Here Monday," *Daily Worker*, January 16, 1941, Martha Graham Collection, box 318, #204, Library of Congress. Also Penitente program, viewable at www.loc.gov/item/ihas .200153245/.

228 *"a lady in white with curls"*: Jean Erdman, interviewed by David Sears, *MGZTL 4–15373, disc 2 of 3, Dance Collection, Performing Arts Library, New York Public Library.

228 *"Don't ask me"*: Ibid.

229 *"The Bible is an antique Volume"*: Emily Dickinson, *The Complete Poems of Emily Dickinson*, ed. Thomas M. Johnson (Boston: Little, Brown, 1960), 344.

230 *"so little has to do"*: Ibid., 157.

230 *"[I am] small"*: "Emily Dickinson's Letters to Thomas Wentworth Higginson," *The Atlantic*, October 1891.

230 *relieved to note*: During Dickinson's early years, her friends included not only Higginson and Newton, but also Daniel Fiske, the "much-loved young director" to whom she referred.

231 *"summer house, to make it dreamlike"*: Martha Graham to Arch Lauterer. See McDonagh, *Martha Graham*, 147.

231 *years later, Erdman said*: Jean Erdman, interviewed by David Sears, *MGZTL 4–15373, disc 2 of 3, Dance Collection, Performing Arts Library, New York Public Library.

233 *"postponeless creature"*: Dickinson, *The Complete Poems*, 186.

234 *"Inebriate of air am I"*: Ibid., 98, from the poem beginning "I taste a liquor never brewed."

235 *"Dear March, come in!"*: Ibid., 572–73.

236 *"I'm wife"*: Ibid., 94.

236 *"There is a pain"*: Ibid., 204.

236 *"Of course I prayed"*: Ibid., 179–80.

237 *"The reading of the poetry"*: Young, *Immortal Shadows: A Book of Dramatic Criticism*, 254.

12. MAKING PLAYS DANCE

239 *"It is rare"*: Morgan, *Martha Graham: Sixteen Dances in Photographs*.

239 *"A break from a certain rigidity"*: Graham, "A Modern Dancer's Primer for Action," in *Dance: A Basic Educational Technique*, ed. Frederick Rand Rogers (New York: Macmillan, 1941).

239 *"Ruth Gordon was the viper"*: Martha Graham to David Zellmer, December 16, 1942, letters from Martha Graham to David Zellmer, 1942–1945, (S) *MGZMD 117, Jerome Robbins Dance Division, New York Public Library.

240 *based his walk*: Richard Boone, cited in "A Chronology by Marian Seldes," introducing Mason, *Martha Graham Remembered*.

240 *"squabble and scuffle"*: John Martin, "Throng Welcomes Martha Graham: Star Lauded as Comedian," *New York Times*, December 29, 1941.

241 *"how to be happy though married"*: Ibid.

241 *"hoped for a score by Aaron Copland"*: Soares, *Louis Horst*, 151.

241 *a silent 1940s film*: *Martha Graham: Punch and the Judy*, copy courtesy of Janet Eilber and Martha Graham Resources.

243 *Walter Terry of the* Herald Tribune *found* Punch and the Judy *"hilarious"*: *New York Herald Tribune*, August 12, 1941, collected in Walter Terry, *I Was There*, comp. and ed. Andrew Mark Wentink (New York: Marcel Dekker, 1978), 119.

243 *"a polished little sinfonia domestica"*: Margaret Lloyd, "Throng Welcomes Martha Graham," *Christian Science Monitor*, January 3, 1942, Martha Graham Collection, box 319, #217, Library of Congress.

243 *"choreography of first class quality"*: Denby, "With the Dancers."

244 *Writing to him from California*: Martha Graham to Erick Hawkins, September [?], 1941, box 55, folder 2, Erick Hawkins Collection, Library of Congress.

244 *"Once the scenery and props came"*: Jane Dudley in de Mille, *Martha*, 236.

245 *The studio floor needs*: Martha Graham to Erick Hawkins, September 5, 1941, box 55, folder 6, Erick Hawkins Collection, Library of Congress.

245 *no virtue in poverty*: Martha Graham to Erick Hawkins, September 18, 1941, box 55, folder 9 (typed), ibid. Library of Congress.

245 *"must learn to limber up"*: Fern McGrath to Erick Hawkins, August [?], 1928, letter (penciled) written while on the Gold Coast Limited. The letterhead identifies Hawkins's sister as Fern McGrath, M.A., consulting psychologist, located in Berkeley, California, and specializing in testing, personal counseling, and marriage problems. Erick Hawkins Collection, Library of Congress.

245 *He wrote her worriedly*: Erick Hawkins to Fern McGrath, January 21, 1929[?], box 54, folder 7, Erick Hawkins Collection, Library of Congress.

245 *she almost fainted*: Fern McGrath to Erick Hawkins, ibid.

245 *competing with a genius was futile*: Fern McGrath to Erick Hawkins ("Fred") on her stationery, December 8, [?], box 54, folder 7, Erick Hawkins Collection, Library of Congress.

245 *his "locked heart"*: Martha Graham to Erick Hawkins (ca. 1939–40), folder 1, item #9, Erick Hawkins Collection, Library of Congress.

246 *"She was lustrous"*: Ben Belitt in Mason, *Martha Graham Remembered*.

246 *"The other teachers [at her studio] are great"*: Robert Moulton interviewed in 1953 by Agnes de Mille about classes he took with Graham for two summers at Bennington and then in New York. Quoted in de Mille, *Martha*, 216.

247 *"She liked contention in the company"*: Cunningham in Mason, *Martha Graham Remembered*.

247 *While in Miami*: Sophie Maslow, quoted in de Mille, *Martha*, 249.

247 *Although Cunningham was eventually declared 1A*: Martha Graham to David Zellmer, December 16, 1942, letters from Martha Graham to David Zellmer, 1942–1945, (S) *MGZMD 117, New York Public Library.

247 *Hawkins's poor eyesight*: De Mille, *Martha*, 225, 249.

248 *The cast list gives you an idea*: McDonagh, *Martha Graham*, 324.

248 *Bennington "has reorganized its summer session"*: Doris Humphrey, letter to Eva Desca Garnet, February 1942, in McPherson, *Bennington School of the Dance*, 208.

249 *"A ballad of a woman's longing"*: Program note for the Graham company's performances at New York's Forty-Fifth Street Theatre, December 26, 1943.

249 *"My love came up from Barnegat"*: Elinor Wylie, "The Puritan's Ballad," in *Collected Poems of Elinor Wylie* (New York: Alfred A. Knopf, 1932), 138.

250 *"A coil of rope or seadrift"*: Margaret Lloyd, *Christian Science Monitor*, collected in *The Borzoi Book of Modern Dance*.

250 *"a twisted circle of sea-drift"*: George Beiswanger, "Moderns in Review: First Performance," *Dance News* (New York), January 1944.

250 *"wonderfully young"*: Edwin Denby, "The Ballet," *New York Herald Tribune*, December 27, 1943.

250 *"Literature cannot be"*: Robert Southey to Charlotte Brontë, December 3, 1837. See "Robert Southey and the Infamous Letter" at www.annebronte.org.

251 *"so much more elemental"*: Martha Graham to David Zellmer, December 14, 1942, letters from Martha Graham to David Zellmer, 1942–1945 (S) *MGZMD 117, New York Public Library.

251 *"situation was unkempt"*: David Vaughan, conversation with Jowitt while on the Eighth Street crosstown bus in New York City, 1980s[?].

252 *"I feel the two days after"*: Martha Graham to David Zellmer, July 22, 1943.

252 *"It isn't often I've seen the lobby"*: Edwin Denby, "Martha Graham's New 'Deaths and Entrances,'" *New York Herald Tribune*, January 16, 1944, reprinted in Edward Denby, *Looking at the Dance* (New York: Curtis Books, 1968), 258.

252 *"an extraordinary experience"*: John Martin, "Brilliant Dance by Martha Graham," *New York Times*, January 27, 1943.

252 *"the public seems baffled"*: Martha Graham to David Zellmer, December 28, 1943.

253 *"The action takes place in a room"*: Program for the Bennington College performances, July 2 and 3, 1943.

254 *"the real open air"*: Edwin Denby, *New York Herald Tribune*, June 20, 1945, reprinted in his *Looking at the Dance*, 266.

254 *In a silent film record*: Video of *Deaths and Entrances* (original cast), courtesy of Janet Eilber and Martha Graham Resources.

255 *"The company dances well"*: Martha Graham to David Zellmer, December 28, 1943.

256 *"she wanted a much darker Heathcliff"*: Bertram Ross in Mason, *Martha Graham Remembered*.

259 *"Sleep brings no strength"*: Emily Brontë. The poem can be read at https://fourteenlines.blog/tag/sleep-brings-no-joy-to-me-by-emily-bronte/.

259 *"certainly no drama in our time"*: John Martin, "The Dance: Second View: On Re-Seeing Martha Graham's Recent 'Deaths and Entrances,'" *New York Times*, January 16, 1944.

13. SPRINGTIME IN APPALACHIA AND A DARKER JOURNEY

260 *"At last, I have my courage up"*: Martha Graham to Aaron Copland, February 9, 1941, Library of Congress 200154072.

261 *like the "revenge plays"*: Ibid., February 17, 1941.

261 *in her typed manuscript*: Martha Graham, "Daughter of Colchis," April 7, 1942, Library of Congress 2001541287.

262 *Copland turned down the* Daughter of Colchis *script*: Pollack, *Aaron Copland*, 391; Aaron Copland and Vivian Perlis, *Copland Since 1943* (New York: St. Martin's Press, 1989), 30.

262 *something less dark*: Howard Isenstein, "Appalachian Spring Redux: Researcher Documents the Art of Collaboration," *Library of Congress Information Bulletin*, April 15, 1996 (interview with Marta Elaine Robertson).

262 *Copland and Paul Hindemith*: Hawkins's suggestion of composers is confirmed by a letter from Elizabeth Sprague Coolidge to Erick Hawkins, June 16, 1942, Library of Congress.

262 *whose music, she wrote to Coolidge, "is so different"*: Martha Graham to Elizabeth Sprague Coolidge, August 12, 1942, Library of Congress.

262 *Copland provisionally accepted*: Aaron Copland to Elizabeth Sprague Coolidge, July 31, 1942, Library of Congress.

262 *"I think I am the most fortunate"*: Martha Graham to Aaron Copland, November 7, 1942, Library of Congress.

262 *she also asked Copland*: Ibid.

263 *advised her against it*: Harold Spivacke to Elizabeth Sprague Coolidge, June 22, 1942.

263 *"I love having you call me Martha"*: Martha Graham to Elizabeth Sprague Coolidge, August 12, 1942.

263 *he learned that he had passed*: Aaron Copland to Harold Spivacke, September 17, 1942.

263 *he wrote to Spivacke*: Aaron Copland to Harold Spivacke, March 3, 1943.

263 *"I approach you"*: Martha Graham to Aaron Copland, May 16, 1943.

264 *"a free world for all men"*: See Wikipedia entry for "The North Star 1943."

264 *Graham's scenario*: Martha Graham, "House of Victory," mailed to Aaron Copland May 16, 1943.

264 *Graham wrote to Spivacke*: Martha Graham to Erick Hawkins, telling him of it, July 7, 1943.

264 *"how fortunate I am"*: Martha Graham to Aaron Copland, May 16, 1942.

264 *His reply shocked her*: Arch Lauterer to Martha Graham in July 1943 from Bennington College.

264 *"If you say that you cannot"*: Martha Graham to Arch Lauterer. Her reply to the above.

265 *She had seen a sculpture*: Alberto Giacometti, *The Palace at 4 a.m.* (1932), Museum of Modern Art.

265 *ready to send him a revised script*: Martha Graham's two scripts titled "Name" and "Name?" are in the Aaron Copland Collection, Library of Congress, dated "between May 29, 1943, and July 10, 1943," which is confusing, and in their online postings, the shorter, seemingly earlier one has been given a higher number. They are similar in many parts, but the second is longer in timing and almost twice as long in terms of pages.

265 *"a telescoped day"*: Appears in both "Name" (4) and "Name?" (8).

266 *To Copland, she wrote*: Martha Graham to Aaron Copland, July 10, 1943.

266 *"she is always with us"*: Martha Graham, "Name?" (2).

266 *what she has planned "will come alive"*: Martha Graham to Aaron Copland, July 22, 1943.

266 *She finds it beautiful*: Martha Graham to Harold Spivacke, October 25, 1943.

266 *Graham had wondered*: Martha Graham to Aaron Copland [?].

266 *Copland later said*: Copland in Mason, *Martha Graham Remembered*. "I have reworked it." Martha Graham to Aaron Copland, May 1, 1945.

267 *advising further postponement*: Harold Spivacke to Elizabeth Sprague Coolidge, August 10, 1943.

267 *Spivacke tells the understandably annoyed Coolidge*: Harold Spivacke to Elizabeth Sprague Coolidge, August 16, 1943.

267 *Copland and Chávez had been exchanging letters*: Aaron Copland to Carlos Chávez, August 23, 1943; March 28, 1944; April 30, 1944.

267 *"in strict musical terms"*: Martha Graham to Harold Spivacke, January 16, 1944.

267 *the scenario based on elements of Shakespeare's King Lear that Graham has offered doesn't suit him*: Martha Graham to Harold Spivacke, March 19, 1944.

267 *"just as bad or worse"*: Martha Graham to David Zellmer, June 6, 1944.

268 *"Martha didn't know beans"*: Erick Hawkins interviewed by Francis Mason.

269 *"It is so beautiful"*: Martha Graham to Aaron Copland, March 5, 1944.

269 *the foundation awarded her*: Guggenheim Foundation files: "Memorandum re: Martha Graham," February 4, 1943.

270 *Graham mentioned this character*: Conversation with Marcia B. Siegel in 1975.

270 *"the folk feeling"*: Aaron Copland handwritten notes with red underlining, Music Division, box 210/20, Library of Congress.

271 *In Nathan Kroll's 1958 film*: "Martha Graham: Dance on Film" (two discs), the Criterion Collection: *A Dancer's World* (1957), *Appalachian Spring* (1958), and *Night Journey* (1961).

272 *"The separateness of the still figures"*: Edwin Denby, "Martha Graham Notes," May 20, 1945, collected in Denby's *Looking at the Dance*, 266.

272 *"small wild animals"*: Ibid.

272 *"a kind of athletic prayer"*: Martha Graham to David Zellmer, September 14, 1944.

273 *"99% sex and 1% religion"*: Graham, quoted in de Mille, *Martha*, 261–62.

273 *"When true simplicity is gained"*: See lyrics on Wikipedia entry for "Simple Gifts."

276 *"the fullest, loveliest"*: John Martin, "The Dance: Washington Festival," *New York Times*, November 5, 1944.

276 *best "dramatic composition" of the year*: Copland and Perlis, *Copland Since 1943*, 46–47.

276 *"I am so very happy"*: Martha Graham to Aaron Copland, September 4, 1945.

277 *"clear, gay, and springlike"*: Darius Milhaud to Aaron Copland re *Jeux de Printemps*.

277 *musicologist Annegret Fauser identifies*: In "I Gained the Ledge," Laura Jacobs reviews Fauser's *Aaron Copland's "Appalachian Spring"* in the *London Review of Books*, November 2017.

277 *According to Marjorie Mazia*: Marjorie Mazia interviewed by Ted Dalbotten for his *To Bear Witness* (Bloomington, IN: Xlibris), 90–91.

277 *Nina Fonaroff was praised*: Patricia Simmons, "Graham Group Dances Trio of New Works," *Star* (Washington, D.C.), October 31, 1944, and Robert Sabin, "Dance at the Coolidge Festival," *Dance Observer*, December 1944.

277 *"solid canvas square changing color"*: Patricia Simmons, "Graham Group Dances Trio of New Works," *Star*, October 31, 1944.

277 *"bits of amusing stage directions"*: John Martin, "Graham Dancers in Festival Finale," *New York Times*, November 1, 1944.

277 *Yuriko, as Chorus, hurried around*: Emiko Tokunaga, *Yuriko, an American Japanese Dancer: To Wash in the Rain and Polish with the Wind* (New York: Tokunaga Dance Ko., 2008), 94–95.

278 *"rather slight and improvisational"*: Sabin, "Dance at the Coolidge Festival."

278 *"not notably successful"*: Martin, "The Dance: Washington Festival."

278 *She found Hindemith's music*: Martha Graham to David Zellmer, June 30, 1944.

279 *"A Mallarmé poem is"*: David Wheatley, "The Poems in Verse by Stéphane Mallarmé, Translated by Peter Manson-Review," *The Guardian*, June 15, 2012.

279 *"Chill water, frozen"*: Stéphane Mallarmé, "Hérodiade," translated by C. F.

MacIntyre, in *Stéphan Mallarmé: Selected Poems* (Berkeley: University of California Press), 31.

280 *"I am staging it"*: Martha Graham to David Zellmer, August 14[?], 1944.

280 *"must have meant himself"*: Deborah Jowitt, "Martha Graham and the Changing Landscape of Modernism," in *Art and Dance* (Boston: Institute of Contemporary Art, 1982), 77–83.

281 *"an x-ray vision of herself"*: Martin Friedman, "Noguchi's Imaginary Landscapes: An Exhibition Organized by Walker Art Center," *Design Quarterly* 106/107 (1978).

281 *saw it as "a skeleton"*: Ibid., 30.

281 *the "moment of choice"*: Frances Wickes, *The Inner World of Choice* (New York: Harper and Row, 1963).

281 *an archival film*: Janet Eilber, artistic director of the Martha Graham Center of Contemporary Dance, and her staff generously provided Jowitt with DVDs of Graham's major dances.

282 *a Woman and Her Attendant*: "A Program Devoted to the Dance." Graham and her dancers performed in the Library of Congress's theater for an invited audience on October 30, 1944. The "three new creations" were *Imagined Wing*, *Mirror Before Me* (later *Hérodiade*), and *Appalachian Spring*. Program viewable at https://www.loc.gov/item/ihas.200153473/.

283 *O'Donnell thought that*: May O'Donnell interviewed by David Sears, *Ballet Review*, Summer 1982, 3.

14. AN ERRAND THROUGH THE MEADOW, THE MAZE,
AND THE HEART'S CAVE

286 *"I loved you to call me"*: Martha Graham to Erick Hawkins, "Wednesday night," n.d. Erick Hawkins Collection, box 55, folder 3, item #1, Library of Congress. A single sentence is the entire message, written from 2024 Garden Street, Santa Barbara, California.

286 *"If you ever feel inspired"*: Martha Graham to Erick Hawkins, written from Bennington College in 1943, Erick Hawkins Collection, box 55, folder 3, item #8, Library of Congress.

286–87 *"I want to write Mr. and Mrs."*: Erick Hawkins, diary entry, August 27, 1945 (possibly a bit later), Erick Hawkins Collection, Hawkins Diary, Library of Congress.

287 *"Dear Honey," he wrote*: Craig Barton to Martha Graham, April 5, 1945.

287 *"There was no especial urgency"*: Martha Graham to Craig Barton about a long-ago evening he may have forgotten, June 11, 1951 (torn upper half of a letter).

288 *"Too much talk"*: Sabin, "Dance at the Coolidge Festival."

288 *"a maze of shivery"*: Elliott Carter, "Scores for Graham" (rest of subtitle obscured), *Modern Music*, Winter 1946.

288 *Horst taught*: His *Pre-Classic Dance Forms* (1937) and *Modern Dance Forms* (1960) were based on choreography classes that he taught at a variety of schools, including the Neighborhood Playhouse and the Juilliard School of Music. The term "pre-classic" relates only to form; the musical structure of a gigue, for example, could result in a contemporary dance.

289 *"Merce says he cannot go"*: Martha Graham to David Zellmer, June 6, 1945,

Letters from Martha Graham to David Zellmer 1942–1945 (S) *MGZMD 117, Jerome Robbins Dance Division, New York Public Library.

289 *"glad to have some freedom"*: Martha Graham to Harold Spivacke, September 13, 1945, in relation to Carlos Chávez, whose music she hopes to use for her *Dark Meadow*.

290 *the program's first page*: Listing the company's performances at the Ziegfeld Theatre, Monday, February 24, 1946, through Sunday, March 2, 1946.

291 *"When I think of the wonder"*: Martha Graham to Frances Wickes, Papers of Frances G. Wickes, Manuscript Division, box 2, folder 15, Library of Congress.

291 *"If our titles"*: Mark Rothko, cited by Dore Ashton in "The Rothko Chapel in Houston," *Studio International* 81 (June 1971), 274.

292 *"falling from the region of light"*: Empedocles, fragments 119, 120, 121, quoted by Martha Graham in *The Notebooks of Martha Graham* (New York: Harcourt Brace Jovanovich, 1973), 177.

292 *"a curious work"*: John Martin, "A World Premiere Dance by Graham," *New York Times*, January 24, 1946.

292 *"beginning to understand* Dark Meadow*"*: Graham wrote this to Frances Wickes on March 28, 1954. Graham, *Blood Memory*, 199.

293 *"biomorphic Stonehenge"*: McDonagh, *Martha Graham*, 187.

293 *"The music is continually danced"*: Carter, "Scores for Graham."

294 *In an early silent film of* Dark Meadow: The Martha Graham Dance Company's black-and-white documentary film of the piece. Courtesy of Janet Eilber and the Martha Graham Company archives.

297 *"We breathe in"*: Isamu Noguchi, *A Sculptor's World* (New York: Harper and Row, 1968), 123.

299 *"Brilliant, bitter"*: Robert Horan, "The Recent Theater of Martha Graham," in Magriel, *Chronicles of the American Dance*, 249.

300 *"frightened flashes"*: Ibid.

301 *according to Agnes de Mille*: De Mille, *Martha*, 258.

301 *"The errand into the maze"*: Ben Belitt, "Dance Piece." Also: Belitt in Mason, *Martha Graham Remembered*.

303 *"There is no telling of a story"*: Martha Graham to William Schuman from Brackett Apartments in Santa Barbara, August 12, 1946.

304 *"The legend concerns those forces"*: Ibid.

304 *"would like best to dance"*: Martha Graham to William Schuman, August 30, 1946.

304 *according to de Mille*: De Mille, *Martha*, 236–37.

305 *"is poetically recalled"*: Faubion Bowers, *Japanese Theatre* (Rutland, VT: Charles E. Tuttle, 1974), 17.

307 *"give Graham exactly what her dance"*: Walter Terry, "The Dance," *New York Herald Tribune*, May 5, 1947.

308 *"It was the violence, the whole ambiance"*: Reminiscences of Ben Belitt Bennington Summer School Project, Oral History Research Office (New York: Columbia University, 1979), 34.

15. ANGELS AT PLAY AND TWO CHRISTIAN HEROINES

310 *"Second for Santa Claus"*: McDonagh, *Martha Graham*, 202.

310 *Ruth Subbie identified*: Ibid.

310 *a United Press writer who cornered her*: Ibid. See Graham's confession about her role at https://artsandculture.google.com/asset/martha-graham-is-miss -hush1947/kgGATeB91dMzsQ?hl=en.

310 *"Miss Graham's complexion"*: McDonagh, *Martha Graham*, 202.

310 *"dismay a literal person"*: Angelica Gibbs, *The New Yorker*, December 27, 1947.

311 *"It is the place of the Rock"*: Ben Belitt, "Dance Piece," in *This Scribe, My Hand: The Complete Poems of Ben Belitt* (1955; Baton Rouge: Louisiana State University Press, 1998), 151.

311 *differentiated by costume color*: Stuart Hodes, *Onstage with Martha Graham* (Gainesville: University Press of Florida, 2021), 69, 72.

312 *of different lengths*: Frances Herridge, "Graham Work Needs Graham," *Star* (New York), August 17, 1948.

312 *Nathan Kroll's 1957 film*: Produced by Kroll and directed by Peter Glushanov for the Criterion Collection. See criterionchannel.com.

314 *"to look like a Chagall"*: Pearl Lang in Mason, *Martha Graham Remembered*.

314 *Graham and Hawkins intervened*: Soares, *Louis Horst*, 171.

315 *On the certificate*: Ibid., 172.

315 *Years later, Hawkins said*: Erick Hawkins to Martha Graham, November [? a Thursday], 1950, Erick Hawkins Collection, box 55, folder 16, item #1, Library of Congress.

315 *tried out her new name*: Martha Graham to Erick Hawkins, April 25, 1954, ibid., box 55, folder 12, Library of Congress.

315 *"I was terrified"*: A dialogue between Martha Graham and Claire Birsh Merrill, Lucy Kroll Papers, December 7, 1971, box 240, reel 1, side B, p. 9 (transcription), Library of Congress.

316 *It was reported that Wiseman*: Joseph Wiseman in Mason, *Martha Graham Remembered*.

316 *"little to do with"*: Martha Graham to David Zellmer, January 30, 1944, Letters from Martha Graham to David Zellmer, archival mix, 1942–45, Performing Arts Research Collections—Dance. (S) *MGZMD 117, New York Public Library for the Performing Arts, Dorothy and Lewis B. Cullman Center.

317 *"There is means, madam"*: Doctor to Cordelia, William Shakespeare's *King Lear*, act IV, scene 4.

317 *"a kind of frantic fantasia"*: John Martin, "Martha Graham Scores in Recital: Receives Ovation After 2-Year Absence—Novelty, 'Eye of Anguish,' Presented," *New York Times*, January 23, 1950.

317 *"tremendous red cloth"*: The cloth is mentioned in many reviews, as well as by Peggy Lyman, interviewed by Jowitt, January 19, 2020.

318 *"The Angst of Eyewash"*: Recounted in Hodes, *Onstage with Martha Graham*, 99.

318 *"Darling—my husband"*: Martha Graham to Erick Hawkins, July 19, 1949, Erick Hawkins Collection, folder 7, no. 1, Library of Congress. Written from The Clift, San Francisco.

318 *Louise Kain, had suggested*: See Wikipedia entry: "Judith (ballet)."

318 *sent him a tentative script*: Martha Graham to William Schuman, October 28, 1946, letter to the composer accompanying *Night Journey* script.

319   *"Slowly, slowly I pulled"*: Martha Graham, quoted in Martin Friedman, ed., "Noguchi's Imaginary Landscapes," *Design Quarterly* 106/107 (1978), 33.

319   *served as a loom*: Ibid., 34.

320   *"little more than an extended gag"*: John Martin, "Graham Presents New Solo Dance: 'Gospel of Eve'—with Music by Paul Nordoff, Featured in Program at 46th Street Theatre," *New York Times*, January 24, 1950.

320   *"in the area of gesture"*: Walter Terry, *New York Herald Tribune*, January 24, 1950.

320   *Ethel Winter thought*: Ethel Winter in Mason, *Martha Graham Remembered*, 3.

321   *Stuart Hodes remembered*: Hodes, *Onstage with Martha Graham*, 128–29.

321   *"I am more grateful to you"*: Martha Graham to Erick Hawkins from the Mission Inn, Santa Barbara, July 27, 1950, Erick Hawkins Collection, 1950, box 55, folder 9, item 2, Library of Congress.

321   *Hawkins sent Graham*: Erick Hawkins to Martha Graham, August 21, 1950, box 55, folder 4, Erick Hawkins Collection, Library of Congress. Its twenty-seven pages, sent August 27, describe in detail all he has done for her and all that she expected from him.

321   *Graham's September 3 answer*: Martha Graham to Erick Hawkins, September 3, 1950, box 55, folder 5, Erick Hawkins Collection, Library of Congress.

322   *she had berated him*: Winter in Mason, *Martha Graham Remembered*. Winter identifies the person being attacked by Graham as the company dancer Barbara Bennion.

322   *"brought a certain agony"*: Martha Graham to Erick Hawkins, September 3, 1950.

323   *"I know of no clearer way"*: Martha Graham to Erick Hawkins, quoting from John Macmurray's *Reason and Emotion* (London: Faber & Faber, 1935).

323   *"not a very satisfactory patient"*: Martha Graham to Frances Wickes from New London, Connecticut, July 16, 1951, Papers of Frances G. Wickes, Manuscript Division, Library of Congress, box 15, folder 12.

323   *"Your hand is on my life"*: Martha Graham to Frances Wickes from Santa Fe, August 26, 1951, ibid.

324   *"All I can do in these five days"*: Martha Graham to Frances Wickes from New London, Connecticut, July 16, 1951, ibid.

325   *"the ageless conflict between"*: Norman Dello Joio, "Challenge of Joan: Composer Relates Effort in Trying to Meet It," *New York Times*, April 1, 1956.

326   *took her title from a poem*: Ben Belitt, *Wilderness Stair: Poems, 1938–1954* (New York: Grove Press, 1955).

326   *These "mobiloids"*: See Anna Kisselgoff, "Dance View: Martha Graham's Affirmation of Life," *New York Times*, January 1, 1987.

327   *"The effect is astoundingly right"*: Ibid. Note: Kisselgoff's review is of a later cast.

327   *"Earth is a serene woman"*: Deborah Jowitt, "Observed with Ceremony," *Village Voice*, October 27, 1987. Note: the original article included the names of each performer (parenthetically) within the text.

327   *movements that Yuriko created*: Tokunaga, *Yuriko*, 96.

328   *"the hungry ones"*: Martha Graham, quoted in Mark Franko, *Martha Graham in Love and War: The Life in the Work* (New York: Oxford University Press, 2012), 152.

328 *As she told Wickes, she had flung out*: Martha Graham to Frances Wickes, from Santa Fe, August 26, 1951. Papers of Frances G. Wickes.

328 *"a grief which turns"*: Robert Payne, *The Wanton Nymph: A Study of Pride* (London: W. Heinemann, 1951).

328 *"to transmute a sentimental experience"*: Martha Graham to Frances Wickes, August 26, 1951. Papers of Frances G. Wickes.

328 *a muezzin calling the faithful*: *The Notebooks of Martha Graham*, 112.

328 *thinking of a bullfight*: Ibid., 105.

328 *"some cool remote room"*: Ibid., 111.

328 *"a meal is finished"*: Ibid., 104.

329 *"the arena of the woman's being"*: Ibid., 111.

329 *"the image of woman"*: Ibid., 136.

329 *"Image—woman seated"*: Ibid., 132.

329 *"As he draws hair pin"*: Ibid., 137.

329 *Decades later, the three men*: Franko, *Martha Graham in Love and War*, 157.

329 *According to Hodes*: Stuart Hodes in Mason, *Martha Graham Remembered*.

329 *"a kind of war dance"*: John Martin, "Martha Graham Begins Dance Engagement at Alvin Theatre with Premiere of 'Voyage,'" *New York Times*, May 17, 1953.

329 *"picked her off"*: Bertram Ross, interview conducted by Selma Jeanne Cohen, June 22, 1971, New York Public Library for the Performing Arts, Dorothy and Lewis B. Cullinan Center.

330 *"I know you could tell me"*: Martha Graham to Frances Wickes, June 1953.

331 *"It has some lovely things"*: Martha Graham to Frances Wickes, from the Hotel des Indes, the Hague, Holland, March 28, 1954. Papers of Frances G. Wickes.

331 *"I conjure every idle"*: Richard Buckle, "Martha Graham: At the Saville," *Sunday Observer* (London), March 14, 1954, reprinted in *Buckle at the Ballet: Selected Dance Criticism* (New York: Atheneum, 1980), 46.

332 *"The weeks in London went by"*: Martha Graham to Frances Wickes, from the Hotel des Indes, the Hague, Holland, March 28, 1954. Papers of Frances G. Wickes.

16. TRAVELING INTO ASIA AND ONWARD WITHOUT ERICK

335 *"'falling domino' principle"*: President Dwight Eisenhower commenting to a reporter. Naima Prevots, *Dance for Export: Cultural Diplomacy and the Cold War* (Middletown, CT: Wesleyan University Press, 1998), 44.

336 *"unbelievable success"*: A handwritten letter from Martha Graham to Frances Wickes from Ceylon, January 10, 1956. Papers of Frances G. Wickes.

337 *Jakarta had been "hot, hot, hot"*: LeRoy Leatherman, *Martha Graham: Portrait of the Lady as an Artist* (New York: Alfred A. Knopf, 1966), 32.

337 *Uday Shankar . . . was at the airport*: Alfonso Umaña, *Helen McGehee Dance* (New York: Editions Heraclita, 1974), n.p.

337 *the great Balasaraswati*: Ibid.

337 *dancer and educator Rukmini Devi*: Ibid.

338 *the monkeys' "concepts of modesty"*: Paul Taylor, *Private Domain* (New York: Alfred A. Knopf), 66.

338 *the company's "wardrobe mistress"*: Ibid.

341 *reveals Clytemnestra*: Brief excerpts from *Clytemnestra* may be viewed on You Tube.com.

343 *"neighbors who share"*: Martha Graham, quoted in Brian Seibert, "Review: Martha Graham's 'Embattled Garden,' Deconstructed," *New York Times*, Aug. 21, 2015.

344 *Lincoln Kirstein jotted down*: Kirstein, *Thirty Years*, 149.

344 *"repelled me so strongly"*: Lincoln Kirstein in Armitage, *Martha Graham*, 24.

345 *lavishly praised her* American Document: Ibid., 76.

345 *"personal intensity . . . exhilarating"*: Ibid.

345 *he found her not only intriguing but also appetizing*: Lincoln Kirstein, handwritten diary, February 10, 1935, New York Public Library.

345 *"fills the air like molecules"*: Ibid.

345 *"traded around like hockey players"*: Taylor, *Private Domain*, 89.

345 *who called him "Geek"*: Ibid.

346 *"Is like fly in glass of milk, yes?"*: Ibid., 91.

346 *"Somehow ghosts"*: John Martin, "'Episodes'; A Challenging Work Choreographed Jointly by Graham and Balanchine," *New York Times*, June 7, 1959.

350 *"I will go lie in wait for Death"*: Robert Browning, "Balaustion's Adventure," including a transfer from Euripides, can be read online.

350 *"stony valley"*: Theodore Morrison, *The Dream of Alcestis* (New York: Viking Press, 1950).

350 *"a liar and ravisher"*: Ibid.

351 *those watching over the queen at her bedside*: Ibid.

351 *She wrote in her notebooks*: Ibid., 45.

351 *"Trio—fight between Herakles & Thanatos"*: Ibid.

17. TO COMBAT THE ONSLAUGHT OF AGING

353 *In 1948 Irving Penn took*: The image appeared in *Vogue*, www.artnet.com /artists/irving-penn/martha-graham-ChBiACCi4-L0S6eueTtSOQ2.

353 *posed for Jack Mitchell*: Dance Magazine. The photograph can be found at gettyimages.com.

354 *"better on a muddy track"*: Graham, *Blood Memory*, 91.

354 *"if there wasn't stress"*: Allen Mead, M.D., in Mason, *Martha Graham Remembered*.

354 *"might be considered"*: John Martin, quoting Martha Graham's program note for *One More Gaudy Night*, "The Dance: Pert Comedy," *New York Times*, April 21, 1961.

355 *Halim El-Dabh's music*: Ibid.

355 *"The myth becomes a festival"*: Program for Martha Graham and Dance Company's *Alcestis* at the Broadway Theater (1962), viewable online at https:// digitalcollections.nypl.org/items/ade95850-bf60-0136-7827-6d6df1a44c68.

355 *"Along the corridors of memory"*: Program for Martha Graham and Dance Company's *Visionary Recital* at the 54th Street Theater (1961), viewable online at https://digitalcollections.nypl.org/items/854e5760-bf60-0136-e705 -7bac7e9f4862.

356 *Some of the terms*: Those terms recur in *The Notebooks of Martha Graham*.

357 *"when I was sitting"*: Ross in Mason, *Martha Graham Remembered*.

357 *the Graham School had to fight*: McDonagh, *Martha Graham*, 266.

358 *"you take that body"*: Martha Graham, quoted in Alan M. Kriegsman, "The Spring of Martha Graham," *Washington Post*, April 8, 1984.

358 *devastatingly witty if affectionate picture*: Taylor, *Private Domain*, 114.

359 *charge of obscenity*: Alan M. Kriegsman, "Martha Graham's 'Phaedra' at Wolf Trap," *Washington Post*, June 25, 1977.

360 *"captured the heart of the Baroness"*: Rena Gluck writes of Jeannette Ordman and Bat-Dor in *Batsheva Dance Company, My Story 1964–1980* (self-published, 2006).

361 *one of the doctors she consulted*: Mead in Mason, *Martha Graham Remembered*.

361 *clutching Robin Howard's hand*: McDonagh, *Martha Graham*, 279.

362 *"wearing heavy boots"*: Gus Solomons, Jr., letter to Jowitt, July 31, 2019.

363 *"red leg"*: *The Notebooks of Martha Graham*, 450.

363 *"Cover Saul with veil"*: Ibid.

363 *"'The Evil spirit was upon him'"*: Ibid., 451.

363 *"beats Saul with her Cape"*: Ibid., 453.

364 *"a dance of great psychological complexity"*: Clive Barnes, "Dance: Martha Graham: 'The Witch of Endor' Is Opener of Season—Story of Saul Is Made Universal," *New York Times*, November 3, 1965.

364 *"a movie of the mind"*: Anna Kisselgoff, "The Dance: Martha Graham's 'Cortege of Eagles,'" *New York Times*, April 6, 1985.

364 *reenvisioned for television*: *Three by Martha Graham*, John Houseman, director, VHS tape or DVD in NTSC format.

365 *"converted them to towers"*: Robert Cohan in Mason, *Martha Graham Remembered*.

366 *"The last time I danced"*: Graham, *Blood Memory*, 238.

366 *"She is the paragon"*: Joseph Campbell, *The Hero with a Thousand Faces* (New York: Pantheon Books, 1949), 310–11.

367 *stage was so full of scenery*: Marcia B. Siegel, "Are Graham's Gods Dead?," *New York*, June 24, 1968, reprinted in her *At the Vanishing Point: A Critic Looks at Dancing* (New York: Saturday Review Press, 1972), 181.

367 *but possibly death*: Anna Kisselgoff, "A Martha Graham Revision: 'Lady in the House of Sleep' Is Performed," *New York Times*, April 17, 1969.

367 *"Miss Graham restricts herself"*: Clive Barnes, "'A Time of Snow': New Work Presented by Martha Graham," *New York Times*, May 27, 1968.

18. CHOREOGRAPHY AS MEAT AND DRINK

368 *At a fundraising gala*: June 21, 1975.

369 *"a complete stage animal"*: Joan Acocella, "Early Spring," *The New Yorker*, February 17 & 24, 2003.

369 *Jim McWilliams . . . told an interviewer*: Jim McWilliams in Mason, *Martha Graham Remembered*.

369 *when her long-ago dancer Bonnie Bird visited*: Bonnie Bird Gundlach, oral history interview conducted by William F. Riess and Suzanne B. Riess, recorded in 2001, 120–21.

369 *"a little Oriental deity"*: De Mille, *Martha*, 398.

369–70 *"began as a whip"*: Ben Garber quoting Jean Rosenthal in Mason, *Martha Graham Remembered*.

370 *"Geordie met me at the ferry"*: Armgard von Bardeleben in ibid.

370 *The doctor who gave her a physical examination prior to the operation was amazed*: Dr. Roy Weston in ibid.

371 *"If you get another"*: Mead in ibid.

371 *"just put[s] herself out of it"*: Garber quoting Dr. Cary Guy in ibid.

371 *"Get me the hell out"*: Martha Graham to Ben Garber from the hospital, after receiving Dr. Allen Mead's surgery on January 15, 1991, Benjamin Garber Papers, 1916–2009, box 3, folder 19–21, Music Division, Library of Congress.

371 *Discovering her asleep*: Garber in Mason, *Martha Graham Remembered*.

371 *a bucket was placed*: Ibid.

371 *"like a snapping turtle"*: Mead in ibid.

372 *"He would call our house"*: Garber in ibid.

372 *Martha accused LeRoy Leatherman*: De Mille, *Martha*, 387.

372 *Harold Taylor, a member of her board of directors, quit*: Ibid., 388.

372 *Gertrude Macy was confronted*: Ibid.

372 *Ralph Gilbert was reprimanded*: Ibid., 389.

373 *she accused the two*: Ibid.

373 *"I think she needed"*: Bethsabée de Rothschild in Mason, *Martha Graham Remembered*.

373 *unhesitatingly replied yes*: Ethel Winter, interviewed by Jowitt in Winter's New York City home, ca. 2013.

373 *"Great age, you lied"*: Saint-John Perse, *Chronique*, translated by Robert Fitzgerald (New York: Pantheon Books, 1961), 29.

375 *"I want the intensification"*: Anna Kisselgoff, "Martha Graham—Still Charting 'The Graph of the Heart,'" *New York Times*, May 15, 1977.

375 *a dancer she cherished*: "Robert Powell Dies: A Leading Dancer for Miss Graham," *New York Times*, October 27, 1977.

376 *"Martha lived for her work"*: Christine Dakin in Mason, *Martha Graham Remembered*.

376 *"When she started making"*: Janet Eilber in ibid.

376 *"For about two seasons"*: Peggy Lyman in ibid.

376 *"We were reviving"*: Peter Sparling in ibid.

377 *Peter London (working on* Night Chant *with her in 1988)*: Ibid.

377 *"If there wasn't a storm"*: Terese Capucilli in ibid.

378 *"a different form"*: Kisselgoff, "Martha Graham—Still Charting 'The Graph of the Heart,'" 65.

379 *"They dined on mince"*: Edward Lear, "The Owl and the Pussy-Cat," in *Nonsense Songs* (London: Frederick Warne, n.d.), n.p.

380 *"stylish schema of her masterpieces"*: Deborah Jowitt, "Refurbishing Your Old Silks," *Village Voice*, July 17, 1978.

380 *"seeking the 'hot points'"*: Belitt in Mason, *Martha Graham Remembered*.

381 *"Very great mendicant tree"*: Saint-John Perse, *Winds*, bilingual edition, translated by Hugh Chisholm (New York: Pantheon Books, 1953), 120.

381 *"Martha had to make that dance"*: Pearl Lang, quoted in Hodes, *Onstage with Martha Graham*, 283.

382 *"in any way inhuman"*: William Schuman quoting Martha Graham in Mason, *Martha Graham Remembered*.

382 *had only to telephone*: Anne O'Donnell in ibid.

383 *"I'm so happy to see you"*: José Aznarez in ibid.

383 *"immensely curious"*: Helen O'Brien in ibid.

384 *The temple's history*: The Metropolitan Museum of Art, "The Temple of Dendur," https://www.metmuseum.org/art/collection/search/547802.

385 *"Give me some music"*: William Shakespeare, *Antony and Cleopatra*, act 2, scene 5.

385 *"Give me my robe"*: Shakespeare, *Antony and Cleopatra*, act 5, scene 2.

386 *audiences, remembered Lyman, loved* Frescoes: Peggy Lyman, interviewed by Jowitt at Lyman's Connecticut house in January 2020.

386 *"In search of herself"*: Anna Kisselgoff, "Dance View: The Gold That Is Graham," *New York Times*, June 20, 1982.

386 *her "Denishawn piece"*: Martha Graham quoted by Anna Kisselgoff, "Martha Graham Pursues New Visions," *New York Times*, May 30, 1982.

387 *She told* The New York Times: Anna Kisselgoff, "Dance View; Graham's 'Rite of Spring' Is a Creative Triumph," *New York Times*, March 11, 1984.

389 *"The Sea, woven in us"*: Saint-John Perse, quoted by Anna Kisselgoff, "Dance: 'Tangled Night,' a Premiere," *New York Times*, June 6, 1986.

BIBLIOGRAPHY

Ackerman, Carl W. *George Eastman*. Boston: Houghton Mifflin, 1930.

Ackerman, Gerald. "Photography and the Dance: Soichi Sunami and Martha Graham." *Ballet Review* 12, no. 2 (Summer 1984): 32. Short essay and many photos.

Allegheny City Society. *Allegheny City, 1840–1907*. Charleston, SC: Arcadia Publishing, 2007.

Anderson, John Murray, and Hugh Abercrombie Anderson. *Out Without My Rubbers: The Memoirs of John Murray Anderson as Told to Hugh Abercrombie Anderson*. New York: Library Publishers, 1954.

Armitage, Merle. *Martha Graham: The Early Years*. New York: Da Capo Press, 1978.

Bannerman, Henrietta. "Martha Graham's House of the Pelvic Truth: The Figuration of Sexual Identities and Female Empowerment." *Dance Research Journal* 42, no. 1 (Summer 2010).

Bell-Kanner, Karen. *Frontiers: The Life and Times of Bonnie Bird; American Modern Dancer and Educator*. London: Harwood Academic Publishers, 1998.

Birchard, Robert S. *Silent-Era Filmmaking in Santa Barbara*. Charleston, SC: Arcadia Publishing, 2007.

Bird, Bonnie. Oral History Interview conducted by William F. Riess and Suzanne B. Riess, Berkeley, California, February 1994.

Bird, Dorothy, and Joyce Greenberg. *Bird's Eye View: Dancing with Martha Graham and on Broadway*. Pittsburgh: University of Pittsburgh Press, 1997.

Champé, Flavia Waters. *The Matachines Dance of the Upper Rio Grande: History, Music, and Choreography*. Lincoln: University of Nebraska Press, 1983.

Copland, Aaron, and Vivien Perlis. *Copland Since 1943*. New York: St. Martin's Press, 1989.

Cornell, Katharine (as told to Ruth Woodbury Sedgwick). *I Wanted to Be an Actress: The Autobiography of Katharine Cornell*. New York: Random House, 1939.

Davis, Bette. *The Lonely Life: An Autobiography.* New York: G. P. Putnam's Sons, 1962.

De Mille, Agnes. *Martha: The Life and Works of Martha Graham.* New York: Random House, 1991.

Dyer, Carlus. "Martha Graham: Eight Lithographs." *Ballet Review* 22, no. 3 (Fall 1994): 42–49.

Easton, Carol. *No Intermissions: The Life of Agnes De Mille.* Boston: Little, Brown, 1996.

Flanagan, Hallie. *Arena: The Story of the Federal Theatre.* New York: Duell, Sloan and Pearce, 1940.

Fowlie, Wallace. *Mallarmé.* Chicago: University of Chicago Press, 1962.

Franko, Mark. *Martha Graham in Love and War: The Life in the Work.* New York: Oxford University Press, 2012.

Friedman, Martin. "Noguchi's Imaginary Landscapes: An Exhibition Organized by Walker Art Center." *Design Quarterly* 106/107 (1978).

Fuller, Loïe. *Fifteen Years of a Dancer's Life: With Some Account of Her Distinguished Friends.* London: H. Jenkins Ltd., 1913.

Garber, Benjamin. Graham Dance Company Papers III, 1966–1976. Benjamin Garber Papers, 1916–2009, box 3, folder 19–21. Music Division, Library of Congress, Washington, D.C.

Geduld, Victoria Phillips. "Dancing Diplomacy: Martha Graham and the Strange Commodity of Cold-War Cultural Exchange in Asia, 1955 and 1974." *Dance Chronicle* 33, no. 1 (2010) (special issue on Martha Graham).

Gluck, Rena. *Batsheva Dance Company 1964–1980: My Story.* Self-published, 2006.

Graff, Ellen. *Stepping Left: Dance and Politics in New York City, 1928–1942.* Durham, NC: Duke University Press, 1997.

Graham, Martha. *Blood Memory: An Autobiography.* New York: Doubleday, 1991.

———. "A Dancer's World—Excerpts from the Script." In *Anthology of Impulse: Annual of Contemporary Dance 1951–1966.* Edited by Marian Van Tuyl. Brooklyn, NY: Dance Horizons, 9–10.

———. "Deaths and Entrances." Typed scenario. Bennington College Library.

———. *The Flute of Krishna.* 1926 film, transferred, and given an appropriate soundtrack by John Mueller, director of the Dance Film Archive at Ohio State University, Columbus.

———. *The Notebooks of Martha Graham.* New York: Harcourt Brace Jovanovitch, 1974.

———, ed. *The Olive and Gold* (Santa Barbara, CA) 7, no. 1 (June 1913). Published by the senior class.

Gundlach, Bonnie Bird. Manuscript, typed by Judith Cederblom. Recorded in 1994.

Hawkins, Erick. Erick Hawkins Collection, 55/1–55/16. Library of Congress, Washington, D.C. https://loc.gov/performingarts/encyclopedia/collections/hawkins.html.

Heckman, Marlin L. *Santa Barbara in Vintage Postcards.* Charleston, SC: Arcadia Publishing, 2000.

Helpern, Alice, ed. "Martha Graham." *Choreography and Dance: An International Journal* 5, part 2 (1999).

———, ed. and author. "Radical Graham: A One Day Symposium on the Work of

Martha Graham," Brooklyn Academy of Music's 1994 Next Wave Festival in Cooperation with the New School, October 1, 1994. Participants included Dorothy Bird, Thelma Babitz, Sophie Maslow, Jane Dudley, Freda Flier, Marie Marchowsky, Nolini Barretto, Helen McGehee, Mark Wheeler, May O'Donnell, and Erick Hawkins.

Hodes, Stuart. *Onstage with Martha Graham*. Gainesville: University Press of Florida, 2021.

Horosko, Marian, comp. *Martha Graham: The Evolution of Her Dance Theory and Training 1926–1991*. Gainesville: University Press of Florida, 2002.

Horst, Louis. "Consider the Question of Communication." In *Anthology of Impulse: Annual of Contemporary Dance 1951–1966*. Edited by Marian Van Tuyl. Brooklyn, NY: Dance Horizons, 1969, 11–21.

"In the American Grain: The Martha Graham Centennial," panel at the University of Michigan, 2019. Program.

Jowitt, Deborah. "Books: Morgan Looks at Graham" *Ballet Review* 9, no. 1 (Spring 1981): 109–12.

———. "A Conversation with Bessie Schönberg." *Ballet Review* 9, no. 1 (Spring 1981): 31–63.

Kendall, Elizabeth. *Where She Danced*. New York: Alfred A. Knopf, 1979.

Kirstein, Lincoln. *Three Pamphlets Collected*, 41–42 ("Blast at Ballet"). Brooklyn, NY: Dance Horizons, 1967.

Kriegsman, Sali Ann. *Modern Dance in America: The Bennington Years*. Boston: G. K. Hall, 1981.

Kroll, Lucy. Lucy Kroll Papers, box 240, reel 10 (transcript), February 10, 1972. Library of Congress, Washington, D.C.

Lamothe, Kimerer L. *Nietzsche's Dancers: Isadora Duncan, Martha Graham, and the Revaluation of Christian Values*. New York: Palgrave Macmillan, 2011.

Lawton, Stephen. *Santa Barbara's Flying A Studio*. Santa Barbara, CA: Fithian Press, 1997.

Leatherman, LeRoy. *Martha Graham: Portrait of the Lady as an Artist*. New York: Alfred A. Knopf, 1966.

Luening, Otto. *The Odyssey of an American Composer: The Autobiography of Otto Luening*. New York: Charles Scribner's Sons, 1980.

Luhrssen, David. *Mamoulian: Life on Stage and Screen*. Lexington: University Press of Kentucky, 1913.

Macmurray, John. *Reason and Emotion*. London: Faber & Faber, 1935.

Magriel, Paul, ed. *Chronicles of the American Dance: From the Shakers to Martha Graham* (1948). New York: Da Capo Press, 1978.

Mallarmé, Stéphane. *Selected Poems*. Translated by C. F. MacIntyre. Berkeley: University of California Press, 1971.

Mantle, Burns. *Best Plays of 1926–1927*. New York: Dodd, Mead, 1927.

Martin, David F. *Invocation of Beauty: The Life and Photography of Soichi Sunami*. Seattle: University of Washington Press, 2018.

McDonagh, Don. *Martha Graham: A Biography* (1973). New York: Popular Library, 1975.

McGehee, Helen. *To Be a Dancer*. Edited by Alfonso Umaña. Lynchburg, VA: Editions Heraclita, 1989.

McPherson, Elizabeth, ed. *The Bennington School of the Dance: A History in Writings and Interviews*. Jefferson, NC: McFarland, 2013.

Meglin, Joellen A., and Lynn Matluck Brooks, eds. "Martha Graham: Perspectives from the Twenty-First Century." *Dance Chronicle* 33, no. 1 (2010).

Morgan, Barbara. *Sixteen Dances in Photographs* (1941). New York: Morgan & Morgan, 1980.

Morrison, Theodore. *The Dream of Alcestis*. New York: Viking Press, 1950.

Nietzsche, Frederic. *Ecce Homo and the Birth of Tragedy from the Spirit of Music*. New York: Modern Library, 1927.

Noguchi, Isamu. *Essays and Conversations*. Edited by Diane Apostolis-Cappadona and Bruce Altshuler. New York: Harry N. Abrams / The Isamu Noguchi Foundation, Inc., 1994.

Perse, Saint-John. *Chronique*. Translated by Robert Fitzgerald. New York: Pantheon Books, 1961.

———. *Winds*. Translated by Hugh Chisholm. New York: Pantheon Books, 1953.

Pollack, Howard. *Aaron Copland: The Life and Work of an Uncommon Man*. New York: Henry Holt, 1999.

Prevots, Naima. *Dance for Export: Cultural Diplomacy and the Cold War*. Middletown, CT: Wesleyan University Press, 1998.

St. Denis, Ruth. *An Unfinished Life: An Autobiography* (1939). Brooklyn, NY: Dance Horizons, 1969.

Schlundt, Christena. "Into the Mystic with Miss Ruth." *Dance Perspectives* 46 (Summer 1971).

Scolieri, Paul A. *Ted Shawn: His Life, Writings, and Dances*. New York: Oxford University Press, 2019.

Sears, David. "Martha Graham and the Golden Thread." *Ballet Review* 14, no. 3 (Fall 1986): 45–64.

Selden, Elizabeth. *The Dancer's Quest*. Berkeley: University of California Press, 1935.

Shawn, Ted. *Dance We Must*. London: Dennis Dobson, 1946.

———, with Gray Poole. *One Thousand and One Night Stands*. Garden City, NY: Doubleday, 1960.

Shelton, Suzanne. *Divine Dancer: A Biography of Ruth St. Denis*. New York: Doubleday, 1981.

Sherman, Jane. "Denishawn Revisited." *Ballet Review* 9, no. 1 (Spring 1981): 97–108.

———. *Denishawn: The Enduring Influence*. Boston: Twayne Publishers, 1983.

———. *The Drama of Denishawn Dance*. Middletown, CT: Wesleyan University Press, 1979.

Shirley, Wayne D. "For Martha." *Ballet Review* 27, no. 4 (Winter 1999): 64–95.

Smith, Wendy. *Real-Life Drama: The Group Theater of America, 1932–1940*. New York: Vintage Books, 2013.

Soares, Janet Mansfield. *Louis Horst: Musician in a Dancer's World*. Durham, NC: Duke University Press, 1992.

———. *Martha Hill and the Making of American Dance*. Middletown, CT: Wesleyan University Press, 2009.

Stewart, Virginia. *Modern Dance* (1935). New York: Dance Horizons, 1970.

Stodelle, Ernestine. *Deep Song: The Dance Story of Martha Graham*. New York: Schirmer Books, 1984.

Story of Old Allegheny City. Pittsburgh: Allegheny Centennial Committee, 1941.

Terry, Walter. *Frontiers of Dance: The Life of Martha Graham*. New York: Crowell, 1975.

Thoms, Victoria. "Martha Graham's Haunting Body: Autobiography at the Intersection of Writing and Dancing." *Dance Research Journal* 40, no. 1 (Summer 2008).

Tobias, Tobi. "A Conversation with May O'Donnell." *Ballet Review* 9, no. 1 (Spring 1981): 64–96.

Todd, Mabel Elsworth. *The Thinking Body*. New York: Dance Horizons, 1975.

Tokunaga, Emiko. *Yuriko, an American Japanese Dancer: To Wash in the Rain and Polish with the Wind*. New York: Tokunaga Dance Ko., 2008.

Torres, Larry. "Understanding Los Matachines." In *Matachines! Essays for the 2008 Gathering*. Edited by Claude Stephenson. Santa Fe: New Mexico Arts: New Mexico Department of Cultural Affairs, 2008.

University of Southern California Yearbook, 1904–1905 (circular of information). Reproduced online.

Warren, Larry. *Anna Sokolow: The Rebellious Spirit*. Pennington, NJ: Princeton Book Company, 1990.

Young, Stark. *Immortal Shadows: A Book of Dramatic Criticism*. New York: Hill and Wang, 1948.

Zellmer, David. *The Spectator: A World War II Bomber Pilot's Journal of the Artist as Warrior*. Westport, CT: Praeger, 1999.

INDEX

A Note About the Author

Deborah Jowitt was the principal dance critic at *The Village Voice* for more than four decades, and her work has appeared in *The New York Times* and *Dance Magazine,* among other outlets. Her previous books include the biography *Jerome Robbins: His Life, His Theater, His Dance*; the essay collection *Time and the Dancing Image*; and the critical works *Dance Beat* and *The Dance in Mind.* A former Guggenheim fellow, she has lectured and conducted workshops worldwide and taught in the Dance Department of New York University's Tisch School of the Arts for forty years. Her recent writings can be found on her *ArtsJournal* blog, *DanceBeat.*